Modern Web Development: Understanding domains, technologies, and user experience

Dino Esposito

PUBLISHED BY
Microsoft Press
A division of Microsoft Corporation
One Microsoft Way
Redmond, Washington 98052-6399

Library of Congress Control Number: 2015934865
ISBN: 978-1-5093-0001-3

First Printing

Microsoft Press books are available through booksellers and distributors worldwide. If you need support related to this book, email Microsoft Press Support at mspinput@microsoft.com. Please tell us what you think of this book at http://aka.ms/tellpress.

Acquisitions and Developmental Editor: Devon Musgrave
Project Editor: Steve Sagman
Editorial Production: Waypoint Press
Technical Reviewer: Marc Young
Copyeditor: Roger LeBlanc
Indexer: Toni Culley
Cover: Twist Creative • Seattle and Joel Panchot

To my wife Silvia.

You make me feel sandy like a clepsydra. I get empty and filled all the time; but it's such a thin kind of sand that even when I'm full, without you, I just feel empty.

—Dino

Contents at a glance

Contents

What do you think of this book? We want to hear from you!

Microsoft is interested in hearing your feedback so we can improve our books and learning resources for you. To participate in a brief survey, please visit:

http://aka.ms/tellpress

PART II   DEVELOPMENT

Chapter 6   ASP.NET state of the art   103

Chapter 9   Core of Bootstrap   171

Chapter 10 Organizing the ASP.NET MVC project   217

What do you think of this book? We want to hear from you!

Microsoft is interested in hearing your feedback so we can improve our books and learning resources for you. To participate in a brief survey, please visit:

http://aka.ms/tellpress

Introduction

No later than the summer of 2008, I gave a few public talks about the future of the web. Customers who hired me at the time heard from this expert voice that the web of the (near) future would be significantly different than what it was looking like in 2008. At the time, the brilliant future of the web seemed to be in the hands of compiled code run from within the browser.

JavaScript? It's dead, at last! ASP.NET? It's gone, thankfully!

The future as I saw it back then (along with many other experts) had only rich-client technologies in store for millions of us. And Microsoft Silverlight stood at the center of the new web universe.

If you started hibernating in 2008 and woke up any time in the past three or even four years, you found a different world than I, or possibly you, had imagined. It was solidly server-side-based and different from what the expectations were. Today, you find a web world in which JavaScript reigns and, with it, a ton of ad hoc tools and frameworks.

Customers who paid good money to hear my expert voice back in 2008 tell them to invest in Silverlight are now paying good money to switch back more or less to where they were in 2008.

Well, not exactly.

This book comes at a weird time, but it's not a weird book. Two decades of web experience taught us that real revolutions happen when, mostly due to rare astral alignments, a bunch of people happen to have the same programming needs. So it was for Ajax, and so it is today for responsive and interactive front ends. JavaScript has been revived because it is the simplest way for programmers to achieve goals. And because it is still effective enough to make solutions easy to sell.

Planning a web solution today means having a solid server-side environment to serve rich and interactive HTML pages, styled with CSS and actioned by JavaScript. Even though a lot of new ad hoc technologies have been developed, the real sticking points with modern applications (which are for the most part web applications) are domain analysis and the supporting architecture. Everything else revolves around the implementation of a few common practices for a few common tasks, some of which are relatively new requirements—for example, push notifications from the server.

In this book, you will find a summary of practices and techniques that guarantee effective solutions for your customers. The point today is no longer to use the latest release of the latest platform or framework. The point is just to give customers what they really want. Tools to build software exist; ideas and plans make the difference.

Who should read this book

This book exists to help web developers improve their skills. The inspiring principle for the book is that today we mostly write software to mirror a piece of the real world, rather than to bend the real world to a piece of technology.

If you just want to do your day-to-day job better, learning from the mistakes that others made and looking at the same mistakes you made with a more thoughtful perspective, then you should definitely read this book.

Assumptions

This book assumes you are familiar with the Microsoft web stack. This experience can range from having done years of Web Forms development to being a JavaScript angel. The main focus is ASP.NET MVC, because that will be the standard with ASP.NET Core and remain so for the future of the ASP.NET platform. Here are some key goals for readers of the book: learning a method general enough so that you can start development projects with a deep understanding of the domain of the problem, select the right approach, and go forward with reliable coding practices.

This book might not be for you if...

If you're looking for a step-by-step guide to some ASP.NET MVC or perhaps Bootstrap, this book is probably not the best option you have. It does cover basic aspects of both technologies, but it hardly does that with the necessary slow pace of a beginner book.

Organization of this book

The book is divided in three parts: understanding the business domain, implementing common features, and analyzing the user experience.

Part I offers a summary of modern software architecture, with a brief overview of domain-driven design concepts and architectural patterns. The focus is on the real meaning of the expression *domain model* and examining how it differs from other flavors of models you might work with. Key to effective design today—an approach that weds domain analysis and user experience—is the separation of commands and queries into distinct stacks. This simple strategy has a number of repercussions in terms of persistence model, scalability, and actual implementation.

Part II begins with a summary of the ASP.NET MVC programming model—the way to go for web developers, especially in light of the new ASP.NET Core platform. Next, it covers Bootstrap for styling and structuring the client side of the views and looks at techniques for posting and presenting data.

Part III is all about user experience in the context of web applications. Web content is consumed through various devices and in a number of situations. This creates a need for having adaptive front ends that "respond" intelligently to the requesting devices. In this book, you'll find two perspectives regarding client responsiveness: a common responsive web design perspective and the server-side device perspective.

So, in the end, what's this book about?

It's about what you need to do and know to serve your customers in the best possible way as far as the ASP.NET platform is concerned. At the same time, the practices and the techniques discussed in the book position you well for participating in the bright future of ASP.NET Core.

Finding your best starting point in this book

Overall, I see two main ways to approach the book. One is reading it from cover to cover, paying special attention to software design and architecture first and then taking note of how those principles get applied in the context of common but isolated programming tasks. The other approach consists of treating Part I—the part on software design and architecture—as a separate book and reading it when you feel it is necessary.

If you are	Follow these steps
Relatively new to ASP.NET development but not to web development	Ideally, you should read the book cover to cover, and be sure not to skip Chapter 4, "Architectural options for a web solution."
Familiar with ASP.NET MVC or Bootstrap	Briefly skim Chapter 8, "Core of ASP.NET MVC," and Chapter 9, "Core of Bootstrap." Also, depending on your personal feelings, you might want to also skim Chapter 6, "ASP.NET state of the art," and Chapter 10, "Organizing the ASP.NET MVC project." Note that the book provides one chapter about ASP.NET Core, but that is mostly to help you form an idea about it.
Interested in practical solutions	Read Part II and Part III.

Most of the book's chapters include hands-on samples you can use to try out the concepts you just learned. No matter which sections you choose to focus on, be sure to download and install the sample applications on your system.

System requirements

To open and run provided examples, you just need a working edition of Microsoft Visual Studio.

Downloads

All sample projects can be downloaded from the following page:

http://aka.ms/ModernWebDev/downloads

Acknowledgments

A bunch of great people made this book happen: Devon Musgrave, Roger LeBlanc, Steve Sagman, and Marc Young. It's a battle-tested team that works smoothly and effectively to turn draft text into readable and, hopefully, pleasantly readable text.

When we started this book project, we expected to cover a new product named ASP.NET vNext, but the new product, now known as ASP.NET Core, is still barely in sight. In light of this, we moved the target along the way, and Devon was smart enough and flexible enough to accept my suggestions on variations to the original plan.

Although you'll find some information about ASP.NET Core in the book, a new ASP.NET Core book is on its way. Ideally, it will be from the same team!

Errata, updates, & book support

We've made every effort to ensure the accuracy of this book and its companion content. You can access updates to this book—in the form of a list of submitted errata and their related corrections—at:

> *http://aka.ms/ModernWebDev*

If you discover an error that is not already listed, please submit it to us at the same page.

If you need additional support, email Microsoft Press Book Support at *mspinput@microsoft.com*.

Please note that product support for Microsoft software and hardware is not offered through the previous addresses. For help with Microsoft software or hardware, go to *http://support.microsoft.com*.

Free ebooks from Microsoft Press

From technical overviews to in-depth information on special topics, the free ebooks from Microsoft Press cover a wide range of topics. These ebooks are available in PDF, EPUB, and Mobi for Kindle formats, ready for you to download at:

http://aka.ms/mspressfree

Check back often to see what is new!

We want to hear from you

At Microsoft Press, your satisfaction is our top priority, and your feedback our most valuable asset. Please tell us what you think of this book at:

http://aka.ms/tellpress

We know you're busy, so we've kept it short with just a few questions. Your answers go directly to the editors at Microsoft Press. (No personal information will be requested.) Thanks in advance for your input!

Stay in touch

Let's keep the conversation going! We're on Twitter: *http://twitter.com/MicrosoftPress*

Understanding the domain

CHAPTER 1

Conducting a thorough domain analysis

Developers have to steep themselves in the domain to build up knowledge of the business.

—*Eric Evans*

More and more developers and managers seem to agree that writing software today is hard and getting harder every day. I, myself, can see that software projects sometimes fail, exceed allocated budgets or, when things don't really go too bad, reach the production stage only a few weeks late. I wonder why development projects so often disappoint in this way and look around. I see some possible answers, but I still I have no certainties to share with confidence.

When I find it hard to understand the mechanics of things, I try to look back at the steps I went through and that reasonably led to the current situation. At some point in my life, I was a teenager learning about driving and parking cars. One day my dad challenged me to take the car out of the tiny space he had parked it in.

"It's impossible," I said after 20 minutes of unsuccessful efforts.

"You're wrong," he said and patiently explained the maneuvers he did to actually park the car. The message was clear: if there was a way to pull it into the spot, there was a way to pull it out.

So the question that this chapter will attempt to answer is this: what should we do to turn the process of writing applications into a reliably successful process? I believe we have to change our current perspective of software and, subsequently, the approach we take to designing it.

Software is increasingly pervasive in our social and business lives. Therefore, software is more frequently expected to mirror social and business processes rather than approximate discrete models. But modeling is what the current generation of software architects grew up with.

Ultimately, writing software is not that difficult. And this is especially true if you stop modeling and start planning it to just mirror what you see in the real world.

Domain-driven design to the rescue

In today's world, software adds value only when it meets true requirements and helps streamline business processes. Software is not necessarily about devising new business processes—there's a specific methodology for that, Business Process Management (BPM). Software, instead, is about faithfully modeling segments of the real world. These segments are effectively referred to as the *business domain*.

Introducing design driven by the domain

As simple as it sounds, if those database-centric, client/server applications we wrote for decades were still the best way to mirror segments of the real world, probably nobody would have spent years thinking and talking about Domain-Driven Design (DDD).

DDD is an approach to software design and development introduced over a decade ago by Eric Evans with the clear intent of finding a more effective way to tackle the inherent complexity of software development. The major strength of DDD lies in the systematic approach it offers to pinpoint and "crunch" aspects of the business domain. DDD is revolutionary because it doesn't rely on increasingly powerful technologies or services to achieve business goals through software. DDD is about understanding the core of the business domain so that you, as a software architect, can find the best tools to build the application. And these concrete tools may or may not be the latest version of a given database or the most recent service added to a given cloud platform.

In the end, DDD is just what its name says it is: design driven by thorough analysis of the business domain. To enable you to conduct such a thorough analysis of the business domain, DDD offers three analysis patterns:

- Ubiquitous language

- Bounded context

- Context mapping

I'll go through all these patterns in the rest of the chapter. However, I can't ignore at this time that some misconceptions exist regarding DDD. Therefore, before I delve deep into what DDD really is, let me first bring up what DDD is not.

Clearing up common misconceptions about DDD

In the original Eric Evans book (*Domain-Driven Design: Tackling Complexity in the Heart of Software*, Addison-Wesley, 2003), DDD is presented as a comprehensive set of best practices and principles for more effectively designing and developing software projects, especially large projects in complex business domains. DDD doesn't push new and revolutionary practices. It simply organizes and systematizes existing and consolidated practices, putting the business domain at the center of the universe.

DDD requires analysis of requirements, and then it goes through the elaboration of a software model that matches the identified business needs. Finally, it ends with the implementation of the elaborated model. In the book, Evans uses the object-oriented paradigm to illustrate the building of the software model for the business domain. He calls the resulting software model the *domain model*.

More or less at the same time, Martin Fowler (who, by the way, wrote the foreword of the book) used the same term—*domain model*—to name a design pattern for organizing the business logic of a system. The Domain Model design pattern builds on the idea of incorporating business rules and processes in the body of objects. The net effect is a graph of interconnected objects that fully represent the domain of the problem. Everything in the model is an object and is expected to hold data and expose a behavior.

As I see things, at the foundation of DDD is the plain notion of a software model for the business domain, and the Domain Model pattern defined by Martin Fowler is just one possible way to implement such a software model.

From here, a few misconceptions arose and contaminated the original idea of DDD. The following sections examine some of them.

It's all about having an object model for the domain

Quite a few people today tend to associate DDD with simply having an object model in the business layer with some special characteristics, as described in the DDD book: aggregates, value types, factories, behavior, private setters, and so on.

DDD has two distinct parts: strategic design and tactical design. *Strategic design* is paramount and revolves around patterns and practices for analyzing the domain and designing the top-level architecture of the system. *Tactical design* is about implementing the results of the strategic design. In this regard, modeling the domain through objects is just one of the possible options. Using a functional approach, for example, is neither prohibited nor patently out of place. You can extract good from DDD even if you end up coding a collection of functions or building an anemic object model with stored procedures to do the hard work.

The database has no impact on the model

I never ran into an application that did not need persistence, though I have run into systems that hid the persistence layer behind an HTTP façade. From a DDD perspective, the business layer and persistence layer are separate parts of the system—interoperating but distinct. That's all of it. Beyond this, there's no declared war between DDD experts and database administrators.

For the sake of design, if you aim at building an object-oriented software model to represent the business domain, persistence certainly isn't your primary concern. At the same time, it's quite likely that the object model you design will need to be persisted at some point. When it comes to persistence, the database and the API you use to go to the database (for example, Entity Framework) are clear constraints and can't always be blissfully ignored.

If you intend to really keep a domain model fully agnostic with regard to database concerns, you should aim at having distinct models—a domain model and persistence model—and use adapters to switch between the two.

Ubiquitous language is about naming conventions

In DDD, the names of classes, properties, and methods are considered to be critical factors. All names are expected to reflect the language of the business and a real step in a real business process. As you'll see in more detail in a moment, the term *ubiquitous language* just refers to a shared vocabulary of terms that is reflected in the conventions used to name classes and members.

By using DDD and discovering the ubiquitous language of the domain, you get to understand the language of the business and know in far greater detail the mechanics of the business. It's correct to say that the ubiquitous language determines naming conventions, but the point of building a ubiquitous vocabulary is to understand the business and mirror the business processes with code. It's much more relevant than just establishing an effective naming convention.

Introducing the ubiquitous language

If you're a doctor or a civil engineer, everything you do each day is strictly related to what you studied and did previously in the course of your career. It's different, instead, if you're a lawyer or a software engineer.

In both these cases, you're regularly called to exercise expertise in areas you know little or nothing about. As a lawyer, you might have to learn about high finance for the closing argument on a bankruptcy case. As a software engineer, you might have to know about international tax rules to implement the business logic of an online store application.

This is where the ubiquitous language fits in.

Creating a vocabulary of domain-specific terms

If the information delivered to you by domain experts and interviewed users was always accurate and unambiguous, all software would probably ship on time and on budget and the world would be a better place. More often than not, though, requirements contain ambiguous definitions, duplicates, foreign terms, acronyms, and jargon. Sometimes, different people within the same organization use different words for the same concept or use the same word to mean different things.

When domain and software experts speak different languages, finding some common ground is crucial to ensure that reliable communication is set up and no loss of information occurs along the way.

Looking at the constituent elements of the ubiquitous language

In spite of the fancy name, ubiquitous language is a simple glossary of all the terms used by experts of a particular business domain. Each term in the glossary is expected to be unambiguous and hold well-defined meaning. Terms are, for the most part, nouns and verbs, and the glossary also includes associations between nouns and verbs so that it's clear which verbs (that is, actions) apply to which noun (that is, entity). While building the glossary, you might also want to look into adverbial phrases found in requirements and user stories. Adverbs might add extra layers of detail to your under- standing and point to relevant aspects of the domain—such as events, processes, and triggers of processes—you might want to account for in the design.

Terms in the glossary should meet the expectations of both domain experts and developers. You have a well-crafted ubiquitous language when the words and verbs in the glossary truly reflect the real semantics of the business domain.

Once it has been defined, the ubiquitous language will be shared by all people participating in the project, whether they are stakeholders, analysts, developers, project managers, or testers. In other words, the language will become the lingua franca of the project and will be used in any form of spoken and written communication, including documentation, email messages, meetings, and project work items.

The development team is typically responsible for developing and maintaining the glossary. The glossary, in fact, is a living thing, and it receives updates and gains new elements as the team learns more and more about the domain.

Choosing terms for the glossary

The ubiquitous language is not an artificial language created in a laboratory. Instead, it emerges from plain discussions in meetings and interviews. In most meetings scheduled to share ideas about a project and the purposes of the project, you typically find two groups of people: domain experts and software experts. Software experts tend to use technical concepts such as "deleting an order." Domain experts tend to use different wording for the same concept. Perhaps they might commonly refer to the removal of an order as "canceling the order."

Another purpose of using ubiquitous language is to remove gray areas. Consider, for example, the following expression, which you might find in a user story or hear at a meeting: "Extra costs should be emphasized in the user account."

The intended business purpose is probably well known to an expert and her colleagues, but it might not be obvious to others outside that circle of experts. What's the intended purpose? In this case, it can be any of the following:

- Show costs when the user logs in.

- List costs on a detail page.

- Mark extra costs in the bill.

The effort of building an unambiguous glossary of terms pays off because it helps clarify a number of possibly obscure points. In addition, it helps ensure different concepts and actions are named in a unique way and, at the same time, ensures matching concepts are detected and named similarly.

The ubiquitous language is neither the raw language of business nor the language of development. Both are forms of jargon, and both—if taken literally—might lack essential concepts, generate misunderstandings, and create communications bottlenecks. Hence, the ubiquitous language is a combination of business and technical jargon. It is expected to contain mostly business terms, but some technical concepts are allowed just to make the final language faithfully express the system behavior. Terms like *caching*, *logging*, and *roles* might not be business specific, yet they are required in the building of the system and might show up in some way in the ubiquitous language.

Sharing the glossary

The value of a language comes from its being used rather than persisted. Just as it might be helpful to have an English dictionary to translate and explain words, stakeholders in a project might find it useful to have a physical place to check for domain-specific terms.

Typically, you should save the glossary to a shared document. It can be a Microsoft Office Excel file placed in a Microsoft OneDrive folder or, better yet, a file collaboratively edited via Microsoft Excel Online. It can even be a wiki. Through an in-house hosted wiki, for example, you can create and evolve the glossary and also easily set up an internal forum to openly discuss features and updates to the language. Also, you can use a wiki to easily set permissions and control how editing takes place and specify who can edit what.

I should point out that any change made to the language should be a business-level decision. As such, that decision should always be made with the full approval of stakeholders and all parties involved.

Keeping business and code in sync

What if you misunderstand a concept or misinterpret a word? At a minimum, you end up building software based on some wrong assumptions. In a DDD scenario, missing a word or a concept is close to creating a bug in the code.

The ultimate goal of the ubiquitous language is neither creating comprehensive documentation about the project nor setting guidelines for naming code artifacts like classes and methods. The real goal for creating the language is to have it be the backbone of the actual code.

Reflecting the ubiquitous language in code

When it comes to turning the ubiquitous language into code, having a naming convention is critical: names of classes, methods, and namespaces should reflect terms in the glossary. It's not really recommended, for example, to name the method that starts a process differently from how users call the same process in the business.

However, the impact of the ubiquitous language on code is not limited to the domain layer. It also helps with the design of the application logic too. For example, imagine the checkout process of an online store. Before proceeding with a typical checkout process, you might want to validate the order and see, for example, if ordered goods are in stock and check the past payment history of the customer.

How would you organize this code? There are a couple of good options to consider:

- Have a single *Validate* step in the workflow for the checkout process. The Validate step will incorporate all required checks. The validation steps are not visible at the process level.

- Have a sequence of individual validation steps right in the workflow.

From a purely functional perspective, both options would work well, but maybe one is ideal in a given business context. The answer about which one to use can be found in the ubiquitous language. If the language refers to a "validate" action to be performed on an "order" during the "checkout" process, you should go with the first option, having a single Validate step. If actions like "check payment history" or "check current stock" exist in the vocabulary, you should have individual steps in the workflow for just those actions.

If nothing in the current version of the language can clarify a coding point, it probably means that more work on the language is required and you should conduct a new round of discussions to break down notions one more level.

> **Note** Using extension methods in languages that support them (C# or Kotlin) helps immensely to keep the code fluent and domain specific. Tools enforce coding rules and conventions. Relevant tools from a DDD perspective are code assistants such as ReSharper, refactoring tools, and even tools that simplify gated check-ins, such as those you find in Team Foundation Server.

Dealing with international teams

So the ubiquitous language is a glossary. But in which language do you build it? Should it be in English or the language of the customer? If the customer speaks, say, German, should the ubiquitous language still be in English? This is not a secondary point, especially in the case of international teams working on the same project. The ubiquitous language needs to be written in the official natural language of the project—which can be either English or German in this example. If translations are necessary for development purposes, a word-to-word table should be created. Having such a table definitely helps, but you do risk introducing some ambiguity.

Dealing with acronyms

In some business scenarios, most notably in the defense industry, acronyms are popular and widely used. Acronyms, however, are hard to remember and understand. In general, acronyms should not be part of the ubiquitous language. Instead, you should introduce new words that retain the original meaning of the acronyms.

If acronyms are common in the business at hand, is not using them a violation of the ubiquitous language pattern? Yes and no. I agree that, strictly speaking, not using acronyms is a violation of the pattern. However, the ubiquitous language is primarily about making the business language and, subsequently, the code easier to use and understand. In this context, acronyms are hard to remember and hinder cross-team communication.

> **Note** Hiring programmers with expertise in a given business domain reduces the problems you might have in creating the ubiquitous language. However, that won't eliminate the root problems, because you'll never find the exact same domain twice.

Introducing the bounded context

The ubiquitous language, in sync with the domain model and code, changes constantly to represent both the evolving business and the architect's growing understanding of the domain. The ubiquitous language, however, cannot change indefinitely to incorporate more and more new concepts and slight variations of existing concepts. If you keep on doing that, you risk having a language with duplicates and creating a language that's less rigorous than it should be.

This is where DDD introduces a new concept: the *bounded context*. The bounded context is the area of the business domain that gives any of the elements of the ubiquitous language a well-defined and unambiguous meaning.

Discovering bounded contexts

Especially in a large organization, you'll find that it's typical that the same term has different meanings for different people or that different terms are used to mean the same thing. When you find this happening, you have probably crossed the invisible boundaries of a *subdomain*. This probably means that the business domain you assumed to be one and indivisible is, in reality, articulated in subdomains.

Using subdomains and bounded contexts

In DDD, the problem space is the business domain. For this domain, you design a software domain model in the solution space. However, the original domain sometimes might be too large to deal with effectively, so you then split it into multiple subdomains. When this happens in the problem space, you have a bounded context in the solution space. (See Figure 1-1.)

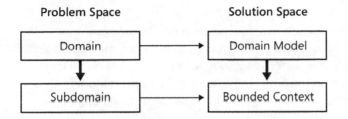

FIGURE 1-1 Problem space and solution space

Examining aspects of a bounded context

A bounded context is the model found in the solution space for a business subdomain. A bounded context is uniquely identified by its own ubiquitous language. Subsequently, outside the boundaries of the bounded context, the ubiquitous language changes. Wherever the ubiquitous language is the same, the context is the same.

Bounded contexts in DDD serve three primary purposes. First, they prevent creating ambiguity and duplicating concepts. Second, bounded contexts divide the domain into smaller pieces, thus simplifying the design of software modules. Finally, a bounded context is the ideal tool to integrate into the system legacy code or external components.

Detecting bounded contexts

In the DDD vision, a bounded context is an area of the application with its own ubiquitous language, its own independent implementation (for example, a domain model) and an interface to talk to other bounded contexts in the software. In some cases, and especially in large organizations, the number and relationships of bounded contexts often reflect the physical organization and departments. In other cases, bounded contexts are discovered along the way as the requirements are processed and differences in the originally unique languages are found.

Generally speaking, in the context of an online store application, the following are good candidates to become a bounded context:

- Store

- Accounting

- Delivery

- Backoffice

However, this is just a guideline. The actual partition results from analysis and depends on the specific context. In general, I'd even say that any web application should be split into at least two contexts: the store and backoffice. The backoffice is the part where administrators feed data and set rules.

> **Important** Each bounded context has its own independent implementation. An independent implementation means having frameworks, technologies, methodologies, and architecture. In other words, it is perfectly acceptable in a DDD context in a large system that one bounded context is implemented following the Domain Model pattern and another one according to a plain, two-tier, CRUD (Create, Read, Update, Delete)–oriented architecture.

Implementing bounded contexts

During the requirements analysis, you might find that some concepts overlap the boundaries of business processes. For example, the same terms might be used to mean different things and to refer to distinct processes.

Figure 1-2 illustrates the scenario.

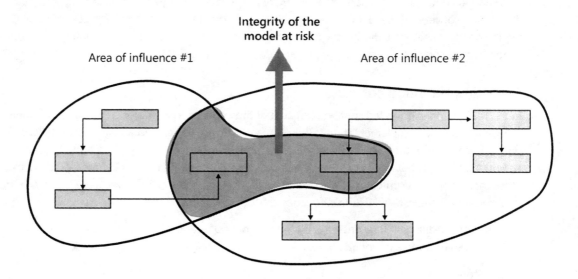

FIGURE 1-2 Overlapping business contexts

In the example, the overall domain is split into two areas of influence that might refer, for example, to the input received from stakeholders in distinct departments. Or it can even be that different development teams are processing different set of requirements and both are trying to define a common piece of domain logic. The two areas have a few concepts in common. You have a few options for addressing this point and to avoid getting a brittle model: an all-encompassing context, a shared kernel, and distinct bounded contexts.

Using an all-encompassing context

Although the concept of a bounded context has always been one of the pillars of DDD, it seems to me that most architects and developers are sometimes scared of splitting the model into pieces. It's as if breaking up the model for simplification reflects poorly on the architect's ability to come up with a well-crafted, unique model.

When multiple definitions exist for a common term or concept, you can still consider them to be part of the same all-encompassing context, but this is a risky choice. Using a single definition for an entity has the side effect of padding the definition with details that might be unnecessary in other contexts.

The net effect is that you expose an API for the domain that potentially allows more than it should and leaves the responsibility of just doing the right thing on the developers' shoulders. When it comes to this, there's a statement I use often that's really close to being another one of Murphy's laws: *if a developer can use an API the wrong way, he will.*

Using a shared kernel

When business concepts are shared across two or more areas of influence, the likelihood of needing to make frequent changes is high. For this reason, implementing the shared concepts in a separated module—a sort of a shared kernel—is a better option from a maintainability perspective, even though it doesn't fix the core issue of having entities with potentially way too many responsibilities.

Opting for distinct bounded contexts

Overall, whenever you recognize concepts that have different definitions in the domain, the best option is just to adopt different bounded contexts. Figure 1-3 provides graphical evidence of the resulting schema.

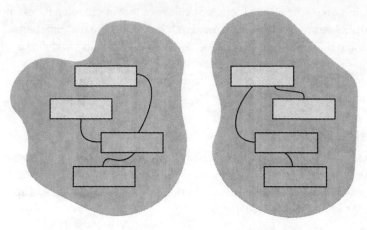

FIGURE 1-3 Distinct bounded contexts for handling shared business concepts

Overlapping concepts are common in business because you won't find two domains that are absolutely identical. In general, the most recommended way to handle overlapping concepts is via distinct bounded contexts. By taking this approach, you guarantee that each concept has the most accurate implementation it can have, with no compromises, no ambiguity, and just the right number of responsibilities.

Any other option might just be the first step toward a true mess.

Giving each context its own architecture

Because a bounded context is a distinct area of the final system, it is expected to have the most appropriate architecture, regardless of what is being done for other bounded contexts. So it can be that the overall software solution is made of two or more contexts, each implemented with different technologies and programming patterns and languages.

For example, the web store of an e-commerce application can be an ASP.NET MVC application with a layered back end based on Command/Query Responsibility Segregation (CQRS) and the Domain Model pattern to organize the business logic. (I'll cover CQRS and the Domain Model pattern in Chapter 2, "Selecting the supporting architecture.") At the same time, the backoffice area of the site can be more effectively coded as a simple two-layer architecture with an ASP.NET Web Forms presentation and ADO.NET data access. Mixing multiple supporting architectures in the realm of a single system is perfectly fine.

Introducing context mapping

DDD serves the purpose of identifying the top-level architecture of the final system. The DDD way of expressing the top-level architecture is through the composition of multiple bounded contexts inter-connected by relationships. The design artifact that expresses the schema is called a *context map*. In other words, the context map is the diagram that provides a comprehensive view of the system being designed.

Figure 1-4 provides a sample context map.

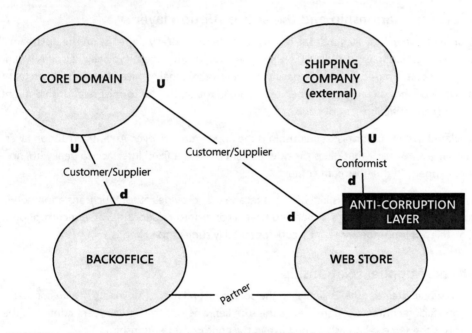

FIGURE 1-4 A sample context map showing some DDD relational patterns

There a few letters in the diagram, specifically *u* and *d*, and a few names. They express various types of relationships that the architect can recognize between bounded contexts.

Examining relationships between bounded contexts

Each DDD relationship between two bounded contexts is like an arc connecting two nodes of a graph. More precisely, the arc has a directed edge characterized by the letter U or D, as shown in Figure 1-4. The *U* indicates an *upstream* context, whereas *D* stands for a *downstream* context.

An upstream context influences a downstream context, but the opposite is not true. Influence can take various forms. For sure, it means that the code in the upstream context is available as a reference to the downstream context. It also means, though, that the schedule of work in the upstream context cannot be changed on demand by the team managing the downstream context. Furthermore, the responsiveness of the upstream team to requests for change might not be as prompt as desired by the downstream team.

Given upstream and downstream contexts, you can identify a few specific relationships:

- The conformist relationship
- The customer/supplier relationship
- The partner relationship

The conformist relationship and the anticorruption layer

A *conformist relationship* indicates that the downstream context totally depends on the upstream context and no negotiation is possible between parties. This arrangement typically happens when the upstream context is based on some legacy code or is an external service. When the same team is taking care of all bounded contexts, or when teams are in touch, the conformist relationship might be found only for really critical pieces of code.

Strictly related to the conformist relationship is the *anticorruption layer*. An anticorruption layer is an additional layer of code that gives the downstream context a fixed interface to deal with, no matter what happens in the upstream context.

Having an anticorruption layer is like having a façade that provides automatic translation between distinct but interfacing data models. When you have a conformist relationship, an anticorruption layer helps to isolate even more the area of the code potentially subject to changes.

The customer/supplier relationship

The *customer/supplier relationship* is similar to the conformist relationship. The upstream context of the two interfacing contexts is identified as the supplier, whereas the downstream context is the customer. This is the same relationship you have in the conformist relationship.

However, in this case some negotiation is possible between the teams that manage the two contexts. For example, the customer team can share concerns and expect that the supplier team addresses them in some way.

The partner relationship

The *partner relationship* refers to a form of mutual dependency set between the two involved bounded contexts. Put another way, both contexts depend on each other for the actual delivery of the code. This means that no team is allowed to make changes to the public interface of the context without consulting with the other team.

An even stricter form of partnership is established when a bounded context is shared by multiple contexts and multiple teams. This situation is referred to as having a *shared kernel*.

Introducing event storming

An emerging practice for effectively exploring the business domain to understand how it works and identify key events, commands, and bounded contexts is *event storming*. Originally developed by Alberto Brandolini, the technique consists of getting developers and domain experts in a room together to ask questions and find answers.

The classic *two-pizza rule* establishes the right number of people to invite. The two-pizza rule says you should never have a meeting that includes more people than you can feed with two pizzas. Generally, this limits the number of participants to less than eight.

Having unlimited modeling space

An event-storming session should take place in a location that has enough modeling space to display a long timeline of events and commands, draw sketches, and jot down notes. If it's a meeting room, you should plan to have a large whiteboard or at least a very long paper roll. Even an empty wall works.

One characteristic of event storming is the use of colorful tape and sticky notes to add business facts, entities, values, rules, and whatever else is needed. An event-storming session consists of talking about observable events in the business domain and listing them on the wall or whiteboard. A sticky note of a given color is applied to the modeling surface when an event is identified. You also do this when other domain-specific information, such as critical entities that aggregate commands and events, are identified.

Finding events in the domain

The primary goal of event storming is identifying relevant domain events. Once a business event is found, a sticky note is put on the wall. For example, in an e-commerce scenario, you will put a sticky note on the wall, say, for the *Order-Created* event.

The next step is to figure out what caused each of the discovered events. For example, a domain event can be caused by a command requested by some user. The Order-Created event, therefore, might be caused by the *checkout* command. In other cases, the event can be caused by some asynchronous occurrence, including a timeout or an absolute time. In both cases, you add a sticky note to the wall that indicates the cause. The event can also be the follower of a previously raised event. In this case, you also add another event note close to the originating event.

In the end, the modeling surface works as a timeline and quite a bit of space is necessary to hold the sticky notes for identified events, commands that caused events, ensuing events, user-interface sketches, notes, and more.

Leading the discussion

A *leader* is required to lead the discussion and stimulate the act of modeling the business. The leader just manages the session, stops long discussions, and ensures that the focus is not lost. The leader will also advance the meeting through the various phases. The leader might or might not be a domain expert or a software expert. She is a person whose goal is to help others understand and formalize the nature of the domain. Along the way, the leader ensures that the emerging model is appropriate and accurate for everyone.

Event storming represents a quick and easy way to gain a comprehensive vision of the business domain. A valuable output of event storming is the list of bounded contexts and the list of aggregates in each context. Looking at the final sticky notes timeline, an aggregate is essentially the software component that handles related commands and events and controls their persistence.

Summary

As shocking as it might sound, the world is being rebuilt in code. To paraphrase the ancient astronomer Galileo, "Software is the alphabet of the world." You can conclude from this statement that it's more important than ever for modern applications to be written to mirror real business processes. This approach is preferable to devising an accurate data model and code components to express the business logic and then, finally, defining workflows for the processes.

Preferring *mirroring* to *modeling* means that you believe focusing on processes is a more direct way to write effective software. It's effective because it creates a model that's closer to the real business and easier to manage because it's simpler and straight to the point.

DDD was introduced a decade ago to tackle the complexity in the heart of software. Although the principles of DDD are correct, DDD never worked in practice the way it worked in theory. I believe this happened mostly because we missed the fact that there are two parts of DDD: strategic design and tactical design. Of the two, strategic design is the most critical, but too many of us focused too much on the tactics portion of DDD.

This chapter looked at DDD strategic design and did it in a way that was technology and framework agnostic. The strategic part of DDD discovers the top-level architecture of the system by using a few analysis patterns and common practices. In the next chapter, I'll look into more concrete supporting architectures to give form and substance to identified architectural blocks.

CHAPTER 2

Selecting the supporting architecture

Does your model start with a root object called "universe"?

—*Greg Young*

In Chapter 1, "Conducting a thorough domain analysis," I focused on the techniques Domain-Driven Design (DDD) offers for exploring the business domain and on the outputs it produces. You've seen that the ideal output of a DDD analysis is a context map and that nodes on the map represent bounded contexts of the domain. You can think of contexts as being connected in some way, whether through a master/subordinate relationship or as partners that are shipped together and equally responsible for deploying the solution.

The context map that results from a DDD analysis is not like a detailed sketch of a bunch of services and their connections. The DDD context map is more general than that. You can certainly take each identified bounded context and implement it as a micro-service, a web service, a Service-Oriented Architecture (SOA) service, or whatever else you can think of. And then you can set up some protocol (for example, HTTP) for them to communicate. Generally, though, a bounded context identifies a segment of the domain and its relationship with other segments.

The next problem to face is giving each segment a software model. Distinct, standalone services are an option, but bounded contexts can also happily live as distinct entities in the context of the same software system.

The question here is slightly different: which way should you go to identify the software model for a bounded context?

It's all about business logic

As obvious as it might sound, the primary reason why customers require architects to devise software is business. Business logic is the part of business that summarizes the rules and functions for the final product to expose. Business logic can be reasonably split into two parts: application logic and domain logic.

Examining the application logic

The application logic is the part of business logic that cares about the implementation of workflows behind application visual endpoints. Anything that users can invoke from the presentation layer triggers some sort of workflow, and the application logic is where the steps are orchestrated.

As an example, consider the classic scenario of an e-commerce application in which the user submits an order. What typically happens next? In many tutorials that try to explain Microsoft ASP.NET, things stay quite simple and a new Order record is added to some database tables. In the real world, on the other hand, you usually go through a few more steps, such as validation, accounting, and delivery. The workflow is more sophisticated, and that's precisely what creates possible gray areas.

Working with the gray areas of application logic

A common aspect of a software system that sometimes becomes confusing is where the logic that prepares data for the presentation belongs. It's a gray area, and in most real-world systems the model used to read and save data is often different from the model used to process and display data. Where does this logic belong? Is it in the business layer or presentation layer?

The application logic layer, or *application layer*, just sits in between the presentation layer and the rest of the system and mediates the flow of data to and from the back end of the system. By design, the application logic is responsible for grabbing data from the presentation layer and sending it as input toward the back end and receiving data to massage to meet the needs of the user interface. (See Figure 2-1.)

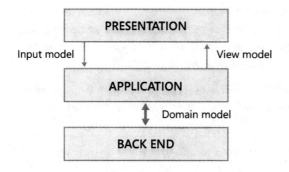

FIGURE 2-1 Flow of data from the presentation layer down to the back end of the system

The figure presents a multilayer architecture in which the presentation layer sends data to the application layer using classes from the input data model. At the same time, the presentation layer receives data for display purposes through the classes of the view data model. Finally, data exchange between the application layer and the back end is based on classes from yet another data model: the domain model.

Splitting the business logic into two parts, the topmost of which is the application logic, helps to keep things as clean and clear as possible and make it obvious who does what and how.

Exploring patterns of the application logic

The application logic consists of a bunch of workflows triggered by public endpoints. The endpoint can be reached via HTTP or in process, and the way it happens depends on the technology stack being employed.

How would you go about coding a workflow?

There are essentially two patterns you can use. One is the classic approach of coding the entire logic of the macro operation in a single place—hard-coding conditions and loops as required. You can do that via plain C# code, or you can use scripts supported by commercial workflow frameworks. The difference with regard to the final effects is not that much, but they are significant with regard to flexibility and in terms of modifying and extending what you have.

Another approach is to use a message-based organization of the workflow. In this regard, you don't have conditions and loops in code, but each action is pushed to a centralized mediator as a command. For example, the mediator can take the form of a bus or a queue. The flow of messages and the order of handlers can guarantee the correct flow of work and also offer a far easier-to-handle and decoupled environment for coding this part of the business logic.

Examining the domain logic

The domain logic is the part of the business logic that deals with business rules and aspects of the domain that are agnostic with regard to other concerns that are not strictly business related. It's also correct to say that the domain logic is the part of the business logic that doesn't vary between use-cases.

Deciding what's domain and what's not

Figure 2-2 is an attempt to illustrate the difference between domain and application logic.

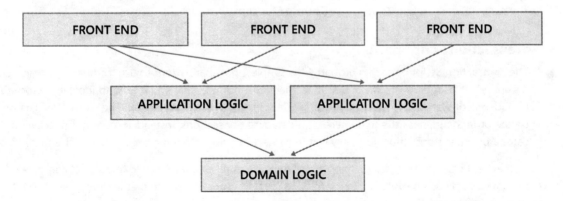

FIGURE 2-2 The difference between domain and application logic at a glance

Given a business domain, the application logic is the implementation of the use-cases for each of the applications that exist to solve the problems or serve the demands for that domain. If you have multiple front ends, such as one web front end and one mobile front end, you might need to have multiple pieces of application logic—typically, one for the use-cases of each front end. All application logic layers, though, will always refer to the same domain-logic implementation as far as the business rules are concerned.

In a banking scenario, for example, multiple front ends, such as the teller application and online banking, might have their own use-cases and might need to have their own application-logic layers. Both, though, will always refer to the same domain-logic API as far as core business entities are concerned, such as accounts and wire transfers.

Addressing persistence concerns

The domain logic is exclusively focused on aspects of the business as described by users and stakeholders through interviews. It is agnostic with regard to concerns such as persistence, and it's also agnostic with regard to dependencies on external services such as web services.

The domain logic, for example, might need to know the current exchange rate of a given currency, but getting that value from an external service is a task that doesn't belong to the domain logic. That's because the domain logic is about how to use currency information, not about how to get that information.

Data types that represent entities in the business domain might need to have their content persisted at some point. This is not a concern of the domain logic. Likewise, materializing instances of domain objects is not a concern of the domain logic, either. All of this belongs to surrounding layers.

Exploring patterns for the business logic

There a few common patterns for organizing the business logic of a layered system. They are the Transaction Script, Table Module, and Domain Model patterns.

Transaction Script pattern

The Transaction Script pattern is probably the simplest possible pattern to use for business logic, and it's entirely procedural. The word "Script" in the name indicates that you intend to logically associate a sequence of system-carried actions (namely, a script) with each user action. The word "Transaction," on the other hand, has little to do here with database transactions. Instead, it more generically indicates a business transaction you carry out from start to finish within the boundaries of the same call.

Inevitably, the pattern has some potential for code duplication. However, this aspect can be easily mitigated with coding discipline by identifying common subtasks and implementing them through reusable routines.

In terms of architectural design, the Transaction Script pattern leads to a design in which actionable user-interface elements in the presentation layer invoke the application layer's endpoints, and these endpoints trigger a transaction for each task.

Table Module pattern

As the same name suggests, the *Table Module pattern* heralds a more database-centric way of organizing the business logic. The core idea is that the logic of a system is closely related to the model used for persistence. So the Table Module pattern suggests you have one business component for each primary database table. Such a component exposes endpoints through which the application layer can execute commands and queries against a given table.

In terms of architectural design, the Table Module pattern leads to a design in which the presentation layer calls into the application layer. Then the application layer for each step of the workflow identifies the tables involved, finds the appropriate table-module component, and works with that.

Domain Model pattern

The Domain Model pattern suggests that, far before you care about persistence, you focus on the expected behavior of the system and on the data flows that make it work. When implementing the pattern, you essentially build an object model. However, the Domain Model pattern doesn't simply tell you to just code a bunch of C# or Java classes. The whole point of the Domain Model pattern is to get to an object-oriented model that fully represents the behavior and the processes of some business domain.

When implementing the pattern, you have classes that represent entities in the domain. The public interface of these classes refers to the actual expected behavior. Subsequently, business rules are incorporated into the body of the classes and the interface reflects ad hoc data types and actions.

The classes in the domain model should be agnostic with regard to persistence. For the content to be persisted, you pair the domain model with additional service classes that contain just the logic to materialize instances of domain classes to and from the persistence layer. A graphical schema of a Domain Model pattern has two elements: a model of aggregated objects, and domain services to carry out specific workflows that span multiple objects or deal directly with persistence. (See Figure 2-3.)

DOMAIN MODEL

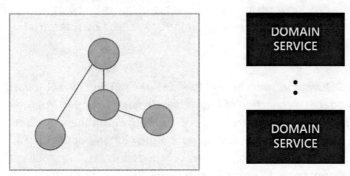

FIGURE 2-3 Graphical schema of the Domain Model pattern

Using a single model

The result of the DDD strategic analysis is having the information for building a software model for the given business domain. The design approach you use for building such a domain-driven software model is referred to as a *supporting architecture*.

The first example of a supporting architecture was presented a decade ago in Eric Evans's seminal book *Domain-Driven Design: Tackling Complexity in the Heart of Software* (Addison-Wesley, 2003). That supporting architecture was a single, object-oriented model designed to cover all aspects and uses of the domain. Such a single, all-encompassing model was referred to as the *domain model*, and it's consistent with the Domain Model pattern for organizing the business logic that I mentioned a moment ago.

Other supporting architectures emerged later in an attempt to solve the problems that people experienced while trying to adapt DDD to an increasingly broader range of problems and business domains. In this chapter, I'll also introduce Command Query Responsibility Segregation (CQRS) and event sourcing (ES)—namely, the foundation for a message-based organization of business logic.

Exploring the elements of an object-oriented domain model

An object-oriented domain model is a software model for a business domain that reflects all the intricacies of real business processes, including tasks performed by personas, roles, and naming conventions. To serve this purpose effectively, the object-oriented model needs to fulfill a few strict requirements.

From the compiler perspective, a domain model is just made of classes and a class is a collection of properties and methods. From the developer perspective, classes are of two main types: entities and value types. Both types of classes work together to express business logic, and persistence is not one of their concerns.

Note Especially back when DDD was introduced and the idea of a domain model started taking root, building that model as a collection of interrelated objects sounded like the perfect fit. However, more recently, the software industry is rediscovering the functional approach to programming. Modern functional languages are growing in popularity (F#, for example), and functional features are being progressively added to existing languages, including C# and Java. In this context, a domain model built using a functional approach is still not a mainstream approach, but it's certainly a viable approach that's being evaluated and put through its paces.

Entities

An *entity* is a class that represents a natural element of the business domain—anything like an invoice, a trade, a wire transfer, or a sports match. The class has public and internal properties and possibly a few methods. Properties are a way to store and expose the current state of the entity. Methods are the public tools available to modify the state.

Among the properties of an entity, there's something that gives the collection of data a unique attribute—*identity*. The identity is a combination of values that uniquely describe the information the entity encapsulates. Overall, it's the same concept you have with a primary key, which you might know from relational databases.

As an example, how would you consider accounting for two money transfers that take place the same day and involve the same amount and bank account? Is it the same operation just repeated? Or are the transactions rather distinct operations occurring independently? It's probably the latter, but whether it is or not strictly depends on the domain.

Entities are typically made of data and behavior. When it comes to behavior, though, I should clarify that *behavior* refers to domain logic and business rules.

> **Important** I can never emphasize the point enough that persistence is not a concern of entities. If an entity has methods, those methods will never be anything like *Load* or *Save*, and they will never be used for CRUD actions. The entirety of persistence concerns in the DDD vision is delegated to domain services and, in particular, to repositories. I'll talk about repositories later in the chapter and also in Chapter 13, "Persistence and modeling."

Value types

In DDD, a *value type* is a type whose instances are fully defined by the values stored in the public properties. However, be aware that the attributes of a value type never change after the instance has been created. If they do change, the value object becomes an instance of another value object fully identified by the new collection of attributes.

DDD value objects are also referred to as *immutable types*. The *Int32* and *String* types are the most popular immutable types in the Microsoft .NET Framework. Here's a sample implementation of a typical value type:

```
public class Score
{
    public Score(int goal1, int goal2)
    {
        Goal1 = goal1;
        Goal2 = goal2;
    }
    public int Goal1 { get; private set; }
    public int Goal2 { get; private set; }

    public override bool Equals(object obj)
```

```
{
    if (this == obj)
        return true;
    if (obj == null || GetType() != obj.GetType())
        return false;
    var other = (Score) obj;
    return Goals1 == other.Goals1 &&
           Goals2 == other.Goals2;
}

// In .NET, you also need to override GetHashCode
// if you override Equals
...
}
```

Behavior is not relevant in value objects; value objects might still have methods, but those are essentially helper methods. Unlike entities, though, value objects don't need identity because they have no variable state and are fully identified by their data.

In the context of a domain model, the role of value types is much more important than many seem to think. Value types are about using more accurate tools to model the real world. The score of a soccer match can be represented with two distinct integer properties, but in the end it's an ad hoc type whose instances are fully identified by two integers. Primitive types, generally, are too often an approximation of the real-world aspect they attempt to model. Some logic is required to validate their use. Having a value type for this purpose is consistent with DDD principles.

Putting business rules inside

The behavior you put in entities is essentially business rules. When you use other patterns for organizing the business logic, you place business rules in standalone components that work as stateless calculators. In a domain model, business rules find their place in the folds of entities.

As an example, let's consider a sports match. How would you devise a software model for a scoring application that referees or assistants use to track the relevant facts of a sports match (score, faults, timeouts, start, finish)? How would you go about defining the behavior of a *Match* class?

Using an anemic entity class

The following class seems to be a good start. Apparently, it's perfect because it lets you store and manage whatever content you typically want to associate with a sports match:

```
public class Match
{
    public int MatchId { get; set; }
    public Score Score { get; set; }
    public int Period { get; set; }
    public string Team1 { get; set; }
    public string Team2 { get; set; }
    public MatchState MatchState { get; set; }
    ...
}
```

The class contains all the pieces that effectively express the state and evolution of the match. You get to know and change the score of the match, the teams or players, the state of the match (scheduled, in progress, finished), and even details such as the current period. With some further refinements, this class could become a good piece of code, especially once you add a factory and maybe a few query methods to read the state, such as *IsInProgress*, *IsTeamLeading*, and so forth.

The entity has some associated behavior. For example, the match starts, finishes, and contains goals scored by one team. Where would you code such behavior? You can add methods to the class, or you can leave the class as is and create a separate engine to consistently modify the state of the class when an action is required. Functionally speaking, both options are good, but if you want to go with a Domain Model pattern, only the former is valid.

Using private setters

If you add methods to the entity class, you must first change the qualifier of public properties. All setters should be made private because you want to ensure that any state change happens only through the business rules engine, which is there to ensure consistency.

As an example, consider the *MatchState* property. Defined with a public setter, it enables any code that gets an instance of the *Match* class to arbitrarily change the state of the match. When you define a domain model, you actually create a public API for the business logic and you should make sure to prevent the API from being misused. A private setter prevents arbitrary changes, and additional methods should be provided to enable developers to alter the state of the match.

In this regard, would a *SetMatchState* method be appropriate?

Using behavior-rich entity classes

From a purely functional perspective, a *SetMatchState* method is appropriate. However, it misses the business perspective of the action. Why would you change the state of the match? What has happened at the business level to require that? It could be, for example, that the match has started. If so, a *Start* method is more appropriate for the following reasons:

- It gives you a behavior-rich design.

- It is business compliant.

- It reflects the ubiquitous language.

- It actually alters the state of the entity consistently.

Here's a way to rewrite the *Match* class:

```
public class Match
{
    public Match( ... ) { ... }
    public Score Score  { get; internal set; }
    public int Period { get; internal set; }
    ...
    public Match Start() { ... }
```

```
    public Match Finish() { ... }
    public Match NewPeriod() { ... }
    public Match Goal( ... ) { ... }
}
```

Now the class exposes a constructor through which you initially put the class in a valid state. There are also read-only properties to get a glimpse of the state:

```
public Match Start()
{
    if (MatchState != MatchState.Scheduled)
      throw new ArgumentException("Cannot start a match that is not currently scheduled");

    MatchState = MatchState.InProgress;
    return this;
}
```

The implementation of methods might not be overly complex at all, as you can see. More importantly, methods are business-oriented and make it so easy for developers to implement use-cases.

Discovering aggregates

As you proceed in acknowledging requirements and turning them into a formal software model, you will often spot a few individual entities being constantly used and referenced together. You can think of them as references within a rich document that contains images, tables, and graphs. At a second look, you might identify a few collections of related objects that always work together. In the Domain Model jargon, this is called an *aggregate*.

Building an aggregate model

You can come up with aggregates in one of two ways, and it all depends on the approach you take to analysis. You can first isolate entities and then see how they work together, and identify aggregates in this way. A more common practice, however, is to decompose a domain model into aggregates first, and then, within any aggregate, identify the domain entities.

Another way to look at aggregates comes from the basic tasks of relational database design. The process of building an aggregate model is the same logical process you use to define tables in a relational database. Not all tables are at the same logical level, and some tables exist only to be used in conjunction with others. The quintessential example is *Orders* and *OrderDetails*.

When you have an aggregate, how do you access the objects and operate on them? If all objects were publicly accessible in the same way, what would be the point of having aggregates? The aggregate model is related to the concept of an *aggregate root*—the primary object in each aggregate.

Creating aggregate roots

An aggregate root is one entity in the collection of related entities and value types that works as the entry point for executing related business tasks. An aggregate root has global visibility throughout the domain model and can be referenced directly. Entities inside the aggregate still have their identity and life, but they can't be referenced directly from outside the aggregate.

At a more abstract level, an aggregate defines a context where a bunch of actions and events are generated and handled. The aggregate root is the entity that defines the transactional boundaries for these actions and events. It also provides a public interface for these actions to be invoked and executed in full respect of business consistency.

Having an aggregate root doesn't necessarily require writing ad hoc code. Recognizing aggregates and roots is primarily something you do as a design aid. Figure 2-4 summarizes the aggregate model.

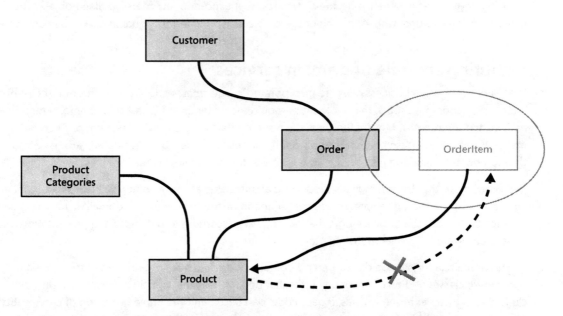

FIGURE 2-4 Relationships between aggregate roots

The four boxes in the figure represent aggregates, three of which are collapsed and just hide their internal entities. The *Customer* and *Order* boxes, for example, might interact but only through the public interface of root objects. The *Order* aggregate includes the *OrderItem* entity. The *Product* aggregate can't reference directly reference *OrderItem*. It can only do that only via the mediation of the *Order* root. Also, the *OrderItem* can reference can still hold a reference to an external aggregate root.

Aggregate root classes hide related classes from callers and require that callers refer to them for any interaction. In other words, an entity is only allowed to reference an entity in the same aggregate or the root of another aggregate. At the same time, a child entity—like *OrderItem* in Figure 2-4—can hold a reference to another aggregate root.

Why have aggregates?

The aggregate root object has a few important responsibilities:

- The aggregate root guarantees that contained objects are always in a valid state according to the applicable business rules. For example, if the business rules state that no detail of the order can be updated after it has shipped, the root must make this update impossible to occur in code.

- The aggregate root is responsible for the persistence of all encapsulated objects, including cascading updates and deletions.

- Any query operation can only retrieve an aggregate root. Access to internal objects must always happen by navigation through the interface of the aggregate root.

Using aggregates is beneficial to the code because it exposes a few coarse-grained objects that developers have to deal with. And each of these objects is—by design—guaranteed to be consistent.

Exploring the role of domain services

In a scenario in which business rules are incorporated in aggregates and exposed through the public interface of aggregate roots, the whole set of requirements tends to be partitioned among identified entities and aggregates. Most of the time, the resulting partitions cover 100 percent of the requirements. What if that doesn't happen? And what if, for business rules to be evaluated, you have to go through durable data and persistence? This is where domain services come into play.

According to the domain model's supporting architecture, at some point a solution has a *domain layer* that sits in between the presentation layer and infrastructure layer. The domain layer is responsible for the part of the business logic that doesn't vary according to use-cases and presentation front ends. (See Figure 2-2 earlier in the chapter.)

The domain layer is made of two parts: a domain model and a set of domain services. *Domain services* are classes and take care of any tasks that don't fit into the domain model. These tasks include dealing with external systems, legacy code, databases, and the implementation of cross-entity business logic. Domain services are part of the domain layer but distinct from domain-model classes. They use and manipulate domain model classes, however. They also might need to have *privileged* access to domain-model classes—for example, for setting properties outside public behavioral methods. This behavior is *internal* to the assembly and, for example, in .NET is achieved through internal (as opposed to private or protected) property setters.

Implementing cross-entity business logic

A good example for seeing where domain services fit is determining whether a given customer reached the status of *gold customer*. Depending on how reaching that status is defined in the requirements, the operation might involve multiple aggregates and database access. As an example, suppose the domain says that a customer earns the status after she exceeds a given threshold of orders on a selected range of products.

You can't reasonably have an *IsGold* method on the *Customer* aggregate that calculates the status. Calculating the status requires accessing the database, and this is not within the duties of an aggregate. A domain service is the perfect fit. A service, in fact, is able to query orders and products for a customer and store results as a Boolean into a newly created instance of a *Customer* aggregate.

In this case, the application-layer method that needs to report a customer's gold-status information back to the user interface invokes a domain service and gets back an instance properly filled with up-to-date data. The constructor of the *Customer* class is invoked internally, and the *IsGold* property is set through an internal setter.

As developers, we tend to consider domain services to be backup solutions for pieces of behavior that we otherwise can't fit in aggregates. However, sometimes the boundary between an entity and a domain service is subtle. The rule of thumb is that when it's not obvious which one is the most appropriate choice, both options can be made to work.

Using repositories

Repositories are the most popular and commonly used type of domain service. Repositories care about persistence of aggregates. When you need to materialize an aggregate from the database or save it back to the database, you use a repository. It's recommended to have one repository per aggregate root—*CustomerRepository*, *OrderRepository*, and so forth. As mentioned before, one repository per aggregate is enough to show you care about consistency and functionality—an aggregate is responsible for the persistence of child objects and cascading options.

There are many ways to write a repository and probably none of them is patently wrong. This said, a repository is often based on a common interface like *IRepository<T>*:

```
public interface IRepository<T> where T:IAggregateRoot
{
    // You can keep the IAggregateRoot interface as a plain marker or
    // you can have a few common methods in it.

    T Find (object id);
    void Save (T item);
}
```

Specific repository classes can then be derived from the base interface:

```
public interface IOrderRepository : IRepository<Order>
{
    // The actual list of members is up to you
    ...
}
```

Members of a repository class will actually perform data access—either queries, updates, or insertions. The technology used for data access is up to you. Most commonly today, you use an Object/Relational Modeling (O/RM) framework like Entity Framework, but nothing prevents you from using ADO.NET, plain stored procedures or, why not, a NoSQL store.

Working with external services and legacy code

When the business logic relies on existing pieces of code or an external service that is reachable over some protocol (TCP, HTTP, and so forth), a domain service class is the ideal wrapper and a good place for storing details about the connection. A good example of external services to wrap and expose to the application layer as services of the domain are web services for things like weather forecasts, stock quotes, currency rates, or perhaps live scores from games in progress.

Legacy code can be treated in the same way as long as there's a way to make the domain service become a sort of façade for the code.

> ### Not just any model—Just the right model for the context
>
> Developers sometimes abstract too much and implement the *God antipattern*, which can be summarized by saying that they come up with a model where the root object is named *GalaxyBase*. The point behind a domain model is having a software model that is a good fit to represent the business scenario. A good example for illustrating this point is a map of the world.
>
> The Mercator projection is a graphical representation of the world map. Its unique characteristics make it suitable for nautical purposes but not for applications like Google Maps. If you look at the world layout through the perspective of the Mercator projection, you would say that Alaska is as large as Brazil. The reality, instead, is that Brazil is five times larger than Alaska. However, when you draw a course on a Mercator world projection, the angle between the course and the Equator remains constant across all meridians. This made it easy—as far back as the 1500s—to measure courses and bearings via protractors.
>
> The Mercator map is a model that distorts both areas and distances; in this regard, it's not suited to faithfully representing the map of the world as it really is. You don't want to use it instead of, say, Google Maps to represent a city on a map. On the other hand, it's a great model for the (domain) context it was created for—nautical cartography.

Implementing command and query separation

For too long, the executive summary of DDD has been that having an object model capable of describing the entire business domain was a winning plan. Some DDD projects succeeded, and some failed. For the most part, it was blind faith in the power of objects that convinced many developers to try that approach. Since the 1990s, the world of software has been obsessed with the idea of objects. So focusing on them sounded like a great idea—except that it didn't work very well in the real world. Having a unique object model that can serve scenarios like processing an order, generating a report of sales, and communicating which products in stock should be promoted is a bit challenging.

Processing an order without gaining access to the persistence layer, external services, or both is highly impractical. Reducing a business transaction to a database transaction (even a distributed database transaction) might be painful because many business transactions are actually long-running transactions.

It's more about the business processes and tasks than the underlying domain model.

The Domain Model supporting architecture suggests you incorporate business logic into classes and define processes through domain services. It's a systematic way to organize business processes and might not be flexible enough to model all real business processes. It's effective when processes stay close to a simple and quick database transaction. Beyond this point, a single model is more of a problem than a solution.

Working with the Command and Query Separation principle

Back in the 1980s, Bertrand Meyer formulated the Command and Query Separation (CQS) principle while elaborating the Eiffel programming language. The principle is simple to explain and understand, yet it has a dramatic impact on the way we plan software.

According to CQS, every action performed by any software should be coded either as a command that alters the state of the system or as a query that reads, without altering, the state of the system. It should never be both things at the same time. Everybody agrees on the formal cleanliness of the principle, but when it's put into practice it might seem a bit too restrictive—especially if you try to apply it at the level of the single class method.

As a result, the CQS principle was blissfully ignored for years.

At some point, in an effort to apply DDD to special business domains (critical 24/7 services with a lot of money involved), somebody has to refresh the CQS principle. Applied at the architecture level, the CQS principle showed its true power and got a slightly different name—CQRS, short for *Command and Query Responsibility Segregation*.

Using distinct stacks in software architecture

As surprising as it might sound, the basic fact that commands and queries are two different things has a deep impact on the overall architecture of a system. Figure 2-5 compares the canonical DDD-inspired layered architecture with the same system redesigned with CQRS in mind. The core difference is that you use a domain model only in the command stack. The query stack is made of plain data-access code and uses simple data-transfer objects (DTO) to bring data up to the presentation layer.

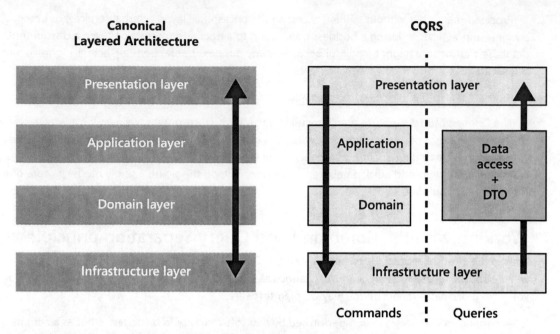

FIGURE 2-5 Contrasting CQRS and a canonical layered architecture

The application layer is responsible for exposing distinct endpoints for commands and queries as triggered from the user interface. The application layer essentially routes requests on distinct workflows. If it's a command, it goes through any implementation of the business logic that suits the need. In most cases, it's just a classic Domain Model pattern with business logic incorporated in aggregates and repositories and other domain services to support the implementation of business processes.

The nice thing about having distinct stacks is that you can use separate object models for implementing commands and queries. This simple split takes away of lot of complexity. You might have two similar objects, but each would be very simple and straight to the point. You typically have a full domain model for commands but plain data-transfer objects tailor-made for the presentation. The structure of DTOs is often directly inferred from the result of SQL queries. In addition, when you need multiple presentation front ends (for example, web, mobile web, and mobile applications), all you do is create additional read models. The complexity results from the summation of individual complexities rather than from the Cartesian product of all of them.

Using distinct databases

The separation of the back end into distinct stacks simplifies design and coding and sets the ground for unparalleled scalability potential. However, this separation raises new issues that should be carefully considered at the architecture level. How can you keep the two stacks in sync so that whatever commands write is read back consistently?

Depending on the business problem you're trying to solve, a CQRS implementation can be based on one or two databases. If a shared database is used, getting the right projection of data for the query's purpose is just extra work in the read stack performed on top of plain queries. A shared database, at the same time, ensures classic ACID (atomic, consistent, isolated, durable) consistency.

In the case of specific issues like performance or scalability, you can consider using different persistence endpoints for the command stack and the read stack. As an example, the command stack might have an event store, a NoSQL document store, or perhaps a nondurable store such as an in-memory cache. The synchronization of command data with read data can happen asynchronously or even can be scheduled periodically, depending on how stale data affects the presentation (and depending on how stale the data is).

In the case of distinct databases, the read database is often a plain relational database that just offers one (or more) projections of data. (See Figure 2-6.)

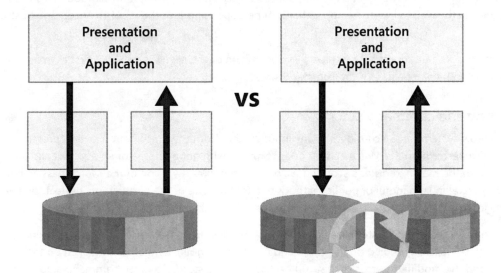

FIGURE 2-6 Comparing two CQRS architectures using shared and distinct databases for the command and query stacks

When is CQRS appropriate?

Unlike DDD, the CQRS principle is not a comprehensive approach to designing an enterprise-class system. CQRS is simply a pattern that guides you in architecting a specific bounded context of a possibly larger system. CQRS is a valid alternative to using the Domain Model approach *tout-court*.

The CQRS architectural pattern was devised primarily to solve performance issues in highly concurrent business scenarios, where handling commands synchronously and performing data analysis was getting more and more problematic. Many seem to think that outside the realm of such collaborative systems, the power of CQRS diminishes significantly. As a matter of fact, the power of CQRS shines in collaborative systems because it lets you address complexity and competing resources in a much smoother way. There's more to it than meets the eye, I think.

CQRS can sufficiently pay the architecture bill even in far simpler scenarios, where the plain separation between query and command stacks leads to simplified design and dramatically reduces the risk of design errors. Put another way, CQRS lowers the level of skills required to implement even quite a sophisticated system. Using CQRS makes implementing scalability and cleanliness an affordable effort for nearly any team.

Implementing CQRS

Let's go back to the *Match* class presented awhile back and take a second look at that from a CQRS perspective. In a scoring application that referees or their assistants might use, there are at least two general goals. One is tracking the score and all relevant events around the match, such as goals, timeouts, or faults. The other goal is reading the score back and displaying it on scoreboards around the venue, via the web in live-score applications, or perhaps using it as the input to encourage or stop bets.

In this context, is it appropriate to have just one version of the *Match* class? Let's first examine the question from the perspective of the command stack.

Exploring the command stack

In the sample system we are considering, any input coming from the presentation layer represents an action to perform on the *Match* class. It doesn't matter whether a referee or an assistant clicks to start or finish the match, register a scored goal, or call a timeout. A version of the *Match* class with a read-only state and a handful of public methods to alter the state of the entity is just perfect for any of these jobs.

A domain service might materialize an instance of the class from the persistence layer, making a query by ID. Next, depending on the command (start, finish, goal), a method is invoked on the instance and the modified state is then saved back to the data store. If a given command algorithm proves to be not particularly effective, changing it has no effect on other parts of the system. And when distinct data stores are used, it doesn't even affect the storage behavior of other parts of the system.

Furthermore, staying focused on the actual behavior and commands that alter the state of the system makes the design become progressively more task-oriented. Even when you end up using a domain model for encapsulating the domain logic, your way of thinking gets more functional in nature and more attention is placed on tasks than on abstract models.

Ultimately, developers are called to write software to solve problems in specific segments of the real world. Most of the time, writing software is about creating artifacts to automate processes. Most of the time, the (high) costs of software originate from misunderstandings and misrepresentation of the segments that the real-world software is called upon to automate. This is why an approach that puts the emphasis on tasks, commands, and events rather than just on models, and often just too abstractly, is welcome. Functional design and separation of concerns between commands and queries are two pillars of tomorrow's software. And you can see more and more examples of this approach even today.

> **!** **Important** Even though CQRS is important, it's not per se such a big thing. It is merely the principle that recognizes the benefits of separating commands from queries. You can achieve this separation, for example, even by simply using different database contexts around a plain Entity Framework solution in which the vision of the final system remains strictly datacentric.

Exploring the read stack

In a single-model scenario, you now have a rich *Match* class that knows how to advance the state of the match by following input from the presentation layer of a given application. The *Match* class, as we designed it earlier in the chapter with methods like *Start* and *Finish*, offers public properties to read the current score and other relevant information, such as faults or requested timeouts.

Passing the class as-is to some O/RM to have it persisted is also a simple operation. What about materializing an instance of the *Match* class from persistence and giving it the last-known-good state it had?

This might not be an easy task.

As it was designed, the internal state of the *Match* class can be altered only via methods, and methods depend on the business logic and actual behavior performed. Initializing a domain-model class to a given state requires a compromise. In particular, setters of some properties should be marked as internal instead of as private, or some internal methods should be provided to be used by domain services within the same assembly.

Even assuming that you work around this problem, though, there's another one to face. The presentation code triggers a query and gets back an instance of the *Match* class. All it needs to do is read the state, the score of the match, and perhaps the names of the teams playing. This information is available, but command methods also are available. The public API of the class offers more than expected, and this enables the client code to do things that potentially would violate the consistency of the system.

To avoid that, you can make the source code of the *Match* class more and more complicated by introducing permissions and conditional write operations. When you head down this slope, though, you soon realize that it's quite slippery. The alternative is using different classes for command and queries. In the read-only domain model you create specifically for queries, you have plain data-transfer objects that reflect as closely as possible the nature of the projection a particular presentation layer requires.

Having distinct object models for commands and queries is exactly what CQRS is all about.

Creating a sample read model

Here's a concrete example of how you can implement a read model that works on top of Entity Framework and always returns *IQueryable* objects up through the layers. The following code shows the typical implementation of an Entity Framework *DbContext* class that exposes a collection of data as *DbSet<T>* objects:

```
public class CommandDatabase : DbContext
{
    public CommandDatabase()
    {
        Products = base.Set<Product>();
        Customers = base.Set<Customer>();
        Orders = base.Set<Order>();
    }

    public DbSet<Order> Orders { get; private set; }
    public DbSet<Customer> Customers { get; private set; }
    public DbSet<Product> Products { get; private set; }
    ...
}
```

The *DbSet* class provides full access to the underlying database and can be used to set up queries and update operations via LINQ-to-Entities. To reduce operations to just queries and then build a read model, some changes are required. Here's an example:

```
public class ReadDatabase : DbContext
{
    private DbSet<Product> _products;
    private DbSet<Customer> _customers;
    private DbSet<Order> _orders;

    public ReadDatabase()
    {
        _products = base.Set<Product>();
        _customers = base.Set<Customer>();
        _orders = base.Set<Order>();
    }

    public IQueryable<Customer> Customers
    {
        get { return _customers; }
    }

    public IQueryable<Order> Orders
    {
        get { return _orders; }
    }

    public IQueryable<Product> Products
    {
        get { return _products; }
    }
    ...
}
```

The key change is that collections of data are exposed and returned as *IQueryable* objects. Any code that receives such references can operate only through the *IQueryable* interface. In particular, it has not access to methods to save changes back. The code in the application layer is requested only to make queries using the *ReadDatabase* root object. Domain services invoked from the command stack, instead, will use the *CommandDatabase* object and gain the rights of reading and writing to the underlying data store.

Introducing message-based formulation

CQRS is only the first step toward a more flexible and revolutionary architecture for modern systems of nearly any level of complexity. Beyond the basic fact of separating the implementation of commands from the implementation of queries, CQRS leads you toward a message-based implementation of the business tasks.

In this context, the read stack is not really different from what I have discussed so far—just a plain layer of queries and data-transfer objects. The command stack, instead, has a significantly different layout. Is a message-based way of organizing the business logic really a new thing? If you look at how Windows has worked (and was programmed) for years, you'll see that messages are nothing new. I'd like to say that CQRS with messages is a new way of doing old things, but it's a new way that's hopefully a lot more extensible and flexible enough to support the evolution of the business.

Ad-hoc infrastructure

In a message-based CQRS design, the application layer doesn't call out any full-fledged implementation of some workflows. It simply turns any input it gets from the callers into a *command* and pushes that command to a new element—the *command processor*.

The command processor can take any form in a concrete implementation. A common implementation is through a *bus*. In software, the term *bus* generically refers to a shared communication channel that facilitates communication between software modules. The bus here is just a shared channel and doesn't need to be a commercial product or an open-source framework. It can simply be your own class.

Commands and messages

A *command* is an action performed against the back end of the system. An example of a command can be registering a new user, processing the content of a shopping cart, or updating the profile of a customer.

A command is represented with a plain data-transfer object class that just contains the input data to be used in the implementation of the command. A command always refers to a monodirectional task that proceeds from the presentation layer down to the domain layer and likely ends up modifying some storage.

Commands are triggered in two ways. One is when the user explicitly acts on some user-interface element, such as a button. The other is when some autonomous services interact asynchronously with the system. As an example, you can think of how a shipping company interacts with its partners. The company might have an HTTP service that partners invoke to place requests, which become commands for the back end of the system.

Generally, a *command* is specific type of a message. Quite typically, the implementation has the *Command* class inherit from a base *Message* class:

```
public class Message
{
    public DateTime TimeStamp {get; set;}
}
public class Command : Message
{
    // Some properties you want all commands to share
    ...
}
public class SomeSpecificCommand : Command
{
    // Properties of the specific command
    ...
}
```

The application layer grabs input from the presentation layer, prepares a command, and pushes the command to the processor. In some common implementations, this sequence of events might mean pushing the command to a bus for further dispatching.

The command processor

The *command processor* is a sort of dispatcher that knows about a list of handlers—with one handler for each supported command. The processor simply checks the type of the message and hands it over to the registered handler. The handler does its job and alters the state of the system the way it's expected to do.

A command is typically directed at one handler and can be rejected by the system or fail while being executed by some handler. Usually, the command brings no response back to the caller except perhaps for some acknowledgment. Commands alone are not enough to implement business processes. When a command executes, it might be necessary to notify other handlers of what has just happened. This raises the need for events.

Notifying events via messages

An *event* is the notification of something that has just happened within the boundaries of some transaction. Unlike a command, though, an event also might be a notification of something happening outside the boundaries of the bounded context that originated it. Here's a sample event:

```
public class Event : Message
{
   // Common properties for all events you want to have
   ...
}
public class OrderCreatedEvent : Event
{
    public string OrderId { get; private set; }
    public string TrackingId { get; private set; }
    public string TransactionId { get; private set; }

    public OrderCreatedEvent(string orderId, string trackingId, string transactionId)
    {
        OrderId = orderId;
        TrackingId = trackingId;
        TransactionId = transactionId;
    }
}
```

As you can see, the structure of event and command classes is nearly the same except for the naming convention—a command is imperative and describes an action to perform, whereas an event refers to something that just happened. In both cases, the name should be very specific about the intended purpose of the message.

A typical example of commands and events that interact is when the user interface triggers the checkout process of an order. The command that starts the process conveys all details about products in the order, shipping address, and customer payment details. The checkout command starts a work-flow that proceeds through actions and events that a given action has been completed. At the end, when the payment has been completed, the *PaymentCompleted* event might be raised. A handler of that will add an *Order* record to the data store, and an *OrderCreated* event will be raised to let possi-bly registered handlers know about the actual order ID and transaction ID. A handler of *OrderCreated* might simply send an email to the customer.

Presenting a sample message-based architecture

As mentioned, a common way to implement the command processor is via a *bus*. At startup, the bus is configured with a collection of listeners. A *listener* is a component that knows what to do with an incoming message. There are two types of message handlers: *sagas* and *handlers*. A saga is an in-stance of a process that is optionally stateful, maintains access to the bus, is persistent, and is poten-tially long-running. A handler is a simpler one-off executor of any code bound to a given message.

The full flowchart behind the business task is never laid out entirely in the application layer. Rather, it's implemented as a sequence of small steps, each calling out the next step or raising an event to indicate it's done. As a result, after a message is pushed to the bus, the resulting sequence of actions is partially predictable and can be altered by adding and removing listeners to the bus. Handlers end immediately. Sagas, which are potentially long-running, will end when the final message is received. Figure 2-7 presents a graphical view of the message-based CQRS architecture.

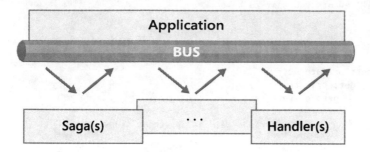

FIGURE 2-7 The command stack of an event-based CQRS architecture

Any interaction that takes place in the user interface generates some requests to the system. For example, in an ASP.NET MVC scenario, these requests take the form of controller actions and methods in the application layer. In the application layer, a command is created and pushed to some machinery for actual processing.

Defining a saga

A saga component looks like a collection of logically related methods and event handlers. Each *saga* is a component that declares the following information:

- A command or event that starts the process associated with the saga

- Commands the saga can handle and events the saga is interested in

Whenever the bus receives a command (or an event) that can start a saga, it creates a new saga object. The constructor of the saga generates a unique ID, which is necessary to handle concurrent instances of the same saga. The ID can be a GUID as well as a hash value from the starter command or anything else, like the session ID. Once the saga is created, it executes the command or runs the code that handles the notified event. Executing the command mostly means writing data or executing calculations.

At some point in the lifetime of the saga instance, it might be necessary to send another command to trigger another process or, more likely, fire an event that advances another process. The saga does that by pushing commands and events back to the bus. A saga also might stop at some point and wait for events to be notified. The concatenation of commands and events keeps the saga alive until a completion point is reached. In this regard, you can also think of a saga as a workflow with starting and ending points.

Introducing event sourcing

Event sourcing (ES) takes events to the next level. ES is not simply about defining events as a tool to express business logic and concatenate actions together to form a workflow. ES goes beyond that and heralds a world in which events are the real items that form the data source of the application. In an ES scenario, you store events and, if required, you process events to extract projections of data that take snapshots of the current state of the system.

The sequence of recorded events is your primary data store. Projections are specific snapshots of data you take at a given time. An event projection is like the SQL projection of a query—the formalization of how you want to see returned data.

As you can guess, persisting events instead of a domain model has a significant impact on the way you organize the back end of a system. Event persistence weds well with CQRS, and with the idea that distinct databases are used to save the state of the application and expose it to the presentation layer. When you add ES to a system, you just change the structure and implementation of the data source.

Considering events as functions

The use of events in software is nothing new. Several sectors of the industry (banking, insurance, and finance) have used events to track the whole history of their activity. Even though the term *event sourcing* is relatively new, these industries found a way to track events in software for decades. Today, with events as a data source, we can write more effective software or software that was impractical to write before. These days, events can do a lot more than just audit—they form the basis of valuable features such as high scalability and, more importantly, new business scenarios.

By using events as the data source, you take one step down the abstraction level of the core data you store. From events, you can build nearly any projection of data you like. With a classic data model, on the other hand, you tend to store a snapshot of the state rather than the sequence of steps that from an initial state brought you to the current state. By going through a list of business events, you can rebuild the current state of the business, of course, but you also can aggregate data in many different ways to conduct many different analyses.

What's an "event," then?

An *event* is more or less a function with a name and parameters that apply to the state and produces a different state. An event is *immutable*, meaning that once it has happened and it has been recorded, it's there and won't change anymore. Because of this, logs of events can be replicated countless times and manipulation software can be applied with no risk of creating concurrency and synchronization issues and inconsistency at the business level. This is the key factor that makes ES so compelling in high-scalability scenarios.

Figure 2-8 gives you an idea of the internal structure of an event data source.

ORDERS audit

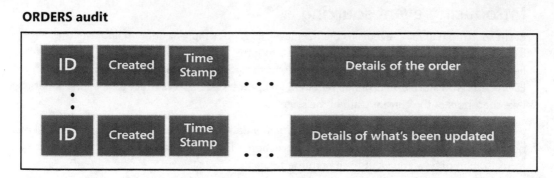

FIGURE 2-8 A sequence of events as they might be stored in a data source

Persisting an event

When persisted, events form an audit log of what happened in the system. Events can be persisted to a relational database, but they ideally go to an ad hoc type of database, called the *event store*. Like a plain database, an event store persists a list of event objects. An event is represented as a plain collection of events. Each event will be made of a different collection of properties, and this irregular schema is exactly what makes relational persistence hard.

An event store has two main characteristics:

- It works as an append-only data store and doesn't have to support arbitrary updates.

- It must be able to return the stream of events associated with a given key.

Event objects must refer in some way to a business object. If you're using the Domain Model pattern to organize the command stack, the event store must be able to return the stream of events associated with an aggregate instance. If you're not using the Domain Model pattern, you still have some key value that uniquely identifies the relevant business object.

Querying for events

As mentioned, persisting events is something that can be done even using a relational database, although a NoSQL document database is perhaps a better option. But anyway, none of this would be a data store *specifically* designed for dealing with events. Saving events is just one aspect of event sourcing; extracting events via queries is just as crucial.

You might want to query events that occurred in a specific timeframe, involved certain amounts of data, or took more than a specified amount of time to complete a business transaction. An event store should provide a query language that is flexible enough to extract just the events you want, not simply the last N events or all events after a given time.

Related to the point of querying events is also the point of building a projection of the data stored in the events. In much the same way you build a SQL query by indicating which columns you want back, you should be able to query an event store to return a given snapshot of data. Today the most effective attempt to create an event store is the Event Store project at *http://geteventstore.com*.

Replaying events

With events in your data source, you don't have the state of the system readymade. However, by reading back the log of messages you can rebuild the state of the system. This aspect is also known as the *replay of the events*. Consider Figure 2-8 shown earlier, and try to figure out what event replay is all about.

The idea is to go through the list of all recorded events, retrieve those related to the specific order, and then in some way replay the events on an empty order instance to turn that into an instance that faithfully represents the real state.

There's no behavior in the event itself because the event is only the summary of a fact that has happened. Replaying events doesn't mean repeating actions that produced events. For example, replaying the order-created event doesn't mean creating a copy of the order. It just means taking a fresh *Order* object and, in some way, making all the changes to it that it would have received because of the actions that produced logged events.

Are there performance concerns with event replay? That's a possibility, and it all depends on the number of events. If performance becomes an issue, you can consider creating durable snapshots that store the state of an aggregate object at a given time and then process only events that occurred after that time. Yet another option to investigate is persisting the entire (or relevant) state of the aggregate with the event itself.

> **Note** Event replay is a powerful concept because it enables *what-if* scenarios that turn out to be very helpful in some business domains (for example, in financial and scientific applications). With event-based storage, you can easily replay events and change some of the run-time conditions to see different possible outcomes.
>
> The nice thing is that what-if scenarios don't require a completely different architecture for the application. You design the system in accordance with the event-sourcing approach and get what-if scenarios enabled for free. The possibility of using what-if scenarios is one of the main business reasons for using event sourcing.

Summary

The real value of DDD is in the tools it provides for discovering the top-level architecture that fits the business needs of a domain. Once you elaborate the context and the relationships between parts, you need to look at ways to actually build the system. Before you look into technologies and practices, you should think about architectures that support the design. In this chapter, I presented three architectural patterns: Domain Model, CQRS, and Event Sourcing. They come one after the next, and each tries to fix issues that arise while extensively using the other.

A single, all-encompassing object-oriented model is the architecture that was initially associated with DDD. Years of experience proved that a single model was too restrictive, and then CQRS was formulated from looking at the basic CQS principle of the Eiffel programming language. CQRS is not a pattern and not even such a big concept: it just suggests you keep commands and queries distinct from one another. This simple observation has huge consequences, though.

Ultimately, CQRS is a middle ground between object-oriented design backed by relational data models and functional design backed by event sourcing. Splitting commands and queries has the effect of shifting the focus onto tasks, and tasks are ultimately a sequence of actions and events. The business logic can be expressed by having components (in-process components and also distinct services) communicate via messages. Any event can be stored and, finally, when you have recorded all events, you have everything you need to build whatever combination of data you need to process: both combinations you know you need today and those you might need to know sometime in the future.

In the rest of the book, I'll use commands and queries in distinct stacks and use different programming approaches to build both. Events and message-based business logic will be demonstrated in some scenarios, too. In the next chapter, I'll be taking a look at the role of user experience in the architecture and design process of a software system.

CHAPTER 3

UX-driven design

Talk is cheap. Show me the code.

—Linus Torvalds

I t's common to hear developers complain that customers change their mind too often. The narrative goes something like this: "We discussed requirements for weeks and signed off on specifications. Then we started coding, and when we delivered the first sprint two weeks later, we found out that the program was only vaguely close to what they really wanted." This experience is summarized in a popular cartoon where the waiter gets a complaint about the coffee he just served. "We use top-quality coffee and the best machine available. What's wrong with the coffee, sir?" And the customer's answer is kind of shocking: "I actually want some tea."

The process of elicitation has always been difficult, and the Ubiquitous Language pattern I discussed in Chapter 1, "Conducting a thorough domain analysis," as the foundation of Domain-Driven Design (DDD) addresses the topic of communication between the various stakeholders involved in a software project. However, agreeing on abstract requirements and specifications is often not enough. When customers actually see the artifact, they might not like it. Despite all the talks you had with the customer, they might have formed an idea that is actually different from yours.

This is to say that to reduce the costs of software development, and further reduce the number of iterations to figure out what exactly users want, an additional level of agreement must be found beyond Ubiquitous Language. Creating a common language shared by all stakeholders and widely used in all spoken and written communications is of immense help to ensure that each word spoken is understood correctly and, subsequently, software specifications are correct.

You know, however, that talk is cheap and to give customers a realistic perspective of what you're going to do you should show some code. But code also is expensive to produce, and nobody likes the idea of writing code that might be thrown away if some assumptions made, and not clearly resolved by specifications, turn out to be wrong.

In this chapter, I'll present UX-Driven Design (UXDD). *UX* stands for *user experience*, and UXDD is a top-down approach to implementing whatever supporting architecture you selected for the system. UXDD differs from most commonly used approaches in that it emphasizes the presentation layer and the actual screens the user will end up working with. The main trait of UXDD is that, before you get into coding mode, you have customers sign off on wireframes and storyboards for each task offered through the presentation.

Why a top-down approach is better than a bottom-up one

In the course of history, many great ideas have been first sketched out on the paper napkins of some cafeterias. This is because hand-drawing is still an excellent way to jot down ideas, whether it's ideas about the top-level architecture of a system or the user interface the actors will use for their interactions. More often than not, customers have a hard time explaining what they want, but on the other hand, they are not expected to explain in full detail the experience they want. It's the development team that should grab the key points and learn from real processes to mirror them in software.

If you agree with this vision of the software world, you also agree that the role of presentation is way more important than it has been in past decades. The term *top-down* is nothing new in software, and it is a term often used in the context of code. Professor Niklaus Wirth—the inventor of Pascal—was among the first to coin and use the term extensively.

The point I want to make here, though, is architectural. Architecturally speaking, I dare say that in past decades we never applied any top-down design approach. Everything we did was done to build the system from the bottom up. It's about time we consider a different approach to reduce development costs.

Foundation of the bottom-up approach

As I see things, we keep on designing and building software as we have done for at least the past 15 years. However, a lot has changed in the same time, both in terms of client and server software and, more than everything else, in terms of the actual users' expectations.

Assets of the 1990s

The onion diagram in Figure 3-1 shows the key architectural assets of the 1990s. Most systems were designed in a way that took the most advantage of the facts depicted in the figure.

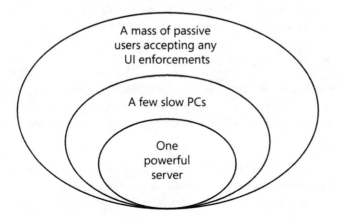

FIGURE 3-1 Assets of the software architecture in the 1990s

In the 1990s, the IT department in most companies was built around a huge powerful server that cost a lot of money and had to be used as much as possible. The server ran all the business logic and took care of all persistence tasks. On top of the server, you typically had a few, and far slower, personal computers acting as dumb terminals with just a nice Microsoft Visual Basic user interface. More than everything else, though, in the 1990s there was a mass of users passively accepting any UI constraints imposed on them by software engineers.

The presentation layer was just disregarded, and all the design efforts focused on getting the most out of that powerful server the company invested all that money on.

What's different today?

Today we live and write software in a totally different world. Take a look at the same onion diagram for modern times in Figure 3-2.

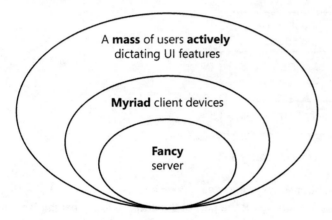

FIGURE 3-2 Assets of the software architecture today

First and foremost, today we have an amazing number of fancy technologies and myriad client devices. This poses new challenges for software architects and also results in users actively dictating user-interface features instead of passively accepting whatever is offered. Today, and even more so in the future, a poor user experience might become a serious issue and undermine the reputation of the software. What you see happening for mobile apps—with many downloaded and soon dismissed—might become the norm for all applications.

Important I'll return to this point later in the chapter, although this is a great time to make such an important clarification: user interface (UI) is not the same as user experience (UX) even though the two things are strictly related. In particular, *user experience* refers to the experience the user goes through while interacting with the application's user interface. A nice UI is not necessarily a sign of a great UX. A great UX might be effective but lack something in terms of aesthetics.

What DDD has changed

DDD has been the first serious attempt to change things and adapt mainstream software architecture to changing times. The mainstream software architecture before DDD was essentially built from the ground up using a solid relational model as the foundation and placing business-logic components on top of that. Business-logic components were mostly vertical components that organized behavior on a per-table basis. Data-transfer object (DTO) or ad hoc data structures like recordsets were used to move data across layers and tiers and up to the presentation layer.

DDD changed a few things, but mostly it contributed to rethinking the overall architecture layout. (See Figure 3-3.)

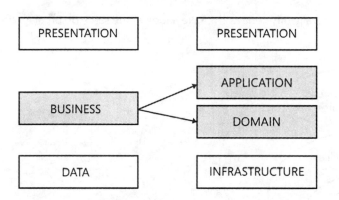

FIGURE 3-3 How DDD changed the core software architecture

DDD led to splitting the monolithic business logic into two smaller and logically distinct pieces—application logic and domain logic. *Application logic* is the part of the business logic that implements the workflows behind use-cases. The *domain logic*, conversely, is the part of the business logic that implements business rules that don't vary according to use-cases. In leading this change of approach, DDD introduced the notion of the domain layer, which is the segment of the architecture where you provide a software model for the business domain. Such a software model doesn't have to be an object-oriented model. It should be whatever you reckon it to be—including an anemic model, a functional model, or even an event-based model.

Ultimately, what years of DDD really changed in software architecture is the perception that the data model is the foundation on which to build software. With DDD, this vision started shifting toward using a domain model to serve as the foundation of software. Today the trend is shifting even more toward using events as the data source and event-based data stores on top of canonical data stores such as relational or document NoSQL data stores.

Planning with a top-down approach

In spite of all the changes we have faced in recent years, I believe we keep on designing code as we used to do back in the 1990s. We develop a good understanding of the system and build a data model that probably works. On top of that, we then build what we consider a good enough user interface. Then we go to the customer and find out we've got something wrong. The more we iterate, the more the software project ends up costing.

To improve things, we have to recognize that what users perceive to be the system is just the user interface they work with. When we can ensure that the UI and subsequent UX is really close to what users expect, the chances of redoing things because we got it wrong are significantly reduced.

To get there, though, we must start planning the system in a top-down way, putting the UX and the presentation at the top of our concerns.

Avoiding a design with square pegs and round holes

When it comes to software, most of users' expectations are met or not met in the screens they use to do the actual job. If you have a mass of passive users, you can afford to build the foundation of the system from the bottom. Whatever model you end up with works for users who have a passive character, but it doesn't work as well if users expect some specific UI/UX to work with. (See Figure 3-4.)

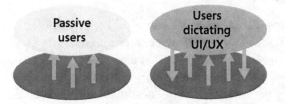

FIGURE 3-4 Role of passive and active users in overall architecture design

If users are willing to accept any UI you offer them, building a system from the bottom up ends up working nicely enough. However, if users expect a specific UI and are not very forgiving on that point, the endpoints developed out of the model built from the bottom-up might not fit with the connection points developed out of the presentation layer approach. This is precisely the conflict that requires a lot of iterative work to be fixed and produces the highest costs and greatest amount of annoyance and misunderstandings. It all looks like trying to fit a square peg into a round hole.

Going the other way around, from top to bottom, instead, ensures that the firm points are those that users want to have. Next, whatever back end you build to support those firm UX points won't diminish the users' level of satisfaction. Put another way, the entire back end of the system becomes a huge black box underneath the agreed-upon presentation screens and forms.

Establishing two architect roles

UXD pushes a top-down design of software architecture. In this scenario, you might find it useful to employ two distinct architect roles on a project. By saying *architect role*, I'm not suggesting you have two distinct professionals; instead, I'm suggesting you have two distinct sets of skills, which possibly could be found in the same individual. One role is the classic software architect role. The other is the UX architect role.

The software architect conducts interviews to collect requirements and business information, with the declared purpose of building the domain layer of the system. The UX architect, on the other hand, conducts interviews to collect usability requirements, with the declared purpose of building the ideal user experience and the ideal presentation layer.

Understanding the responsibilities of a UX architect

The pillars of a good user experience are summarized in the following list. Note that the order is not coincidental:

- Organization of the information

- Interaction model

- Review of the actual usability

For a UX architect, the first point to look at is the organization of the information presented to the users, including identifying the *personas*—namely, the types of users working on the application. Next comes the way in which users are allowed to interact with the displayed information and the graphical tools you provide for that to happen.

All this work is nothing without the last point—*usability reviews*. A UX expert can interview customers a million times—and should do that, actually—but that will bring about only an understanding of the customers' basic needs. This leads to some sketches that can be discussed and tweaked. A high rate of UX satisfaction is achieved only when the interface and interaction form a smooth mechanism so that neither has usability bottlenecks nor introduces roadblocks in the process.

For a UX expert, talking to users is fundamental, but it's not nearly as important as validating any user interface live from the field, observing users in action and, if possible, even filming them in action.

Looking at user experience from an architectural perspective

Usually, the term *UX* refers to behavior and emotions the user goes through when she uses a product, including a software product. UX is mostly about interaction, and interaction with a computer is mostly made of visual controls. And visual controls are the interface of the system. So UI and UX are tightly related but distinct.

My point is that UX is more relevant for users than actual UI, which mostly is there to please the eye. Unlike UI, the user experience is also relevant at the architecture level. Because to give users an objectively positive experience, you might want to reconsider the order in which design steps take place and the importance assigned to the presentation layer.

UX is not UI

Some 30 years ago, graphical user interfaces (GUI) changed the rules, and both developers and users learned the importance of visual design. Up until a few years ago, and surely before the advent of smartphones and tablets, well-designed visual interfaces were sufficient to ensure a good experience to users of software applications. The road ahead seems to indicate that a good UI is no longer sufficient for delivering a well-designed presentation layer.

To stay on the cutting edge, we have to replace *UI* with *UX*.

Defining wireframes and other similar terms

When it comes to UI and UX, we hear and use a few terms constantly, not always using each with its precise meaning. Sometimes what we actually mean is clear from the context, yet terms like *wireframe* and *mockup* refer to slightly and subtly different things. From a ubiquitous language perspective, let me clarify what is commonly intended with terms like sketch, wireframe, and mockup:

- **Sketch**   A sketch is typically a freehand drawing done primarily to jot down ideas for a user interface. Overall, it's a necessary step for every designer to do in order to translate the original idea into a graphical user interface.

- **Wireframe**   A wireframe is a more precise type of sketch. It contains additional information and is focused on layout, navigation, and content to present. A wireframe is often related to other wireframes to form a storyboard. In a wireframe, you won't find many details about the actual aesthetics of the final product.

- **Mockup**   A mockup is a wireframe with a specific look and feel. A mockup offers a preview of the final product with a clear idea of layout, content organization, navigation, and aesthetics.

These terms are sometimes used interchangeably. Even though interchangeable use might even be acceptable, I think it's important to know what each term means specifically.

Defining prototypes and other similar terms

After elicitation, the first required synchronization that must be arranged between development teams and stakeholders involves the presentation. If the complexity of the domain logic is not really high and if tasks are relatively trivial to figure out and implement, a sign-off at the level of presentation might be enough. In other cases, a second synchronization step might be required before going into the final acceptance procedure.

When it comes to needing a second synchronization, a few other terms are often used interchangeably. A misunderstanding about whether you're expected to provide a prototype or proof of concept (PoC) might be much more expensive than any misunderstanding about wireframes or mockups. Let me clarify the terms, then:

- **Proof of concept**   A proof of concept is essentially a small piece of code created to test the feasibility of an idea and to verify that some theoretical points have the potential of being or becoming a useful production feature. Sometimes, a PoC is also done to put a new technology or framework through its paces.

- **Prototype**   A prototype is a partially fake system that tries to simulate the full system. Like a PoC, it is done to test the viability or usefulness of a system. It seems to behave like the full system except that most features are partially implemented or use canned data or hard-coded logic. The point is to show how the whole thing will work. Compared to a PoC, a prototype is a lot more sophisticated and complex, though it might cost a fraction of the full system.

- **Pilot** A pilot is a full production system tested only against a subset of the general intended audience and possibly working on a subset of the full data set. A pilot can easily be the full application running on a staging system, database or both.

Sometimes, any of these terms is replaced by a more generic (as well as popular) term: *demo*. Proofs of concept, prototypes, and pilots are all demos. When the customer asks for a demo, try to have them be more—a lot more—specific about they want. And demos, usually, are not effortless.

Experience is about interaction

If UX analysis is the central point of modern presentation layers, the *usability review* is the central point of UX analysis. Here's a quick true story I often tell during conference talks and classes. A customer asked for a tool to cherry-pick tweets based on hashtags. They wanted to see a list of tweets, click on those of interest, and have those saved to a database table. We even worked out a wireframe for the main user interface of the webpage. (See Figure 3-5. By the way, the wireframe in the figure was created with Balsamiq.)

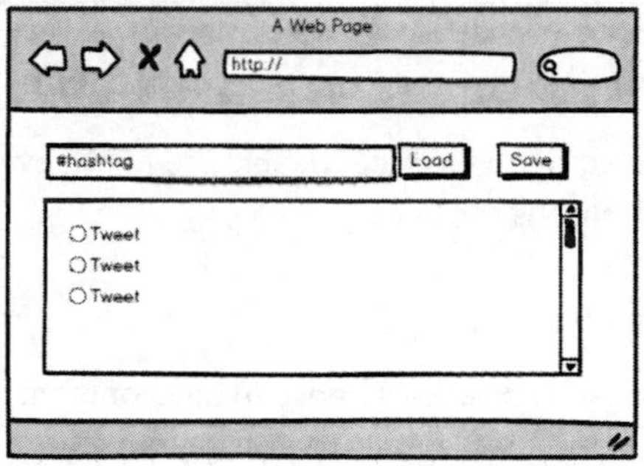

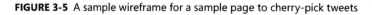

FIGURE 3-5 A sample wireframe for a sample page to cherry-pick tweets

After the first test, everyone was happy and the application was seen as just perfect. After a few days of intense use, though, it started looking quite a bit less compelling. To cut a long story short, two key features were missing that apparently everybody ruled out because they were too advanced for a first run of the app. One was the ability to select and hide unwanted tweets so that picking really interesting tweets became an easier task. The other missing feature was the ability to hide tweets in the stream that had been already picked.

The first lesson I learned from this is that only by looking at users using the application can you reliably say whether the UX you offer is good or not. The second lesson is that the word *requirements* is less and less expressive of what users and developers need to talk about. Gathering requirements is only the starting point of a far longer workflow that involves building tasks and business processes.

Finally, the third lesson relates to the UX prioritization of features that don't work. A given feature is either useful or not. And if it is determined to be useful, it must be planned from the beginning. Otherwise, you'll be doing the work—any work—at least twice.

Explaining UXDD in three steps

In essence, UXDD is a top-down, three-step design workflow. First, you work out screens and storyboards to get approval and feedback from users about the effectiveness of the interface and underlying processes. Second, based on screens, you formalize what comes in and out of those screens and build application layer endpoints that perfectly match that expected data flow.

In other words, the first step lets you discover shape and type of the pegs you're going to have, while the second step ensures you use compatible holes as well. What about the third step? It's about building the back end of the system in a way that is completely transparent to the front end and its pegs and application layer holes. (See Figure 3-6.)

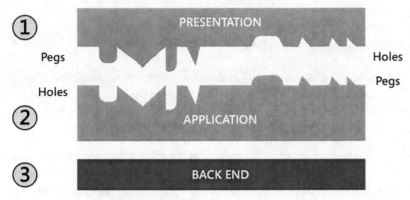

FIGURE 3-6 The three steps of UXDD

Understanding the importance of screens and storyboards

One of the most important things I've learned from UX experts is that requirements are better when they're actively generated through discussion than when they're passively gathered through interviews. Years of real-world experience taught many of us that being too passive during elicitation of feedback from stakeholders leads users to deprioritize a feature so that they can have the software as soon as possible. Even though users might make that decision, it doesn't stop them from complaining that the system is barely usable when they finally get it.

Figure 3-7 presents an example we can use as a starting point for discussion, and you might spot the weak points in it at first glance. Despite the shortcomings of the wireframe shown, by generating this type of outline you enable users to let you know whether you missed something important—say, a particular aggregation of data. The user can tell you right away so that you have plenty of time to organize the back end to make that particular data easier to grab.

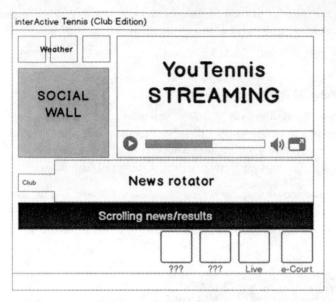

FIGURE 3-7 A sample wireframe to give users a clear idea of the screen being planned

Showing screens and storyboards to users as early as possible, iteratively running them later, and incorporating feedback are critical steps you need to perform to move from sketches to wireframes, and even mockups. You might think this is more or less already done in many projects, but is it more or is it less? I think it's mostly less. And usually the missing part is the storyboards.

The experience of a user results from using the UI tools to accomplish a task. Very few tasks are entirely accomplished through a single screen. You'll likely find that just looking at the wireframe of a screen might not provide you with enough information to spot possible bottlenecks in the process implementation. Concatenating screens in a storyboard is a better idea. The problem you'll encounter is the lack of tools available for easily and effectively connecting screens to build storyboards.

Table 3-1 presents a list of some tools available today.

TABLE 3-1 Short list of tools for UX development

Tool	More information	Description
Axure	*http://www.axure.com*	Creates wireframes and mockups, and links them to create true storyboards with animation and even calculations. You can use it to create HTML-based realistic prototypes from wireframes for users to experience the design.
Balsamiq	*http://balsamiq.com*	A rapid wireframing tool that reproduces the experience of sketching on a whiteboard. It provides a toolbox of readymade visual elements you can combine to construct a shareable wireframe. By linking wireframes and saving the result to a PDF, you get a very cheap but simple and effective solution to gather feedback from customers.
UXPin	*http://uxpin.com*	More ambitious than Balsamiq, it can be classified as another wireframing tool. It offers a highly sophisticated UI, readymade screen templates, and collaborative options.

Tool	More information	Description
JustInMind	http://www.justinmind.com	Another prototyping tool on the same functional level as UXPin and Axure. It focuses on creating design and prototypes for multiple devices.
Indigo Studio	http://www.infragistics.com/products/indigo-studio	A fully featured product for creating animated UI prototypes, screens, and storyboards. You can use its features to share your work with team members and stakeholders and receive annotations.
Wirify	http://www.wirify.com	A bookmarklet you install on a web browser and use to capture wireframes of existing sites. Any captured wireframe can be exported to drawing tools such as Visio and Balsamiq.

Screens are, at best, HTML or just XML content rendered in some graphical way. In any case, they are purely static content with no life and no action in them. You can use some of the tools in Table 3-1, most notably Indigo Studio and UXPin, to turn wireframes into true storyboards to demonstrate the flow of UI screens. Sometimes, this is only the first step, though.

Turning views into prototypes

Keep in mind that even the best and most widely agreed-upon user interface might turn bad when used extensively. When in doubt, you can go with a working software prototype and you might even be able to film users while they're using the prototype to get a realistic indication of their actual experience when using your software.

> **Note** Regardless of tiers, layers, frameworks, databases, and technologies, for end users the only thing that matters about a software system is the user interface—specifically, the user experience and perceived speed of the application.

In terms of concrete technologies, a prototype can be anything that serves the purpose of gathering early and informative feedback. It can be a set of HTML pages as well as a XAML-based application. A prototype consists only of the presentation layer and uses canned data or just a fake back end to simulate some behavior. Depending on the level of fidelity you want to offer, creating wireframes and prototypes for an agreed-upon set of sketches is usually takes only a few days of work. Not a big effort, in the end.

The hardest part of turning views into prototypes is probably not creating the prototypes themselves, but making it clear to the customer that what they're seeing is only a prototype and nowhere near to being even halfway complete.

Tasks and workflows

Suppose that at some point the customer decides they like the prototype and gives you the go-ahead to build the application. The more that you have validated and accurately created the screens and related storyboard to respond to realistic needs, the less (re)work you'll need to do later. This is the key point that makes UXDD financially worthwhile. If you're looking for where the return on any UXDD investment might lie, well, this is the place.

Having the screens ironed out brings a lot benefits, and one in particular. You know exactly what the back end of the application has to produce.

Each screen you have can be easily mapped to an outbound class, which becomes the input of the application layer and, in turn, the entry point in the back end of the system. The application layer forwards the input to the back end, and that input proceeds down the stack. Any calculated response is carried up the stack to the application layer, packaged in a view model object, and returned to the presentation.

Now look back at Figure 3-6. What I called pegs and holes in the figure are just classes going in and out of the presentation as they are passed to, and returned by, application-layer methods. Application-layer methods are responsible for orchestrating the tasks behind use-cases.

The rest of the back end

In terms of the actual code you would write within an ASP.NET MVC application, the essence of UXDD is summarized in the following few lines of a controller method:

```
public class SomeController
{
    private ApplicationLayerService _service = new ApplicationLayerService();

    public ActionResult SomeTask(InputModel input)
    {
        var model = _service.GetActionViewModel(input);
        return View(model);
    }
}
```

In ASP.NET MVC, any controller is still part of the presentation layer. More precisely, it is the repository of any presentation logic you might need to have. Any actionable UI elements end up calling into one of the controllers, and the invoked controller forwards the call and input data to the application layer. The _service_ variable in the code snippet is an instance of the segment of the application layer associated with a given controller. The service has one method for each action in the UI that can trigger the controller. The method will receive an input model and return a view model. The input model is a class that contains all data that flows out of the screen. The view model is a class that gathers all data that fills out the screen when it's rendered back to the user.

The link between the controller and the application-layer helper class is then more elegantly established via any form of dependency injection, including the simplest of all, which is shown in the following lines of code:

```
public class SomeController
{
    private IApplicationLayerService _service;

    public SomeController(IApplicationLayerService service)
    {
        _service = service;
    }
```

```
    public SomeController() : this(new ApplicationLayerService())
    {
    }

    public ActionResult SomeTask(InputModel input)
    {
        var model = _service.GetActionViewModel(input);
        return View(model);
    }
}
```

Once you have this code architecture in place, the rest of the system that lies underneath the application layer is just an implementation detail, even though it's the segment of the system that fully contains the entire domain logic and all the business rules of the domain. The idea depicted in Figure 3-8 might seem quite minimalistic, but it's true.

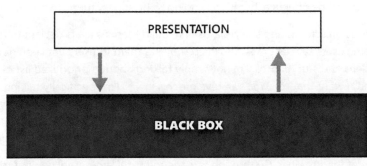

FIGURE 3-8 The overall layout of a system architected following UXDD principles

Why UXDD is beneficial to nearly everybody

Like many other buzzwords ending with *DD* for "driven design," UXDD also is born with the declared goal of saving the world of software or, at a minimum, reducing its costs. In this regard, UXDD shares the same noble goal of DDD.

UXDD, however, doesn't force you to switch to any significantly different way of thinking about and writing software. It doesn't require any significant preliminary training, either. When I present UXDD principles at conferences or during classes, more often than not I'm approached by people saying that some core ideas I refer to as *UXDD* are just what they are doing or have been doing for years.

There's no strict need to label the practices outlined in this chapter with a resounding new name like *UX-Driven Design*. Yet, a new and resounding name might help attract attention to it.

Where are the benefits of UXDD?

We write software, and we all would like to write it as effectively as possible and in a sustainable way. Software is a complex matter and an engineering project. We can't reasonably cut down the actual costs of engineering, though this is exactly what often happens. (Smile.) If our customers perceive that software costs too much, and if we all perceive that software development is not being financed well enough, then somewhere, somehow both developers and customers are doing something wrong.

What exactly are we doing wrong?

My two cents' worth of opinion on the matter is that the problem lies with UXDD principles. I start from the fact that all that users are concerned about is the experience and how easily they can do their work. The success of any software is determined by its ability to perform business tasks in a way that is constantly appropriate—which is just a bit of wordplay to avoid using the more popular term *scalability*—and convenient for the user. If the software fails at providing a satisfactory user experience, it can still be used and can still be effective, but it's not going to be successful software.

UXDD recommends you focus on screens and storyboards first, build them as users declare to love them, and run them by the same users several times. You keep showing them to users until you get them to sign off on those screens and storyboards. I'm not simply talking about a prioritized list of intentions like "I want this" and "I want that" or "You can give me this in v2." I'm specifically talking about wireframes and possibly animated sequences of wireframes. In this way, you show users how they're going to use the system once it's deployed.

This first step is not free, of course, but the cost is a fraction of developing any software at any level and that has any number of features in it. Go through screens and wireframes until you get really close to ideal user experience. Then decide whether it's good to invest some more time and money and build some lightweight software prototypes. I consider this step optional but in large projects it can really be a lifesaver.

What next?

Once you have users' approval for screens, you know exactly what output the system is going to produce and what input it is going to receive. The next step is simply about organizing the layers underneath the presentation to handle this data.

There's very little in UXDD that you won't do anyway. But for the extra cost of dealing with screens and animated wireframes, you get to write software that users might like perfectly well the first time. And you can be quite sure of that because, well, the users just signed off on that! But even if users don't like the software the first time they see the screens or wireframe, the chances are great that the number of iterations you have to go through to fix it will be significantly reduced. What else would you call it if not "cost saving"?

Figure 3-9 shows the overall diagram of UXDD development.

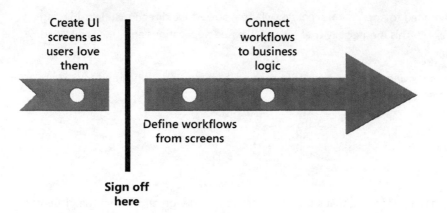

Create UI screens as users love them

Connect workflows to business logic

Define workflows from screens

Sign off here

FIGURE 3-9 The overall diagram of UX-Driven Design

> **Note** The sign-off step seems more essential with regard to return on investment (ROI) in a consulting scenario than it is in a corporate development scenario. However, when you write software for internal customers, it's still about coming to a mutually satisfactory agreement with them that reduces the overall time needed to have software up and running in its final form.

MVC, MVP, MVVM, and other patterns

Short for *Model-View-Controller*, *MVC* is a pattern devised in the 1980s to originally architect the entire application. Applications of the time, though, were essentially monolithic and MVC as a general pattern totally made sense. The primary goal of MVC is to split the application into distinct pieces—the model, the view, and the controller.

The *model* refers to state of the application, wraps the application's functionalities, and notifies the view of state changes. The *view* refers to the generation of any graphical elements displayed to the user, and it captures and handles any user gestures. The *controller* maps user gestures to actions on the model and selects the next view. These three actors are often referred to as the *MVC triad*.

The MVC pattern evolved into Model-View-Presenter (MVP) where the presenter element replaced the controller and took more responsibility, essentially summing the orchestration of tasks to the rendering of the view. In MVP, view and model are neatly separated and the presenter mediates between them.

Model-View-ViewModel (MVVM) is a much more popular name for a pattern that was originally introduced as Presentation Model. In MVVM, you have a class that incorporates both the commands and view model for the UI. A single class—the view model object— exposes properties to bind to UI visual components and methods to bind to UI events. MVVM is particularly suited to application scenarios where a powerful bidirectional data-binding mechanism exists. This is especially true for XAML-based applications and Universal Windows applications.

Don't get me wrong: in the context of layered applications, MVC, MVP, and MVVM are all patterns for the sole presentation layer.

Summary

UX-Driven Design is a philosophy that suggests you start your design effort from the presentation layer and proceed in a top-down way toward the bottom of the stack. In doing so, you run the preliminary domain analysis on a double track: collecting business domain data and UX data. Collected UX data will guide the team as they design interaction models that work for the user before they are made to work for the system.

The primary goal of UX-Driven Design is building screens in such a way that users decide that they love them. After wireframes and mockups of screens are signed-off on, you start defining data workflows and then domain logic, services, and storage. The benefit is that you know as early as possible for which output you are going to create the system, and the user guides you to discovering needs and ideal solutions. This cuts down the number of iterations to fix what users don't actually like when you deploy the system. Today, the key to saving money on software projects is ensuring as early as possible, and as reliably as possible, that you are creating exactly what users want. And users judge the system primarily from their user experience.

CHAPTER 4

Architectural options for a web solution

The future depends on what you do today.

—*Mahatma Gandhi*

Quite frankly, when developing software these days, what's more important than knowing technology is knowing how to do concrete things. This means it's more important to learn about design and architecture patterns, best practices, supporting architectures, and applicable solutions that have a successful record. More and more, software is merging with business and knowing the technology alone is not sufficient to solve real-world problems. More often than not, a real-world business solution comes from the combination of multiple, even heterogeneous, technologies. So, if you don't perform a careful analysis, you won't go anywhere, at least not on time and on budget.

Performing a careful analysis is not something new in software development—reasonable, analysis has been around for as long as software itself. As summarized in Chapter 1, "Conducting a thorough domain analysis," and Chapter 3, "UX-Driven Design," the analytical tools of Domain-Driven Design (DDD) and the top-down design of UXDD tend to move the focus a lot more on concrete things like business processes rather than models that are sometimes too abstract.

You accomplish concrete software things via technologies, but just upgrading a single technology today is no longer a guarantee of success. There was surely a time when just upgrading to the newest database management system (DBMS), operating system, or library would magically solve any pending issues. These days, software makes more sense to users the more it captures real-world processes. It's time for architects to learn to mirror, rather than model, the real world.

In this chapter, I'll look into a few options you have for architecting web solutions. I'll do that in light of the new Microsoft ASP.NET Core 1.0 framework and the related runtime pipeline.

Assessing the available web solutions

Today when it comes to planning a web solution using the Microsoft stack, you have the following options available:

- ASP.NET Web Forms

- ASP.NET MVC

- Single-Page Application (SPA)

These are the primary options, and they deal with creating the skeleton of the solution and how entry points are made available for users to interact with the application. The popular ASP.NET Web API and the newest ASP.NET Core 1.0 framework add two more dimensions to the picture, multiplying the scenarios in which you can use the primary options.

Deciding on the best framework

Any of these options work. Determining whether one is preferable to the other depends on the specific problem you need to solve and the constraints you have around it, not the least of which is the skills of the people you work with.

A team that is familiar with ASP.NET Web Forms can probably build the same front end in a fraction of the time it takes to rebuild it with ASP.NET MVC. The paradigm of each technology is different. You'll probably find that, by design, it takes more time to learn ASP.NET MVC and create solid code with it than when you use ASP.NET Web Forms. Forcing yourself or your team to switch to using ASP.NET MVC might be a painful decision, but ASP.NET MVC is a more modern framework.

ASP.NET Web Forms is not going to receive much attention from Microsoft in the future. It's an old framework whose latest significant update dates back to 2010, and its very first release occurred over a decade ago. However, just because a framework has not been significantly updated is not a reason to stop using it, especially if the framework still does well what is supposed to do.

There's a general sentiment that Web Forms is gone. No matter what you might hear, though, my humble opinion is that there's no clear business reason to abandon Web Forms if you have good reasons to keep using it.

> **Note** The release of Microsoft Visual Studio 2015 and ASP.NET Core 1.0 also come with a slightly updated Web Forms framework. As I see things, Web Forms isn't frequently updated because not much else can be added to a framework devised the way Web Forms was.

You might find it difficult to see the big picture of web frameworks today, and it's even more difficult to try to explain it. A common scenario is that, after spending years in the cave of a long-term ASP.NET Web Forms project, you now look around and see alternatives and approaches to planning a significant refresh of the project. You see so many new frameworks that you wonder which one is the best fit for another long-term project.

Well, the first point I should make is that you might not need to determine which framework is ideal for you. Likely, a combination of frameworks, languages, and storage technologies is what you should use. Nearly everything is polyglot these days, and the burden of learning languages and figuring out which one to use is up to you.

Laying out a solution

Nearly any software solution today results from the application of a layered architecture. A *layered architecture* is simply an evolution of the classic three-tier architecture, where the application is separated into three segments: presentation, business, and data access.

In a layered architecture, you still have a presentation layer and the data-access layer is renamed as infrastructure and extended to contain additional services, such as queues and caching. The business-logic layer is split into two distinct segments: application logic and domain logic. The application logic is where you find the implementation of user-interface use-cases. The domain logic is any logic you need to have that doesn't vary across use-cases. (I'll say more about this architecture in Chapter 5, "The layered architecture.")

Whatever archetypal solution you opt for—Web Forms, MVC, or a single-page application (SPA)—you then have the problem of defining the API of your application as a set of publicly callable HTTP endpoints. From a technology perspective, this is where ASP.NET Web API can be helpful. However, before you focus on the ideal technology to use to expose HTTP endpoints, you should focus on the processes you want to implement and evaluate supporting architectures for these processes, such as Command/Query Responsibility Segregation (CQRS) and event-driven architectures. Also, the architecture of the storage is critical, whether it is state-based or whether it's better to introduce some level of support for event sourcing (ES).

In Chapter 3, I focused on the role of user experience when you're designing an architecture. I suggested a top-down approach that starts from the iterative definition of the user-interface screens, and then recommended you subsequently design and build the back end code starting from the data coming into and going out of screen forms. I recently came across a cartoon about the different perspectives of software that users and developers can have. I tried to capture the different visions more seriously in Figure 4-1.

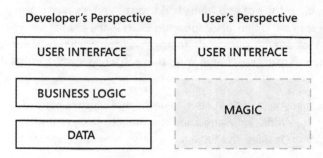

FIGURE 4-1 How users and developers perceive software

The users' perspective represented in Figure 4-1, which illustrates their lack of understanding for the intricacies of software, typically makes developers chuckle at the lack of understanding users have regarding the intricacies of software. Yet, when looking for options to plan a real-world web solution, developers find the allure of a UX-first, top-down approach is quite powerful. That's because such an approach lets you build the "magic" after making sure that whatever tricks the magic ends up doing will make users happy.

> **Important** Especially if Figure 4-1 made you smile at the naiveté of users, or just smile, I'd recommend you reconsider the core points of UX-Driven Design (UXDD) discussed in Chapter 3. It's probably the only way we have today to cut the costs of software development without also cutting the relevant aspects of development (such as testing and debugging).

Examining the role of ASP.NET Core 1.0

ASP.NET Core 1.0 is a new open source and cross-platform framework for building web applications using the Microsoft .NET Framework. It stands side by side with ASP.NET and just represents a second option that developers and architects can choose when it comes to using the Microsoft stack for building web solutions. In other words, choosing ASP.NET is not enough: you also have to choose which flavor of the ASP.NET platform you want to rely on.

Considering ASP.NET as the starting point

Figure 4-2 provides an overview of the classic ASP.NET platform and highlights aspects of it that are going to change with ASP.NET Core 1.0. In particular, the figure focuses on the host environment and the model for interactions between the host and core application.

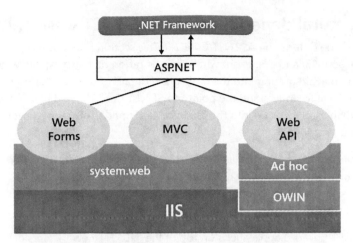

FIGURE 4-2 Overall diagram of the classic ASP.NET platform

The figure shows the dependencies between the ASP.NET Core framework and other .NET libraries. In particular, the ASP.NET platform contains the Web Forms and ASP.NET MVC libraries that developers use to build HTML-based views. The framework also encompasses the Web API module that can be used to create an HTTP-based API. The relevant thing to notice here, especially in light of the changes coming with ASP.NET Core 1.0, is that Web Forms and ASP.NET MVC run on a runtime pipeline that is different from Web API. In particular, Web API can be hosted under ASP.NET, but it also can be self-hosted if needed or run from other containers. The pipeline of the Web API engine is not tightly integrated with ASP.NET and Microsoft Internet Information Services (IIS), and it doesn't strictly rely on the services of the *system.web* assembly. Furthermore, the classic ASP.NET Core framework can run applications only on top of the full-fledged .NET Framework and Common Language Runtime (CLR).

> **Note** Short for *Open Web Interface for .NET*, the acronym *OWIN* defines a standard interface within which a web server and a web application can interact. OWIN was defined with the praiseworthy intent of decoupling the server and application, leading to a world in which the same web application can be hosted within a generic container that just exposes an OWIN interface. Put another way, OWIN is the exact opposite of that "integrated ASP.NET/IIS pipeline," which was pushed as a major achievement of ASP.NET development only a few years ago.
>
> No irony is intended here. I just want to acknowledge how quickly things are changing right before our eyes.

Examining the architectural dependencies in ASP.NET Core 1.0

I want to show you in brief what will be different in ASP.NET Core 1.0. This section provides a high-level perspective of ASP.NET Core 1.0 and points out what's new or different. I also explain why certain things are different and try to avoid getting into the nitty-gritty details of the new features. In the end, I suppose it's a lot more critical to understand the point of ASP.NET Core 1.0, and figure out whether or not it can be helpful, than to delve deep into the technical descriptions of this new set of tools for developers to become acquainted with.

First and foremost, ASP.NET Core 1.0 has a more flexible and cross-platform host environment than its predecessors, and it's an environment that doesn't depend in any way on IIS and the *system.web* assembly. In addition, ASP.NET Core 1.0 can run applications on top of a few different flavors of the .NET Framework and the CLR.

For example, you can run ASP.NET Core 1.0 applications on top of the .NET Framework (version 4.5.2 and newer) and leverage the full API set. This guarantees that your solution will have the maximum compatibility with existing code. At the same time, you can run ASP.NET Core 1.0 on top of the newest .NET Core and enjoy the new features in it and the much smaller memory footprint. Finally, at some point in the future, you'll also be able to run ASP.NET Core 1.0 on a cross-platform implementation of the .NET Core running on Linux and Mac.

Figure 4-3 shows the big picture of ASP.NET Core 1.0 using the same language as in Figure 4-2.

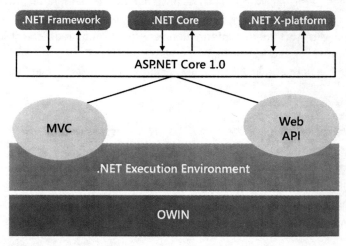

FIGURE 4-3 Overall diagram of the ASP.NET Core 1.0 platform

The ASP.NET Core 1.0 platform contains the ASP.NET MVC library used to build HTML-based views and Web API, which is the main building block for HTTP-based APIs. As you can see, it doesn't include any support for Web Forms. So, if you embrace the ASP.NET Core 1.0 platform, you must be able to create web front ends using ASP.NET MVC or plain HTML and JavaScript. In addition, both ASP.NET MVC and Web API now share the same runtime environment—the .NET Execution

Environment (DNX)—written from the ground up to be best-of-breed and offer unprecedented levels of flexibility and customization.

ASP.NET was entirely rewritten to get rid of all the issues that limit scalability and, subsequently, the adoption of ASP.NET beyond its current usage. This rewrite, dubbed *ASP.NET Core 1.0*, makes total sense because the original core infrastructure of ASP.NET was devised in the late 1990s and shipped for the first time in the early 2000s. That is well over a decade ago, which sounds like an insane amount of time no matter how you look at it.

Because ASP.NET Core 1.0 is essentially a new framework, it might create a few issues for developers in terms of compatibility and evolution. Jumping on the ASP.NET Core 1.0 bandwagon has its pros, but you might not want to choose it with a light heart. It's an inevitable choice, but that doesn't mean the time for you to adopt it is right now.

Exploring the reasons to choose ASP.NET Core 1.0

The new ASP.NET stack is definitely cleaner and less bulky than the current stack and attempts to do a bit of overdue housekeeping. The configuration infrastructure is based on JSON files and is fully customizable so that there's no longer a single entry point such as web.config. In addition, as Figure 4-3 illustrates, the new ASP.NET stack can run distinct versions of the .NET Framework.

In my attempt to find an appropriate catchphrase, I'm tempted to summarize the ASP.NET Core 1.0 platform as a very important minor update. I don't expect everybody to agree with me on this point, but let me explain.

Looking at ASP.NET Core 1.0 from a CTO perspective

ASP.NET Core 1.0 doesn't add anything to the programming power the average web developer has today. If you're already on the ASP.NET stack, ASP.NET Core 1.0 is the starting point of a slow transition toward a better core platform. It introduces changes such as lack of support for Web Forms, a different runtime pipeline, and a richer extensibility model. Also, it arranges a convergence between ASP.NET and ASP.NET Web API in a single model. Finally, it supports different flavors of the .NET Framework and even versions of the .NET Framework running on platforms other than those based on Microsoft Windows.

For some people, some of these changes might be significant breaking changes. For other people, these changes might be so insignificant that they can be blissfully ignored for the time being. In a nutshell, I see two options ahead for a Chief Technology Officer (CTO) to consider.

- Ignore ASP.NET Core 1.0 entirely, and do business as usual: use the same frameworks, same coding experience, and same deployment options, and implement no additional features. You don't lose any of what you have and can do today.

- Embrace ASP.NET Core 1.0 entirely, and look at it as a new platform concept—compatible with, but possibly requiring changes in, your coding approach. Realize also that it's a platform that isn't particularly hard to learn, especially for anyone with some good MVC experience.

ASP.NET Core 1.0 lays the groundwork for the Microsoft web stack for the next 10 years at least. It inherits enough from the current stack, adds some breaking changes, and sets new goals and a new direction. Like it or not, you won't be able to ignore ASP.NET Core 1.0 for too long.

The most intricate part of ASP.NET Core 1.0 involves the choice of the .NET CLR to work with.

Understanding the DNX runtime environment

The DNX runtime environment—the new ASP.NET runtime—is a host process that, among other things, is responsible for loading the CLR. As mentioned, it can run ASP.NET applications across different flavors of .NET. If the DNX environment is available on different platforms (for example, Linux or Mac), the same ASP.NET application source can run on any of those platforms as well.

Support for multiple flavors of the .NET Framework, though, doesn't mean that the code is normalized to a common intermediate language. It just means that you can write an ASP.NET application using three different sets of class libraries on top of the same (new) runtime.

Using the full .NET Framework

The easiest and smoothest transition to ASP.NET Core 1.0 passes through the use of the full .NET Framework as the CLR target. ASP.NET Core 1.0 supports any version of the .NET Framework equal to or newer than version 4.5.2. When making this transition, you can use the complete set of .NET Framework classes. In other words, you upgrade to the newest platform without modifying a single line of code if you are porting existing applications. If you are writing new applications, on the other hand, you don't have to learn any new API.

So what's the point of upgrading to ASP.NET Core 1.0 if you still want or need to target the full .NET Framework?

First and foremost, your applications will run on a faster and more configurable runtime pipeline. Second, by upgrading to ASP.NET Core 1.0 you use the new JSON-based configuration model and new tooling tailor-made for ASP.NET Core 1.0. The "very important minor update" definition I offered earlier in the chapter descends from this last point.

> **Important** Keep in mind that, as shown in Figure 4-3, ASP.NET Core 1.0 doesn't support Web Forms. Therefore, if you currently have a Web Forms application that can't be ported as is to ASP.NET Core 1.0, you must at least rewrite the most superficial part of the presentation layer to target ASP.NET MVC or plain HTML.

Introducing .NET Core

The .NET Core is a new and cross-platform version of the .NET Framework with a significantly smaller footprint. Without beating around the bush, targeting the .NET Core just means learning a new set of APIs that only look similar to the familiar .NET Framework. The gap between .NET Core and the full .NET Framework is similar to the gap between classic Microsoft Visual Basic and Microsoft Visual Basic .NET.

There are a few key benefits to choosing the .NET Core framework.

First, any of your applications can be packaged to include just the .NET Framework version it uses. This makes it possible for the application to run regardless of the version of the runtime installed on the server. Therefore, your application can run side by side with any other version of the .NET Framework installed. This also means you no longer need to be concerned if you update your application to a different version of the runtime. Likewise, it's no longer a concern if another version of the framework is installed on the same server. It won't affect your application.

The .NET Core makes it easier for you to pick just the features you need, which results in you being in total control of the footprint and the features you depend on. Finally, the .NET Core version of the .NET Framework is designed to be cross-platform. So when you finalize the application, it can run on any platform that hosts a compatible version of the DNX runtime. But it doesn't work this way only for deployment. It's the same for development, too. Developers, in fact, can write and test applications locally on any supported platforms.

> **Important** If you plan to target .NET Core, first get into the mood to (re)write your entire application from scratch—presentation layer, business layer, and back end. Doing so will probably be less difficult than you expect, but the scope of the effort is closer to a full rewrite than just an update. Obviously, for developing a new application, .NET Core is a serious candidate, with the sole cost of learning a new flavor of the ASP.NET API.

A cross-platform version of .NET

Plans are in the works to one day have a cross-platform version of the .NET Core runtime. Development is being done with a significant community effort, but there's a long way to go before such a runtime exists at the production level. If you're looking to use .NET in a cross-platform fashion, you also better look at Mono. The good news, however, is that cross-platform .NET Core is coming.

Determining if you should use ASP.NET Web Forms

It is estimated that the general ASP.NET platform is only second in usage to PHP. Most of the available ASP.NET web applications, however, are based on the ASP.NET Web Forms framework. The new ASP.NET Core 1.0 framework, conversely, focuses on a new pipeline, where ASP.NET MVC is used to serve both HTML views and data and where the Web API remains an option for data-only services.

Web Forms, therefore, is not included in ASP.NET Core 1.0.

Although Web Forms will be fully supported, and even slightly improved, for the foreseeable future, the direction ASP.NET Core 1.0 is headed sends a clear message: move away from ASP.NET Web Forms as soon as your business allows. That strategy is the right move for any organization and for the people in and around the organization. In this context, though, there are many different scenarios that might lead to different decisions. Let's take a look at some of them.

Examining a common scenario

Here's one of the most common user stories you will hear in the wild these days:

> The company has a web application that is a few years old but still works well. Because the application has been properly fine-tuned over the years, its performance is acceptable and it doesn't even raise any major scalability concerns. In addition, people on the team know how to maintain and evolve it. Everything seems to be OK.

As the company faces new business challenges, however, the need for a remake emerges. The new business challenge is sometimes as simple as making the presentation comply with new responsiveness standards, and sometimes the challenge is more intricate, like adding new pieces of business or application logic.

Within the Microsoft web stack, ASP.NET Web Forms is by far the most well-known and commonly used framework. The lion's share of application remakes start from large ASP.NET codebases. After years of hard work on a single system, though, software architects will raise their heads and clearly see that ASP.NET Web Forms is now a thing of the past. So they'll diligently look around for alternatives, and they'll find nothing that is clearly better than ASP.NET Web Forms. More precisely, they won't find a strong business reason for choosing ASP.NET MVC over Web Forms. It's not an attractive option when they consider the costs of retraining and rewriting that a significantly different programming paradigm inevitably poses. And for the most part, they're exactly right.

If you encounter these scenarios, how should you go about remaking the application? Should you stick to Web Forms, or should you invest in ASP.NET MVC or SPA? And what is the role of Web API? Let's pinpoint the pros and cons of ASP.NET Web Forms, leaving out any biases.

ASP.NET Web Forms at a glance

ASP.NET Web Forms was first devised in the late 1990s in the thick of the browser wars. At that time, any development approach that included writing web applications, while minimizing the impact of learning web-related stuff and coming to grips with specific features of browsers, was warmly welcomed. ASP.NET Web Forms did make the cut, and the winning move was the introduction of server controls.

Server controls produce user interfaces without the need to learn much HTML. Server controls were the web counterpart of Visual Basic visual components, and they made page prototyping quick and easy to do, while enabling developers to do it in a WYSIWYG way. Properties of server controls also could be configured programmatically using Microsoft C# or Visual Basic. In the end, any server developer could create webpages just by learning a slightly new API and with nearly no exposure to HTML and JavaScript. At run time, server controls generated any necessary HTML and JavaScript for the browser to display. In the end, server controls were conceived to work as plain factories of HTML running on the server side.

Server controls proved to be a strong paradigm. Microsoft packaged a bunch of core controls while offering the API to create custom ones. An entire branch of the industry sprouted nearly overnight to produce and sell richer and richer families of server controls. For Web Forms developers, the presentation layer was never a problem to be really concerned about.

Well beyond the role of server controls, the Web Forms framework was characterized by the post back interaction model. Devised as the junction point between web and desktop programming, it enabled a programming model similar to what developers did for years: render the user interface, wait for some commands, have the system do some work, and render back. Other aspects of web programming—such as session state, authentication, and statefulness—were managed within the host runtime environment, and over the years it ended up being backed into IIS.

ASP.NET Web Forms reached its climax with version 2.0 back in 2005. Since then, the framework received no significant updates except for some minor improvements to reduce the impact of the viewstate—a viable part of the postback model—and to provide more control over the generation of HTML and CSS.

What's still good with Web Forms

ASP.NET Web Forms "just works," but for sure it encompasses design principles for web applications that are becoming more outdated every day. You can still build web applications using ASP.NET Web Forms, and you can still find and buy plenty of commercial libraries and tools. The platform is mature and reliable and, although it won't likely receive more treatment in the future, it won't die overnight either.

You might have read, or you might even think yourself, that any product that has not received updates for years is a dead product. Well, that depends. An absence of improvements certainly shows that a role is no longer considered to be strategic. But a lack of improvements also indicates there's no more to add without rewriting the product from scratch according to new principles and a more up-to-date vision. Yet, the old product works. It's like a TV a few years old. It won't give you the best experience, but you can still use it to watch your favorite shows. You can get a new TV, but you shouldn't be too critical of those who don't. It all depends on how crucial it is, business-wise, to jump on a new platform and how much it will cost you.

Web Forms is obsolete from a design perspective, but it can still let you quickly arrange solutions with its own tools. If you can use these tools to achieve your business goals, why should you drop them? Sticking to Web Forms strictly depends on the business needs you're facing. The question to ask is, "Will Web Forms be up to performing the new tasks?"

If your purpose is to build a SPA or, more simply, a JavaScript-intensive application, you might find that difficult to do if you stick with Web Forms. Similarly, you might encounter difficulty if you need to ensure full accessibility to all pages of the site or if having SEO-friendly URLs is critical.

The requirements of the presentation layer—responsiveness, gestures, and touch-first user experience in particular—are other possible sore points. Moving away from Web Forms might have the cost of retraining people and the difficulty of having people learn a new paradigm (whether it's MVC or new frameworks like AngularJS) and become proficient in JavaScript. On the other hand, if you look at ASP.NET Core 1.0, you see clearly that the direction is toward ASP.NET MVC. In this regard, I dare say the sooner you make the transition the better off you will be.

Why you should move away from Web Forms

ASP.NET Web Forms was designed at a time when abstraction over HTML and JavaScript was perceived as an excellent benefit. This is no longer the case. Therefore, if you see the Web Forms programming model encountering limits in the business scenario you're facing, look to ASP.NET MVC or a SPA. If achieving what you want is hard with Web Forms, even if it's doable, you should just move to ASP.NET MVC. Moving this way, with an eye on ASP.NET Core 1.0, you will be well positioned for the future.

ASP.NET Web Forms is not a CSS-friendly framework by design, and CSS and responsive pages are a common presence in websites today. You can hardly be creating CSS effects on top of server controls. Likewise, if you just use an ASPX file as a container of plain HTML in a SPA scenario, why not jump to Razor and ASP.NET MVC?

Anyway, the major reason for moving away from Web Forms is not strictly technological. The major challenge in modern software, and the major aspect we'd love to fix in legacy code, is the architecture of information and the back end. As you can see, this has little to do with choosing Web Forms or ASP.NET MVC. Yet Web Forms encourages, even though it doesn't mandate, using a programming model that is essentially database-driven and often heralds a two-tier schema (presentation and data access layers).

The problem I see here is not that a two-tier schema is wrong or inappropriate in principle. It's that such a schema doesn't likely let you address the real challenges of modern software. Most of the software we write can still fall under the umbrella of the Create, Read, Updated, Delete (CRUD) paradigm, but it realistically involves a lot more than just implementing CRUD operations. Web Forms shines at plain CRUD, and most modern applications only look like CRUD. With that said, just because this point is about architecture it doesn't have much to do with how you arrange the presentation layer and whether you use server controls or plain HTML.

Today success in software comes mostly from adherence to business scenarios. Web Forms might still be used to address some business scenarios, but planning a migration to ASP.NET MVC is becoming necessary to stay in business and to stay in it comfortably.

A word or two about Microsoft Silverlight

Silverlight is another symbol of the fleeting nature of software technology. Back in 2008, it was heralded as the new way of writing web software. Within a couple of years, it became the place to be and the technology of the century. Then a poisoned arrow shot it in the heel, and it just died overnight. Yet a bunch of companies out there are stuck with significant investments in presentation layers built with Silverlight.

Silverlight still works and will work for the foreseeable future. As mentioned, just because a technology is not updated, it doesn't mean it stops working all of a sudden. At the same time, as a user of that technology, you must consider what you should do and how to move away from it. You need to find a valid alternative approach to rebuilding your presentation at some point.

How should you replace Silverlight?

There are not all that many options. I'd say there's just one option—using HTML5. The next issue, then, is how to package up the user interface defined with HTML5. In this case, too, I don't see that many options. There are just two.

You can go with a full single-page application (SPA) or use a mix of server and client code hosted in some ASP.NET container. Which container? ASP.NET MVC.

In this context, you can still find a bunch of component suites that simplify development and deliver a development experience similar to Silverlight. Quite likely, the same vendors who helped you with Silverlight can help you build a nice user interface on top of HTML5.

Later in the chapter, I'll define this approach—which is a mix of server and client code—for creating a hybrid SPA.

Determining if you should use ASP.NET MVC

ASP.NET MVC was introduced about a decade ago to give developers an alternative way of writing web applications. The move, I guess, was inspired by a long list of open-source frameworks available at the time that used the Model-View-Controller (MVC) pattern. ASP.NET MVC, though, was not bad at all and became a powerful development framework for the web from 2010 forward.

The changes coming with ASP.NET Core 1.0 reinforce and confirm this vision. To be a web developer today and tomorrow on the Microsoft stack, you need to master ASP.NET MVC.

ASP.NET MVC at a glance

ASP.NET Web Forms owed its success to the thick abstraction layer it built over the core web infrastructure. ASP.NET MVC makes a point of doing just the opposite; it makes the same abstraction layer as thin as possible. Whereas Web Forms aims to shield developers from the details of HTML, CSS, and JavaScript, ASP.NET MVC strives to give developers total control over markup by including HTML, JavaScript, and CSS.

ASP.NET MVC uses the *controller* as the entry point in the server-side chain of tasks that process an incoming request. As a developer, you have total control over the building of the URL and how it is mapped to a controller. Internally, the controller has access to the surrounding HTTP context—including the session state, request, response, and user information—and it orchestrates the processing of the request. Any results generated by the request processing are delivered back to the controller, which decides about the next step. The next step involves generating an HTML view, packaging data in JSON or XML format, or delivering anything else the caller expects to receive—for example, binary data.

Compared to using Web Forms, the building of the view is a lot trickier because the developer is responsible for just about everything. The often-blamed viewstate in Web Forms actually saved a lot of work for developers. It is not part of ASP.NET MVC, and all the viewstate's maintenance work now has to be manually coded. Aside from this, ASP.NET MVC doesn't use HTML factory components and any HTML markup is under the total control of the developer.

Figure 4-4 summarizes the programming model of ASP.NET MVC and contrasts it to that of ASP.NET Web Forms.

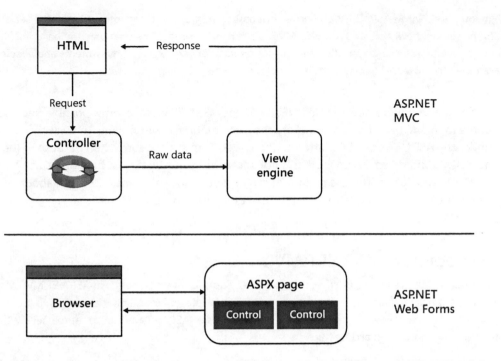

FIGURE 4-4 Contrasting the architecture and programming model of ASP.NET MVC and ASP.NET Web Forms

What's good with ASP.NET MVC

The web today is oriented toward an intensive use of JavaScript to empower and render pages and the use of CSS to style pages. Quite simply, these tasks are much easier to achieve with ASP.NET MVC than with ASP.NET Web Forms. And even if you opt for a SPA—plain JavaScript calling into web services—you still need a host. The most likely option you have is still an ASP.NET MVC application within IIS.

By using ASP.NET MVC, you probably can achieve what you need to achieve these days. It doesn't prevent you from using frameworks like AngularJS, Knockout, or even React. It works beautifully with Twitter Bootstrap and jQuery. And as long as you stay away from ASP.NET Core 1.0, it also works side by side with Web Forms.

This is an important factor to consider for CTOs.

If you have a large ASP.NET Web Forms codebase to migrate, you can import the entire set of ASPX pages in a newly created ASP.NET MVC project and rewrite piecemeal only the parts you need to rewrite. It's a slow transition that preserves most of your existing investments and allows developers to grow and gain new skills at their best pace.

> **Important** A mix-up between ASP.NET MVC and ASP.NET Web Forms is possible because, at the moment, both frameworks share the same runtime environment. This will change under the ASP.NET Core 1.0 platform, where Web Forms is not supported because of the new DNX runtime environment that is not based on *system.web*—the beating heart of ASP.NET Web Forms. This is a point that can help you make a business decision about whether or not to upgrade to ASP.NET Core 1.0 in the short term.

Weak points of ASP.NET MVC

From a purely functional perspective, I don't find any significant weak points in ASP.NET MVC. As a framework, it has been around for quite a few years, it's well stabilized, and it conforms to the needs of today's server-side web development. The weak points of ASP.NET MVC occur at two levels: the infrastructure and coding architecture.

Since the beginning, ASP.NET MVC was created not to be intrusive and to work side by side with ASP.NET Web Forms. For this reason, the two frameworks share the same runtime environment, which is heavily based on the *system.web* assembly and tightly integrated with IIS. As a sign that times do change, not that many years ago the integrated pipeline between ASP.NET and IIS was touted as a strong measure of improved performance and a positive evolution of the ASP.NET stack. Today, though, the tight dependency that exists between the ASP.NET stack and the host environment is seen as a major weakness of ASP.NET MVC.

For the time being, you have two choices. You can choose to stay with the current ASP.NET stack and runtime environment and still run the latest version of the ASP.NET MVC framework on top of it. Or you can jump to the ASP.NET Core 1.0 stack and enjoy a cleaner pipeline based on the OWIN standard for communication with the host environment. In this context, IIS is just one of the possible hosts and Windows Server is just one of the possible operating systems.

Another aspect of ASP.NET MVC that is less than ideal, in my opinion, relates to the patterns you use most to architect web solutions. ASP.NET MVC as a framework certainly is not related in any way to architecture, but the communication being made around it transmit some ideas that might be hard to modify. ASP.NET MVC is often associated with building up a sort of REST interface around a data model and using the controller classes to implement the core CRUD operations.

The problem I see is that a REST interface with core CRUD operations performed over the web is only sometimes a model that works well in real-world business domains. If you grow up with this idea in mind, you might run into serious problems when you face a domain where the query stack is quite different from the command stack and ideally requires completely different models. Getting rid of the REST idea and focusing on tasks—which is more like adopting a remote-procedure-call (RPC) style than a REST style—is a better approach because focusing on tasks doesn't prevent you from doing REST if that is all that the application requires, and at the same time it keeps you open to more sophisticated things if that's the case.

I suggest using a layered architecture, which I'll cover in the next chapter, and using ASP.NET MVC as the framework for the presentation layer. And in the context of the layered architecture, I recommend Command Query Responsibility Segregation (CQRS) as the supporting architecture to have commands and queries split and implemented separately.

Examining the role of ASP.NET Web API

ASP.NET Web API is a framework created to facilitate the exposure of an API over the web. Put another way, it's an API used to build and expose web services for webpages to consume. An ASP.NET Web API solution still needs to be hosted somewhere, and this is most likely, though not necessarily, within an IIS application.

An ASP.NET Web API front end typically exists to provide HTTP-reachable endpoints to webpages that return raw data (for example, JSON, XML, or plain text). Raw data is then rendered into a nice-looking format within the browser.

What's the ideal way to set up such a web-service front end?

Moving from WCF to Web API

Over the years, different frameworks have been worked out and regularly presented as the definitive solution to the issue of exposing HTTP-reachable endpoints. In the beginning, there was Windows Communication Foundation (WCF). WCF was built and sold as a framework for exposing services that could work the same regardless of the transportation layer. In other words, any WCF service can be reached using TCP or HTTP without changing anything but the configuration parameters.

To work this way, WCF requires a rich and generic infrastructure that is too complex and expensive for scenarios where you just want to use a single protocol. In other words, WCF has never been focused on HTTP.

Over the years, WCF went through a number of extensions aimed at simplifying HTTP programming, such as Web HTTP binding and the REST starter kit. But, in the end, it was always WCF running over HTTP. It never was a solution that was optimized for HTTP and built from scratch with that goal in mind. ASP.NET Web API is probably the best attempt to provide an ideal framework for web services exposed over HTTP.

Although sometimes perceived as an ASP.NET MVC branch, ASP.NET Web API is a general framework and is not even limited to working in web scenarios. ASP.NET Web API can be hosted in any flavor of a .NET application, including a Windows service or a console application. If it's hosted in a Web Forms application, you'll find it's a lot easier to write web services to be consumed from HTML pages via jQuery functions. In fact, you can use ASP.NET Web API as a replacement for WCF and stop relying on JavaScript proxies and experiencing configuration difficulties.

Hosting ASP.NET Web API in an ASP.NET MVC application is a different story that has yet to be fully written. And it might even have quite a surprise ending.

> **Note** Thanks to ASP.NET Web API, it is safe and even recommended to limit the use of WCF services to just those scenarios where a non-HTTP communication is required or likely to be requested. If you're definitely going to stay with HTTP as the transportation protocol, by all means drop WCF for ASP.NET Web API. It's far easier and quicker to write with ASP.NET Web API, and it also offers better performance because of the significantly smaller footprint and workload.

Comparing ASP.NET Web API and ASP.NET MVC

ASP.NET Web API is a framework that, once hosted in a listener application, handles requests to its endpoints delivered via HTTP. Its overall architecture is close to that of ASP.NET MVC. Both frameworks make use of controllers and actions. Both frameworks rely on model binding and have an internal and configurable routing system and various extensibility points.

There are some important differences, too.

In particular, the runtime of Web API is completely separated from ASP.NET MVC. You meet classes with similar names and behavior, but namespaces are different and so are assemblies. The differences between ASP.NET MVC and ASP.NET Web API can be summarized in the following three points:

- Processing code and serializing results are decoupled steps at the runtime level.

- Content negotiation is different.

- Hosting outside of IIS is possible.

An ASP.NET Web API layer is made of a collection of controller classes derived from a base class called *ApiController*. HTTP GET methods defined on a controller can just return raw data, without explicitly passing from an *ActionResult* container as in ASP.NET MVC. Here's an example:

```
// NewsController class
public IList<News> Get()
{
    // This is processing code for the request
    var url = ...;
    var client = new WebClient();
    var rss = client.DownloadString(url);
    var news = DoSomethingToParseRssFeed(rss);

    // Just return data and let the runtime do any required HTTP packaging/formatting
    return news;
}
```

Let's compare an analogous method written within an ASP.NET MVC controller:

```
public ActionResult Index()
{
    // This is processing code for the request
    var url = ...;
    var client = new WebClient();
    var rss = client.DownloadString(url);
    var news = DoSomethingToParseRssFeed(rss);

    // Explicit JSON serialization step
    return Json(news, JsonBehavior.AllowGet);
}
```

The differences illustrate the first two bullet points in the earlier list.

Any data returned from a Web API action method passes through a formatting layer—a process known as *content negotiation*—that ultimately determines the stream to be served back to the caller. Content negotiation, for the most part, is invisible to the developer. Standard conventions default any returned data to JSON. However, if the HTTP request indicates XML as the preferred format for returned data, the framework automatically switches to XML using a built-in schema.

Extensibility points exist to replace the native JSON formatter or serialize to a custom XML formatter. You register your own formatters at the startup of the application, as part of the configuration effort. If you want to use a custom XML schema for each method, you need to tweak the configuration every now and then.

Under the folds of ASP.NET Web API there are a lot of conventions. For example, all methods whose name starts with *Get* are automatically bound to an HTTP GET operation, and the URL becomes the method name without the *Get* prefix. In the example, both methods are called via a URL such as */news*. If you renamed the ASP.NET Web API method to *GetAll*, the URL to call it would be */news/all*.

If you already have an ASP.NET MVC application, exposing the API of the domain via Web API doesn't really give you any significant benefit. It's doable, it works, and it's not even the wrong choice. But I don't see any special benefit. Additionally, I see some complications deriving from the fact that two runtime environments are involved to process requests.

If you already have an ASP.NET MVC application, you can still expose an HTTP front end, writing it easily and quickly, just using the same controller classes you would use for rendering HTML. Content negotiation doesn't happen, but it's the controller that determines the format of data being returned. Here's an example where the controller chooses between JSON and XML:

```
public ActionResult Index(Boolean xml = false)
{
    // This is processing code for the request
    var url = ...;
    var client = new WebClient();
    var rss = client.DownloadString(url);
    var news = DoSomethingToParseRssFeed(rss);
```

```
// Explicit JSON serialization step
if (xml)
  return Content(new ThisMethodXmlFormatter(rss), "text/xml");
return Json(news, JsonBehavior.AllowGet);
}
```

Everything is under your total control. There are no places where magic happens, and you use just one runtime environment.

A web service still needs to be hosted somewhere. If you decide to host the web service outside IIS or under Web Forms, using ASP.NET Web API to implement it is acceptable. If you, instead, plan to host the web service within ASP.NET MVC, you better build the service using an ad hoc controller within the same ASP.NET MVC application.

Talking about REST

ASP.NET Web API is often associated with REST. In other words, one of the points made about the use of ASP.NET Web API to build a web service is that it makes it easier to build a REST interface around a data model you might have in the back end and want to expose.

This is true.

I'm not a lover of REST, and I have no issues admitting I strongly prefer an RPC lifestyle because I find the "free" language of an RPC API to be more flexible and ideal for expressing the intricacy of business domains and their tasks. For me, REST is more about modeling than it is about mirroring the business scenarios.

Anyway, if you love coding the REST way—having basic HTTP operations performed on entities you own on the server side—using the ASP.NET Web API even in the context of ASP.NET MVC is an acceptable choice. I just want to clarify and, in some way, demystify the point that you need ASP.NET Web API if you want a tier of services distinct from the core site. It's the same story: it's all about deciding how to host the web service and whether to create it around a REST or RPC interface.

In this regard, it's interesting to look at the development of in ASP.NET Core 1.0.

Using Web API in ASP.NET Core 1.0

Apparently, if you read some documentation about ASP.NET Core 1.0, it all seems to be in line with what Figure 4-3 shows. In ASP.NET Core 1.0, you have support for ASP.NET MVC and ASP.NET Web API, and both run on top of the same runtime environment and pipeline. If you take a closer look, however, all that you have is a single framework that starts from the core features of ASP.NET MVC and just extends them with some specific features borrowed from Web API. What does it mean concretely?

Web API is disappeared, and you just create a controller class and decide what it has to return—either an *IActionResult* type or plain CLR objects. If it's a plain CLR object, the actual serialization format is negotiated, as in today's Web API, by looking at HTTP headers. Put another way, the statement, "We have an ASP.NET MVC site and a Web API," makes no sense in ASP.NET Core 1.0. All that you're going to have is a set of controller classes in an ASP.NET Core 1.0 application. Here's how to write a controller in ASP.NET MVC that runs under ASP.NET Core 1.0:

```
[Route("api/[controller]")]
public class NewsController : Controller
{
    [HttpGet]
    public IEnumerable<NewsItem> All()
    {
        var data = ...;
        return data;
    }

    [HttpDelete("{id}")]
    public IActionResult DeleteNews(int id)
    {
        // Delete the item
        ...

        return new HttpStatusCodeResult(204);
    }
}
```

The *Route* attribute on top of the controller class defines the default routing mechanism for anything that passes through the controller. As specified in the example, any URL mapped to this controller class begins with */api/news*, where *news* is the nickname of the controller.

If you drop the *Route* attribute, the default routing is the same as in ASP.NET MVC or as specified in the configuration of the application. As you can see, there's no base controller class to inherit from that is specific to Web API. The controller class is the same whether it returns HTML or data. You have a richer API in the controller class to shape up the response and decide how to map requests to methods. For example, the method *DeleteNews* is mapped to an HTTP DELETE action.

I admit that my earlier statement, "Web API is disappeared," is (deliberately) a bit too harsh. Web API doesn't disappear but is merged into the core ASP.NET MVC API. As a result, though, it no longer makes sense to consider Web API as something different from ASP.NET MVC. At least in ASP.NET Core 1.0.

Single-page applications

A *single-page application (SPA)* is just what the name suggests. It's a web application based on a single HTML page.

Upon loading, the page connects to some remote endpoint and downloads any data it needs to prepare programmatically and, dynamically, any user interface. Next, the DOM of the page is updated as the user interacts with the displayed content. The "single page" is what you download once from the server at the beginning and never change. Every interaction results in updating views within the page container by downloading HTML chunks or generating client-side HTML from downloaded data. There's nearly no navigation except to jump to another HTML page with a different but related set of functions. Instead, you switch between HTML views following controls (Back buttons as well as hyperlinks) that implement JavaScript code to hide and show HTML views.

The primary goal of a SPA is to give users a much more fluid experience, removing all full-page refreshes and making interaction quite similar to a desktop application.

Setting up a SPA

The canonical SPA is made of one page, or perhaps just a few pages, hosted on a web server as plain HTML files or endpoints of some ASP.NET server application. The HTML option often means that the container is a half-empty HTML body with a HEAD section and an empty DIV as the body. The page loads up a bunch of script code, and the script code, in turn, starts downloading data and markup to display to users.

Any data requested for startup makes the loading of the site take a bit longer—sometimes too long for the user. After the first view has been rendered, though, interaction goes much faster and smoother because most of the content has been downloaded and rendered and, more importantly, it won't be modified any more.

Setting up a SPA is much more complicated than it might appear at first, and realistically only the use of ad hoc frameworks—for example, AngularJS—can make it worthwhile. However, once you de-liver such a solution, usually users are happy. A SPA is significantly different from classic ASP.NET code and is mostly made of JavaScript code and client-side data-binding techniques.

Hybrid SPA

A hybrid SPA is something in between a classic ASP.NET site and a SPA. It relies on a server-side ASP.NET application that serves up a few HTML pages connected together via hyperlinks. You start building a hybrid SPA in exactly the same way you build a plain ASP.NET site, except that the content of some HTML views is highly dynamic and based on Ajax interaction and dynamic updates of the client-side DOM.

In a hybrid SPA, you might still be using client-side JavaScript libraries to do data binding and Ajax calls, but you use these features to optimize specific views rather than using this pattern throughout the entire application.

For users, the benefits are that at least critical pages are highly dynamic and much faster than a classic set of server pages. Initialization is the same as with a regular server website, and there's no need to preload the entire set of pages.

In terms of skills, the transition toward JavaScript is limited to learning one of two data-binding frameworks, the most popular of which is certainly AngularJS. You don't have to learn all of AngularJS, however. Also, from the SEO perspective, you are halfway home and can effectively decide how many distinct HTML views (and HTTP endpoints) you need to have based on SEO requirements.

Weak points of a SPA

Paradoxically, the weakest points of a SPA are exactly the same points that contribute to its strength. The fluidity of the user interface that descends from having predownloaded content might introduce a delay in the first display or might even block interactivity for a few seconds if the remote server is occasionally slow to respond.

I agree that a slow response certainly isn't an issue specific to a SPA. But on a regular ASP.NET server site, once the markup is displayed you can read and interact smoothly until you click to post or navigate elsewhere. In a SPA, it could even be that some content is hidden and will be downloaded on demand. So there's a greater chance of making remote requests and, subsequently, a greater chance you'll encounter slow responses. This issue can be quite annoying on mobile devices.

Another issue I see with a SPA is selling it to management. Marketing usually loves the idea of a website that promptly reacts to any user input, but sometimes management might argue that a website requires many pages and not a single page. It might be hard to explain that a SPA is one page (or just very few pages) and dozens of distinct HTML views routed and navigated in some way.

Another objection I'd expect is about skills. Writing a SPA requires strong JavaScript skills and familiarity and mastering of the SPA framework of choice. To build a true SPA, you need help from one of the SPA professional frameworks, such as AngularJS, Durandal, or Ember. Learning to use any of these is analogous to learning a new programming language. It's perhaps easy to get started, but becoming proficient might take a bit of time. And time is money.

If you opt for a hybrid, instead, I see a far easier learning curve. First because you still write quite a bit of server-side code, and next because you can limit your efforts to using on the client side only a specific data-binding library (say, Knockout or Moustache) or just the data-binding module of larger frameworks.

Summary

This chapter illustrated the options you have for building a web solution. In the end, you can build web solutions these days in many equally effective ways. The critical point is defining what makes a solution "effective" in the context of the business domain.

A large number of systems built using Web Forms are waiting for a remake. At the same time, there are new systems just being architected that have an expected long lifespan. And there are more and more websites built to last only for a few weeks. What should you do?

Short-lived web applications and sites should be created using whatever approach the team manages well, regardless of the present and future of the frameworks being used. New systems for the ASP.NET stack should definitely take the route of ASP.NET MVC and consider Web API to be just an extension of ASP.NET MVC. Web API is going to disappear because it will be incorporated into ASP.NET MVC in ASP.NET Core 1.0.

For existing large Web Forms codebases, I assume that the costs of changing the framework are high. On the other hand, you're going to pay its costs at some point. A good middle ground could be starting the transition to ASP.NET MVC without going to ASP.NET Core 1.0. By doing that, you can mix and match ASP.NET Web Forms and ASP.NET MVC, thus moving the company on the right track but at a sustainable pace.

I'm not a big fan of SPAs, but I do recommend hybrid SPAs. To me, a hybrid SPA on top of ASP.NET MVC represents the best approximation of a web stack these days. It's better if it's backed by a layered architecture focused on CQRS.

Finally, I spent a word or two writing about what in Chapter 3 I called *UX-Driven Design*. The main issue I see with software today is the gap between the business view and the software view. For many years, we hoped that we could come up with an all-encompassing single model for the entire domain. Sometimes it worked, and sometimes it didn't.

I think we'd better focus on screens and expected interactions between users and applications. This is what I recommended in Chapter 3 in the form of UX-Driven Design. The point is not so much about doing things right but doing as many things as possible right the first time. This approach won't lower development costs to near zero, but it will surely make estimating costs a much more predictable experience.

CHAPTER 5

The layered architecture

We shape our buildings; thereafter they shape us.

—*Winston Churchill*

It has been quite a few years since computer programs have been the result of monolithic software. Monolithic software is an end-to-end sequence of procedural instructions that achieve a goal. While nearly no professional developers or architects would seriously consider writing end-to-end programs today, building monoliths is the most natural way of approaching software development for newbies. Monoliths are not bad per se—it's whether the program achieves its mission or not that really matters—but monoliths become less and less useful as the complexity of the program grows. In real-world software architecture, therefore, monoliths are simply out of place. And they have been out of place for decades now.

In software, a layer hides the implementation details of a given set of functionality behind a known interface. Layers serve the purpose of Separation of Concerns and facilitate interoperability between distinct components of the same system. In an object-oriented system, a layer is essentially a set of classes implementing a given business goal. Different layers may be deployed to physical tiers, sometimes in the form of services or micro-services available over a known network protocol such as HTTP.

A layer is a segment of software that lives in-process with other layers. Layers refer to a logical, rather than physical, separation between components. The *layered architecture* I present in this chapter is probably the most widely accepted way to mix functionality and business to produce a working system.

Beyond classic three-tier systems

You might have grown up with the idea that any software system should be arranged around three segments: the presentation, business, and data layers. The *presentation* segment is made of screens (either desktop, mobile, or web interfaces) used to collect input data and present results. The *data* segment is where you deal with databases and save and read information. The *business* segment is where everything else you need to have fits in. (See Figure 5-1.)

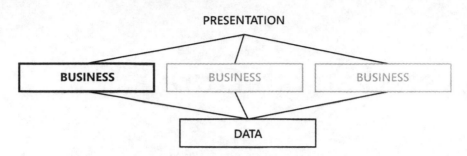

FIGURE 5-1 The classic three-tier segmentation of software architecture

Industry literature mostly refers to the architecture depicted in Figure 5-1 as a *three-tier architecture*. However, you can allocate segments both on physical tiers and logical layers. It just depends on your needs.

Working with a three-tier architecture today

The three-tier architecture has been around for a long time, but it originated at a time when most business work was either database related or restricted to external components such as mainframes. For the most part, the three-tier architecture uses a single data model that travels from the data store up to the presentation and back.

The architecture certainly doesn't prevent you from using other flavors of data-transfer objects (DTOs), but for the most part the three-tier architecture is emblematic of just one data model and is database-centric. The challenge you face these days—foreseen by Domain-Driven Design (DDD)— is matching persistence with presentation needs. Even though the core operations of any system remains Create-Read-Update-Delete (CRUD), the way in which business rules affect these core operations require the business layer to take care of way too many data transformations and way too much process orchestration.

Even though a lot of tutorials insist on describing an e-commerce platform as a plain CRUD regarding customers and orders, the reality is different. You never just add an order record to a database. You never have just a one-to-one match between the user interface of an order and the schema of the Orders table. Most likely, you don't even have the perception of an order at the presentation level. You more likely have something like a shopping cart that, once processed, produces an order record in some database tables.

Business processes are the hardest part to organize in a three-tier mental model. And business processes are not simply the most important thing in software; they're the only thing that really matters and they're the thing for which no compromises are possible. At first glance, business processes are the heart of the business tier. However, more often than not, business processes are too widespread to be easily restricted within the boundaries of an architecture that likes to have layers that can easily turn into physical tiers. Different presentation layers can trigger different business processes, and different business processes can refer to the same core behavior and the implementation of a few rules.

Although the meaning of business logic seems to be quite obvious, the right granularity of the reusable pieces of business logic is not obvious at all.

Fifty shades of gray areas

In a plain three-tier scenario, where would you fit the logic that adapts data to presentation? And where does the logic that optimizes input data for persistence belong? These questions highlight two significant gray areas that some architects still struggle with these days.

A *gray area* is an area of uncertainty or indeterminacy in some business context. In software architecture, the term also refers to a situation in which the solution to apply is not obvious and the uncertainty originates more from the availability of multiple choices than the lack of tools to solve the problem.

To clear the sky of gray areas, a slightly revisited architecture is in order. When Eric Evans first introduced Domain-Driven Design (which I discuss in Chapter 1, "Conducting a thorough domain analysis"), he also introduced the layered architecture, as depicted in Figure 5-2.

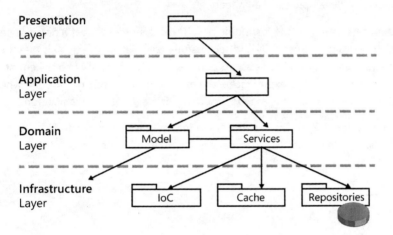

FIGURE 5-2 The layered architecture

The layered architecture has an extra layer and expands the notion of a data-access layer to that of just the provider of any necessary infrastructure, such as data access via object-relational mapping (ORM) tools, implementation of inversion of control (IoC) containers, and many other cross-cutting concerns such as security, logging, and caching.

The business layer exploded into the application and domain layers. This trend is an attempt to clear up the gray areas and make it clear that there are two types of business logic: application and domain. The *application* logic orchestrates any tasks triggered by the presentation. The *domain* logic is any core logic of the specific business that is reusable across multiple presentation layers.

The application layer aligns nearly one-to-one with the presentation layer and is where any UI-specific transformation of data takes place. The domain logic is about business rules and core business tasks using a data model that is strictly business oriented.

The presentation layer

The presentation layer is responsible for providing some user interface to accomplish any necessary tasks. The presentation layer consists of a collection of screens, either HTML forms or anything else. Today, more and more systems have multiple presentation layers. This is an ASP.NET book, so you might think that, at least in the current context, there's just one presentation layer. Not exactly, I'd say.

The mobile web is another presentation layer that must be taken into account for a web application. A mobile web presentation layer, then, can be implemented through responsive HTML templates or a completely distinct set of screens. However, that doesn't change the basic fact that the mobile web is an additional presentation layer for nearly any web application.

The user experience

No matter what kind of smart code you lovingly craft in the middle tier, no applications can be consumed by any users without a presentation front end. Furthermore, no applications can be enjoyable and effective without a well-designed user experience. However, for a long time the presentation layer has been the last concern of developers and architects.

Many architects consider presentation as the less noble part of the system—almost a detail once the business and data-access layers have been fully and successfully completed. The truth is that the presentation, as well as the business logic and data-access code, is equally necessary in a system of any complexity. These days, though, the user experience—the experience the users go through when they interact with the application—is invaluable, as I explained in Chapter 3, "UX-Driven Design."

At any rate, whether you develop the system in a top-down manner (as recommended in Chapter 3) or in a more classic bottom-up fashion, you need to understand the purpose of the presentation. Take a look at Figure 5-3.

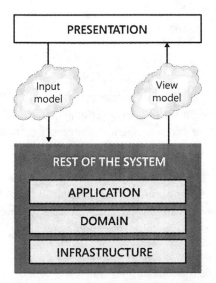

FIGURE 5-3 Describing the data that goes into and out of presentation screens

The presentation layer funnels data to the rest of the system, ideally using its own data model that reflects the structure well and organizes the data in the screens. You should render the user interface as an order entity, and not just because you end up storing date in an Orders table. For example, when you submit an order, you typically collect information like the shipping address that might or might not be related to the customer that is paying for the order. And the shipping address doesn't necessarily get stored with the order. It could be that the shipping address is communicated to the shipping company and the reference number is stored with the order.

Generally speaking, each screen in the presentation that posts a command to the back end of the system groups data into an input model and receives a response using classes in a view model. The input and view models might or might not coincide. At the same time, they might or might not coincide with any data model being used in the back end to perform actual tasks.

The input model

In ASP.NET MVC, any user's clicking originates a request that a controller class will handle. Each request is turned into an action mapped to a public method defined on a controller class. What about input data?

In ASP.NET, any input data is wrapped up in the HTTP request, either in the query string, in any form-posted data, or perhaps in HTTP headers or cookies. Input data represents the data being posted for the system to take an action on. Whatever way you look at it, it is just input parameters. You can treat input data as loose values and variables, or you can group them into a class acting as a container. The collection of input classes form the overall input model for the application.

As you'll see in a lot more detail in upcoming chapters, in ASP.NET MVC a component part of the system infrastructure—the model-binding layer—can automatically map sparse and loose variables in the HTTP request to public properties of input model classes. Here are two examples of a controller method that are equally effective:

```
public ActionResult SignIn(string username, string password, bool rememberme)
{
    ...
}

public ActionResult SignIn(LoginInputModel input)
{
    ...
}
```

In the latter case, the *LoginInputModel* class will have public properties whose names match the names of uploaded parameters:

```
public class LoginInputModel
{
    public string UserName { get; set; }
    public string Password { get; set; }
    public bool RememberMe { get; set; }
}
```

The input model carries data in the core of the system in a way that aligns one-to-one with the expectations of the user interface. Employing an input model makes it easier to design the user interface in a strongly business-oriented way. The application layer (shown in Figure 5-3) then takes care of unpacking any data and consuming it as appropriate.

The view model

Any request gets a response and, more often than not, the response you get from ASP.NET MVC is an HTML view. (Admittedly, this is not the only option, but it's still quite the most common.) In ASP.NET MVC, the creation of an HTML view is governed by the controller, which invokes the back end of the system and gets back some response. It then selects the HTML template to use and passes the HTML template and data to an ad-hoc system component—the view engine—which will mix the template and data and produce the markup for the browser.

In ASP.NET MVC, there are a few ways to pass data to the view engine that will be incorporated in the resulting view. You can use a public dictionary such as *ViewData*, a dynamic object such as *ViewBag*, or a made-to-measure class that collects all properties to pass. Any class you create to carry data to be incorporated in the response contributes to creating the view model. The application layer is the layer that receives input-model classes and returns view-model classes:

```
public ActionResult Edit(LoginInputModel input)
{
    var model = _applicationLayer.GetSomeDataForNextView(input);
    return View(model);
}
```

More and more, in the future the ideal format for persistence will be different from the ideal format for presentation. The presentation layer is responsible for defining the clear boundaries of acceptable data, and the application layer is responsible for accepting and providing data in just those formats. If you take this approach extensively, you then fall in line with the principles outlined in Chapter 3 regarding UX-driven software design.

> **Note** Putting the presentation layer at the center is an approach that pays off whether you use a server-side approach to the building of the web solution or a client-side solution.

The application layer

To carry on business operations, the presentation layer needs a reference to the back end of the system. The shape and color of the entry point in the business layer of the application depends on how you actually organized that.

In an ASP.NET MVC solution, you can call the infrastructure layer directly from the controller via a few repository classes. Generally, though, you want to have an intermediate layer or two in between controllers (for example, as part of the presentation layer) and repositories (for example, as part of the infrastructure layer). Have a look at Figure 5-4.

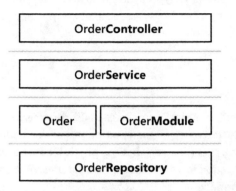

FIGURE 5-4 An aggregate-based section of the layered architecture

As you can see from the picture, you can access repositories from within controllers, but that's just a way to simplify things when the simplification of the design doesn't end up adding more pain than gain. A layered architecture is generally based on four logical layers. Each layer has its own place, and if you don't use any it should be because you have good reasons (mostly because of simplification) to do that.

Entry point in the system's back end

Each interactive element of the user interface (for example, buttons) triggers an action in the back end of the system. In some simple scenarios, the action that follows some user's clicking takes just one step to conclude. More realistically, though, the user's clicking triggers something like a workflow.

The application layer is the entry point in the back end of the system and the point of contact between the presentation and back end. The application layer consists of methods bound in an almost one-to-one fashion to the use-cases of the presentation layer. You can group methods in any way that makes sense to you.

I tend to organize application-layer methods in classes that go hand in hand with controller classes. In this way, the *OrderController* class, for example, has its own private instance of an *OrderService* class. (See Figure 5-4.)

Methods in the *OrderService* class get classes in the input model and return classes from the view model. Internally, this class performs any necessary transformation to make data render nicely on the presentation and be ready for processing in the back end.

Orchestration of business processes

The primary purpose of the application layer is abstracting business processes as users perceive them and mapping those processes to the hidden and protected assets of the application's back end. In an e-commerce system, for example, the user expects a shopping cart, but the physical data model might have no entity like the shopping cart. The application layer sits in between the presentation and the back end and performs any necessary transformation.

Accepting an order is typically a multistep workflow and never a single step. If it's a single step, you might not find any benefit in passing through the application layer. Otherwise, the application layer helps immensely to keep workflows distinct from business rules and domain-specific processes. To better understand the difference between application logic and domain logic, consider the following example from a banking scenario.

As a customer, you can talk to a teller and ask to deposit a paper check. Ultimately, some money will be withdrawn from one account and added to another one. But actual processes might be quite different. At a minimum, the teller will go through a process that first places a request to the issuing bank and then adds some money to your account. So you have two operations:

- Cash check from a bank.

- Add money to a bank account.

Both operations are domain-level operations, and both are core tasks of the business domain. The combination of the two, on the other hand, is a workflow that is bound to a specific use-case of the presentation layer—letting users deposit a check. The resulting workflow represents a statement like "Deposit a check" and, depending on the implementation and external services involved, might or might not be a core domain operation. That's an architectural decision after all.

Splitting the business logic into application and domain logic gives you the logical tools to better model the business logic as close as possible to the real world and, more than everything else, close to the user's expectations.

Note These days, the user experience is more important than it once was for the success of any application at any level of complexity. So, to provide an excellent user experience, the golden rule is, "You better have an application layer."

The domain layer

Any software—even the simplest data-entry application—is written against a business domain. Each business domain has its own rules. The number of rules is sometimes close to zero, but as an architect you should always reserve room for a collection of business rules. Finally, each business domain exposes a sort of an application programming interface (API). The way in which the presentation allows end users to interact with such an API—use-cases—determines the application layer.

In a nutshell, the domain layer hosts the entire business logic that is not specific to one or more use-cases. Typically, the domain layer consists of a model (known as the *domain model*) and possibly a family of services (known as *domain services*).

The mythical domain model

Frankly, I find that there's a lot of confusion around the intended role and purpose of the domain model. Abstractly speaking, the domain model is a plain software model that helps render the business domain. The software model can be defined using an object-oriented paradigm (the most common scenario) or any other approach you might find appropriate, such as the functional paradigm. The domain model is the place where you implement the business rules and common, reusable business processes.

Even when you use an object-oriented paradigm, the domain model might or might not be a plain entity-relationship model and might or might not have a one-to-one relationship with the persistence model. The domain model is not strictly related to persistence; the domain model must serve the supreme purpose of implementing business rules. Persistence comes next and is one of the concerns of the infrastructure layer.

In terms of technologies, there's a lot of hype about Entity Framework Code First, which makes it easy to create your classes and then instruct the runtime to create database tables accordingly. This is not domain modeling—it's persistence modeling. As an architect, you should be well aware of logical layers: domain models are a different thing than persistence models. However, the two models can match—and usually match in simpler scenarios—and this brings Entity Framework Code First into play.

In a domain model that focuses on the logic and business rules, inevitably you have classes with factories, methods, and read-only properties. *Factories*, more than constructors, let you express the logic necessary to create new instances. *Methods* are the only way to alter the state of the system according to business tasks and actions. *Properties* are simply a way to read the current state of an instance of the domain model.

An object-oriented domain model is not necessarily an entity relationship model. It can be simply a collection of sparse and loose classes that contain data and store any behavior in separate classes with only methods. A model with entities devoid of any significant behavior—that is, mere data structures—form an *anemic domain model*.

A domain model lives in memory and is, to a great extent, stateless. Yet, some business-relevant actions require database reads and writes. Any interaction with the database—including the canonical example of determining whether a given customer has reached the status of "gold" customer (whatever that means in the business)—should happen outside the domain model. It should occur within the domain layer. This is why, along with a domain model, the domain layer should also feature domain services.

The equally mythical concept of domain services

It's quite simple to explain what a domain model is. Typically, developers nearly instantaneously and completely understand the concept of a software model that renders a business domain. The trouble emerges at a later time when you insist on the ideal separation between domain and persistence.

The point is that a significant part of the business logic is related to the manipulation of information that is persistently saved in some data store or held and controlled by some external web services. In an e-commerce system, to determine whether a customer has reached the status of gold customer, you need to count the amount of orders placed in a given timeframe and compare it to a selected range of products. The output of such a complex calculation is a plain Boolean value that you store in a fresh instance of the Customer domain-model class. Yet you still have a lot of work to do to get that value.

Which module is in charge of that?

Domain service is the umbrella under which a number of helper classes fall. A *domain service* is a class that performs reusable tasks related to the business logic, and it performs them around the classes in the domain model that implement business rules. Classes in the domain services segment have free access to the infrastructure layer, including databases and external services. A domain service, for example, orchestrates repositories—plain classes that perform CRUD operations on entities in the persistence model.

A simple rule for domain services is that you have such a domain service class for any piece of logic you need that requires access to external resources, including databases.

A more pragmatic view of domain modeling

I've probably been too rigorous and abstract in describing the domain layer. Whatever I stated is correct, but in the real world you often apply some degree of simplification. Simplification is never a bad thing, as long as you know exactly which logical layers you are removing for simplicity. If you look at a simplified model, you risk missing some important architectural points that exist even though they might be overkill in that scenario.

There are two terms I need to further explain here in the context of simplifying the architecture of the domain layer: *aggregates* and *repositories*.

Both terms have some DDD heritage. An *aggregate* is a whole formed by combining one or more distinct domain objects that are relevant in the business. It's a logical grouping you apply to simplify the management of the business domain by working with fewer coarse-grained objects. For example, you don't need to have a separate set of functions to deal with the items of an order. Order items make little sense without an order; therefore, orders and order items typically go in the same aggregate. Also, products might be used in the context of an order but, unlike order items, a product might also be acted on outside of orders—for example, when users view the product description before buying.

A *repository* is a component that manages the persistence of a relevant domain object or aggregation of domain objects. You can assign repositories any programming you like, though many developers design these classes around a type *T* being a relevant domain type.

In DDD domain modeling, the concept of an aggregate is a key concept. The vision I'm trying to convey here is more task-oriented and subsequently less centered on entities. The role of an aggregate, therefore, loses importance in the context of the domain layer but remains central in the realm of the infrastructure layer.

In the domain layer, you should focus on classes that express business rules and processes. You should not aim at identifying aggregations of data to persist. Any aggregation you identify should simply descend from your business understanding and modeling. Next, you have the problem of persisting the state of the system.

And when it comes to this, you have at least two options. One option is the classic persistence of the last-known-good-state of the system; the other option is the emerging approach known as *event sourcing*, in which you just save what happened and describe what has happened and any data involved. In the former case, you need aggregates. In the latter case, you might not need aggregates as a way to keep related data together in the description of the event that has happened.

The infrastructure layer

The infrastructure layer is anything related to using concrete technologies, whether it's data persistence (ORM frameworks like Entity Framework), external web services, specific security API, logging, tracing, IoC containers, caching, and more.

The most prominent component of the infrastructure layer is the persistence layer—nothing more than the old-faithful data-access layer, possibly extended to cover a few data sources other than plain relational data stores. The persistence layer knows how to read or save data and is made of repository classes.

Current state storage

If you use the classic approach of storing the current state of the system, you'll need one repository class for each relevant group of entities—this is the aggregate concept. By *group of entities*, I mean entities that always go together like orders and order items.

The structure of a repository can be CRUD-like, meaning you have Save, Delete, and Get methods on a generic type *T* and work with predicates to query ad hoc sections of data. Nothing prevents you from giving your repository a remote procedure call (RPC) style with methods that reflect actions—whether the actions are reads, deletes, or insertions—that serve the business purpose.

I usually summarize this by saying that there's no wrong way to write a repository. Technically, a repository is part of the infrastructure layer. However, from the perspective of simplifying things, a repository can be seen as a domain service and can be exposed up to the application layer so that the application can better orchestrate complex application-level workflows.

Event stores

I would bet that event sourcing will have a dramatic impact on the way we write software. As discussed in Chapter 2, "Selecting the supporting architecture," event sourcing involves using events as the primary data source of the application.

Event sourcing is not necessarily useful for all application. In fact, developers blissfully ignored it for decades. Today, however, more and more domain experts need to track the sequence of events the software can produce. You can't do this with a storage philosophy centered on saving the current state. When events are the primary data source of your application, a few things change and the need for new tools emerges.

Event sourcing has an impact on two aspects: persistence and queries. *Persistence* is characterized by three core operations: insert, update, and delete. In an event-sourcing scenario, insert is nearly the same as in a classic system that persists the current state of entities. The system receives a request and writes a new event to the store. The event contains its own unique identifier (for example, a GUID), a type name or code that identifies the type of the event, a timestamp, and associated information such as the content that makes up the data entity being created. The update exists in another insert in the same container of data entities. The new entry simply indicates the data—which properties has changed, the new value and, if relevant in the business domain, why and how it changed. Once an update has been performed, the data store evolves as in Figure 5-5.

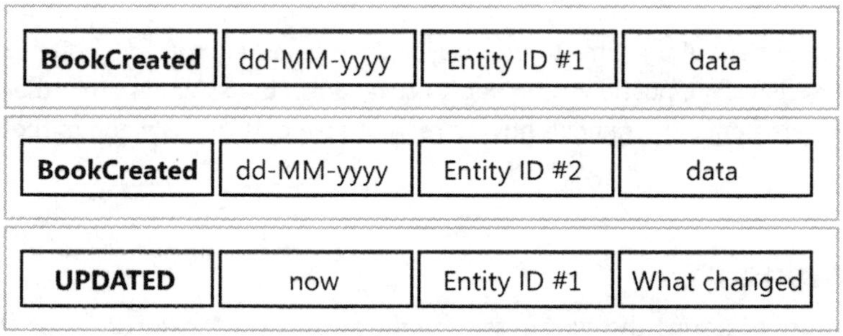

FIGURE 5-5 A new record to indicate the update to the book entity with ID #1

The delete operation works in the same way as an update except that it has different type information.

Making updates in an event-based data store immediately creates a few issues when it comes to queries. How do you get to know if a given record exists or, if it exists, what its current state is? That requires an ad hoc layer for queries that conceptually selects all records with a matching ID and then analyzes the data-set event after the event. For example, it could create a new data entity based on the content of the Created event and then replay all successive steps and return what remains at the end of the stream. This technique is known as *event replay*.

The plain replay of events to rebuild the state might raise some concerns about performance because of the possible huge number of events to process. The problem is easy to understand if you think of the list of events that make up the history of a bank account. As a customer, you probably opened the bank account a few years back and went through hundreds of operations per year. In this context, is it acceptable to process hundreds of events every time you want to see the current balance? The theory of event sourcing has workarounds for this scenario, the most important of which consists of creating snapshots. A *snapshot* is a record that saves the known state of the entity at any given time. In this way, to get the current balance you process only the events recorded since the latest snapshot was taken.

Event sourcing gives architects and domain experts a lot more power to design effective solutions, but for the time being it requires a lot of extra work to create and operate the necessary infrastructure. Event sourcing requires a new family of tools—*event stores*. An event store is another type of database with a public API and a programming language tailor-made for event data items.

Caching layers

Not all data you have in a system changes at the same rate. In light of this, it makes little sense to ask the database server to read unchanged data each and every time a request comes in. At the same time, in a web application requests come in concurrently. Many requests might hit the web server in a second, and many of those concurrent requests might request the same page. Why shouldn't you cache that page or at least the data it consumes?

Very few applications can't survive a second or two of data caching. In a high-traffic site, a second or two can make the difference. So caching, in many situations, has become an additional layer built around ad hoc frameworks (actually, in-memory databases), such as Memcached, ScaleOut, or NCache.

External services

Yet another scenario for the infrastructure layer is when data is accessible only through web services. A good example of this scenario is when the web application lives on top of some customer relationship management (CRM) software or has to consume proprietary company services. The infrastructure layer, in general, is responsible for wrapping external services as appropriate.

In summary, architecturally speaking, these days we really like to think of an infrastructure layer rather than a plain data-access layer that wraps up a relational database. Caching, services, and events are all emerging or consolidated aspects of a system, and they work side by side with plain persistence.

Summary

Software will never be what it was some 10 years ago. Software is destined to be more and more integrated with real life. For this to happen—and it will happen—we have to revisit our architectural principles and change some of them.

In this chapter, I presented a general and generic architecture that can be adapted to any type of software you might write today. It's an evolutionary phase of the classic multitier architecture we grew up with. Although it apparently adds only an extra layer, it has a deep impact on the way we think and do things.

I encourage you to form a clear picture of the purpose of the layered architecture and all its parts before you move further into the book. The issue I see is not that you might miss the point of what a layered architecture represents. That's well-known, at least at a big-picture level. It's the little-known details of the layered architecture—the parts subject to simplification—that represent the sore point and the aspects of the architecture I recommend you spend some time on. Even spending time to decide you don't need those parts is more productive than ignoring them.

PART II

Development

CHAPTER 6

ASP.NET state of the art

There is an almost universal quest for easy answers and half-baked solutions.

—*Martin Luther King*

In Chapter 4, "Architectural options for a web solution," I listed and discussed the options we have today for architecting and building web solutions. If you are looking for concrete suggestions and use-cases, you can refer back to that chapter and probably skip this one entirely.

This brief chapter serves the purpose of introducing the next chapter and the bunch of chapters that come after the next one. The next chapter is a quick guide to ASP.NET Core 1.0, the new runtime environment, and the breaking changes you might face if you opt for targeting the Microsoft .NET Core Framework. The chapters following the next one move back to "classic" ASP.NET MVC programming topics that are updated to ASP.NET MVC 6 and remain equally valid whether you stay on the current ASP.NET platform and related runtime or upgrade to the ASP.NET Core 1.0 platform and related runtime.

In Chapter 4, I introduced ASP.NET Core 1.0 and also discussed it from the perspective of architects and chief technology officers (CTOs). In that chapter, though, I engaged in a discussion about the concrete options you have today for building applications. I listed and discussed them, but I didn't illustrate my choice or give any explicit recommendation.

This chapter presents my personal view of the state of ASP.NET technology and some of my gut feelings about it. The point I start from is with the question, "Where's ASP.NET going?"

Web flavors

Overall, the ASP.NET Framework has been around for almost two decades. It was an incredibly successful platform when it first came out in the early 2000s. It was the right thing at the right time and literally taught web development to a mass of C, C++ and Visual Basic developers. Over the years, ASP.NET changed skin quite a few times, incorporated new features, and made developers more and more capable of achieving amazing results.

We had ASP.NET MVC breaking up the black boxes of server controls and taking development one abstraction level down and closer to the actual HTTP metal. We also witnessed some underlying changes to Web Forms that made it possibly more interactive and gave it more Ajax-style features. We then saw the explosion of HTML5 and the number of lines of JavaScript code in webpages.

The web could have been different

In the past decade, at some point the web had a (great?) chance of becoming something completely different. This could have happened by getting rid of HTML and JavaScript and embracing richer and more powerful templating and programming languages. It was the time of Microsoft Silverlight, to be clear.

We know how Silverlight worked. Yet, at least hundreds of companies all over the world invested a lot of money on Silverlight front ends, and they did it at the same time the tech world was betting the farm on Silverlight and analogous rich-client technologies. Now these companies have just one option—unrolling Silverlight and embracing HTML5 and classic web development.

Oh yes, there's also the single-page application (SPA) option. Frankly, I wouldn't recommend that as a mainstream development strategy for a company. I find it surely works occasionally on spot projects, but you need a totally different skill set and good people on the team. This is not common, though. And if this is not common, using SPA is risky. And getting a faster and responsive *single* page for the entire application, well, is a great challenge too.

I don't really know if dropping rich-client web development (and Silverlight) has been right or wrong. I take it as fact and look ahead. To me, SPAs are just a shrink-wrapped version of a rich client web. It might not be as powerful or as fast and responsive. But, then again, feel free to disagree.

The important fact is quite a different one.

Classic web is the winner

The industry decided to stick to the classic web model, where browsers send stateless requests and receive JSON or HTML responses. Related responses are aggregated around the virtual concept of a webpage. A webpage is no longer a physical concept—say a URL—but it is a bunch of related responses served by the same controller.

Most responses are padded with JavaScript and cool frameworks that help to render web views on the client. AngularJS is the most prominent framework, but React is another decent one. In addition, there's also an ecosystem of more or less popular and trendy frameworks that grow (and die) spontaneously. Many even claim to have seen a bottle of milk last longer than some must-have JavaScript frameworks.

Like it or not, the winner is a revisited version of a classic web. It's just a plain old, request-response web made more interactive via Ajax-style calls. Some call this model *hybrid SPA*, which is just as good as calling it Ajax. The core is having views padded with some JavaScript to quickly show and hide sections and make changes to the view occur automatically and in real time.

An aspect of the modern web that didn't exist for quite a long time is real-time updates. In this regard, ASP.NET SignalR is absolutely awesome and a real must-have. It is not intrusive at all in your code and has an amazingly simple and natural programming model. It really makes a webpage look live and up to date.

This is the web of today. To build HTML responses with chunks of JavaScript, expose JSON endpoints, and receive live updates, you can use plain ASP.NET. By *plain ASP.NET*, I just mean the same ASP.NET you used for years, either through the filter of Web Forms or MVC.

Why, then, do we hear all this hype about ASP.NET Core 1.0 being new and cool and revolutionary? Let me say it up front: no, ASP.NET Core 1.0 is not changing the flavor of the web. Additionally, it doesn't even bring a gram of really new functionality. Yet, it has a purpose and possibly a role for companies.

ASP.NET is feature-complete

Recently, I was engaged in a long thread on what to do with technologies that are not going to receive (significant and major) updates any more. As you might guess, there were two strongly opinionated camps. One camp considered these technologies dead and favored abandoning them as soon as possible, like jumping from a sinking ship. The other camp favored using these technologies as long as they were serving a business purpose.

My gut feeling and first thought was to join the second camp and start yelling as loud as I could. Fortunately, a second thought came soon that calmed me down and let me see a broader perspective of things.

No more to add is no more to add

The original subject of the thread I just described was ASP.NET Web Forms, but the thread soon expanded to swallow up ASP.NET MVC as well. To be forgiving, the last major update to ASP.NET Web Forms came with version 4 back in 2010. Only a bit later, the last update to ASP.NET MVC showed up that I would surely call *major*. It was ASP.NET MVC 3, and it was the last update even though some good features on routing, bundling, and display modes came with version 4. Since then, we've had a few additional releases that just increased the version number at the low cost of minor functional changes.

What's the real health of a technology when there's simply no more to add and its technology teams are scratching the bottom of the barrel to find something that can be added?

As in the thread, some believe the technology is dead and some are happy because they can keep on using it without any risk of incurring face-breaking changes, spend time learning new things, and use their time in a more productive way.

So is anybody wrong? Is anybody right?

I believe a better question is, "Why is there no more to add to a given technology?" ASP.NET just reached its full potential. Because of this, there's not much the team can add to make it more power-ful. ASP.NET, whether you're talking about Web Forms or MVC, is there, is mature and consolidated, has tools and frameworks supporting it, and has Visual Studio to build solutions. You can take any flavor of ASP.NET you like and go with it.

Is it full potential or software obsolescence?

As mentioned in Chapter 4, you can still use Web Forms if it serves your needs. But, as an architect, you should make sure you're making the right choice in using a technology that has already expressed its full functional potential.

The border line between full potential and obsolescence is thin, and obsolescence comes right after having expressed full potential. In software, obsolescence is different than in hardware because there's nearly no physical damage or consumption involved. Obsolete software can still be running and working and sustaining an entire company or business. (By the way, we usually call it *legacy code*!)

From an architect and CTO perspective, it's key to see what's next for the business you're in. The technology is a tool; the business is the deal. You should look at the evolution of the business (including the people you have on board) and evaluate and pick up the right technology. The business dwarfs the age of the technology, so as long as the technology works and is up to handling the tasks, it is usable.

ASP.NET Core 1.0 has no new functions

ASP.NET Core 1.0 is presented as a framework for developing web applications using the sole MVC pattern. ASP.NET Core 1.0 also offers the infrastructure for exposing RPC and REST services and real-time functionalities.

Well, this is nothing new. We have exactly the same capabilities today in the classic ASP.NET platform. ASP.NET Core 1.0 won't give you any new function that will increase your programming power. Because it's a rewrite of the Microsoft web stack, it offers a different way of doing some of the things you typically want to do in the context of a web application. If there's a reason to upgrade to ASP.NET Core 1.0, well, it's not a functional one.

It's about the new runtime

Current ASP.NET runs on top of the same runtime that was devised in the late 1990s. At some point, with Internet Information Services (IIS) 7, that runtime was integrated with IIS and this integration presented as the best way to achieve better performance.

The scenario changed quite significantly in only a few years. Today, the reality is that way too many assemblies are loaded in memory and the average footprint of each HTTP request that goes through ASP.NET and IIS is about 20 KB. These numbers work for some people and businesses, and they don't work for others.

ASP.NET Core 1.0 offers a new runtime environment that runs applications more efficiently on top of the same feature set. It is estimated that the memory footprint might be as low as 3 KB per request. But wait a moment before you say, "Wow!"

The point is that to get the most out of ASP.NET Core 1.0 you should target a different version of the .NET Framework, the aforementioned .NET Core. This framework eliminates some little-used APIs and rewrites other APIs to achieve the same functionality in a different way. These are breaking changes, period. If you make this change, however, you're well positioned to experience that insane decrease of memory footprint. If you don't have reasons to complain about IIS and how well it hosts for you today, well, you can still ignore ASP.NET Core 1.0 and be happy, no matter the hype.

It's about the business model

The next question one might ask at this point is why? Why do we need ASP.NET Core 1.0, and why is Microsoft embarking on such a huge refactoring? Is it because some customers asked for that? Maybe, but there's more to it, I believe.

It's the business model, baby.

And it's not just the Microsoft business model that involves switching to cloud and mobile services. It's also the business model of many companies that are Microsoft shops. To offer modern services, and scale when and how you need, you must leverage cloud platforms, which are paid per use. Memory footprint and execution time become crucial.

That's why a cloud-optimized ASP.NET platform makes sense. But it cannot simply be the same platform of today expanded. It has to be completely new. And ASP.NET Core 1.0 is just the external container of up to three flavors of the .NET Framework: the classic .NET Framework, the .NET Core cloud-optimized framework and, at some point, the cross-platform .NET Core Framework.

If you don't have a business model that is exportable to, and growable through, the cloud you might not be in the strict need of looking into ASP.NET Core 1.0. Or can take your time to evaluate the transition.

It's about the development model

Another aspect of ASP.NET Core 1.0, and more specifically an aspect of its runtime environment, is its independence from the host. This means that it becomes realistic to write and test ASP.NET applications using a machine equipped with a non-Windows operating system and without using virtual machines. Again, it is not as easy and quick to write and test as it might sound, but it's definitely going to happen.

I consider this an interesting feature to have, but not one of those that really count when it comes to making a decision. Yet, it's better to have than not, but it works only if you target the cross-platform .NET Framework that is still in development.

What is the state of ASP.NET?

I believe ASP.NET as a platform is close to being feature complete. If you check out the list of features new to the latest versions of MVC and Web Forms (those that also ship with the ASP.NET Core 1.0 runtime), you see minor things such as tag helpers and view components. Those are good features to have and definitely make Razor development easier and more enjoyable, but they are not critical features that justify an upgrade given the burden you'll bear in terms of performing regression tests and configuring compatibility.

When a technology is close to being feature-complete, the question becomes, "What's next?" You can keep on using the technology, but you should look elsewhere the moment you need to unlock the new level of service and deliver it to your customers.

With the industry having lost a great chance to change the web by stopping development using HTML and JavaScript and restarting with XAML and C#, I really have no idea of what we can find beyond ASP.NET and JavaScript. If I had to guess what the next stage is beyond the current state of the art, I'd look for cloud services and cloud-based deployment of services—if that make sense for the business you run or for continually improving the user experience.

If I had to predict the next step beyond technology, I'd say it will involve taking into even more careful account the business and the processes. And I'd say it also will involve designing web, social, and mobile integrated solutions that make users feel at home when they use your software and your services. Technology is the means, not the end. And ASP.NET Core 1.0 is no exception.

CHAPTER 7

Whys, wherefores, and technical aspects of ASP.NET Core 1.0

If the facts don't fit the theory, change the facts.

—Albert Einstein

Let's face it without fear of being pessimistic or even seeming defeatist. We're scratching the bottom of the barrel as far as web development is concerned. There's not much left that can be realistically added to make programming richer and more powerful in the current paradigm. The future of web programming will require that we pass through great change and at a number of levels.

The first aspect of web programming we might want to change is HTML and JavaScript. If, instead, we stick with those, we can adopt (and perhaps write for ourselves) more and more different flavors of a framework, but only slightly different ones. Expecting that any JavaScript framework can be a silver bullet for innovation is pure illusion. If we add server-side programming to the bill, we'll see that once we integrate some mechanism to intelligently serve markup to devices and push data back to the client we're done. Everything else is the same, and it has been for the last decade. There's no new revolutionary programming feature on the horizon for current web platforms.

While awaiting something completely different, and frankly well beyond my imagination, the future of the web seems like it's all about performance. I'd say it's about performance much more than scalability. I'm not convinced that every website on the face of the earth needs to be immensely scalable as if they all were a popular billion-user social network. Cloud platforms make it easy and cost-effective to manage load balancing and fire up new instances of the application on demand. But the cloud is not magic if the application instance is poorly designed or bound to some clogged infrastructure.

The quest for better performance certainly passes through the introduction of a new version of the HTTP protocol. The HTTP/2 draft is ready, and it addresses all the known issues of today's use of the web and promises to solve all the issues of web development for which we developed workarounds and a wave of ad hoc tools. What today we call *optimization* (bundling, minification, sprites, and push notifications) will be part of the infrastructure with HTTP/2. But it will take years until HTTP/2 becomes mainstream.

The quest for better performance also must pass through a modernized host for web applications. This is where ASP.NET Core fits in.

The background of ASP.NET Core

ASP.NET was first devised in the late 1990s. The core of the runtime pipeline that still works today dates back to over a decade ago—a very long time in software. Moreover, in the beginning ASP.NET was devised to be tightly integrated with Internet Information Services (IIS). Only a few years ago, Microsoft celebrated with the release of IIS 7 the full merger of ASP.NET and IIS. It was called the *integrated pipeline*.

A few years later, we're now told that the scenario is completely different and that an integrated pipeline is no longer desirable, maybe even detrimental, and also the heart of any performance problem we might face over the web.

In my humble opinion, it's really hard here to separate the wheat of true performance issues from the chaff of just underlying business strategies requiring different programming models. Let me present a few deeper considerations.

The cost of a large memory footprint

The current ASP.NET pipeline was devised at a time in which the only expected web server had to be IIS and hosting costs were not based on memory and actual use. Having ASP.NET based on the full Microsoft .NET Framework seemed like a plus rather than an issue, and *system.web* was the magical tool that allowed web applications to run.

It turns out that initializing a plain web request via the current *system.web*-based infrastructure has a peak memory consumption that is in the order of 100 KB. In addition, the memory footprint of the entire Microsoft .NET Framework is in the order of 200 MB.

ASP.NET Core attempts to reduce these numbers so that hosting applications in the cloud—paying per use and per resources used—will become cheaper. ASP.NET Core applications can be built to use a core version of the .NET Framework that is less than one-tenth of the full framework. At the same time, the cost of initializing a web request outside the realm of *system.web* went down by the same ratio to just a few kilobytes.

ASP.NET Core is here to give development teams a way to deploy web applications in the cloud and gain a lot more control over the resources used and, subsequently, the bill for that usage. It's not just because you rewrite applications for ASP.NET Core that you face lower hosting and maintenance costs—you have the opportunity to drop hidden costs and pay just for what you need.

This opportunity, though, comes at the cost of more painful development—or more exactly, a more painful start to the development and configuration of new projects. More control, in fact, means less automation.

Reconsidering the cloud as the silver bullet

Not all companies use the cloud to host or need the infinite scalability potential the cloud can provide. In other words, the silent majority of applications are still OK as they are today. Bringing these apps to the cloud and rewriting them for the cloud might not deliver any tangible benefit. At any rate, the stimulus to change should always come from real issues and needs and never from marketing hype.

If you're not having performance issues with your websites and you're happy with the current hosting model, there's probably nothing in ASP.NET Core that is worth the cost of migrating or even rewriting the application. At the same time, if you're planning a significant rewrite or new development, ASP.NET Core is the newest framework in the Microsoft web stack.

There's no silver-bullet solution, and good architecture and smart implementation are still the best ways to ensure you have effective applications. They're also the best ways to ensure that the applications deployed to the cloud are the ones that will benefit the most from that environment.

Making the case for the necessity of a different programming model

To put the cloud at the center of the software universe and to drive people toward it, the entire .NET platform had to be reworked while keeping it fully backward compatible. Not an easy task at all. The result is a twofold framework. There is the classic .NET Framework as we know it today that is strictly bound to the Windows platform. And there is a new smaller framework—the .NET Core. The .NET Core is built from scratch to be cross-platform also and capable of being hosted on non-Windows platforms.

The huge difference between the two is the set of libraries available, which is clearly smaller in the .NET Core. That's the key factor that enables using a smaller memory footprint for applications and cloud-optimized workloads.

What's the role of ASP.NET?

ASP.NET Core is the first framework that supports the .NET Core framework. ASP.NET Core is a new framework for web programming and is a deep refactoring of today's ASP.NET, centered on a rewritten HTTP pipeline. ASP.NET Core applications don't rely on *system.web* and are not even specifically bound to IIS. As you'll see later in the chapter, when you create a new ASP.NET Core project, you can choose to target the full .NET Framework as well as the .NET Core. For the most part, the code is the same and an underlying infrastructure takes care of mapping application code to the actual CLR.

The programming model of ASP.NET applications is based on ASP.NET MVC, and a brand new ASP.NET Core application doesn't look really different from an old ASP.NET MVC application. Migrating an existing application is not seamless, but it mostly works once you understand the foundation of the new HTTP pipeline.

Note It's useful to recall what CLR is and what .NET Framework is. Especially in the case of ASP.NET Core, the terms are sometimes used interchangeably or, at least, they are perceived as interchangeable.

The term *.NET Framework* comprises the CLR, base libraries, and tools such as the JIT compiler and garbage collector. The *.NET Core framework* comprises a smaller CLR, named *CoreCLR*, and the same tools as the full .NET Framework. However, it has a different set of libraries, and it's also slated to be cross-platform. ASP.NET Core is a web framework that can run on top of both versions of the .NET Framework.

The impact on everyday work

The steps to develop and deploy a new ASP.NET Core project are similar overall to the steps for developing and deploying an ASP.NET project these days. At the same time, though, you might find that many things about the two approaches are completely different.

The configuration of the application and the overall startup phase, for example, require different code and a different API. In addition, you have new features available, such as a built-in infrastructure for injecting components into other components in an Inversion-of-Control (IoC) fashion.

Because the HTTP pipeline is totally different in ASP.NET Core, and inspired by the Open Web Interface for .NET (OWIN) standard, many common practices of web applications need to be coded differently. A great example of this is authentication.

The bottom line is that switching to ASP.NET Core these days without a strong business reason (but simply for the thrill of doing something new) might turn out to be a painful experience given the current stage of the technology. In the long run and with the succession of major releases, eventually ASP.NET Core will stabilize and reach a decent state with regard to documentation, use-cases, and best practices. That will make it definitely worthwhile for the masses.

Frankly, making a brownfield migration to ASP.NET Core is not a mission-impossible task, but it's not free of issues. The most striking one to me is that you have to learn new ways of doing old basic things. This necessity just wastes your time and adds a sense of uncertainty, because at this time the documentation is mostly in blog posts and StackOverflow answers.

Note An aspect to consider in a brownfield migration scenario is the cost of rewriting the entire data-access layer to use the newest Entity Framework Core (EF Core). You can port to the new platform the old code based on Entity Framework 6, but that probably would invalidate some benefits of the migration itself. On this point, however, nobody today can show real facts.

The ASP.NET Core runtime at a glance

ASP.NET Core is based on a runtime host that supports a few different CLRs. The runtime host is also cross-platform, thus enabling ASP.NET Core applications to also be hosted well outside the IIS server and also well outside the Windows operating system. The runtime host is named *DNX*, short for *.NET Execution Environment*.

The DNX host

DNX provides the infrastructure required for an ASP.NET Core application to run. DNX is essentially a host process and contains the logic necessary to load and host the appropriate CLR, whether it's the full CLR or the CoreCLR. DNX also contains the logic to discover the entry point in the code and to actually invoke it.

Looking at DNX simply as a proxy for launching ASP.NET Core applications is limiting, as Figure 7-1 attempts to explain.

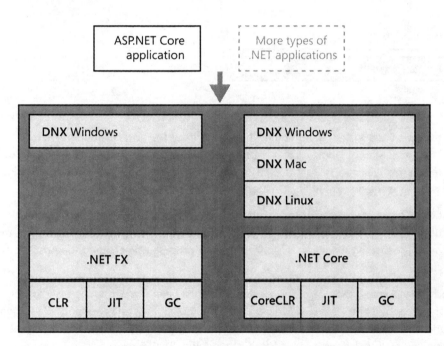

FIGURE 7-1 How DNX manages the execution of ASP.NET Core applications

For the time being, ASP.NET Core applications are the only type of application that can leverage the DNX. Console applications and other types of applications might be available in the near future. This means that, in the end, DNX is the foundation of a new (and cross-platform) .NET rather than just the foundation of a new ASP.NET.

Layers of the DNX

The internal structure of the DNX application is layered as illustrated in Figure 7-2. At the top, you find the application's source code, and at the bottom there's the operating system. DNX sits in between and uses five logical layers to run the logic for launching the application.

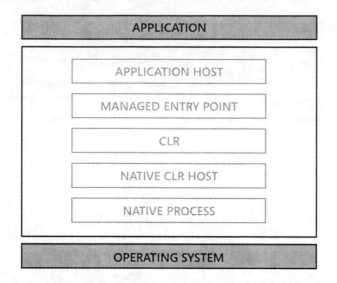

FIGURE 7-2 The five layers of a DNX application

The native process is code written according to the standards of the host operating system, whether that is Windows, Mac, or Linux. All that happens at this level is the finding and invoking of the CLR host—another native process—and the passing of any available argument to it. In Windows, the DNX native process is the dnx.exe utility. On Mac and Linux, it's a shell script.

The CLR host is another native piece of code with the primary responsibility of booting the CLR. Though the actual process changes depending on the type of CLR (full, CoreCLR, or even Mono), the key steps performed are loading the libraries, starting the CLR process, and creating the AppDomain to manage the code.

The managed entry point is made of .NET code and is the first layer not written natively for the host platform. The managed entry point is invoked by the native CLR host and is responsible for loading system libraries and setting up the dependency-injection infrastructure. When the entry point returns, the native CLR host is also responsible for shutting down the CLR process.

Finally, the application host completes the loading of the application, resolving dependencies on NuGet packages or preexisting compiled DLL code. The application host walks the list of project dependencies and calls the entry point of the startup assembly. In ASP.NET Core applications, this step consists of the instantiation of the startup class.

Tools of the DNX environment

A bunch of other tools completes the equipment of the DNX environment. In particular, you find tools named *DNVM* (.NET Version Manager) and *DNU* (.NET Development Utility). DNVM installs and updates the versions of the .NET Framework available on a given machine.

This tool is key to having various versions of the .NET Framework up and running at the same time bound to a specific instance of DNX and running applications. This is, in fact, an important change coming up with ASP.NET Core and the new .NET as a whole: the possibility of running different versions of the .NET Framework side by side. So far, to run an application based on a given version of the framework you are required to install that version in the Global Assembly Cache (GAC). This is no longer required with the new .NET.

DNU is the package manager tool of the new .NET runtime environment. It allows you to pull down and restore all project dependencies in the machine execution environment. In other words, it's the new NuGet manager tool.

> **Note** For compatibility reasons, side-by-side versions of the .NET Framework are allowed only if you target the CoreCLR. In other words, side-by-side versions of the .NET Framework should be read as side-by-side versions of the .NET Core framework.

Hosting web applications in DNX

At the top of Figure 7-1, you see two blocks representing types of DNX applications. In Figure 7-2, on the other hand, I generically refer to DNX applications. When the DNX application is a web application, there's an additional layer that must be taken into account—the ASP.NET hosting layer.

Role of the ASP.NET hosting layer

A web application needs a web server to spring to life. The web server is the application that receives HTTP requests on port 80 and pushes requests through the canonical request pipeline until some response is generated. This is the part of the new ASP.NET infrastructure that got the most changes and even a brand new philosophy.

ASP.NET was devised to work tightly bound to IIS and to be hosted in IIS. However, the first version of ASP.NET shipped with a distinct host application conceptually analogous to today's Kestrel tool. In ASP.NET 1.x, IIS listened to port 80 and passed requests along to the host process via named pipes. The host process was in charge of loading the CLR, finding the managed entry point, and actually processing the request. ASP.NET 1.x was close to being decoupled from IIS, but interestingly that was perceived as a bad thing at the time.

The hosting layer is invoked directly from the application host you see in Figure 7-2. Figure 7-3 shows an updated diagram of the runtime environment.

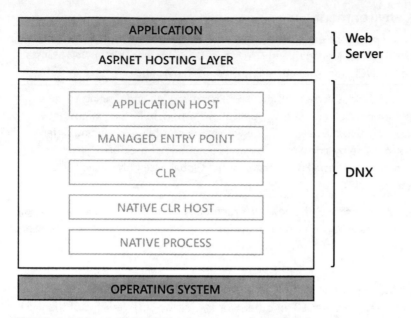

FIGURE 7-3 Adding the ASP.NET Hosting Layer to the DNX diagram

Responsibilities of the ASP.NET hosting layer

In ASP.NET Core, the hosting layer is primarily responsible for finding the web server the application will run on—whether it's IIS or Apache—and the web listener for incoming requests. Next, the hosting layer will find the startup logic and fire up the application.

Through the hosting layer, you can configure the web server to be used and pass it any initialization data. The web-server component must implement a known factory interface through which it will be started. Once the web server is up and running, it starts listening for incoming requests and triggers the application pipeline.

The hosting layer also needs to start up the application code, and to do this it needs to locate the entry point in the application. In ASP.NET Core, the entry point in the application is the *Configure* method on a *Startup* class.

ASP.NET Core HTTP pipeline

ASP.NET Core applications leverage a brand new application pipeline, meaning that incoming requests go through a configured list of runtime modules that are given a chance to read and alter the request along the way. At the end of the pipeline, the request is executed by the application.

The new pipeline replaces HTTP handlers and HTTP modules supported in the current version of ASP.NET. Interestingly, in the ASP.NET Core pipeline, modules are called in sequence from the code of the *Startup* class rather than being just listed in a section of the *web.config* file.

Collectively, all modules callable from within the pipeline form the application's middleware. After performing its own tasks, each middleware component can hand the request on to the next component or just force a response back to the caller. That mostly depends on the role played by the middleware component.

ASP.NET comes with a bunch of predefined middleware components, one of which is an exception handler. You want to call this one quite early in the pipeline to have more chances to catch exceptions. At the same time, you don't want it to short-circuit the call and fail to yield to the next component.

Modules in the pipeline can be called on the way to executing the request and back, as it is summarized in Figure 7-4.

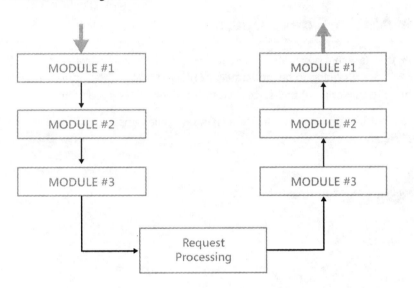

FIGURE 7-4 Each module can perform operations before and after the next module

You can register pipeline modules by calling a *UseXxx*, *Run*, or *MapXxx* extension method. Most middleware components come in the form of predefined *UseXxx* extension methods exposed out of the *IApplicationBuilder* object that the startup class receives from the ASP.NET hosting layer. Commonly used extension methods are *UseExceptionHandler* and *UseStaticFiles* that you'll see in action in a moment.

Alternatively, you can pass lambda code to be executed. In this case, you use the *UseXxx* extension method and indicate the lambda as an argument. The *Run* extension method works like *UseXxx* except that it immediately ends the pipeline and doesn't call the next module (if there are any) in the pipeline. Finally, the *Map* and *MapWhen* extension methods let you configure under which conditions a middleware component must be added to the pipeline.

> **Note** The new HTTP pipeline marks an important difference with existing applications. Any existing framework or functionality that relies on HTTP modules must be rewritten to work on ASP.NET Core. An illustrious example of a common component that won't work in ASP.NET Core unless fully rewritten is Error Logging Modules and Handlers (ELMAH). ELMAH is a popular exception-handling tool that captures and persistently logs any unhandled exceptions. Because it's written as an HTTP module, it can't be used as-is in any new ASP.NET Core application.

ASP.NET Core for ASP.NET developers

Ultimately, I don't think there's such a huge difference between greenfield and brownfield development in ASP.NET Core. It's going to be moderately painful in any case. The primary reason for such pain is the new runtime environment that forces you to learn new tricks to perform known tasks.

Some programming areas that underwent significant changes, while remaining concept-compatible, are those listed here:

- Application startup
- Storage of global application settings
- Authentication
- HTTP request pipeline
- Data access

In addition, ASP.NET Core reduces to ASP.NET MVC and Razor for the production of views and processing logic. In ASP.NET Core, there's no support for ASP.NET Web Forms, and Web API and its stack are now fully merged with ASP.NET Core controllers. As a matter of fact, Web API is kind of dead or, at least, it now lives under a different identity.

Let's get a taste of ASP.NET Code starting from a blank new project. In this way, you'll experience the pleasure of selective runtime modules—the key to reduced memory footprint.

> **Note** For the first release of ASP.NET Core, Web Pages and SignalR are not part of the package. But unlike Web Forms, both will be added to the framework shortly.

Creating a new project

After you create a new project for ASP.NET Core in Microsoft Visual Studio 2015, the Solution Explorer view looks like the one shown in Figure 7-5.

FIGURE 7-5 The Solution Explorer view of an empty ASP.NET Core new project in Visual Studio 2015

The *wwwroot* folder

The first new thing you might notice is the *wwwroot* folder, which also gets a special icon in Visual Studio. The folder plays no special functional role and is there by default only to clearly indicate the root of your website. It's recommended that you place there all static resources your site needs— images, CSS, script, fonts, and plain HTML pages. Code files, such as controllers and Razor views, should be placed outside of the *wwwroot* folder. In other words, the *wwwroot* folder aims to keep code files and static resource files separated.

> **Note** Storing static resources in a separate folder like *wwwroot* is a common practice encouraged, if not enforced, in ASP.NET Core at the project level. ASP.NET Core, however, requires you to set a project folder to be the webroot folder of the deployed site so that any path is considered relative to it. The *wwwroot* folder is only the conventional name. You can change it by editing (manually) the *webroot* property in the *project.json* file.

The Bower file

The *bower.json* file is another new entry. Technically, Bower is a front-end package manager and does exactly the same job as NuGet does except that it works only with client-side resources. Its only purpose in life is reading your text instructions and ensuring that all referenced script packages are available in the project and up to date. If you don't mind managing, say, the jQuery or Bootstrap files yourself, you can happily live and code without Bower. Bower just downloads scripts and client files for you.

The *bower.json* file is conceptually equivalent to *packages.config* for client-side files only.

> **Note** Why is Bower being added in the default project configuration of a new ASP.NET Core project? It's nothing more than a trendy choice. You can just drop the *bower.json* file and keep on using NuGet to download Bootstrap, jQuery, or Angular files. Or you can still copy required files manually to specific project folders of your choice.
>
> The biggest difference between Bower and NuGet is that Bower is considered more specific to client-side programming, so framework developers are more used to releasing updates through the Bower channel than NuGet's. But this makes a bit of a difference only if it's crucial for you to have the latest version of any framework applied upon release. However, it could even be that in the future Microsoft stops updating NuGet with JavaScript frameworks that are already on the Bower repository.

The Gulp file

ASP.NET Core tooling in Visual Studio that deals with Bower files intelligently copies any referenced resource right under the *wwwroot* folder, nearly in the most reasonable place where you expect files to be. As you can see in Figure 7-6, the JS folder is reserved for user-defined JavaScript files, while the LIB folder contains full libraries referenced via Bower.

FIGURE 7-6 Expanding the *wwwroot* folder with the content brought in through Bower

What if you don't like the default distribution of resource files? What if you need minification and bundling? Or need to perform any other tasks on resources like running JSLint to check your JavaScript files? Gulp and Grunt are two tools that allow scripting tasks through different approaches. Grunt requires configuration, while Gulp is a plain JavaScript file you can use to code what you want.

Like Bower, Gulp (or Grunt) is of no value if you don't want to deal with manually copying, moving, and minifying tasks. As such, Gulp files can be safely removed from an ASP.NET Core project if you don't feel comfortable using them.

> **!**
>
> **Important** My suggestion is to just drop Bower and Gulp files from ASP.NET Core projects until you get familiar with those tools and start appreciating what they can do for you. When doing so, another file you might want to consider dropping entirely from a new project is *package.json*, which initially contains the list of Gulp packages required to write automation scripts to move downloaded files around.

The *project.json* file

For many years, we had a *.csproj* text file to keep track of external references, versioning, and folder preferences. Other than in exceptional situations, there never was a need to manually edit the file. Visual Studio provided a graphical interface to edit the settings physically saved to the file.

In an ASP.NET Core project, the project configuration file is treated like a regular file and is available to be edited freely. If you open up *project.json* in the text editor, you see a JSON string describing the structure of the project. In the JSON source, you distinguish the actual name of the *wwwroot* folder, the version of the application, and the NuGet packages it depends on. You also find listed the versions of the .NET Framework to support—either full, .NET Core, or both. A basic *project.json* file looks like this:

```
{
  "version": "1.0.0-*",
  "compilationOptions": {
    "emitEntryPoint": true
  },
  "dependencies": {
    "Microsoft.AspNet.IISPlatformHandler": "1.0.0",
    "Microsoft.AspNet.Server.Kestrel": "1.0.0"
  },
  "commands": {
    "web": "Microsoft.AspNet.Server.Kestrel"
  },
  "frameworks": {
    "dnx451": { },
    "dnxcore50": { }
  },
  "exclude": [
    "wwwroot",
    "node_modules"
  ],
  "publishExclude": [
    "**.user",
    "**.vspscc"
  ]
}
```

Unless some specific tooling is provided in the near future, for the most part, updates to the *project.json* file must be made manually by typing code in. However, as you refer to classes in your code belonging to missing packages, Visual Studio offers to add those packages and silently edits the project files.

Minimal dependencies of ASP.NET Core applications

As you can see, at a minimum an ASP.NET Core project depends on the IIS platform installer and something called *Kestrel*. Figure 7-7 illustrates in more detail the hosting model of ASP.NET Core applications across Windows and non-Windows platforms. To host in IIS, you need to install the *IISPlatformHandler* component, which must also be referenced from the application. The component is responsible for launching DNX and forwarding requests.

The platform installer ultimately forwards requests to web command as specified in the *project.json* file for the application.

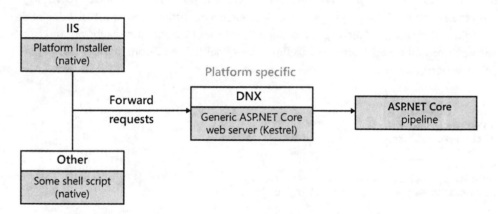

FIGURE 7-7 Detailed hosting architecture for ASP.NET Core applications on IIS and other web servers

The DNX process hosts a generic ASP.NET Core web server (cross-platform) that knows how to deal with requests through the ASP.NET Core pipeline. This generic web server is called *Kestrel*.

Application startup

To fire up the web application, the hosting layer needs to identify an entry point in the user's application. This entry point is a static method named *Main*. The method is conventionally defined in a class named *Startup*. However, it can—and I think it should—be moved elsewhere to better emphasize its role, which is distinct from the role of the *Startup* class. Let's say you add a class like this to the empty project template you invoke in Visual Studio 2015:

```
public class App
{
    public static void Main(string[] args) => WebApplication.Run<Startup>(args);
}
```

The *WebApplication* class is defined in the hosting layer and is responsible for instantiating a class named *Startup*.

The *Startup* class contains two methods: *Configure* and *ConfigureServices*. Both methods are invoked from the ASP.NET Core runtime. The former is used to configure the HTTP request pipeline. The latter is used to inject services into the ASP.NET Core request stack.

Configuring the HTTP pipeline

At a minimum, the pipeline must reference the IIS platform installer, but most likely it also needs to enable the serving of static files and MVC routes:

```
public void Configure(IApplicationBuilder app)
{
    app.UseIISPlatformHandler();
    app.UseStaticFiles();
    app.UseMvc(routes =>
        routes.MapRoute( name: "default",
                         template: "{controller=Home}/{action=Index}/{id?}")
    );
}
```

To enable serving static files and routes, you must add new packages. Thankfully, Visual Studio detects missing packages and offers to restore them at the cost of a click. The overall experience is analogous to having ReSharper installed as in earlier versions of Visual Studio. Another package you want to have is the diagnostics package so that detailed exception pages can be displayed at development time. (See Figure 7-8.)

```
app.UseDeveloperExceptionPage();
```

Note that without the previous line of code, you won't even be able to get the classic yellow error page you've received countless times in classic Web Forms and ASP.NET MVC.

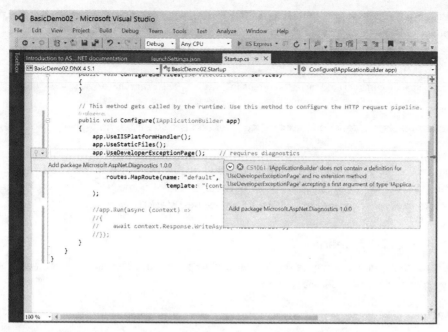

FIGURE 7-8 Adding a missing package in a Visual Studio 2015 ASP.NET Core project

Before ASP.NET Core, after creating a new project from scratch you couldn't see any concrete output until you arranged a view infrastructure, including a controller method and a layout. In ASP.NET Core, if you run an empty new project as soon as it loads in Visual Studio, you still see something, most likely a *hello-world* message. This is because of the following code, which you find by default in the *Configure* method of the *Startup* class:

```
app.Run(async (context) =>
{
    await context.Response.WriteAsync("Hello World!");
});
```

You remove this code when you start adding controller classes and Razor views.

Note The *Configure* method must accept at least an *IApplicationBuilder* parameter. However, you can optionally add two more parameters of type *IHostingEnvironment* and *ILoggerFactory*, which will be passed to you by the runtime.

Adding services to the ASP.NET request stack

The sole configuration of the application builder is not enough to make the website produce anything significant. At this stage, the application is not even qualified as an ASP.NET MVC application. You need to explicitly inject a reference to the MVC core services:

```
public void ConfigureServices(IServiceCollection services)
{
    services.AddMvc ();
}
```

At this point, as soon as you add a controller you start getting some visible output.

There are a few other services you might want to add to the ASP.NET stack, such as a service to handle application options and share object instances globally across controllers, additional layers of code, and views.

In ASP.NET Core, a *service* is a shared component that various parts of an application might consume. Services are made available to the application through dependency injection. ASP.NET Core comes with an integrated container, but it can be replaced with one of your choice. There are three flavors of a service that relate to how each instance is managed by the container.

An instance of a transient service is created each and every time it's required within the application. A new instance of a service marked as a scoped service, instead, is created only if no instance exists in the current scope. In the context of a web application, current scope is equivalent to the current request. Finally, a singleton service is a service that allows just one instance per application.

Displaying the home page

In ASP.NET Core, controllers and views are not much different from the controllers and views you might know from classic ASP.NET MVC. A minor but visible difference is the base return type of controller methods, which is now an interface—*IActionResult*:

```
public class HomeController : Controller
{
    public IActionResult Index()
    {
        ViewBag.Title = "Hello World";
        return View();
    }
}
```

The view engine works in the same way as in classic ASP.NET MVC, and Razor view files must be organized in the same way—that is, in controller-specific folders under the root folder *Views*.

The Razor syntax in ASP.NET Core has some additional features, such as tag helpers and the *@inject* method, but any existing code works the same way.

Application settings

In old ASP.NET applications, developers used to store global settings in the *appSettings* section of the *web.config* file or, when safe enough, in global static members exposed out of the application object. This is no longer possible in ASP.NET Core.

Reading settings from a persistent store

Dealing with application settings in ASP.NET Core is a two-step procedure you perform from the *Startup* class. First you read information from a persistent file, and then you copy data into an in-memory container that then injects it as a service into the ASP.NET container.

The new configuration infrastructure is built around the concept of builders, and you can have a custom builder for nearly any data format, whether it's JSON, XML, or even a database schema. By default, you save data in a JSON file. Suppose you have the following JSON file added to the project and call it *MyAppSettings.json*:

```
{
  "Data": {
    "Title": "Hello, world",
    "Build":  "1.0.0.0"
  }
}
```

The following code added to the constructor of the *Startup* class will read it:

```
public class Startup
{
    private IConfigurationRoot _appSettings;
    public Startup(IHostingEnvironment env, IApplicationEnvironment appEnv)
    {
        var builder = new ConfigurationBuilder()
                        .AddJsonFile("MyAppSettings.json");
        _appSettings = builder.Build();
    }
}
```

The *_appSettings* variable is a mere pointer in the JSON stream and doesn't contain any explicit value extracted from the actual file. Another step is necessary to map the content of the JSON file to an object. Let's add a C# class that maps the content of the JSON file—for example, the *MyAppSettings* class:

```
public class MyAppSettings
{
    public string Title { get; set; }
    public string Build { get; set; }
}
```

To copy the JSON content to an instance of *MyAppSettings*, you proceed as follows. You add the following code to the *ConfigureServices* method of the *Startup* class:

```
services.Configure<MyAppSettings>(settings =>
{
    settings.Title = _appSettings["Data:Title"];
    settings.Build = _appSettings["Data:Build"];
});
```

The just-created instance of the *MyAppSettings* class is now ready to be injected into the ASP.NET application stack. It must be wrapped in a common interface, though, and the service for this wrapper interface must be added as well:

```
services.AddOptions();
```

Now some more work is required on any class (for example, controllers) that need to consume the global application settings.

Consuming application settings

Application settings are now injectable in any component created under the control of the ASP.NET container. This is certainly true for controllers and for classes injected in a controller. Here's how to rewrite the controller class to make it use any data configured from the JSON file:

```
public class HomeController : Controller
{
    private MyAppSettings _settings;

    public HomeController(IOptions<MyAppSettings> accessor)
    {
        _settings = accessor.Value;
    }

    public IActionResult Index()
    {
        ViewBag.Title = String.Format("{0} [{1}]", _settings.Title, _settings.Build);
        return View();
    }
}
```

The constructor of the controller now receives an *IOptions<T>* parameter and saves the wrapped content to a local member. Other members of the controller class can then use the injected values.

> **Note** Although I won't really recommend it for the sake of code modeling, you can even inject object instances directly into Razor views through the *@inject* command. My favorite approach is to pass a view-model class down to the view and build the instance of the view-model class right in the controller, passing any injected data that is required.

Authentication

ASP.NET Core also introduces some changes to the authentication process. To be precise, changes are not introduced for the pleasure of just making things in a different way but because of the support for the OWIN standard. In brief, OWIN is an abstract interface that defines the interaction model between web servers and web applications.

As mentioned, ASP.NET was initially devised in the late 1990s to be tightly coupled to IIS. Later on, such a tight coupling turned out to be a pain rather than a benefit and OWIN was introduced to define a general interaction model for the same concrete things, such as authentication and authorization. As a result, in ASP.NET Core you have to indicate explicitly which form of authentication you expect and how you expect the identity token to be saved and carried. Ultimately, it's not much different from what you were expected to do in the *authentication* section of the *web.config* file; you just do it through a different API.

ASP.NET Identity vs. plain authentication

Most examples of ASP.NET Core applications use the ASP.NET Identity framework to implement login forms and validation of credentials. I consider the ASP.NET Identity to be an overwhelming complexity at least for those basic scenarios where you just need to check a plain user name and password pair. If you're interested in trying out ASP.NET Identity (and some of its more advanced features such as two-factor authentication), you can simply go with the Visual Studio 2015 ASP.NET Core template and enabled an authentication mechanism. If you want to learn how to build plain cookie-based authentication step by step in ASP.NET Core, just read on.

Enabling cookie authentication

Cookie authentication is part of the application configuration. You need to enable it via a specific call you perform from the *Configure* method of the *Startup* class:

```
app.UseCookieAuthentication(new CookieAuthenticationOptions
{
    LoginPath = "/account/login",
    AuthenticationScheme = "Cookies"
});
```

These settings you see are not really different from the typical entries you enter in the *web.config* file in classic ASP.NET. You also use the usual *Authorize* attribute to restrict access to specific controller sections only to authenticated and authorized users.

To create the authentication cookie, you use different code that is a functional replacement for the now unsupported methods of the old faithful *FormsAuthentication* class:

```
public async Task<IIActionResult> PostLogin(LoginInputModel input)
{
    // Validate credentials
    if (!ValidateCredentials(input.Username, input.Password)
        return RedirectToAction("login", "error");
```

```
    // Create the authentication cookie
    var claims = new List<Claim>
    {
        new Claim("username", input.Username)
    };
    var id = new ClaimsIdentity(claims, "local", "name", "role");
    await HttpContext.Authentication.SignInAsync("Cookies", new ClaimsPrincipal(id));
    return Redirect("/");
}
```

The *LoginInputModel* class is simply a class that wraps up the content coming from the input fields of the login form. The *async/await* interface is required because of the internal implementation of the *Authentication* object in the HTTP context.

Detecting authenticated users

To detect whether or not the current user is authenticated, you use the canonical *User.Identity* object and check the *IsAuthenticated* property:

```
@{
    if (User.Identity.IsAuthenticated)
    {
        <a class="btn-lg btn-primary" href="@Url.Action("logout", "account")">
            @User.Identity.Name
        </a>
    }
    else
    {
        <a class="btn-lg btn-primary" href="@Url.Action("login", "account")">
            Log In
        </a>
    }
}
```

Every other aspect of the authentication process remains unaltered, including the detection of the return URL and validation of the model state.

Other aspects of web programming

A few other aspects of web programming are also touched by the advent of ASP.NET Core. As mentioned, ASP.NET Web Forms is no longer an option. So before you jump on the ASP.NET Core bandwagon, it's recommended you get familiar with the patterns of ASP.NET MVC programming. If you're coming from an ASP.NET MVC background, however, there are a few other aspects of programming to take into account.

Web API

Up until ASP.NET Core, Web API and ASP.NET MVC were distinct frameworks with a common class name and compatible concepts but radically different pipelines. As someone who mostly did ASP.NET MVC programming in the past five or six years, I never considered Web API a framework to seriously focus on. All, or at least most, of what I needed could be achieved via plain ASP.NET MVC controllers.

I was just looking at OData facilities on top of Web API as a plus that could have led me to use a standalone web service based on Web API. From a purely logical perspective, I couldn't make sense of two distinct flavors of controllers, though Web API was based on a more modern pipeline really close to the one you find in ASP.NET Core.

In ASP.NET Core, with the framework to produce HTML (ASP.NET MVC) and Web API sharing the same newer pipeline, there's really no reason to have two distinct controller classes. In the end, in ASP.NET Core you have just one base controller class that you can configure to return either Razor views, plain JSON, or XML via content negotiation.

The bottom line is that in ASP.NET Core you just get requests and figure which response they should receive from the server environment. Talking Web API might still happen, but it would mostly be for backward-compatibility reasons. Logically and functionally speaking, Web API is dead in the sense that it has been merged (and relives) in a newer and all-encompassing ASP.NET MVC stack.

Middleware

In classic ASP.NET, you have two types of components that can be used to customize the way each request is processed: HTTP handlers and HTTP modules. An *HTTP handler* is a piece of code that is invoked when a request comes in whose URL matches a given pattern. An *HTTP module* is a component that is registered with the runtime pipeline, hooks up any request, and processes it.

HTTP handlers play a relevant role mostly in the context of ASP.NET Web Forms. This is because in Web Forms each request is designed to target a specific page or view; hence, an HTTP handler is a way to place a request for an action that might or might not return a view. In ASP.NET MVC, the emphasis is on actions instead, so every request is for an action and will then be served, returning HTML views or JSON data. HTTP handlers lose all their appeal in the context of ASP.NET MVC.

HTTP modules are a different thing. They are components used to preprocess a request. The ASP.NET pipeline raises a list of application events, and registered modules hook up one or more events and perform their own logic.

In ASP.NET Core, the HTTP pipeline has been redesigned from the ground up, so it's the gamma of runtime components. The term *middleware* is now used to denote components assembled into a pipeline to handle requests and responses. A middleware component behaves according to one of the following patterns:

- It performs some action and then passes the request on to the next component in the pipeline.

- It performs some action, passes the request on to the next component in the pipeline, and performs some more work afterward.

- It passes the request on to the next component in the pipeline and performs some more work afterward.

- It performs some action and then stops the chain, returning a response to the caller.

A middleware component represents a task, and tasks are combined to actually assemble the pipeline for the requests of a given application. In the old ASP.NET, a bunch of HTTP modules were automatically applied and removing them required some configuration tweaks. In ASP.NET Core, the configuration of the pipeline is entirely programmatic and takes place in the *Configure* method of the *Startup* class.

The bottom line is that HTTP modules you might have, whether they're standalone products or parts of applications, must be rewritten as middleware components in an ASP.NET Core application.

Data access

Most .NET applications work with data through the services of Entity Framework. There are many versions of Entity Framework out there. From the standpoint of ASP.NET Core, the versions to consider are these: Entity Framework 6 and Entity Framework Core (and newer). The guideline is to use Entity Framework 6 to bring in some legacy code and use Entity Framework Core for any new development. However, both versions work just fine, but some differences do exist.

First and foremost, if you opt for using Entity Framework 6, your ASP.NET Core application can target only the full .NET Framework. The .NET Core framework doesn't support Entity Framework 6. Put another way, you have no chance to turn your Entity Framework 6 code into cross-platform code.

You import Entity Framework 6 via NuGet as you would do in an old ASP.NET project based on Code First. This means you should have (or create) *DbContext* classes that gets the connection string via a constructor. Likewise, you should have (or adapt) a Code First class ,adding a data-annotations attribute where appropriate and necessary.

The connection string will be stored in a JSON file and passed around to data-access classes via the Options service, as demonstrated earlier in the "Application settings" section. Here's some sample code for a repository class:

```
public class CountryRepository
{
    private string ConnectionString { get; set; }
    public CountryRepository(IOptions<AppConfig> accessor)
    {
        ConnectionString = accessor.Value.DbConnectionString;
    }

    public IList<Country> All()
    {
        using (var db = new CountryContext(ConnectionString))
        {
            var list = (from c in db.Countries select c).ToList();
            return list;
        }
    }
}
```

Entity Framework Core is a new version of Entity Framework rewritten from the ground up to be cross-platform. It's still an O/RM, and it builds on the experience matured through years of Entity Framework development. In this regard, therefore, Entity Framework Core is largely concept compatible with old versions. It also fully integrates with the dependency injection mechanism of ASP.NET Core, though passing for the dependency injection engine certainly isn't a strict requirement.

The latest documentation for Entity Framework Core can be found at the following URL: *http://docs.efproject.net/en/latest/getting-started/index.html*.

Summary

For developers coming from an ASP.NET MVC background, most of the differences between old and new ASP.NET are summarized here. Beyond what's outlined in this chapter, programming is really close to what you would do in a traditional ASP.NET MVC application.

Sounds like moving to ASP.NET Core is a no-brainer? Well, it depends.

As it appears after the first step of a clearly longer development route, ASP.NET Core is completely different than ASP.NET under the hood, but more or less the same at the cover level. Unless you really have reasons to blame the current ASP.NET for the performance it provides and the memory (and money) it costs—and unless it's really crucial for your business to offer the same web application on a non-Windows platform—I don't see any huge benefit to making the change.

Moreover, moving to ASP.NET Core at this time surely means you'll incur the costs of migration and some sort of a learning curve for no tangible benefits unless, as mentioned, you are actively looking for alternatives to traditional ASP.NET.

Remember the Who moved my cheese novel? The ASP.NET cheese at some point will be terminated, and we all will be forced to look for other cheese elsewhere. We can start our quest today, tomorrow, or just later, and only time will tell which approach was actually right. For sure, I would be scared to move to another, albeit familiar, platform without complete and well compiled documentation. At this time, ASP.NET Core looks like a work in progress to me, no matter which 1.0 hat it might wear.

You can write modern and effective applications even if you ignore ASP.NET Core for another year or two. Architecture and design can do much more for you at this time and even at a later time when you eventually move to ASP.NET Core.

CHAPTER 8

Core of ASP.NET MVC

It does not matter how slowly you go, so long as you do not stop.

—*Confucius*

ASP.NET Web Forms and ASP.NET MVC envision the HTTP request in different ways, although both frameworks share the same runtime environment up until ASP.NET Core 1.0. In ASP.NET Web Forms, each request is directed at displaying a given ASPX page. As a developer, you design a website around a bunch of pages. Each page offers a bunch of clickable elements to trigger an action. No action is clearly identified by name and parameters; all actions, instead, are postbacks the page makes to itself. Put another way, in ASP.NET Web Forms you handle a user's clicking, modify the state of the page, and render it back.

In ASP.NET MVC, the granularity is different, and each request results in the execution of an action—ultimately, a method on a specific controller class. The results of executing the action are passed down to the view subsystem along with a view template. The results and template are then used to build the final response for the browser. Users of an ASP.NET MVC application don't request pages but just place a request for the server to execute an action.

Another big difference between ASP.NET Web Forms and ASP.NET MVC is the lack of server controls--black-boxed components capable of generating markup out of parameter values. In ASP.NET MVC, instead, you use raw HTML templates to generate views for the browser. In this way, you gain total control over the markup and can apply styles and inject script code at will using the JavaScript frameworks you like most.

Unlike Web Forms, ASP.NET MVC is made of various layers of code connected together but not intertwined and not forming a single monolithic block. For this reason, it's easy to replace any of these layers with custom components that enhance the maintainability as well as the testability of the solution. This chapter will guide you to discovering the role and structure of the controller—the foundation of ASP.NET MVC applications—and show you how requests are routed to controllers and rendered back to browsers.

Routing incoming requests

Even though the whole ASP.NET platform was originally developed around the idea of serving requests for physical pages, it is not limited to just calling into resources identified by a specific location and file. For example, by writing an ad hoc HTTP handler and binding it to a fixed URL, you can have ASP.NET process a request regardless of the dependencies on physical files. This is exactly the aspect of ASP.NET that allowed the building of a different programming framework inspired by the Model-View-Controller (MVC) pattern. In a web framework like ASP.NET MVC that emphasizes the role of actions, it is crucial to have a routing system that maps incoming requests to a method on some actual class.

Before exploring the routing system of ASP.NET MVC, let's briefly see how to simulate the ASP.NET MVC behavior in ASP.NET Web Forms through an HTTP handler. This example is recommended for all readers trying to catch on to ASP.NET MVC with a significant background in ASP.NET Web Forms. If you're just trying to learn ASP.NET MVC, you can skip the next section and proceed directly to the section "The URL routing HTTP module."

Simulating the ASP.NET MVC runtime

Let's build a simple ASP.NET Web Forms application and use HTTP handlers to figure out the internal mechanics of ASP.NET MVC applications. You can start with an empty web project and just add the ASP.NET Web Forms dependencies.

Defining the syntax of recognized URLs

In a world in which requested URLs don't necessarily match up with physical files on the web server, the first step to take is listing which URLs are meaningful for the application. To avoid being too specific, let's assume you support only a few fixed URLs, each mapped to an HTTP handler component. The following code snippet shows the changes required to be made to the default *web.config* file:

```
<system.webServer>
    <validation validateIntegratedModeConfiguration="false" />
    <modules runAllManagedModulesForAllRequests="true" />
    <handlers>
      <add name="MvcEmule"
          path="home/test/*"
          verb="*"
          type="MvcEmule.MvcEmuleHandler" />
    </handlers>
</system.webServer>
```

Whenever the application receives a request that matches the specified URL, it will pass the request on to the specified handler—namely, the *MvcEmuleHandler* class.

Defining the behavior of the HTTP handler

In ASP.NET, an HTTP handler is a component that implements the *IHttpHandler* interface. The interface is simple and consists of two members, as shown here:

```
public class MvcEmuleHandler : IHttpHandler
{
    public void ProcessRequest(HttpContext context)
    {
        // Logic goes here
        ...
    }

    public Boolean IsReusable
    {
        get { return false; }
    }
}
```

Most of the time, an HTTP handler has a hardcoded behavior influenced only by some input data passed over the query string. Nothing prevents us, however, from using the handler as an abstract factory for adding one more level of indirection. The handler, in fact, can use information from the request to determine an external component to call to actually serve the request. In this way, a single HTTP handler can serve a variety of requests and just dispatch the call among a few more specialized components.

The HTTP handler could parse out the URL in tokens and use that information to identify the class and method to invoke. Here's an example of how it could work:

```
public void ProcessRequest(HttpContext context)
{
    // Parse out the URL and extract controller, action, and parameter
    var segments = context.Request.Url.Segments;
    var controller = segments[1].TrimEnd('/');
    var action = segments[2].TrimEnd('/');
    var param1 = segments[3].TrimEnd('/');

    // Complete controller class name with suffix and (default) namespace
    var fullName = String.Format("{0}.{1}Controller",
                        this.GetType().Namespace, controller);
    var controllerType = Type.GetType(fullName, true, true);

    // Get an instance of the controller
    var instance = Activator.CreateInstance(controllerType);

    // Invoke the action method on the controller instance
    var methodInfo = controllerType.GetMethod(action,
        BindingFlags.Instance |
        BindingFlags.IgnoreCase |
        BindingFlags.Public);
    string result;
    if (methodInfo.GetParameters().Length == 0)
```

```
    {
        result = methodInfo.Invoke(instance, null) as String;
    }
    else
    {
        result = methodInfo.Invoke(instance, new Object[] { param1 }) as String;
    }

    // Write out results
    if (result != null)
        context.Response.Write(result);
}
```

The preceding code just assumes the first token in the URL past the server name contains the key information to identify the specialized component that will serve the request. The second token refers to the name of the method to call on this component. Finally, the third token indicates a parameter to pass.

Invoking the HTTP handler

Given a URL such as *home/test/**, *home* identifies the class, *test* identifies the method, and whatever trails is the parameter. The name of the class is further worked out and extended to include a namespace and a suffix. According to the example, the final class name is *MvcEmule.HomeController*. This class is expected to be available to the application. The class is also expected to expose a method named *Test*, as shown here:

```
namespace MvcEmule
{
    public class HomeController
    {
        public String Test(Object param1)
        {
            var message = "<html><h1>You passed '{0}'</h1></html>";
            return String.Format(message, param1);
        }
    }
}
```

Figure 8-1 shows the effect of invoking a page-agnostic URL in an ASP.NET Web Forms application.

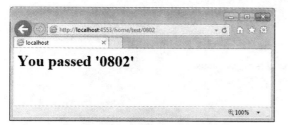

You passed '0802'

FIGURE 8-1 Processing page-agnostic URLs in ASP.NET Web Forms.

This simple example demonstrates the basic mechanics used by ASP.NET MVC. The specialized component that serves a request is the controller. The controller is a class with just methods and no state. A unique system-level HTTP handler takes care of dispatching incoming requests to a specific controller class so that the instance of the class executes a given action method and produces a response.

What about the scheme of URLs? In this example, you just use a hardcoded URL. In ASP.NET MVC, you have a flexible syntax you can use to express the URLs the application recognizes. In addition, a new system component in the runtime pipeline intercepts requests, processes the URL, and triggers the built-in ASP.NET MVC HTTP handler. This component is the URL routing HTTP module.

Exploring the URL routing HTTP module

The URL routing HTTP module processes incoming requests by looking at the URLs and dispatching them to the most appropriate executor. The URL routing HTTP module supersedes the URL rewriting feature of older versions of ASP.NET. At its core, URL rewriting consists of hooking up a request, parsing the original URL, and instructing the HTTP runtime environment to serve a "possibly related but different" URL.

Routing the requests

What happens exactly when a request knocks at the Internet Information Services (IIS) door in the context of an ASP.NET MVC application? Figure 8-2 gives you an overall picture of the various steps involved.

The URL routing HTTP module intercepts any requests for the application that could not be served otherwise by the hosting environment, most likely IIS. If the URL refers to a physical file (for example, an ASPX file), the URL routing HTTP module ignores the request unless it's configured otherwise. In any other case, the URL routing HTTP module attempts to match the URL of the request to any of the application-defined routes. If a match is found, the request goes into the ASP.NET MVC space to be processed in terms of a call to a controller class. If no match is found, the request will be served by the standard ASP.NET runtime in the best possible way and likely will result in an HTTP 404 error.

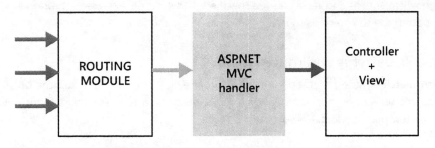

FIGURE 8-2 The role of the URL routing HTTP module in ASP.NET MVC.

In the end, only requests that match predefined URL patterns (also known as *routes*) are allowed to enjoy the ASP.NET MVC runtime. All such requests are routed to a common HTTP handler that instantiates a controller class and invokes a defined method on it. Next, the controller method, in turn, selects a view component to generate the actual response.

Examining the internal structure of the URL routing HTTP module

In terms of implementation, I should note that the URL routing engine is an HTTP module that wires up the *PostResolveRequestCache* event. The event fires right after checking that no response for the request is available in the ASP.NET cache.

The HTTP module matches the requested URL to one of the user-defined URL routes, and it sets the HTTP context to use the ASP.NET MVC standard HTTP handler to serve the request. As a developer, you're not likely to deal with the URL routing HTTP module directly. The module is system provided and doesn't need you to perform any specific form of configuration. You are responsible, instead, for providing the routes that your application supports and that the URL routing HTTP module will actually consume.

Using application routes

As mentioned, in ASP.NET MVC users place requests to act on resources. The framework, however, doesn't mandate the syntax for describing resources and actions. I'm aware that the expression "acting on resources" will likely make you think of Representational State Transfer (REST). And, of course, you will not be too far off the mark in thinking so.

Although you can definitely use a pure REST approach within an ASP.NET MVC application, ASP.NET MVC is loosely REST-oriented in that it acknowledges concepts like resource and action, but it leaves you free to use your own syntax to express and implement resources and actions. As an example, in a pure REST solution you use HTTP verbs to express actions—GET, POST, PUT, and DELETE—and the URL to identify the resource. Implementing a pure REST solution in ASP.NET MVC is possible but requires some extra work on your part.

The default behavior in ASP.NET MVC is using custom URLs, which makes you responsible for the syntax through which actions and resources are specified. This syntax is expressed through a collection of URL patterns, also known as routes.

Working with URL patterns and routes

A route is a pattern-matching string that represents the absolute path of a URL—namely, the URL string without protocol, server, and port information. A route might be a constant string, but it will more likely contain a few placeholders. Here's a sample route:

```
/home/test
```

The route is a constant string and is matched only by URLs whose absolute path is /home/ test. Most of the time, however, you deal with parametric routes that incorporate one or more placeholders. Here are a couple of examples:

```
/{resource}/{action}
/Customer/{action}
```

Both routes are matched by any URLs that contain exactly two segments. The latter, though, requires that the first segment equals the string *Customer*. The former, instead, doesn't impose specific constraints on the content of the segments.

Often referred to as a *URL parameter*, a placeholder is a name enclosed in curly brackets ({ }). You can have multiple placeholders in a route as long as they are separated by a constant or delimiter. The forward slash (/) character acts as a delimiter between the various parts of the route. The name of the placeholder (for example, *action*) is the key your code will use to programmatically retrieve the content of the corresponding segment from the actual URL.

Here's the default route for an ASP.NET MVC application:

```
{controller}/{action}/{id}
```

In this case, the sample route contains three placeholders separated by the delimiter. A URL that matches the preceding route is the following:

```
/Customers/Edit/ALFKI
```

You can add as many routes as you want with as many placeholders as appropriate. You can even remove the default route.

Defining application routes

Routes for an application are usually registered in the *global.asax* file, and they are processed at the application startup. Let's have a look at the section of the *global.asax* file that deals with routes:

```
public class MvcApplication : HttpApplication
{
    protected void Application_Start()
    {
        RouteConfig.RegisterRoutes(RouteTable.Routes);

        // Other code
        ...
    }
}
```

RegisterRoutes is a method on the *RouteConfig* class defined in a separate folder, usually named App_Start. (You can rename the folder at will, though.) Here's the implementation of the class:

```
public class RouteConfig
{
    public static void RegisterRoutes(RouteCollection routes)
    {
        // Other code
        ...

        // Listing routes
        routes.MapRoute(
          "Default",
          "{controller}/{action}/{id}",
          new {
                  controller = "Home",
                  action = "Index",
                  id = UrlParameter.Optional
          });
    }
}
```

As you can see, the *Application_Start* event handler calls into a public static method named *RegisterRoutes* that lists all routes. Note that the name of the *RegisterRoutes* method, as well as the prototype, is arbitrary and can be changed if there's a valid reason.

Supported routes must be added to a static collection of *Route* objects managed by ASP.NET MVC. This collection is *RouteTable.Routes*. You typically use the handy *MapRoute* method to populate the collection. The *MapRoute* method offers various overloads and works well most of the time. However, it doesn't let you configure every possible aspect of a route object. If there's something you need to set on a route that *MapRoute* doesn't support, you might want to resort to using the following code:

```
// Create a new route and add it to the system collection
var route = new Route(...);
RouteTable.Routes.Add("NameOfTheRoute", route);
```

A route is characterized by a few attributes, such as a name, a URL pattern, default values, constraints, data tokens, and a route handler. The attributes you set most often are the name, the URL pattern, and default values. Let's expand on the code you get for the default route:

```
routes.MapRoute(
        "Default",
        "{controller}/{action}/{id}",
        new {
                controller = "Home",
                action = "Index",
                id = UrlParameter.Optional
        });
```

The first parameter is the name of the route; each route should have a unique name. The second parameter is the URL pattern. The third parameter is an object that specifies default values for the URL parameters.

Note that a URL can match the pattern even in an incomplete form. Let's consider the root URL—*http://yourserver.com*. At first sight, such a URL wouldn't match the route. However, if a default value is specified for a URL parameter, the segment is considered optional. As a result, for the preceding example, when you request the root URL, the request is resolved by invoking the method *Index* on the *Home* controller.

Processing routes

The ASP.NET URL routing HTTP module employs a number of rules when trying to match an incoming requested URL to a defined route. The most important rule is that routes must be checked in the order they were registered in *global.asax*.

To ensure that routes are processed in the right order, you must list them from the most specific to the least specific. In any case, keep in mind that the search for a matching route always ends at the first match. This means that just adding a new route at the bottom of the list might not work and might also cause you a bit of trouble. In addition, be aware that placing a catch-all pattern at the top of the list will make any other patterns—no matter how specific—pass unnoticed.

Beyond the order of appearance, other factors affect the process of matching URLs to routes. As mentioned, one is the set of default values you might have provided for a route. Default values are simply values that are automatically assigned to defined placeholders in case the URL doesn't provide specific values. Consider the following two routes:

```
{Orders}/{Year}/{Month}
{Orders}/{Year}
```

If in the first route, you assign default values for both *{Year}* and *{Month}*, the second route will never be evaluated because, thanks to the default values, the first route is always a match regardless of whether the URL specifies a year and a month.

A trailing forward slash (/) is also a pitfall. The routes *{Orders}/{Year}* and *{Orders}/{Year}/* are two very different things. One won't match to the other, even though logically, at least from a user's perspective, you'd expect them to.

Another factor that influences the URL-to-route match is the list of constraints you optionally define for a route. A route constraint is an additional condition that a given URL parameter must fulfill to make the URL match the route. The URL not only should be compatible with the URL pattern, it also needs to contain compatible data. A constraint can be defined in various ways, including through a regular expression. Here's a sample route with constraints:

```
routes.MapRoute(
    "ProductInfo",
    "{controller}/{productId}/{locale}",
    new { controller = "Product", action = "Index", locale="en-us" },
    new { productId = @"\d{8}",
          locale = "[a-z]{2}-[a-z]{2}" });
```

In particular, the route requires that the *productId* placeholder be a numeric sequence of exactly eight digits, whereas the *locale* placeholder must be a pair of two-letter strings separated by a dash. Constraints don't ensure that all invalid product IDs and locale codes are stopped at the gate, but at least they save you a good deal of work.

Introducing the route handler

The route defines a bare-minimum set of rules according to which the routing module decides whether or not the incoming request URL is acceptable to the application. The component that ultimately decides how to remap the requested URL is another one entirely. Precisely, it is the route handler. The route handler is the object that processes any requests that match a given route. Its sole purpose in life is returning the HTTP handler that will actually serve any matching request.

Technically speaking, a route handler is a class that implements the *IRouteHandler* interface. The interface is defined as shown here:

```
public interface IRouteHandler
{
    IHttpHandler GetHttpHandler(RequestContext requestContext);
}
```

Defined in the *System.Web.Routing* namespace, the *RequestContext* class encapsulates the HTTP context of the request plus any route-specific information available, such as the *Route* object itself, URL parameters, and constraints. This data is grouped into a *RouteData* object. Here's the signature of the *RequestContext* class:

```
public class RequestContext
{
    public RequestContext(HttpContextBase httpContext, RouteData routeData);

    // Properties
    public HttpContextBase HttpContext { get; set; }
    public RouteData RouteData { get; set; }
}
```

The ASP.NET MVC framework doesn't offer many built-in route handlers, and this is probably a sign that the need to use a custom route handler is not that common. Yet, the extensibility point exists and, in case of need, you can take advantage of it. I'll return to custom route handlers and provide an example later in the chapter.

Handling requests for physical files

Another configurable aspect of the routing system that contributes to a successful URL-to-route matching is whether or not the routing system has to handle requests that match a physical file.

By default, the ASP.NET routing system ignores requests whose URL can be mapped to a file that physically exists on the server. Note that if the server file exists, the routing system ignores the request even if the request matches a route.

If you need to, you can force the routing system to handle all requests by setting the *RouteExistingFiles* property of the *RouteCollection* object to *true*, as shown here:

```
// In global.asax.cs
public static void RegisterRoutes(RouteCollection routes)
{
    routes.RouteExistingFiles = true;
    ...
}
```

Note that having all requests handled via routing can create some issues in an ASP.NET MVC application. For example, if you add the preceding code to the *global.asax.cs* file of a sample ASP.NET MVC application and run it, you'll immediately face an HTTP 404 error when accessing *default.aspx*.

Preventing routing for defined URLs

The ASP.NET URL routing HTTP module doesn't limit you to maintaining a list of acceptable URL patterns. It also allows you to keep certain URLs off the routing mechanism. You can prevent the routing system from handling certain URLs in two steps.

First, you define a pattern for those URLs and save it to a route. Second, you link that route to a special route handler—the *StopRoutingHandler* class. All it does is throw a *NotSupported* exception when its *GetHttpHandler* method is invoked.

For example, the following code instructs the routing system to ignore any *.axd* requests:

```
// In global.asax.cs
public static void RegisterRoutes(RouteCollection routes)
{
    routes.IgnoreRoute("{resource}.axd/{*pathInfo}");
    ...
}
```

All that *IgnoreRoute* does is associate a *StopRoutingHandler* route handler to the route built around the specified URL pattern.

Finally, a little explanation is required for the *{*pathInfo}* placeholder in the URL. The token *pathInfo* simply represents a placeholder for any content following the *.axd* URL. The asterisk (*), though, indicates that the last parameter should match the rest of the URL. In other words, anything that follows the *.axd* extension goes into the *pathInfo* parameter. Such parameters are referred to as *catch-all parameters*.

Using attribute-based routing

In classic routing, any time a request comes in, the URL is matched against the template of registered routes. If a match is found, the appropriate controller and action method to serve the request are determined. If a match is not found, the request is denied and the result is usually a 404 message. Now, in large applications, or even in medium-sized applications with a strong REST flavor, the number of routes can be quite large—easily in the order of hundreds.

You might quickly find that classic routing becomes a bit overwhelming to handle. Attribute routing is an alternative approach to routing that is all about defining routes directly on controller actions via attributes, as shown here:

```
[HttpGet("orders/{orderId}/show")]
public ActionResult GetOrderById(int orderId)
{
    ...
}
```

The code sets the method *GetOrderById* to be available over an HTTP GET call only if the URL template matches the specified pattern. The route parameter—the *orderId* token—must match one of the parameters defined in the method's signature. There are a few more attributes available—for each HTTP verb—but the gist of attribute routes is all here.

More powerful attributes are *Route*, *RoutePrefix*, and *RouteArea*. You can use the *Route* attribute at the controller-method or action-method level. If you do that at the controller level, the route definition has an impact on all methods, but each method can customize the route on a per-verb basis, as shown here:

```
[Route("info/[controller]")]
public class NewsController : Controller
{
    [HttpGet("{id}")]
    public ActionResult Get(int id)
    {
        ...
    }
}
```

The method *Get* is now invoked through the URL *info/news/{id}*. The attributes *RouteArea* and *RoutePrefix* are typically used to speed up configuration. This is because they add, once per controller, the string to use as an area name and the prefix to use for all methods to be extended by *Route* and other verb-specific attributes. Finally, note that attribute routing in ASP.NET MVC must be enabled explicitly. Here's the common way of doing that:

```
public static void RegisterRoutes(RouteCollection routes)
{
    routes.IgnoreRoute("{resource}.axd/{*pathInfo}");
    routes.MapMvcAttributeRoutes();

    // Classic convention-based routes
    ...
}
```

If you use attribute routing along with classic routing, you also define route conventions in the same place as you do when enabling the attribute-based routing.

> **Note** In ASP.NET MVC, an *area* is simply a name that identifies a group of controllers and views that you want to keep separated from other areas and the rest of the application. In a way, defining an area is like creating a logical subapplication within the application. I say "logical subapplication" because ultimately you always deploy it as a single comprehensive application. You register an area by calling the *RegisterAllAreas* method in *global.asax* and creating a matching project folder with its own subset of controller and view folders.

Exploring the controller class

If the routing module is the place where the system makes sense of the request, the controller class is the place where developers write the code required to actually serve a request. Let's briefly explore some characteristics of controller classes, including implementation details.

Looking at aspects of a controller

As the core of an ASP.NET MVC application, the controller is a delicate part of the design. The granularity of controllers affects the organization of the project and the distribution of code and implementation of use-cases. The state being held (or not held) in the controllers might affect the way operations are coded and, to some extent, even the scalability and testability of the application.

Finally, just because ASP.NET MVC as a framework is inspired by the MVC pattern, that doesn't mean you're getting a perfectly layered system. There's a lot of work to be done on your own and a lot of forethought.

Working with the granularity of controllers

An ASP.NET MVC application is usually made of various controller classes. How many controller classes should you have? The actual number is up to you and depends only on how you want to organize your application's actions. In fact, nothing prevents you from arranging an application around a single controller class that contains methods for any possible requests.

A common practice consists of having a controller class for any significant functionality your application implements. Defining what "significant functionality" really means is problematic, though. I suggest that, as a first approximation, you consider having a controller class for each use-case you're implementing. In an e-commerce system, for example, you might want to have a controller for all login and membership operations, one controller to handle orders or shopping carts, and one controller to let customers edit their profile. You also should have yet another controller class to handle products in stock. Another way to look at the granularity of controllers is that you should have one class for each item you expect to have in the main menu of the application.

In general, the granularity of the controller is a function of the granularity of the user interface. Plan to have a controller for each significant source of requests you might have from the user interface you provide.

> **Note** Be aware that there's no objectively correct number of controller classes for an application. You can build any application with a single controller class or with a long list of one-method controller classes. The "right" number of classes is the number that minimizes maintenance efforts while staying as close as possible to the actual business logic you're exposing.

Working with the statelessness of controller classes

An important point to keep in mind is the inherent statelessness of the web and, subsequently, of controller classes. Every time a new request is captured by the routing module and mapped to a controller action, a new instance of the selected controller class is created.

Any state you might add to the class, therefore, is bound to the same lifetime of the request. The controller class, then, must be able to retrieve any data it needs to work from the HTTP request stream and the HTTP context. The controller class is dependent on the HTTP context, so it can have access to whatever information is bound to the context, whether it is fresh information coming with the request or stored in the ASP.NET infrastructure, such as session state or cache information.

As a general rule, consider that making the controller class dependent on state reduces the scalability of the application, because it makes spinning up a new server in a cloud environment more difficult to do and less immediate.

Deciding whether to use further layering

Often ASP.NET MVC and controller classes are presented as a magic wand you wave to write layered code that is cleaner and easier to read and maintain. The stateless nature of the controller class helps a lot in this regard, but it is not enough.

In ASP.NET MVC, the controller is isolated from both the user interface that triggered the request and the engine that produces the view for the browser. The controller sits in between the view and the back end of the system. Although this sort of isolation from the view is welcome and fixes a weak point of ASP.NET Web Forms, it alone doesn't ensure that your code will respect the venerable principle of separation of concerns (SoC).

By design, the system gets you a minimal level of separation from the view but everything else is up to you. Keep in mind that nothing, not even in ASP.NET MVC, prevents you from using direct ADO.NET calls and plain T-SQL statements directly in the controller class. The controller class is not the back end of the system, and it is not the business layer. It should be considered, instead, as the MVC counterpart of the code-behind class of Web Forms. As such, it definitely belongs to the presentation layer, not the business layer.

Examining the testability of controllers

The inherent statelessness of the controller and its neat separation from the view, make the controller class potentially easy to test. However, the real testability of the controller class should be measured against its effective layering. Let's have a look at Figure 8-3.

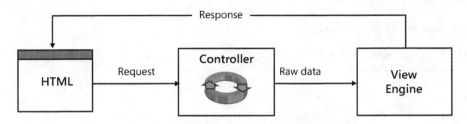

FIGURE 8-3 Controllers and views in ASP.NET MVC.

Although the controller class can be easily fed any fixed input you like and its output can be asserted without major issues, nothing can be said about the internal structure of action methods. The more the implementation of these methods is tightly bound to external resources (for example, databases, services, or components), the less likely it is that testing a controller will be quick and easy.

As you'll see in more detail in Chapter 10, "Organizing the MVC project," an ideal way to build controller classes is to put all the orchestration logic into distinct classes—application layer classes—and keep the controller classes as thin as possible. The benefit is that the controller class is the only place where you're bound to the HTTP context. Application-layer classes, and therefore the work-flow behind each request, can be tested without worry because there are no dependencies on the surrounding environment.

Testing the controller becomes optional. You don't strictly need it unless there are special controller features (such as response and action filters) you want to test. For the most part, writing tests against application-layer classes does the job.

Writing controller classes

The writing of a controller class can be summarized in two simple steps: creating a class that inherits (either directly or indirectly) from *Controller* and adding a bunch of public methods.

Mapping actions to methods

The final output of the ASP.NET MVC pipeline applied to an incoming request is a pair of elements, made of the name of the controller class to instantiate and the name of the action to perform on it. Executing an action on a controller invokes a public method on the controller class. There are a few different ways to map an action name to a class method, however.

The core rule is that any public method on a controller class is a public action with the same name. For example, a public method named *Index* corresponds to an action named *Index*. Sometimes, you need to have a public method on a controller class but don't want it to be invoked from the outside as an action. In this case, all you do is decorate the method with the *NonAction* attribute.

Finally, you can associate an action name with any public method, thus decoupling the method name from the action name. In this case, you decorate the method with the *ActionName* attribute. Here's an example:

```
public class HomeController : Controller
{
    // Implicit action name: Index
    public ActionResult Index()
    {
        ...
    }

    [NonAction]
    public ActionResult About()
    {
        ...
    }

    [ActionName("About")]
    public ActionResult LoveGermanShepherds()
    {
        ...
    }
}
```

Public and not decorated with any attributes, the method *Index*, therefore, is implicitly bound to an action with the same name. The method *About*, instead, is marked as public, but the *NonAction* attribute makes it invisible from the outside. You can call it from within the server-side code of the application, but it is not bound to any action that can be called from browsers and JavaScript code.

The third public method in the sample class has a fancy name, but the *ActionName* attribute binds it explicitly to the action *About*. The net effect is that every time the user requests the action *About*, the method *LoveGermanShepherds* runs.

Another level of method-to-action mapping is the HTTP verb.

Mapping actions to HTTP verbs

ASP.NET MVC is flexible enough to let you bind a method to an action only for a specific HTTP verb. To associate a controller method with an HTTP verb, you either use the parametric *AcceptVerbs* attribute or direct attributes such as *HttpGet*, *HttpPost*, and *HttpPut*. The *AcceptVerbs* attribute allows you to specify which HTTP verb is required to execute a given method. Let's consider the following example:

```
[AcceptVerbs(HttpVerbs.Post)]
public ActionResult Edit(Customer customer)
{
    ...
}
```

Given that code, it turns out that the *Edit* method can't be invoked using a GET. Note also that you are not allowed to have multiple *AcceptVerbs* attributes on a single method. Your code won't compile if you add multiple *AcceptVerbs* attributes (or analogous direct HTTP verb attributes) to an action method.

The *AcceptVerbs* attribute takes any value from the *HttpVerbs* enum type:

```
public enum HttpVerbs
{
    Get = 1,
    Post = 2,
    Put = 4,
    Delete = 8,
    Head = 0x10
}
```

The *HttpVerbs* enum is decorated with the *Flags* attribute. So you can combine multiple values from the enumeration using the bitwise OR (|) operator and still obtain another *HttpVerbs* value:

```
[AcceptVerbs(HttpVerbs.Post|HttpVerbs.Put)]
public ActionResult Edit(Customer customer)
{
    ...
}
```

Using *AcceptVerbs* or multiple individual attributes, such as *HttpGet* or *HttpPost*, is entirely a matter of preference. The following code is absolutely equivalent:

```
[HttpPost]
[HttpPut]
public ActionResult Edit(Customer customer)
{
    ...
}
```

Over the web, you perform an HTTP GET command when you follow a link or type the URL into the address bar. You perform an HTTP POST when you submit the content of an HTML form. Any other HTTP command can be performed from the Web only via AJAX, and from a Microsoft Windows client that sends requests to the ASP.NET MVC application. Here's a common scenario you'll face in nearly every HTML scenario that involves an HTML form. You need a method that renders the view that displays the form, and you also need a method that processes the posted values. How do you handle that?

An option might be to have a single method bound to any possible HTTP verb:

```
public ActionResult Edit(Customer customer)
{
    ...
}
```

In the body of the method, you manage to figure out whether the user intended to display the form or process posted values. There's not much information available to figure this out; the best source you have is the HTTP verb you figure out from the *Request* object:

```
[HttpGet]
public ActionResult Edit(Customer customer)
{
    ...
}

[HttpPost]
public ActionResult Edit(Customer customer)
{
    ...
}
```

There are two methods now bound to distinct actions. This is acceptable for ASP.NET MVC, which will invoke the appropriate method based on the verb. It is not acceptable for a Microsoft C# compiler, though, which won't let you have two methods with the same name and signature in the same class. Here's a rewrite:

```
[HttpGet]
[ActionName("edit")]
public ActionResult DisplayEditForm(Customer customer)
{
    ...
}

[HttpPost]
[ActionName("edit")]
public ActionResult SaveEditForm(Customer customer)
{
    ...
}
```

Methods now have distinct names, but both are bound to the same action, albeit for different verbs.

Action methods

Let's have a look at a sample controller class with a couple of simple but functional action methods:

```
public class HomeController : Controller
{
    public ActionResult Index()
    {
        // Process input data
        ...

        // Perform expected task
        ...
```

```
    // Generate the result of the action
    return View();
}

public ActionResult About()
{
    // Process input data
    ...

    // Perform expected task
    var results = ...

    // Generate the response from calculated results
    return View(results);
}
}
```

An action method grabs available input data using any standard HTTP channels. Next, it arranges for some action and possibly involves the middle tier of the application. The template of an action method can be summarized as follows:

- **Process input data**   An action method can get input arguments from various sources, including collections exposed by the *Request* object. ASP.NET MVC doesn't mandate a particular signature for action methods. For testability reasons, however, it's highly recommended that any input parameter be received through the signature. If you plan to have tests on controller classes, which might not be necessary most of the time, you should avoid methods that retrieve input data programmatically from *Request* or other sources. In this regard, you can leverage the services of the model-binding layer that I'll discuss in a moment.

- **Perform the task**   The action method does its job based on input arguments and attempts to obtain expected results. In doing so, the method likely needs to interact with the middle tier. It is recommended that any interaction takes places through ad hoc, dedicated application-layer services. At the end of the task, any (computed or referenced) values that should be incorporated in the response are packaged as appropriate. If the method returns JSON, data is composed into a JSON-serializable object. If the method returns HTML, data is packaged into a container object and sent to the view engine. The container object is often referred to as the *view-model*, and it can be a plain dictionary of name/value pairs or a view-specific, strongly typed class.

- **Generate the results**   In ASP.NET MVC, a controller's method is not responsible for producing the response itself. It is, however, responsible for triggering the process that will use a distinct object (often, a view object) to render content to the output stream. The method identifies the type of response (file, plain data, HTML, JavaScript, or JSON) and sets up an *ActionResult* object as appropriate.

A controller's method is expected to return an *ActionResult* object or any object that inherits from the *ActionResult* class. Often, though, a controller's method doesn't directly instantiate an *ActionResult* object. Instead, it uses an action helper—that is, an object that internally instantiates and returns an *ActionResult* object.

Processing input data

The signature of a controller action method is free. If you define parameterless methods, you make yourself responsible for programmatically retrieving any input data your code requires. If you add parameters to the method's signature, ASP.NET MVC will offer automatic parameter resolution.

In this section, I'll first discuss how to manually retrieve input data from within a controller action method. Next, I'll turn to automatic parameter resolution via model binders—the most common choice in ASP.NET MVC applications.

Manual parameter binding

Controller action methods can access any input data posted with the HTTP request. Input data can be retrieved from various sources, including form data, a query string, cookies, route values, and posted files. Let's get into some details.

Getting input data from the *Request* object

When writing the body of an action method, you can directly access any input data that comes through the familiar *Request* object and its child collections, such as *Form*, *Cookies*, *ServerVariables*, and *QueryString*. As you'll see in a moment, ASP.NET MVC offers quite compelling facilities (for example, model binders) that you might want to use to keep your code cleaner, more compact, and easier to test. Having said that, though, nothing at all prevents you from writing old-style *Request*-based code as shown here:

```
public ActionResult Echo()
{
    // Capture data in a manual way
    var data = Request.Params["today"] ?? String.Empty;
    ...
}
```

In ASP.NET, the *Request.Params* dictionary results from the combination of four distinct dictionaries: *QueryString*, *Form*, *Cookies*, and *ServerVariables*. You can also use the *Item* indexer property of the *Request* object, which provides the same capabilities and searches dictionaries for a matching entry in the following order: *QueryString*, *Form*, *Cookies*, and *ServerVariables*. The following code is fully equivalent to the code just shown:

```
public ActionResult Echo()
{
    // Capture data in a manual way
    var data = Request["today"] ?? String.Empty;
    ...
}
```

Note that the search for a matching entry is case insensitive.

Getting input data from the route

In ASP.NET MVC, you often provide input parameters through the URL. These values are captured by the routing module and made available to the application. Route values are not exposed to applications through the *Request* object. You have to use a slightly different approach to retrieve them programmatically:

```
public ActionResult Echo()
{
    // Capture data in a manual way
    var data = RouteData.Values["data"] ?? String.Empty;
    ...
}
```

Route data is exposed through the *RouteData* property of the *Controller* class. Also in this case, the search for a matching entry is conducted in a case-insensitive way.

> **Note** The *RouteData.Values* dictionary is a String/Object dictionary. The dictionary contains only strings most of the time. However, if you populate it programmatically (for example, via a custom route handler), it can contain other types of values. In this case, you're responsible for any necessary type cast.

Model binding

Using native request collections of input data is functional but not ideal from a readability and maintenance perspective. You'll find it's better to use an ad hoc model to expose data to controllers. This model is often referred to as the *input model*. ASP.NET MVC provides an automatic binding layer that uses a built-in set of rules for mapping raw request data from any value providers to properties of input model classes. As a developer, you are largely responsible for the design of input model classes.

> **Note** Most of the time, the built-in mapping rules of the model-binding layer are enough for controllers to receive clean and usable data. However, the logic of the binding layer can be customized to a large extent, thus adding unprecedented levels of flexibility as far as the processing of input data is concerned.

The default model binder

Any request passes through the engine of a built-in binder object that corresponds to an instance of the *DefaultModelBinder* class. Figure 8-4 provides an overall view of the parameter binding process.

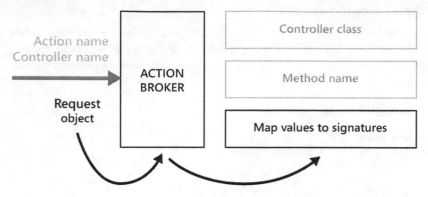

FIGURE 8-4 The process of mapping request values to a controller method's signature.

The action invoker is an ASP.NET MVC internal pipeline component that has the goal of turning action and controller names into a call to a method on a controller class instance. In doing so, it needs to investigate the signature of the controller method and look at formal parameter names in an attempt to find a match with the names of any data uploaded with the request, whether through the query string, form, route, or cookies.

The model binder uses convention-based logic to match the names of posted values to parameter names in the controller's method. The *DefaultModelBinder* class knows how to deal with primitive and complex types, as well as collections and dictionaries. In light of this, the default binder works just fine most of the time.

Binding primitive types

Admittedly, it sounds a bit magical at first, but there's no actual wizardry behind model binding. The key fact about model binding is that it lets you focus exclusively on the data you want the controller method to receive. You completely ignore the details of how you retrieve that data, whether it comes from the query string or the route.

Let's suppose you need a controller method to repeat a given string a given number of times. The input data you need is a string and a number. Here's what you do:

```
public class BindingController : Controller
{
    public ActionResult Repeat(string text, int number)
    {
        ...
    }
}
```

Designed in this way, there's no need for you to access the HTTP context to grab data. Where do the values for *text* and *number* come from? And which component is actually reading them into *text* and *number* parameters?

The actual values are read from the request context, and the default model-binder object does the trick. In particular, the default binder attempts to match formal parameter names (*text* and *number* in the example) to named values posted with the request. In other words, if the request carries a form field, a query string field, or a route parameter named *text*, the carried value is automatically bound to the *text* parameter. The mapping occurs successfully as long as the parameter type and actual value are compatible. If a conversion cannot be performed, an argument exception is thrown. The next URL works just fine:

```
http://server/binding/repeat?text=Dino&number=2
```

Conversely, the following URL causes an exception:

```
http://server/binding/repeat?text=Dino&number=true
```

The query string field text contains *Dino*, and the mapping to the String parameter *text* on the method *Repeat* takes place successfully. The query string field *number*, on the other hand, contains *true*, which can't be successfully mapped to an *int* parameter. The model binder returns a parameters dictionary, where the entry for *number* contains null. Because the parameter type is *int*—that is, a non-nullable type—the invoker throws an argument exception.

Dealing with optional values

Note that an argument exception that occurs because invalid values are being passed is not detected at the controller level. The exception is fired before the execution flow reaches the controller. This means you won't be able to catch it with *try/catch* blocks.

If the default model binder can't find a posted value that matches a required method parameter, it places a *null* value in the parameter dictionary returned to the action invoker. Again, if a value of *null* is not acceptable for the parameter type, an argument exception is thrown before the controller method is even called.

What if a method parameter has to be considered optional?

A possible approach entails changing the parameter type to a nullable type, as shown here:

```
public ActionResult Repeat(string text, Nullable<int> number)
{
    var model = new RepeatViewModel {Number = number.GetValueOrDefault(), Text = text};
    return View(model);
}
```

Another approach consists of using a default value for the parameter:

```
public ActionResult Repeat(String text, Int32 number=4)
{
    var model = new RepeatViewModel {Number = number, Text = text};
    return View(model);
}
```

Any decisions about the controller method's signature are up to you. In general, you might want to use types that are very close to the real data being uploaded with the request. Using parameters of type *Object*, for example, will save you from argument exceptions, but it will make it hard to write clean code to process the input data.

The default binder can map all primitive types, such as string, int, double, decimal, bool, DateTime, and related collections. To express a Boolean type in a URL, you resort to the *true* and *false* strings. These strings are parsed using .NET Framework native Boolean parsing functions, which recognize *true* and *false* strings in a case-insensitive manner. If you use strings such as *yes/no* to mean a Boolean, the default binder won't understand your intentions and will place a *null* value in the parameter dictionary, which might cause an argument exception.

Binding complex types

There's no limitation on the number of parameters you can list on a method's signature. However, a container class is often better than a long list of individual parameters. For the default model binder, the result is nearly the same whether you list a sequence of parameters or just one parameter of a complex type. Both scenarios are fully supported. Here's an example:

```
public class ComplexController : Controller
{
    public ActionResult Repeat(RepeatText inputModel)
    {
        var model = new RepeatViewModel
                    {
                        Title = "Repeating text",
                        Text = inputModel.Text,
                        Number = inputModel.Number
                    };
        return View(model);
    }
}
```

The controller method receives an object of type *RepeatText*. The class is a plain data-transfer object defined as follows:

```
public class RepeatText
{
    public String Text { get; set; }
    public Int32 Number { get; set; }
}
```

As you can see, the class just contains members for the same values you passed as individual parameters in the previous example. The model binder works with this complex type as well as it did with single values.

For each public property in the declared type—*RepeatText* in this case—the model binder looks for posted values whose key names match the property name. The match is case insensitive. Here's a sample URL that works with the *RepeatText* parameter type:

```
http://server/Complex/Repeat?text=ASP.NET%20MVC&number=5
```

Binding collections

What if the argument that a controller method expects is a collection? For example, can you bind the content of a posted form to an *IList<T>* parameter? The *DefaultModelBinder* class makes it possible, but doing so requires a bit of contrivance of your own. Have a look at Figure 8-5.

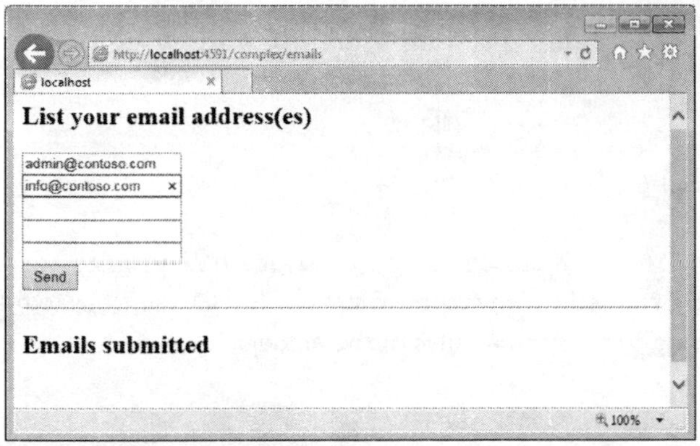

FIGURE 8-5 The page will post an array of strings.

When the user clicks the Send button, the form submits its content. Specifically, it sends out the content of the various text boxes. If the text boxes have different IDs, the posted content takes the following form:

```
TextBox1=admin@contoso.com&TextBox2=info@contoso.com&TextBox3=&TextBox4=&TextBox5=
```

In classic ASP.NET, this is the only possible way of working because you can't assign the same ID to multiple controls. However, if you manage the HTML yourself, nothing prevents you from assigning the same ID to the five text boxes in the figure. The HTML DOM, in fact, fully supports this scenario (though it is not recommended). Therefore, the following markup is entirely legal in ASP.NET MVC and produces HTML that works on all browsers:

```
@using (Html.BeginForm())
{
    <h2>List your email address(es)</h2>
    foreach(var email in Model.Emails)
    {
        <input type="text" name="email" value="@email" />
        <br />
    }
    <input type="submit" value="Send" />
}
```

What's the expected signature of a controller method that has to process the email addresses typed in the form? Here it is:

```
public ActionResult Emails(IList<String> email)
{
    ...
}
```

Figure 8-6 shows that an array of strings is correctly passed to the method thanks to the default binder class.

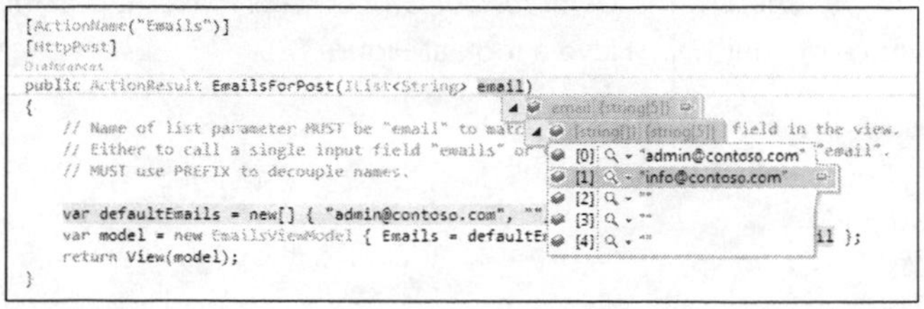

```
[ActionName("Emails")]
[HttpPost]
public ActionResult EmailsForPost(IList<String> email)
{
    // Name of list parameter MUST be "email" to match       field in the view.
    // Either to call a single input field "emails" or             "email".
    // MUST use PREFIX to decouple names.

    var defaultEmails = new[] { "admin@contoso.com", ""
    var model = new EmailsViewModel { Emails = defaultEr                 il };
    return View(model);
}
```

FIGURE 8-6 An array of strings has been posted.

In the end, to ensure that a collection of values is passed to a controller method, you need to ensure that elements with the same ID are emitted to the response stream. The ID, then, has to match the controller method's signature according to the normal rules of the binder.

Producing action results

An action method can produce various results. For example, an action method can just act as a web service and return a plain string or a JSON string in response to a request. Likewise, an action method can determine that there's no content to return or that a redirect to another URL is required. In these two cases, the browser will just get an HTTP response with no significant body of content. This is to say that it's one thing to produce the raw result of the action (for example, collecting values from the middle tier), and it is quite another case to process that raw result to generate the actual HTTP response for the browser.

Wrapping results

An action method typically returns an object of type *ActionResult*. The type *ActionResult* is not a data container, though. More precisely, it is an abstract class that offers a common programming interface to execute some further operations on behalf of the action method. All these further operations relate to producing some response for the requesting browser.

Taking a look inside the *ActionResult* class

Here's the definition of the *ActionResult* class as it appears in the ASP.NET MVC framework:

```
public abstract class ActionResult
{
    protected ActionResult()
    {
    }

    public abstract void ExecuteResult(ControllerContext context);
}
```

By overriding the *ExecuteResult* method, a derived class gains access to any data produced by the execution of the action method and triggers some subsequent action. Generally, this subsequent action is related to the generation of the response for the browser. Because *ActionResult* is an abstract type, every action method is actually required to return an instance of a more specific type.

Table 8-1 lists all predefined *ActionResult* types.

TABLE 8-1 Predefined *ActionResult* types in ASP.NET MVC

Type	Description
ContentResult	Sends raw content (not necessarily HTML) to the browser. The ExecuteResult method of this class serializes any content it receives.
EmptyResult	Sends no content to the browser. The ExecuteResult method of this class does nothing.
FileContentResult	Sends the content of a file to the browser. The content of the file is expressed as a byte array. The ExecuteResult method simply writes the array of bytes to the output stream.
FilePathResult	Sends the content of a file to the browser. The file is identified via its path and content type. The ExecuteResult method calls the TransmitFile method on HttpResponse.
FileStreamResult	Sends the content of a file to the browser. The content of the file is represented through a Stream object. The ExecuteResult method copies from the provided file stream to the output stream.
HttpNotFoundResult	Sends an HTTP 404 response code to the browser. The HTTP status code identifies a request that failed because the requested resource was not found.
HttpUnauthorizedResult	Sends an HTTP 401 response code to the browser. The HTTP status code identifies an unauthorized request.
JavaScriptResult	Sends JavaScript text to the browser. The ExecuteResult method of this class writes out the script and sets the content type accordingly.
JsonResult	Sends a JSON string to the browser. The ExecuteResult method of this class sets the content type to the application or JSON and invokes the JavaScript serializer to serialize any provided managed object to JSON.
PartialViewResult	Sends HTML content to the browser that represents a fragment of the whole page view. A partial view in ASP.NET MVC is a concept that's similar to a user control in Web Forms.
RedirectResult	Sends an HTTP 302 response code to the browser to redirect the browser to the specified URL. The ExecuteResult method of this class just invokes Response.Redirect.
RedirectToRouteResult	Like RedirectResult, it sends an HTTP 302 code to the browser and the new URL to navigate to. The difference is in the logic and input data employed to determine the target URL. In this case, the URL is built based on action/controller pairs or route names.
ViewResult	Sends HTML content to the browser that represents a full page view.

Note that *FileContentResult*, *FilePathResult*, and *FileStreamResult* are derived from the same base class, *FileResult*. You use any of these action result objects if you want to reply to a request with the download of some file content or even some plain binary content expressed as a byte array. *PartialViewResult* and *ViewResult* inherit from *ViewResultBase* and return HTML content. Finally, *HttpUnauthorizedResult* and *HttpNotFoundResult* represent common responses for unauthorized access and missing resources, respectively. Both derive from a further extensible class, *HttpStatusCodeResult*.

Examining the mechanics of executing action results

To better comprehend the mechanics of action result classes, let's dissect one of the predefined classes. I chose the *JavaScriptResult* class, which provides some meaningful behavior without being too complex. The *JavaScriptResult* class represents the action of returning some script to the browser. Here's a possible action method that serves up JavaScript code:

```
public JavaScriptResult GetScript()
{
    var script = "alert('Hello')";
    return JavaScript(script);
}
```

In the example, *JavaScript* is a helper method in the *Controller* class that acts as a factory for the *JavaScriptResult* object. The implementation looks like this:

```
protected JavaScriptResult JavaScript(string script)
{
    return new JavaScriptResult() { Script = script };
}
```

The *JavaScriptResult* class supplies a public property—the *Script* property—that contains the script code to write to the output stream. Here's its implementation:

```
public class JavaScriptResult : ActionResult
{
    public String Script { get; set; }

    public override void ExecuteResult(ControllerContext context)
    {
        if (context == null)
            throw new ArgumentNullException("context");

        // Prepare the response
        HttpResponseBase response = context.HttpContext.Response;
        response.ContentType = "application/x-javascript";
        if (Script != null)
            response.Write(Script);
    }
}
```

As you can see, the ultimate purpose of the *ActionResult* class is preparing the *HttpResponse* object to return to the browser. This entails setting content type, expiration policies, and headers as well as content.

Returning HTML markup

Most ASP.NET MVC requests require that HTML markup be served back to browsers. In ASP.NET MVC, the action method produces the raw results for the user and the view engine composes raw results into an HTML template. Finally, the final artifact is composed and served as the request's response.

Examining the structure of the view engine

The view engine is the component that physically builds the HTML output for the browser. The view engine kicks in for each request that ends up in a controller action that returns HTML. It prepares the output by mixing together a template for the view and any data the controller passes in. The template is expressed in an engine-specific markup language (for example, Razor); the data is passed packaged in dictionaries or in strongly typed objects. Figure 8-7 shows the overall picture of how a view engine and controller work together.

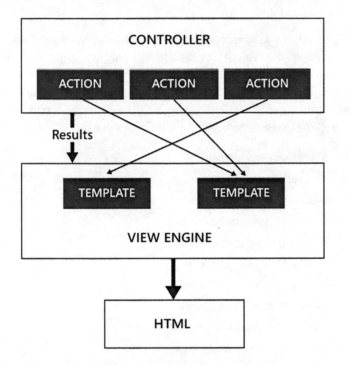

FIGURE 8-7 Controllers and view engines.

In ASP.NET MVC, a view engine is merely a class that implements a fixed interface—the *IViewEngine* interface. Each application can have one or more view engines and use all of them in different views. In ASP.NET MVC, each application is armed by default with two view engines: Razor and ASPX. The aspect of the view engine that most affects the development is the syntax it supports for defining the template of the view. The ASPX view engine uses the same syntax of code blocks in Web Forms. The most commonly used engine, though, is Razor. The Razor syntax is far cleaner and more effective than ASPX.

Exploring general aspects of the Razor view engine

In Razor, a view template is essentially an HTML page with a few placeholders. Each placeholder contains an executable expression—much like a code snippet. The code in the snippets is evaluated when the view gets rendered, and the resulting markup is integrated into the HTML template.

The Razor engine reads view templates from a physical location on disk. The path is retrieved using the ASP.NET virtual path provider. Any ASP.NET MVC project has a root *Views* folder where the view templates are stored in a specific structure of subdirectories. The *Views* folder usually has a number of subfolders—each named after an existing controller. Each controller-specific subdirectory contains physical files whose name is expected to match the name of an action. The extension has to be *.cshtml* for the Razor view engine. (If you're writing your ASP.NET MVC application in Microsoft Visual Basic, the extension must be *.vbhtml*.) ASP.NET MVC requires that you place each view template under the directory of the controller that uses it. If you expect multiple controllers to invoke the same view, move the view template file under the *Shared* folder.

Note that the same hierarchy of directories that exists at the project level under the *Views* folder must be replicated on the production server when you deploy the site. The Razor view engine defines a few properties through which you can control how view templates are located. For the internal working of the Razor view engine, you need to provide a default location for master, regular, and partial views, both in a default project configuration and when areas are used. Table 8-2 shows the location properties supported by the Razor view engine with the predefined value.

TABLE 8-2 The default location formats of the Razor view engine

Property	Default location format
AreaMasterLocationFormats	~/Areas/{2}/Views/{1}/{0}.cshtml
	~/Areas/{2}/Views/Shared/{0}.cshtml
	~/Areas/{2}/Views/{1}/{0}.vbhtml
	~/Areas/{2}/Views/Shared/{0}.vbhtml
AreaPartialViewLocationFormats	~/Areas/{2}/Views/{1}/{0}.cshtml
	~/Areas/{2}/Views/{1}/{0}.vbhtml
	~/Areas/{2}/Views/Shared/{0}.cshtml
	~/Areas/{2}/Views/Shared/{0}.vbhtml
AreaViewLocationFormats	~/Areas/{2}/Views/{1}/{0}.cshtml
	~/Areas/{2}/Views/{1}/{0}.vbhtml
	~/Areas/{2}/Views/Shared/{0}.cshtml
	~/Areas/{2}/Views/Shared/{0}.vbhtml
MasterLocationFormats	~/Views/{1}/{0}.cshtml
	~/Views/Shared/{0}.cshtml
	~/Views/{1}/{0}.vbhtml
	~/Views/Shared/{0}.vbhtml
PartialViewLocationFormats	~/Views/{1}/{0}.cshtml
	~/Views/{1}/{0}.vbhtml

Property	Default location format
	~/Views/Shared/{0}.cshtml
	~/Views/Shared/{0}.vbhtml
ViewLocationFormats	~/Views/{1}/{0}.cshtml
	~/Views/{1}/{0}.vbhtml
	~/Views/Shared/{0}.cshtml
	~/Views/Shared/{0}.vbhtml
FileExtensions	.cshtml, .vbhtml

As you can see, locations are not fully qualified paths, but they can contain up to three placeholders. The placeholder *{0}* refers to the name of the view because it is being invoked from the controller method. The placeholder *{1}* refers to the controller name because it is used in the URL. Finally, the controller *{2}*, if specified, refers to the area name.

Invoking the view engine

From within a controller method, you invoke the view engine by calling the *View* method, as shown here:

```
public ActionResult Index()
{
    return View(); // same as View("index");
}
```

The *View* method is a helper method responsible for creating a *ViewResult* object. The *ViewResult* object needs to know about the view template, an optional master view, and the raw data to be incorporated into the final HTML. Just because the method *View* in the code snippet is parameterless doesn't mean no data is actually passed on. Here's the complete signature of the method:

```
protected ViewResult View(String viewName, String masterViewName, Object viewModel)
```

Here's a more common pattern for a controller method:

```
public ActionResult Index(...)
{
    var model = GetRawDataForTheView(...);
    return View(model);
}
```

In this case, the name of the view defaults to the name of the action, whether it's implicitly inferred from the method's name or explicitly set through the *ActionName* attribute. The master view defaults to *_Layout.cshtml*. Finally, the variable *model* indicates the data model to be incorporated in the final HTML.

The master view is the common template that a view is based on. A master view file is located in the *Shared* folder. In its simplest form, a master view is as shown here:

```html
<html>
  <head>
    <link href="@Url.Content("~/Content/site.css")" rel="stylesheet" type="text/css" />
    <script src="@Url.Content("~/Scripts/jquery.js")" type="text/javascript"></script>
  </head>
  <body>
      @RenderBody()
  </body>
</html>
```

The *@RenderBody* call indicates the insertion point where the specific view is injected into the master template. The *@Url.Content* expression is a facility that completes the relative URL with the root path of the site. The tilde symbol, in fact, just refers to the root of the site.

Any data model being used in the view must be declared through the *@model* directive:

```html
@model MySite.Models.ViewModel
<html>
<head>
    <title>@Model.Title</title>
  </head>
  <body>
      @RenderBody()
  </body>
</html>
```

The type you declare in the directive must be compatible with the type of the object you pass in the call to the *View* method from the controller. In the body of the view, you reference properties of the view model object using the *@Model.XXX* syntax.

Let's find out more about the @ character in a Razor view or master template.

Using Razor code snippets

In a Razor template, you find plain HTML markup emitted verbatim and code snippets. The @ character denotes the start of a Razor code snippet. The interesting thing is that in Razor you need to indicate the start of a code snippet, but after that the internal parser uses the Visual Basic or C# parsing logic to figure out where a line of code finishes. Here's an example:

```html
<html>
<head>
    <title>@ViewBag.Title</title>
</head>
<body>
    ...
</body>
</html>
```

In the code snippet, the *ViewBag.Title* expression refers to another way you have to pass data from the controller. *ViewBag* is a dynamic object shaped up from the controller to contain data to be consumed in the view:

```
public ActionResult Index(...)
{
    // Get data for the view
    ...

    // Package data for the view
    ViewBag.Title = ...;
    ViewBag.Xxx = ...;
    ...

    // ViewBag is implicitly passed to the view engine
    return View();
}
```

ViewBag is an object of type *dynamic*, meaning that any expression that involves it is not compiled up front, but it is interpreted at run time.

Any Razor code snippet can be mixed with plain markup, even when the snippet contains control flow statements such as *if/else* or *for/foreach*. Here's a brief example that shows how to build an HTML table:

```
<body>
    <h2>My favorite cities</h2>
    <hr />
    <table>
        <thead>
            <th>City</th>
            <th>Country</th>
            <th>Ever been there?</th>
        </thead>
    @foreach (var city in ViewBag.Cities) {
        <tr>
            <td>@city.Name</td>
            <td>@city.Country</td>
            <td>@city.Visited ?"Yes" :"No"</td>
        </tr>
    }
    </table>
</body>
```

Note that the closing curly brace, placed in the middle of the source (which you can see in the line of *@foreach*), is correctly recognized and interpreted by the parser.

In a Razor template, you can use any C# or Visual Basic instructions as long as the expression is prefixed by @. Here's an example of how you import a namespace and create a form block:

```
@using MyApp.Components;
...
<body>
    @using (Html.BeginForm()) {
        <div class="editor-field">
            <span>...</span>
        </div>
    }
</body>
```

You can insert a full segment of code made of multiple lines anywhere by wrapping it within a @{ code } block as shown here:

```
@{
    var user = "Dino";
}
...
<p>@user</p>
```

Any variable you create can be retrieved and used later as if the code belonged to a single block. Multiple tokens (for example, markup and code) can be combined in the same expression using round brackets:

```
<p> @("Welcome, " + user) </p>
```

Any content being processed by Razor is automatically encoded, so you have no need to take care of that. If your code returns HTML markup that you want to emit as is without being automatically encoded, you should resort to the *Html.Raw* helper method:

```
@Html.Raw(Strings.HtmlMessage)
```

Finally, when inside multiline code snippets using @{ ... }, you use the C# or Visual Basic language syntax to place comments. You can comment out an entire block of Razor code using the @* ... *@ syntax. Here's how:

```
@*
<div> Some Razor markup </div>
*@
```

There are some minor differences between a C#-based Razor view and one based on the Visual Basic language. In Visual Basic, you can directly write XML literals in the source code; this creates ambiguity in the resolution of some Razor markup. The following expression would be acceptable in C#, but it can't be ported literally to Visual Basic:

```
@if (isHelloWorld) {
    <h1> Hello world <h1>
}
```

In Visual Basic, you need to prefix HTML literals with an additional @ symbol, as shown here:

```
@If (isHelloWorld) Then
    @<h1>Hello world</h1>
End If
```

As you might know, most Visual Basic constructs require a closing tag. This is the case for *For..Each*, *If*, *Using*, and others. The closing tag doesn't need to be prefixed with an @ symbol.

Partial views

Sometimes it is useful to isolate some common pieces of Razor markup to a separate file and just link it from within a master or a view. If you're familiar with ASP.NET Web Forms programming, this is the same service that user controls can provide. In ASP.NET MVC, you achieve the same effect by using the *Partial* helper method on the *Html* internal object:

```
@Html.Partial("name_of_the_view")
```

The *Partial* method returns a string that is incorporated in the stream being manipulated by the view engine. A partial view is a plain file with the same structure and syntax of a view or a template. The typical location for a partial view is the *Shared* folder under *Views*. It is also acceptable, however, that you store a partial view under the controller-specific folder. This happens when the partial view is not used outside the realm of the views handled by a given controller.

Returning JSON content

ASP.NET MVC lends itself well to implementing simple web services to be called back from jQuery snippets in an Ajax context. All you need to do is set one or more action methods to return JSON strings instead of HTML. Here's an example:

```
public JsonResult GetCustomers()
{
    // Grab some data to return
    var customers = _customerRepository.GetAll();

    // Serialize to JSON and return
    return Json(customers);
}
```

The *Json* helper method gets a plain .NET CLR object and serializes it to a string using the built-in *JavaScriptSerializer* class.

Note What if your controller action method doesn't return an *ActionResult* type? First and foremost, no exceptions are raised. Quite simply, ASP.NET MVC encapsulates any return value from the action method (numbers, strings, or custom objects) into a *ContentResult* object. The execution of a *ContentResult* object causes the plain serialization of the value to the browser. For example, an action that returns an integer or a string will get you a browser page that displays data as-is. On the other hand, returning a custom object displays any string resulting from the implementation of the object's *ToString* method. If the method returns an HTML string, any markup will not be automatically encoded and the browser will likely not properly parse it. Finally, a void return value is actually mapped to an *EmptyResult* object whose execution causes a no-op.

Asynchronous operations within a controller

The primary purpose of a controller is to serve the needs of the user interface. Any server-side functions you need to implement should be mapped to a controller method and triggered from the user interface. After performing its own task, a controller's method selects the next view, packs some data, and tells it to render.

This is the essence of the controller's behavior. However, other characteristics are often required in a controller, especially when controllers are employed in large and complex applications with particular needs, such as long-running requests. In earlier versions of ASP.NET MVC, you had to follow a specific pattern to give controller methods an asynchronous behavior. In recent versions of ASP.NET and the .NET Framework, you can leverage the *async/await* language facilities and the underlying .NET Framework machinery. Here's how you write a controller class with one or more asynchronous methods:

```
public class HomeController : AsyncController
{
    public async Task<ActionResult> Rss()
    {
        // Run the potentially lengthy operation
        var client = new HttpClient();
        var rss = await client.GetStringAsync(someRssUrl);

        // Parse RSS and build the view model
        var model = new HomeIndexModel();
        model.News = ParseRssInternal(rss);
        return model;
    }
}
```

Note that using asynchronous controller methods is not strictly beneficial to the method itself, which won't run faster just because of that. It is highly beneficial, instead, for the whole application because it won't keep any ASP.NET thread locked up waiting for some potentially lengthy task to complete. The entire application will be more responsive if you use asynchronous controller methods.

Summary

One characteristic feature of ASP.NET MVC is that it doesn't match URLs to disk files; instead, it parses the URL to figure out the next requested action to take. An action is then mapped to a method on a controller class. Each method execution then terminates, with a result being serialized back to the requesting browser. The most common type of action result is an HTML view, but other types of responses are possible, including JSON, plain text, binary data, and redirects.

In this chapter, I touched on the components that make up the workflow of a typical ASP.NET MVC request. First the URL routing HTTP module examines the incoming request and figures out the controller that will handle it and the method being invoked. Next, the binding layer kicks in and maps data being posted (such as a query string, a form, cookies, headers, or a route) to the signature of the controller method. If the mapping is successful, the controller method runs and produces raw results. Raw results are any data you want to be presented back to the user—collections, strings, number, dates, or whatever. Finally, the view engine picks up a view template and generates HTML for the browser. Controllers are not limited to just returning HTML. In ASP.NET MVC, a controller can easily return any type of data serialized as XML, plain text, or JSON.

This chapter barely scratched the surface of ASP.NET MVC, but it provided an overview of how things go. In the next chapter, I'll give a go to explaining Twitter Bootstrap—a CSS and graphical library you can use to arrange effectively the layout and user interface of HTML views. Starting with Chapter 11, "Presenting data," I'll return to Razor and discuss common ways to present and edit data in views.

Core of Bootstrap

Part of the inhumanity of the computer is that, once it is competently programmed and working smoothly, it is completely honest.

—Isaac Asimov

Originally developed for internal purposes at Twitter, Bootstrap is a CSS and JavaScript library aimed at simplifying the building of modern webpages. But what is a "modern webpage," anyway?

Quite simply, a modern webpage is a webpage constructed as most users like to have it these days. The HTML language is still the foundation of webpages and the core language. However, the building blocks of the HTML markup language are less and less adequate for quickly and directly expressing the complexity and sophistication that make up modern pages. For example, drop-down menus, segmented option buttons, tab strips, accordions, and modal dialogs are all common elements of most pages, yet there's no direct HTML element for having them readily available.

Bootstrap provides a direct way to turn chunks of HTML into more sophisticated visual elements as required by modern websites.

Bootstrap at a glance

Bootstrap is a modular web library made of CSS and JavaScript files. The CSS files contain classes to redesign common HTML elements to make them look different and possibly nicer. The JavaScript files come in the form of a collection of jQuery plugins and support more sophisticated features that can't be achieved with CSS only.

Bootstrap was originally developed as a collection of LESS files, and you can still get the CSS part of the library as a collection of LESS files. Essentially, you have a LESS or CSS file for each module the Bootstrap library is made of: forms, buttons, navigation bars, dialog boxes, and so forth. Before getting into the details of the Bootstrap library, let's first take a quick look at LESS.

LESS and the foundation of Bootstrap

A LESS file is an abstraction over plain CSS syntax and provides developers the ability to declare how a CSS file will ultimately be used. You can consider LESS to be a programming language that, once compiled, produces CSS. In a LESS file, you can use variables, functions, and operators, thus wildly streamlining the process of creating and maintaining large and complex CSS stylesheets.

Variables

One of the biggest issues developers address with LESS is the repetition of information. As a software developer, you probably know very well the "Don't Repeat Yourself" (DRY) principle and apply it every day. The major benefit of DRY is that it reduces the number of places where the same information is stored, and thus the number of places where it should be updated. In plain CSS, you simply have no DRY. For example, if a given color is used in multiple CSS classes—and at some point you have to change it—you likely have no better way to do that than by updating it in every single occurrence.

The problem with CSS classes is that they operate at the level of the semantic HTML element. In the building of the various CSS classes, you often must repeat small pieces of information, such as colors or widths. You can't easily create a class for each of these repeatable small pieces. Even if you manage to have a CSS class for nearly any repeatable style, such as colors and widths, when it comes to styling the semantic element—say, a container—you need to concatenate multiple CSS classes together to achieve the desired effect.

Consider the following CSS example:

```
.container {
    color: #111;
}
.header {
    background-color: #111;
}
```

Both the *container* and *header* CSS classes depend on the same color. If that color has to change, you must go through all the places where it's used and edit it. Here's how you can rewrite the same feature in a LESS fashion:

```
@black: #111;
.container {
    color: @black;
}
.header {
    background-color: @black;
}
```

Now the color is defined in a single place, as a global variable. LESS, therefore, is a language that adds programmer-friendly concepts to CSS coding, such as variables. But it can do even more.

Imports

You can split your LESS code across multiple files and reference them where necessary. Suppose, for example, that you create a *container.less* file with the following content:

```
@black: #111;
.container {
   background-color: @black;
}
```

In another LESS file—say, *main.less*—you can reference the entire CSS by importing the file:

```
@import "container";
.body { .container; }
```

If the *container.less* file (the extension isn't strictly required) lives in a different folder, you should indicate path information in the call to *@import*.

Mixins

Especially at a time when webpages must adapt to different screen sizes, the ability to adapt CSS styles to different resolutions is critical. For example, it's common for developers to increase padding around buttons when buttons are viewed on tablets and subject to coarse-grained pointers, such as fingers. Generally speaking, how can you make the same CSS class change and look different depending on some runtime conditions? This is where LESS mixins come to the rescue.

Here are a couple of mixins:

```
.shadow(@color) {
  box-shadow: 3px 3px 2px @color;
}
.text-box(@width) {
  .shadow(#555);
  border: solid 1px #000;
  background-color: #dddd00;
  padding: 2px;
  width: @width;
}
```

From here, you can derive more specific CSS classes, as shown here:

```
.text-box-mini {
  .text-box(50px);
}
.text-box-normal {
  .text-box(100px);
}
.text-box-large {
  .text-box(200px);
}
```

This is precisely what Bootstrap does internally to support different flavors of common elements such as buttons and input fields.

Turning LESS into CSS

Although LESS can be used as a meta-language for CSS, LESS is not CSS. It must be processed in some way to produce plain CSS. LESS code can be downloaded as-is and processed on the client through JavaScript code, or it can be preprocessed on the server and downloaded to the client as plain CSS. In the former case, everything works as if you were using plain CSS files: server-side changes are applied to the client with the next page refresh.

The server-side preprocessing, though, might be a better option if you have performance concerns and large, complex CSS files to deal with. Server-side preprocessing is an operation that takes place every time you modify the CSS on the server. Usually, you perform the extra step at the end of the build process using the LESS compiler from the command line. Tools like Gulp help to extend the build process with JavaScript-related steps. Another popular tool like Microsoft Web Essentials—a Visual Studio plugin—can be used to add ad hoc menu commands to deal with web resources like CSS and script files.

In ASP.NET MVC, however, there's another possible route. You can integrate the LESS framework with the bundle and minification mechanism. As you'll see in more detail in the next chapter, bundling is the process of rolling up a number of distinct resources into a single, downloadable resource. For example, a bundle might consist of multiple JavaScript or CSS files you bring down to the local machine by making a single HTTP request to an ad-hoc endpoint. Minification is a special transformation applied to a resource. In particular, minification is the removal of all unnecessary characters from a text-based resource in a way that doesn't alter the expected functionality. This means removing comments, white-space characters, new lines and, in general, all characters that are usually added for readability but take up space and don't really serve any functional purpose.

Setting up Bootstrap

You get Bootstrap from NuGet or as a direct download from *http://getbootstrap.com*. In this case, you can more easily take just the portions of the framework you need. It's quite common to have Bootstrap used throughout the entire website. In this case, you link it from the master view, as shown here:

```
<meta name="viewport" content="width=device-width, initial-scale=1.0">
<link rel="stylesheet" src="@Url.Content("~/content/styles/bootstrap.min.css")">
```

The *viewport* meta tag sets the width of the browser viewport to the actual device width and sets the zoom level to Normal. The *link* element just brings in the minified version of the Bootstrap style sheet. If you intend to also use the more advanced features of Bootstrap that require JavaScript, you link the script file as well, along with the jQuery file it depends on:

```
<script type="text/javascript"
        src="@Url.Content("~/content/scripts/jquery-2.1.4.min.js")"></script>
<script type="text/javascript"
        src="@Url.Content("~/content/scripts/bootstrap.min.js")"></script>
```

If you are using the full Bootstrap library, once you link the CSS and script files you're pretty much done. If you're using only portions of the Bootstrap library, you must ensure that all parts you need are correctly linked. Note that some features of the Bootstrap library—for example, tooltips and pop-overs—require some startup JavaScript code that must be added in individual pages.

> **Note** Bootstrap is not supported in the old Internet Explorer compatibility mode. The best way to make sure that your pages are being viewed in the best possible rendering mode under Internet Explorer is to add the following *meta* tag in your pages:
>
> ```
> <meta http-equiv="X-UA-Compatible" content="IE=edge">
> ```
>
> CSS classes of Bootstrap make use of the latest CSS features (such as rounded corners), which might not be available on older browsers. A good example of an older browser partially supported by Bootstrap is Internet Explorer 8.

Putting Bootstrap into perspective

Twitter Bootstrap is close to being a must-have today. The reason for this is that Bootstrap makes it quick and easy to add advanced features to a modern website. Bootstrap has a relatively short learning curve, and many templates based on it are available for free. For any web designer, though, customizing the basic Bootstrap template to get unique artwork is not a big deal.

Whether Bootstrap is the perfect fit for your project depends on how important aesthetics is. If you're building for a customer that demands its own look and feel, Bootstrap might or might not be ideal. In this case, the development team just receives a graphical template and uses it. Bootstrap, on the other hand, is perfect for quick projects where aesthetics are important but not fundamental.

Put another way, Bootstrap is a great achievement, but it doesn't remove the need for great design. At the same time, it doesn't remove the need for a great user experience defined on a per-device basis. It's easy to find websites that offer free or paid templates based on Bootstrap. If you limit yourself to using the styles of the default Bootstrap library—with no changes to the CSS or LESS source code—the risk is that all sites might end up looking the same.

Deciding whether or not to use Bootstrap is an architectural decision that must be made early in the project and is a decision that's hard to change later. It's quite problematic, though not impossible, to add Bootstrap to or remove it from ongoing projects. Finally, consider that the full Bootstrap library is about 100 KB of CSS plus 30 KB of script. It's not a huge resource, but it's not a lightweight resource, either—especially for smaller devices working over potentially slower connections.

One of the key reasons for the rapid adoption of Bootstrap is the low cost of having pages that can be viewed well from different families of devices.

Responsive layouts

All websites these days are expected to be at least responsive to changes in the width of the host screen. As a member of a development team, you can achieve this functionality in two main ways. You can just order an HTML-responsive template from a vendor, stick to that, and keep the implementation details transparent, or you can undertake in-house development of the template.

In the latter case, which framework would you use? Bootstrap is probably the first framework one should consider, but it's not the only one. Other equally popular and effective responsive frameworks are Foundation, Skeleton, and Gumby. Any approach to learning Bootstrap starts with the services it provides to give HTML views a responsive layout.

The grid system

Bootstrap comes with a flexible grid system that splits the available horizontal space into 12 equally sized physical columns. Bootstrap offers predefined CSS classes for you to lay out templates as you wish by creating logical columns. Put another way, Bootstrap gives you a way to space your template columns through a measurement system that ranges from 1 unit to 12 units. The actual size of Bootstrap units depends on the actual screen size of the device.

The screen size is actually the *viewport*—the visible area of content. On mobile devices, the device screen and viewport match because devices typically do not support resizable windows. On desktop computers, conversely, you can have a resized window that takes less than the maximum available space. In this case, Bootstrap considers the viewport—namely, the available rendering space.

Overall template

Any Bootstrap content that intends to be responsive to changes in screen size is based on a matrix of rows and columns. The overall container—the *matrix*—is a DIV element styled as *container*. (See Figure 9-1.)

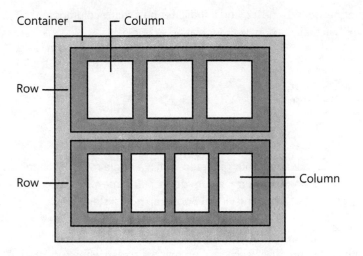

FIGURE 9-1 Schema of a fluid grid in Bootstrap

Containers and rows

The outermost container takes care of any necessary alignment and is also responsible for padding. If you don't explicitly define a row, just one full-height row is assumed. Any user-interface content is placed within columns. Note that only columns are allowed to be immediate children of rows. Any content in Bootstrap is usually laid out according to the following schema:

```
container > row > column
```

Each of the words in the preceding line of code refers to a Bootstrap class name you typically apply to a DIV element. In particular, *container* manages the width of the page and padding. The *row* style ensures that the content is placed within the same row and multiple rows are stacked up vertically. Without a row element in your code, any content within the container will flow horizontally and wrap to the next line when the end of the screen is reached.

Finally, the *column* element identifies monolithic blocks of content within a row. Bootstrap defines several actual classes for columns. To define a column in a row, you use class names according to the following pattern: *col-XX-N*. In the pattern, *XX* stands for the prefix of the device family and can be any of the values in Table 9-1. As you'll see in a moment, each of the XX codes is bound to a specific width in pixels, known as a *breakpoint*.

TABLE 9-1 Bootstrap codes for devices

Code	Generic screen size
XS	Extra small devices
SM	Small devices
MD	Medium devices
LG	Large devices

The *N* in the template is a number between 1 and 12, and it indicates how many columns in the virtual grid the column of content is actually taking. Let's look at an example:

```
<div class="container">
  <div class="row">
    <div class="col-xs-6 col-md-4"> First </div>
    <div class="col-xs-6 col-md-4"> Second </div>
    <div class="col-xs-6 col-md-4"> Third </div>
  </div>
</div>
```

In this case, you want to have a three-column layout rendered within a single row. All columns will be equally sized. All columns display in a single row on medium devices. The *col-md-4* style makes each column as wide as four columns (out of 12) in the virtual Bootstrap grid system.

What about smaller and larger devices?

On XS devices, the three columns of content will each take up half the screen when rendered. As you might have guessed, three layout columns can't fit in the screen if each one has to take up half of it. The third column in this case will overflow onto the following line. The same will happen on SM devices. On LG devices, on the other hand, the rules are set by MD styles.

The bottom line is that each column in a fluid row can be styled for width using multidevice attributes. Those attributes always hold for larger devices until more specific settings are entered. In light of this, if you don't need to distinguish layouts on a per-device basis, the best you can do is always use the XS styles. The sum of *N*s in the column styles should always be at most 12. If it's larger than that, any column beyond the twelfth one will overflow to the next line.

Container and fluid containers

So far, we've considered only the *container* class for DIV elements. There's also a slight variation of it you might want to consider in some cases: the *container-fluid* class. The plain container has a fixed width for each breakpoint, and the viewport width changes only when the user crosses a breakpoint while resizing the browser.

A fluid container, on the other hand, takes up the full width of the parent, typically 100 percent of the available browser viewport. The viewport width is recalculated and updated for each resize. When a fluid container is used, the user experience is smoother, but using a fluid container mostly makes sense for desktop devices.

Screen-based rendering

Why should you use multiple column settings? The answer to that mostly depends on the actual content you have to show. With reference to the previous example, a three-column layout might be fine to have on medium-sized devices, but columns might to be too rich in content to render on a third of a smaller screen. This is why I added *col-xs-6* to the DIV style. The net effect is that Bootstrap will change the final behavior depending on the actual size of the screen.

You'll have a three-column layout on medium and large devices and only two columns per row on small and extra small devices. The third column will wrap to the next line on small and extra small devices. If this is not what you want, you can consider hiding the third column on small and extra small devices. Let's see how.

Virtual measurement and actual screen sizes

The entire grid system and the device families in Bootstrap are based on *breakpoints*, as shown in Table 9-2. As you can see, each screen code corresponds to a breakpoint that identifies the intended width for extra small, small, medium, and large devices.

TABLE 9-2 Codes to use for breakpoints

Code	Breakpoint in pixels	Type of device
XS	< 768	Smartphones
SM	< 992	Tablets
MD	< 1200	Desktops
LG	> 1200	Large desktops

If no *col-xx-n* style is specified, an XS screen is assumed. A common reaction to these coded categories is that Bootstrap doesn't let you easily handle the very small devices listed here as 768 pixels or less in width. Old devices fall in this range, and they might deserve more specific treatment that's different from larger devices that have a width larger than 768 pixels.

To monitor how Bootstrap changes the page layout, you can use the following script code. Just add it to a webpage and go:

```
<script type="text/javascript">
    updateSize();
    $(window).resize(function() {
        updateSize();
    });

    function currentBootstrapScreenClass() {
        var screen = "LG";
        var width = $(window).width();
        if (width <= 768)
            screen = "XS";
        else if (width <= 992)
            screen = "SM";
        else if (width <= 1200)
            screen = "MD";
        return screen;
    }

    function updateSize() {
        var info = currentBootstrapScreenClass();
        $('#currentScreenWidth').text($(window).width() + "px");
        $('#currentViewport').text(info);
    }
</script>
```

Obviously, the webpage must have some elements with matching IDs:

```
<span id="currentScreenWidth"></span>
<span id="currentViewport"></span>
```

Figure 9-2 shows an example.

FIGURE 9-2 Showing the link between screen size and Bootstrap classes

The *col-xx-n* classes are the primary tool Bootstrap provides for adapting the layout of the page to the size of the screen. More powerful tools also exist to hide and nest columns only at specific screen sizes.

Multiresolution views

As mentioned, you can assign multiple settings to containers and rows as far as the columnar layout is concerned. Let's look at an interesting example:

```
<div class="container">
    <div class="row">
        <div class="col-xs-6 col-md-4"> Column #1 <br /> Column #1 <br /></div>
        <div class="col-xs-6 col-md-4"> Column #2 </div>
        <div class="col-md-4"> Column #3 </div>
    </div>
</div>
```

The first column takes up half the space in XS and SM modes and one-third in MD and LG modes. However, the content of the first column contains some BR elements, which make the column taller than other columns. In MD and LG, the display is exactly what one expects—three columns in a row. But in XS and SM, where is the third column going to show? Have a look at Figure 9-3.

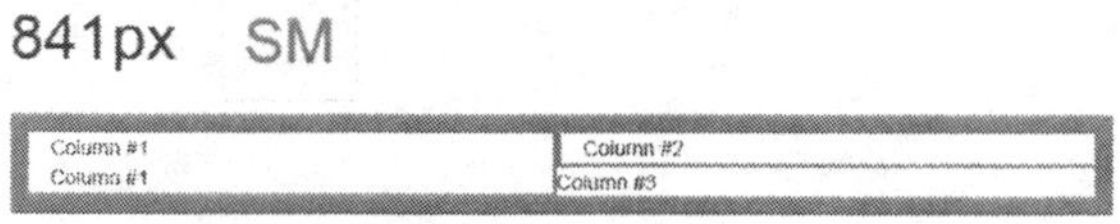

FIGURE 9-3 The third column floats to the immediate left of the row, taking up any available space.

In XS and SM mode, the first two columns take up the entire screen because of their *col-xs-6* class. Subsequently, the third column flows to the next line. However, in this particular example, the first column is taller than the others and this would leave some space to the right. Bootstrap reuses that screen real estate to fit the column that wraps to the next line.

Generally, whenever you use a *col-xx-n* class, you are actually playing with the CSS *float* attribute set to *left* (or *right*) and telling the browser to find the leftmost (or rightmost) available space to fit a given element. Note that to align to the right, you just add the *pull-right* class to the desired elements.

Size-specific classes

What if you want to force the third column to go on the next line but be leftmost? You have to explicitly stop the default alignment and restore the block nature of DIV elements. In plain CSS, you achieve this by using an empty DIV with the *clear:both* attribute. The equivalent in Bootstrap is the *clearfix* class:

```
<div class="clearfix"></div>
```

Figure 9-4 shows what you get if you blindly use the *clearfix* class to force the third row to the start of the next line.

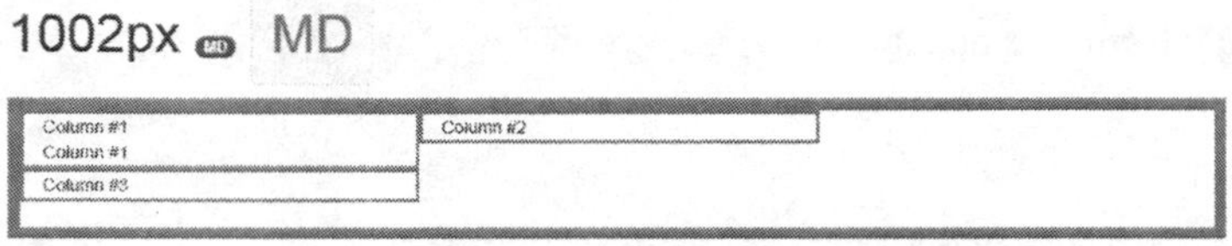

FIGURE 9-4 The third column now starts at the very beginning of the next line.

If you resize the browser window to be in XS or SM mode, all works well. However, Figure 9-4 just shows what happens in MD and LG mode. As you can see, the use of the *clearfix* class leaves empty space to the right where the third column would nicely fit. Ideally, you might want to clear the floating of DIV elements, but only for XS and SM modes.

In Bootstrap, you have the *visible-xx* and *hidden-xx* classes just for this purpose:

```
<div class="clearfix visible-xs"></div>
```

The effect now is just what you want. The DIV with the *clearfix* class is now emitted only on XS and SM screens. Analogously, you can hide elements and entire rows using the *hidden-xx* class.

> **Note** The *hidden-xx* classes alone are a formidable tool that Bootstrap offers to let you create ad hoc, responsive web templates that adjust content as the user resizes the viewport or when the same content is viewed on smaller full-screen devices. As I'll discuss in a lot more detail in Chapter 15, though, Responsive Web Design comes at the cost of hiding unwanted content. The effect is great for the user but not necessarily for the application, especially when RWD is used on mobile devices.

Flexible rendering

Let's briefly look at a concrete example of using the *hidden-xx* classes. Imagine you have a login form with a lot of introductory text and a picture to surround the classic user/password form:

```
<div class="container">
    <h1 class="hidden-xs">WELCOME to CONTOSO Industries</h1>
    <h4 class="visible-xs">WELCOME to CONTOSO</h4>
    <div class="col-md-4 hidden-xs hidden-sm">
        <div class="center">
            <img src="~/Content/Images/contoso.png" />
        </div>
    </div>
</div>
```

Figure 9-5 presents the login form as it appears on an LG screen.

FIGURE 9-5 A flexible login form displayed in MD and LG modes

The H1 element is displayed only on SM and larger devices. On XS devices, instead, the H1 element is replaced with a smaller H4 element. The image, then, is displayed only on MD and LG screens. You see the difference as you resize the browser window.

Offsetting and pulling columns

The Bootstrap grid system also supports nesting of columns. All you have to do is embed a child row within a column. Beyond that point, everything proceeds as usual according to the rules discussed so far. The offsetting of columns is supported too. It happens through the *col-XX-offset-N* set of classes. For example, *col-md-offset-2* will skip the next two grid columns on MD and larger devices.

In general, columns are rendered in the order they appear in the HTML source. However, *col-XX-pull-N* and *col-XX-push-N* classes can be used to alter the natural order of columns by pushing forward or pulling back columns. This is sometimes useful to modify existing pages in production. If you're still in development, in fact, you can more easily move columns around in the source code and render them in the natural order of definition.

> **Note** When you use Bootstrap, it's assumed that you stick to the four predefined visual breakpoints of XS, SM, MD, and LG. Those breakpoints are defined in the source CSS file you link from your pages, and they don't need to be redefined. If you want to make changes, you can just edit your own copy of the CSS file.

Taxonomy of today's web elements

Bootstrap is far too large a library to be summarized effectively in a single book chapter. I definitely invite you to bookmark the *getbootstrap.com* link in your favorite browser to gain quick access to online documentation. Overall, there are two ways to work with the library. One way is by using plain, single HTML elements (for example, buttons and anchors) and just styling them differently. The other way is by creating ad hoc HTML chunks that a predefined combination of Bootstrap CSS and script code can turn into a completely different and functional piece of the user interface.

All in all, Bootstrap contributes to defining the taxonomy of modern web user-interface elements, including basic elements such as input fields and buttons, and also more sophisticated components such as navigation bars, drop-downs, tab strips, and popovers. Finally, some extensions have been created to the core Bootstrap library that can hardly be ignored these days. Two of them are the autocompletion library called *typeahead* and the date-picker component.

Restyling basic HTML elements

Let's get into the nitty-gritty details of Bootstrap HTML programming by exploring the ad hoc styles available to characterize input fields, buttons, navigation bars, and text elements.

Input fields

Input fields are typically used within HTML forms. I said "typically" because some modern web applications tend to post content to a remote endpoint via JavaScript, which doesn't strictly require the use of an HTML form. If you decide to serialize content to post yourself, you don't strictly need to have an HTML form to gather content. However, whether you post via the browser or programmatically, HTML forms are the most common container of input fields.

Here's a typical input form in Bootstrap, for a login page:

```
<form class="form-inline" method="post"
    action="@Url.Action("login", "account")">
  <div class="form-group">
      <div class="input-group">
          <label for="username">User name</label>
          <div class="input-group-addon">
             <span class="glyphicon glyphicon-user"></span>
          </div>
          <input type="text" class="form-control" id="username" name="username"
                 maxlength="30" placeholder="User name">
      </div>
  </div>
  <div class="form-group">
      <div class="input-group">
          <label for="password">Password</label>
          <div class="input-group-addon">
             <span class="glyphicon glyphicon-lock"></span>
          </div>
          <input type="password" class="form-control" id="password" name="password"
                 maxlength="30" placeholder="Password">
      </div>
  </div>
  ...
</form>
```

The HTML form can take two classes: *form-inline* or *form-horizontal*. As the names suggest, both tend to instruct the library to optimize the rendering of child input elements on just one line (as shown in Figure 9-5) or on multiple horizontal lines where labels and input fields are laid out vertically.

A Bootstrap HTML form is made of multiple groups. Each group typically consists of a label and an input field—which can be *text*, *date*, *password*, *checkbox*, *hidden*, and the like. Input elements should be decorated with the *form-control* class and sized using the *input-lg* or *input-sm* classes:

```
<input type="password" class="form-control input-lg" id="password">
```

All other attributes you can have on input fields—such as *maxlength*, *placeholder*, *id*, *name*, and *value*—are used and processed as usual.

An interesting feature you have in Bootstrap is input add-ons. An input add-on is the combination of input fields with buttons, static text, or both. All elements in a single input group are treated by Bootstrap as segments of the same HTML element, as shown in Figure 9-6.

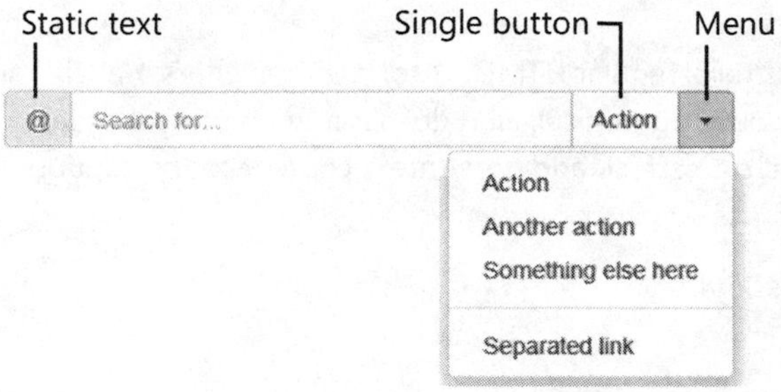

FIGURE 9-6 A Bootstrap input group with add-ons

Here's the overall markup you need to have for Bootstrap to produce the artifact shown in Figure 9-6:

```
<div class="input-group input-group-lg">
  <span class="input-group-addon">@</span>
  <input type="text" class="form-control" placeholder="Search for...">
  <span class="input-group-btn">
     <button class="btn btn-default" type="button">Action</button>
  </span>
  <div class="input-group-btn">
     <button type="button" class="btn btn-default dropdown-toggle" data-toggle="dropdown">
       <span class="caret"></span>
     </button>
     <ul class="dropdown-menu">
         <li><a href="#">Action</a></li>
         ...
     </ul>
  </div>
</div>
```

You use the class *input-group-addon* to create a text placeholder and the class *input-group-btn* to add buttons or menus to an input field. Applied to a SPAN element, the *caret* class renders the classic downward triangle that indicates more content. The UL element defines the list of drop-down items. The caret button is styled with *dropdown-toggle* to indicate it has content to show on demand. Finally, the *data-toggle* class indicates the modality of the content display. In this case, it's a drop-down display.

> **Important** You still can use plain input fields, buttons, and HTML elements in a page that is subject to the action of Bootstrap. As long as you don't add Bootstrap-specific classes to elements, Bootstrap doesn't interfere with the browser rendering. However, the overall graphical effect might clash with that of other parts of the page or other pages in the application and make the user unhappy overall. If you choose Bootstrap, it should be permanently in all views you're going to have.

Buttons

In Bootstrap, the class *btn* turns submit buttons, regular HTML buttons, and anchors into clickable square areas. The effect of the class *btn* is purely graphical; all it does is add padding, borders, rounded corners, and colors. As a pleasant side effect, adding nontext content to the caption of a button couldn't be easier.

Here's the simplest ways to use the class *btn*:

```
<button class="btn">
   Log in
</button>
<a href="#" class="btn" role="button">
   ...
</a>
```

The class *btn* comes with a few other helper classes that characterize the button in terms of size and colors. By default, a Bootstrap button takes the space it needs to render the assigned content plus regular padding. Classes like *btn-xs* and *btn-lg* just remove or add some extra padding from the default *btn*. As for colors, *btn-primary*, *btn-danger*, *btn-alert*, *btn-success*, and *btn-info* style buttons with different colors to indicate the relevance of the operation being achieved through the button. From a developer perspective, it's a quick and easy way to give a more consistent design to a page.

Here's a common way of defining a Bootstrap button. (See Figure 9-7.)

```
<button class="btn">
   <span class="glyphicon glyphicon-ok"></span>
   Log in
</button>
```

FIGURE 9-7 A sample Bootstrap button

As you can see, mixing small pictures and text in the caption of a button couldn't be easier. With Bootstrap buttons, you often use *glyphicons*, a special embedded font that comes with the library that renders icons and very small clip art. If you don't use native Bootstrap icons, you can add any of the numerous icon libraries currently available. One of the most popular icon libraries is FontAwesome, which you can read more about at *http://fontawesome.io*. Once you have FontAwesome on board, you can rewrite the login button as shown here:

```
<button class="btn">
   <i class="fa fa-lg fa-ok"></i>
   Log in
</button>
```

Grouping buttons

More often than not, a webpage needs to display several buttons that are somewhat related. You can certainly treat buttons individually and style them as you like most. However, a few years ago the iOS user interface introduced the concept of *segmented buttons*; now segmented buttons are, if not a must, a feature that's desirable to have. A segmented button is essentially a group of buttons acting individually but rendered as a single strip of buttons. The nicest effect is that the first and last buttons of the strip have rounded corners, whereas the middle buttons are fully squared. In Bootstrap, you use the following HTML-based markup:

```
<div class="btn-group">
  <button type="button" class="btn btn-success">Agree</button>
  <button type="button" class="btn btn-default">Not sure</button>
  <button type="button" class="btn btn-danger">Disagree</button>
</div>
```

Each button will have its own click handler added either explicitly through the *onclick* attribute or unobtrusively via jQuery. To have a button group, all you need to do is wrap the list of buttons with a DIV element styled as *btn-group*.

The size of buttons in the group can be controlled with an additional class: *btn-group-lg* or *btn-group-xs*. By default, buttons are stacked horizontally. To stack them vertically, you just add the *btn-group-vertical* class to group buttons together. Multiple groups can be placed side by side by wrapping them in a button toolbar container:

```
<div>
  <div class="btn-group">...</div>
  <div class="btn-group">...</div>
  <div class="btn-group">...</div>
</div>
```

From looking at Figure 9-6, you probably can guess that Bootstrap buttons can be used to implement drop-down menus as well. Here's how you accomplish that:

```
<div class="btn-group">
  <button type="button" class="btn btn-default">One</button>
  <button type="button" class="btn btn-default">Two</button>
  <div class="btn-group">
    <button type="button" class="btn dropdown-toggle" data-toggle="dropdown">
      Numbers
      <span class="caret"></span>
    </button>
    <ul class="dropdown-menu">
      <li><a href="#">1</a></li>
      <li><a href="#">2</a></li>
      <li><a href="#">3</a></li>
    </ul>
  </div>
</div>
```

The first two items in the group are plains buttons. Next, a nested, drop-down group follows. The button group is made of a button with an attached drop-down menu. Interestingly, the button features a *caret* segment that visually delivers the message that there are more options to see. By adding the *dropup* class to the button group that wraps up the list, you can have the list display upward.

> **Important** When you look at drop-down button lists in Bootstrap, you might think of two common elements of user interfaces: drop-down menus and drop-down lists. Button groups are plain drop-down menus. A drop-down list—like the artifact you obtain with SELECT/OPTION elements in plain HTML—is a slightly different thing. For selection, Bootstrap has no built-in facilities. This is an issue because you might end up having SELECT elements in a form with a clearly different style than other visual elements. What makes SELECT different from a plain menu is it keeps track of the selected item and shows that to users and programs.

Option buttons

A common element in many user interfaces is option buttons. It's a list of mutually exclusive buttons that work together: only one can be selected at a time and selecting a new one automatically removes the selection from the current button. HTML provides an ad hoc type of input element for implementing option buttons. With Bootstrap, you can add a nicer user interface by mixing together native HTML input option buttons and grouped buttons.

Here's how to arrange an option button list to select the gender in a user-profile editor:

```
<div class="btn-group" data-toggle="buttons">
    <label class="btn btn-primary @active1">
      <input type="radio" id="gender" name="gender" value="X" @checked1>
      Don't show
    </label>
    <label class="btn btn-primary @active2">
            <input type="radio" id="gender" name="gender" value="M" @checked2>
            Male
        </label>
        <label class="btn btn-primary @active3">
            <input type="radio" id="gender" name="gender" value="F" @checked3>
            Female
        </label>
    </div>
```

Figure 9-8 shows the result. Note that, by design, buttons are not equally sized. You can obtain that through the addition of some extra customized styles.

FIGURE 9-8 Bootstrap option buttons

As mentioned, Bootstrap grouped buttons are plain buttons rendered side by side. Option buttons, instead, require a bit of logic. You need both logic and grouped buttons to have option buttons styled the Bootstrap way. In the code snippet just shown, you see two groups of Razor variables used. Ideally, the markup of Figure 9-8 is preceded by the following code:

```
@{
    var active1 = "";
    var active2 = "active";
    var active3 = "";

    var checked1 = "";
    var checked2 = "checked";
    var checked3 = "";
}
```

The variables *active1*, *active2*, and *active3* serve the purpose of adding the attribute *active* to the *label* element that represents the current selection. The *active* attribute has a visual effect and instructs Bootstrap to switch the style of the button to make it look like it's selected. At the same time, you should consider that an option button is an official HTML input element. An option button list is typically hosted in an HTML form and, at some point, the content of the form is posted to the server for further work. Only the option button with the *checked* attribute is uploaded, though. The variables *checked1*, *checked2*, and *checked3* track the checked status of individual buttons and guarantee the proper button is shown to be checked or active when the page is rendered into the browser.

Navigation bars

Most websites feature a navigation bar, typically at the top of the pages. Bootstrap offers some facilities to add a header to webpages. Additionally, Bootstrap navigation bars are flexible enough to collapse and expand as the available viewport width changes. In smaller views, the navigation bar automatically collapses to a button and requires JavaScript support to be expanded. If for some reason JavaScript is disabled, a Bootstrap navigation bar that gets collapsed cannot be expanded anymore.

The navigation bar is a plain HTML container, mostly a DIV element. However, it's recommended that you wrap the header in a NAV element:

```
<div role="navigation">
   ...
</div>

<nav class="navbar navbar-default">
   ...
</nav>
```

The *role* attribute customizes the generic DIV element to declare it as a navigational component for screen readers. Here's a possible structure for a navigation bar, with two lists of links and a search bar:

```
<nav class="navbar navbar-default">
  <div class="container-fluid">
    <div class="navbar-header">
      <button type="button"
              class="navbar-toggle collapsed"
              data-toggle="collapse"
              data-target="#content">
        <span class="sr-only">More</span>
        <span class="icon-bar"></span>
        <span class="icon-bar"></span>
        <span class="icon-bar"></span>
      </button>
      <a class="navbar-brand" href="#">Home</a>
    </div>
    <div class="collapse navbar-collapse" id="content">
      <ul class="nav navbar-nav">
        <li> <a href=""> Button #1 </a> </li>
        ...
      </ul>

      <form class="navbar-form navbar-left">
        <div class="form-group">
          <input type="text" class="form-control" placeholder="Search for...">
        </div>
        <button type="submit" class="btn btn-primary">Find</button>
      </form>
      <ul class="nav navbar-nav navbar-right ">
        <li class="dropdown">
          <a href="#" class="dropdown-toggle" data-toggle="dropdown">
            I want to <span class="caret"></span>
          </a>
          <ul class="dropdown-menu">
            <li><a href="#">Create a record</a></li>
            ...
          </ul>
        </li>
      </ul>
    </div>
  </div>
</nav>
```

A common navigation bar is made of two parts—the collapse/expand infrastructure and the actual content that can be hidden on smaller viewports:

```
<nav class="navbar navbar-default">
  <div class="container-fluid">
    <div class="navbar-header">
      <!-- Collapse/Expand button to toggle on smaller viewports -->
    </div>

    <div class="collapse navbar-collapse" id="content">
```

```
        <!-- Actual content being collapsed on smaller viewports -->
      </div>
  </div>
</nav>
```

The content area is identified with a unique ID (in the example, the ID is *content*). The collapsible area is linked to the collapse/expand infrastructure through the *data-target* attribute of the clickable button that does the toggling. The triple SPAN elements shown next render the canonical three horizontal bars of such collapse/expand buttons:

```
<div class="navbar-header">
    <button type="button"
            class="navbar-toggle collapsed"
            data-toggle="collapse"
            data-target="#content">
      <span class="sr-only">More</span>
      <span class="icon-bar"></span>
      <span class="icon-bar"></span>
      <span class="icon-bar"></span>
    </button>
</div>
```

The content area can contain whatever you like, most notably quick-access buttons, drop-down buttons, and search forms. All buttons are often rendered as anchors embedded in UL/LI elements.

A navigation bar can be fixed to the top of the page by adding the *navbar-fixed-top* class to the NAV element. Note that when you intend to fix the header to the top, you must also pad the body of the page accordingly. In other words, you must move down any visible content of the body by the same amount of pixels that bar takes. If you don't do so, that content would be covered by the absolute positioning of the navigation bar:

```
body { padding-top: 100px; }
```

You might not need it to happen as often as with top alignment, but you can also stick the navigation bar to the bottom of the page. In this case, you just add the *navbar-fixed-bottom* class to the NAV element.

Text elements

Bootstrap provides three artifacts to render structured text: panels, alerts, and wells. A panel is the combination of three elements: the title, body, and footer. Each element is styled accordingly. Here's a sample panel. Note that title and footer elements are optional:

```
<div class="panel panel-info">
  <div class="panel-heading">
    <span class="panel-title">Title</span>
  </div>
  <div class="panel-body">
    Any content goes here
  </div>
```

```
     <div class="panel-footer">
        Footer
     </div>
  </div>
</div>
```

The panel can be styled using the same meta classes I identified for buttons: *panel-default*, *panel-primary*, *panel-info*, *panel-danger*, *panel-warning*, and the like. You can also create your own meta classes as well.

An alert is a plain DIV element with some HTML content, except that it enjoys some predefined styles, configured as shown here:

```
<div class="alert alert-success" role="alert">
   Any content goes here
</div>
```

Also, with alerts you can use Bootstrap meta classes for context (success, warning, danger, info, and similar). In Bootstrap pages, alerts are often used to display messages. An interesting feature is that alerts can be dismissible:

```
<div class="alert alert-warning alert-dismissible" role="alert" id="alert-id">
  <button type="button" class="close" data-dismiss="alert" aria-label="Close">
      <span>&times;</span>
  </button>
  <strong>Warning!</strong> This is message for you.
</div>
```

In this case, the alert is a bit larger and in the top-right corner encompasses a closing button. By clicking there, the user dismisses the DIV and the page content shifts up. Another nice feature you can add is a timer that slides the alert up after a given number of milliseconds:

```
window.setTimeout(function () {
   $("#alert-id").slideUp();
}, 4000);
```

> **Note** If you need to have links in alerts, you can have them properly styled in sync with the context information of the parent alert by simply adding the *alert-link* class to the anchor.

Finally, wells are plain text surrounded by a border and some padding. It's a very quick and easy way to present some text in an emphasized way:

```
<div class="well">
   ...
</div>
```

With wells, also, you can use sizing classes such as *well-lg* and *well-xs*.

Restyling list HTML elements

Call it an artificial need created by the first iOS user-interface architects, but scrollable lists segmented in groups of related items spread through the realm of devices and conquered the entire web in just a few years. jQuery Mobile first realized the value of segmented and scrollable lists and provided ad hoc components to build them. Today, Bootstrap also offers ad hoc CSS classes to render plain unordered HTML lists and plain lists of anchor tags into nice-looking blocks that mimic the iOS lists.

Lists

In a Bootstrap-based page, a plain sequence of list items is automatically turned into a bordered table. Let's consider the following markup:

```
<ul class="list-group">
  <li class="list-group-item">First item</li>
  <li class="list-group-item">Second item</li>
  <li class="list-group-item">Third item</li>
  <li class="list-group-item">Fourth item</li>
  <li class="list-group-item">Fifth item</li>
</ul>
```

The *list-group* class is responsible for drawing the border all around the content. The *list-group-item* class, instead, takes care of spacing and fonts. All list items are rendered as plain text. The output of a *list-group* class is similar to a good-old list box, where a list of options is presented and one or more items can be rendered as selected. To mark a list item as selected, you add the *active* CSS class. You can add the class to as many list items as you wish.

A plain list group is essentially a static list that has no user interaction. An interesting variation of list groups is linked list groups. The key difference is that items in a linked list are anchors instead of plain text:

```
<li class="list-group-item">
  <a href="...">First item</a>
</li>
```

To prevent one or more items from being clickable, you can use a SPAN element instead of the A element. Here's an example:

```
<div class="list-group">
  <span class="list-group-item list-header">Just Items</span>
  <a href="..." class="list-group-item">First item</a>
  <a href="..." class="list-group-item active">Second item</a>
</div>
```

You can use nonclickable elements to create headers along the list. Headers identify segments within the list box in much the same way iOS allows you to do. In line with the iOS user interface, badges can be used to make the text in each item richer and nicer for the user. A *badge* is small text in a colorful balloon that indicates the count of something that is relevant for the page, such as messages in the inbox. To obtain this effect, you just mark a SPAN element with the *badge* class, as shown here:

```
<a href="..." class="list-group-item">
   First item <span class="badge">22</span>
</a>
```

The content of any A element you use in lists can be customized at will. It can be plain text as well as HTML markup and can contain images or media as well:

```
<a href="#" class="list-group-item">
    <p class="list-group-item-text">Some small text</p>
    <h4 class="list-group-item-heading">Some bigger text here</h4>
</a>
```

To achieve a more uniform graphical effect ,you can use some predefined styles such as *list-group-item-text* and *list-group-item-heading*. However, whether or not to use them is up to you because it's purely a matter of aesthetics.

Media objects

Another common feature of most webpages is a list of mixed markup made of text and media content, mostly images. Aligning text and images is usually boring. Bootstrap attempts to make it a far smoother process with a few classes:

```
<div class="media">
  <div class="media-left">
    <a href="#">
      <img class="media-object" src="..." alt="...">
    </a>
  </div>
  <div class="media-body">
    <h4 class="media-heading">Title of the image</h4>
    <span>Description of the image</span>
  </div>
</div>
```

The *media-left* class sticks the image to the left edge of the container. You can use the *media-right* class to stick the image to the right. If you intend to do so, though, you should place the rightmost DIV after the media body DIV in the markup. Media content, by default, is top aligned. You can change the alignment to the middle or bottom by adding *media-middle* or *media-bottom* classes to the image DIV.

You also can use media content in lists to create a list of items with images and text. You use the *media* class to wrap the list item and the *media-list* class for the entire list. The *media-object* class is placed around the IMG element. The class *media-body*, on the other hand, decorates the text alongside the image or any other media object you might have (for example, video).

Here's an example:

```
<ul class="media-list">
  <li class="media">
    <div class="media-left">
      <a href="#">
        <img class="media-object" src="..." alt="...">
      </a>
    </div>
    <div class="media-body">
      <h4 class="media-heading">Title of the image</h4>
      <span>Description of the image</span>
    </div>
  </li>
  ...
</ul>
```

Note that lists, with or without media content, can be easily embedded in panels too.

The class *thumbnail*, on the other hand, can be used to present related images with or without additional markup. Here's a sample layout that presents four images in medium and large screens and two or three in smaller screens:

```
<div class="row">
  <div class="col-xs-6 col-sm-4 col-md-3">
    <a href="#" class="thumbnail">
      <img src="..." alt="...">
    </a>
    <div class="caption">
        <h3>Thumbnail label</h3>
        ...
    </div>
  </div>
  ...
</div>
```

Tables

For years, many developers used plain HTML tables as a tool to lay out the content of webpages. Today, DIV elements and CSS positioning attributes are more flexibly used for the same purpose. It doesn't mean, however, that HTML tables have become useless. Tables still serve the purpose of presenting tabular data, for example, in the context of data grids.

In Bootstrap, you find a few basic classes to style HTML tables and, in particular, to control padding and row coloring:

```
<table class="table table-condensed">
   <tr> ... </tr>
</table>
```

The *table-condensed* class keeps padding and spacing to an absolute minimum. Additional classes exist for more sophisticated, yet common, effects—such as alternate row coloring and hovering. Note that Bootstrap for tables, as well as for many other HTML artifacts, is purely graphical. This means that you find tools to render elements in a given way, but binding styles with data is up to you. The best way to data-bind styles to actual data is via Razor variables and ad hoc classes or even, if no better way exists, inline styles.

A look at more advanced components

Even though HTML is the official language of the web, and it might even become the common language of mobile applications at some point in the near future, it doesn't offer all the syntactical elements you need to create modern pages. Earlier in the chapter, I covered drop-down menus. As discussed, in Bootstrap you can create drop-down menus by combining buttons and unordered HTML lists of anchors. Not even in HTML5 do you find any native element to set up a drop-down menu. The story is the same for a few other common visual elements—popular in pages but not natively supported by HTML, at least not at an abstraction level that would minimize markup. In this chapter, I'll present how to set up modal dialog boxes, tabs, and custom tooltips in Bootstrap.

Modal dialogs

A modal window is a window that displays on top of everything else and captures the input focus for the time it's up. Underlying elements can regain the input focus only when the modal window is dismissed. An excellent example of a modal window is the message box that browsers display when the code invokes the *window.alert* JavaScript method. More and more pages, though, render a topmost rich DIV element to emphasize messages for the user or as a way to perform tasks without fully refreshing the current page.

All in all, the most common scenario for modal dialog boxes is to implement input forms in the body of the current page. In Chapter 12, "Editing data," I'll return to the topic of modal dialog boxes as a way to implement input forms and touch on the implementation of actions subsequent to posts. In this chapter, instead, I will focus mostly on the steps you need to take to display and populate a modal dialog box in Bootstrap.

A modal dialog is made of two elements: a trigger and content. The content is a plain DIV decorated with some ad hoc attributes that mostly keep it hidden until the trigger fires. The trigger is typically a button or an anchor equipped with a few special attributes.

Here's an example:

```
<button class="btn btn-primary btn-lg"
        data-toggle="modal"
        data-target="#dialogBox">
    Launch modal
</button>
@Html.Partial("pv_rateitemmodal")
```

The *data-toggle* attribute set to *modal* indicates that the button is just used to pop up a modal element. The *data-target* element is the CSS expression that selects the DIV element to pop up. For the trigger to work in the preceding example, the current DOM must be able to find a DOM subtree rooted in an element whose ID is *dialogBox*. The DIV for the modal content can be placed inline in the current page or imported as a partial view through the *Html.Partial* Razor method. The final effect is the same, but using partial views lets you have more, though far simpler, HTML views to maintain.

Here's some sample content for the modal dialog:

```
<div class="modal" id="dialogBox">
    <div class="modal-dialog">
        <div class="modal-content">
            <div class="modal-header">
                <button type="button" class="close" data-dismiss="modal">&times;</button>
                <h4 class="modal-title">Rate the article</h4>
            </div>
            <div class="modal-body">
            </div>
            <div class="modal-footer">
                <button type="button" class="btn btn-default" data-dismiss="modal">Close</button>
                <button type="button" class="btn btn-primary" onclick="...">Vote</button>
            </div>
        </div>
    </div>
</div>
```

A modal dialog results from three levels of nested DIV elements. The outermost DIV is styled with the *modal* class. Here you can add some specific styles for the appearance—for example, the *fade* or *slide* class. Its direct child is styled as *modal-dialog*, and yet another level of DIV is *modal-content*. Within the content DIV, you find a header, body, and footer. The header and footer are optional, but you typically have both and use the header to add a title to the dialog and the close button. The footer, instead, is usually filled with buttons that dismiss the dialog either abruptly or by launching a server-side operation.

In the example, the footer has two buttons: *Close* and *Vote*. Because of the *data-dismiss* attribute, the *Close* button can be used only to close the dialog. The *Vote* button, on the other hand, will typically have some *onclick* handler attached to perform some JavaScript tasks.

Especially if you use the modal dialog to edit records inline, you need a way to initialize the elements of the modal to the actual data to show. If the modal has some fixed content to show, you can put any initialization logic in the Razor view that produces the modal or the containing page. If you have, instead, a list of records and want to show a modal when the user clicks on a given record, initialization must ideally take place on the client grabbing data via JSON. This can be done in JavaScript by hooking up some events that the modal Bootstrap component fires.

Here's an example:

```
$('#dialogBox').on('show.bs.modal', function (e) {
        $.ajax({
            url: "...",
            cache: false
        }).done(function(json) {
            // Update the user interface
            // with downloaded data
        });
    });
```

As soon as the modal component fires the *show.bs.modal* event—just before the content is shown—an Ajax call is made to some URL to download data. Next, the user interface of the dialog is updated with fresh content and then presented to the user.

> **Note** If you're simply looking for an alternative to the system's alert message box that is even more flexible in terms of rendering, you can try *Toastr*. Toastr is a jQuery plugin that displays plain text in a colorful way and offers numerous options as far as positioning and timers are concerned. Here's some code that shows how it works:
>
> ```
> toastr.options.positionClass = "alert-center";
> toastr.success("Isn't this popup much better than a plain alert()?", "Better alert!");
> ```
>
> The *toastr* library offers several display methods in addition to "success," each characterized by a different set of icons and colors. The message can stay on screen until users dismiss it, or it can be associated with a timer. Properties like *showDuration* and *hideDuration* indicate the milliseconds it should take to show and hide the content. Content is typically made of a title and a text message.

Tab strips

Tabs are a collection of views displayed one at a time with a top menu to allow selection. Bootstrap supports a few variations of tabs, including the classic tab strip and navigation pills. The required HTML template is similar.

Let's see classic tab strips first:

```
<div class="tabbable">
  <ul class="nav nav-tabs" id="myTabStrip">
    <li><a class="btn btn-primary" href="#profile" data-toggle="tab">Profile</a></li>
    <li><a class="btn btn-primary" href="#preferences" data-toggle="tab">Preferences</a></li>
    <li><a class="btn btn-primary" href="#friends" data-toggle="tab">Friends</a></li>
  </ul>
</div>
```

A first DIV wrapping a UL element defines the list of clickable tabs. Any time the user clicks any tab, the current content is hidden so that the content related to the clicked tab can be displayed. The *href* attribute of the LI element indicates the path to the child DIV that stores the tab content. The *data-toggle* attribute set to *tab* is also crucial because it instructs the component to act as a tab and hide and show content on demand.

Tab content follows in the same page, one after another. The visibility of these DIVs is automatically managed by the script code that comes with the tab-strip component:

```
<div class="tab-content">
  <div id="profile" class="tab-pane">
    ...
  </div>
  <div id="preferences" class="tab-pane">
    ...
  </div>
  <div id="friends" class="tab-pane">
    ...
  </div>
</div>
```

It's important to specify the *tab-content* and *tab-pane* CSS classes in the content DIV elements for the tabs. The tab strip gets its own styles from Bootstrap defaults. From the outside, you can select the colors of the tabs using button styles such as *btn-primary*, *btn-danger*, and the like. As usual, though, the default Bootstrap styles can be overridden in the application's or single page's scope. The tab that's initially selected is indicated via the *active* class.

An interesting feature you might want to consider is adding a JavaScript call to remove the outline that typically decorates any clickable area after the click. Here's the call you need to add to the LI elements of the tab strip:

```
onclick="this.blur()"
```

A tab strip renders horizontally, one tab after the next. Another slightly different view is navigation pills. In this case, the text of tabs is rendered without borders and a separator and only the selected pill has some padding and different colors. The behavior is the same; it's just the aesthetics are different:

```
<ul class="nav nav-pills" role="tablist">
  <li class="active">
    <a class="btn btn-primary" href="#profile" data-toggle="tab">Profile</a>
  </li>
  <li> ... </li>
  <li> ... </li>
</ul>
```

The pills also can be stacked vertically. You achieve that by adding the style *nav-stacked*.

Tooltips

Tooltips have been available in webpages since the early days of browsers, but they haven't changed since those early days. Native browser tooltips, today as in the 1990s, are plain popover windows of a short line of static text.

You display a tooltip by simply wrapping some plain text in an HTML element (even a plain SPAN element) decorated with the *title* attribute. The tooltip is displayed by the browser, and it's subject to the browser's implementation. There's no way to change that. The advent of jQuery led to the creation of a variety of plugins for implementing nice tooltip effects. The problem for developers became how to choose the best and most appropriate tooltip plugin. Bootstrap authors made a choice themselves and incorporated some features in the library. So today, once you choose Bootstrap, you also find in the package a nice infrastructure for tooltips.

In Bootstrap, a tooltip is any HTML element decorated with the *data-toggle* attribute set to the keyword *tooltip*. Needless to say, the HTML element must also have the *title* attribute to indicate the text to display.

Here's an example:

```
<p>
   This is a message about
   <span data-toggle="tooltip" title="Some extra information">
      something
   </span>
   incorporated in the web page ...
</p>
```

The *data-toggle* attribute set to the keyword *tooltip* does the trick. When the user hovers over the sensitive element, the content is displayed. However, if you just copy the markup into a running Bootstrap page, nothing happens. The reason is that, by design, Bootstrap architects decided to make tooltips an opt-in feature. It means that some script is required to activate custom tooltips. Note that as long as the default *title* attribute is found, the browser displays the built-in user interface for tooltips.

In Bootstrap, the following script code is required to enable tooltips. You might want to run that code in the *ready* event handler for the page:

```
$(document).ready(function () {
    $("[data-toggle=tooltip]").tooltip();
});
```

As you can see, the code doesn't simply enable one particular tooltip. Instead, it extends to cover all tooltip occurrences in the page. The Bootstrap tooltip supports various features you don't find in regular browser tooltips. In the first place, it allows you to add an arrow indicator and place the tooltip at a particular position around the text it refers to. Placement can be top, left, bottom, or right. If you choose "auto" instead it's placed in the most appropriate location according to the framework.

Another interesting feature is HTML content. Basically, Bootstrap allows you to place any HTML content in the *title* attribute. The content, however, will be rendered as HTML only if you set the *html* flag in the tooltip options:

```
$("[data-toggle=tooltip]").tooltip({
    placement: 'auto',
    html: true
});
```

Furthermore, you can use the *trigger* option to specify how you want the tooltip to be triggered. The default configuration displays the tooltip when the mouse hovers over the element and when the element gets the focus. You can change, or just add, the option to trigger it by clicking:

```
$("[data-toggle=tooltip]").tooltip({
    placement: 'auto',
    html: true,
    trigger: 'click focus hover'
});
```

Finally, tooltips can be controlled programmatically via methods and fire events when being displayed or dismissed.

Popovers

Tooltips and popovers are close relatives in spite of having quite different names. *Tooltips* appear as you hover over a given element; *popovers* support a richer set of formatting options and can be triggered in various ways, including when the user hovers over a given HTML element. More generally, popovers are DIV elements that get displayed as a drop-down blocks near an element. What makes popovers particularly interesting is that they can be populated with live data if you add a bit of data-binding logic via JavaScript.

You start by creating a DIV element that has to be hidden initially. Next, you configure the trigger of the popover: it can be a button or a clickable element. This is much like what you do with tooltips. The only difference is that the *data-toggle* attribute must be set to *popover*:

```
<div id="popover-content" class="hidden">
    ...
</div>
```

You then add some script to initialize the popover from the content of a specified DIV element:

```
$("#sensitive").popover({
    html: true,
    title: "More Details",
    placement: 'right',
    trigger: 'click',
    content: function () {
        return $("#popover-content").html();
    }
});
```

In the code snippet, the *#sensitive* path refers to the element that the popover refers to. Basically, the code automatically attaches the content of the DIV element named *popover-content* to the *#sensitive* element so that whenever the item is clicked the popover shows up. The popover is given a default size. You can change that by changing the *.popover* CSS class in the Bootstrap library. The trigger mechanism you select for the popover determines the way the content is dismissed. Options for triggering are the same as for tooltips: *hover*, *click*, and *focus*.

Bootstrap extensions

Bootstrap is a comprehensive CSS and HTML library that defines the taxonomy of modern webpages. However, it doesn't provide built-in components and classes for all common needs of web developers. From my experience with Bootstrap, I identified three key pieces that are currently missing: autocompletion, date picking, and drop-down lists. For the first two, you can use a couple of Bootstrap-based additional frameworks. For drop-down lists, instead, you should create your own custom extension to the Bootstrap library.

Autocompletion

Usability is increasingly important in webpages. One of the most important usability aspects is simplifying data entry and selection, especially when a long list of options is available. For example, instead of presenting users a drop-down list of choices several hundred items long, you can offer a text box and let users type the name of what they want. This is the role of autocompletion.

The *typeahead* component

The best way to achieve autocompletion with Bootstrap is through a separate download known as the *typeahead.js* library. Let's start adding the NuGet package for the latest *typeahead.js* library and see what it takes to arrange a simple search form:

```
<form action="@Url.Action("Query", "Home")" method="post">
    <input type="hidden" id="queryCode" name="queryCode" />
        <input type="text" name="queryString" id="queryString">
        <button id="queryButton" type="submit">Go get it!</button>
</form>
```

Note that to use autocompletion on a webpage for something useful, you also need a complementary hidden field to collect some unique ID for the selected hint. To use the library, you must reference jQuery 1.9.1 or newer and the *typeahead.js* script. The minimal amount of code you need in a view that uses *typeahead.js* is shown here:

```
var hints = new Bloodhound({
    datumTokenizer: Bloodhound.tokenizers.obj.whitespace('value'),
    queryTokenizer: Bloodhound.tokenizers.whitespace,
    remote: "/yourServer/...?query=%QUERY"
});
hints.initialize();
$('#queryText').typeahead(
    null,
    {
        displayKey: 'value',
        source: hints.ttAdapter()
});
```

Although you can bind data from any JavaScript array, autocompletion mostly makes sense to use when data is downloaded from a remote data source. Downloading from a remote source raises a bunch of issues—same-origin browser policy, prefetching, and caching, to name a few. *typeahead.js* comes with a suggestion engine named Bloodhound, which does most of this work for you and does it transparently. If you get the bundle JavaScript file from NuGet, you can just start calling into Bloodhound without worrying about its download and setup.

The *hints* variable in the previous code snippet results from the following, rather standard initialization of Bloodhound:

```
var hints = new Bloodhound({
    datumTokenizer: Bloodhound.tokenizers.obj.whitespace('value'),
    queryTokenizer: Bloodhound.tokenizers.whitespace,
    remote: "/yourServer/...?query=%QUERY"
});

hints.initialize();
```

Note the *remote* attribute. It refers to the server endpoint responsible for returning hints to display in the drop-down list. Also note the syntax %QUERY, which indicates the string in the input field being sent to the server for hints. In other words, %QUERY is a placeholder for whatever text happens to be in the input field. The code snippet assumes that a field named *value* exists in the downloaded data. If that's not the case, you should replace *value* with the name of the downloaded field that you're interested in.

In the *typeahead.js* initialization, you indicate two key pieces of information: the aforementioned collection of hints as managed by Bloodhound, and the display field used to fill the input field. In the code snippet just shown, the display field is *'value'*. By default, *typeahead.js* starts getting hints as soon as a single character is typed. If you want to wait for characters to be in the buffer before autocompletion starts, you add a settings object as the first argument of the plugin:

```
$('#queryString').typeahead(
   {
      minLength: 2,    // Wait for 2 characters to be typed
      limit: 15     // Don't return more than 15 hints
   },
   {
      displayKey: 'value',
      source: hints.ttAdapter()
   }
});
```

When the buffer is full enough to start remote calls, Bloodhound begins to work, downloads JSON data, and adapts it for display. At this point, you have a barely working autocompletion engine that pops up suggestions based on some logic you have on the server. There's a lot more to do, however, before you can use autocompletion effectively in a real page.

The remote endpoint that returns hints to be displayed is a collection of C# classes serialized to JSON. You can package hint data the way you like, but at a minimum the type you use has to contain the following information:

```
public class AutoCompleteItem
{
    public string id { get; set; }
    public string value { get; set; }
    public string label { get; set; }
}
```

The *id* property contains a unique ID that, when posted, is meaningful to the receiving controller. If your hints refer to products that users are finding by name, *id* might just be the product ID. The property *value* is the string content to show in the drop-down list and the text being copied in the input field. The *label* property is optional, and you should look at it as a sort of cargo property for whatever else you might need to have handy on the client side. Most of the time, it can be dropped without pain. Sometimes I use it to carry server-generated HTML formatting for hints.

> **Note** Check out some documentation and examples of how to use *typeahead.js* at the following URL: *http://github.com/twitter/typeahead.js*.

Fixing the CSS

Any sufficiently complex plugin needs a bit of CSS to look nice, and *typeahead.js* is no exception. The plugin comes with its own default user interface, but especially if you use it combination with Bootstrap, you need to apply some fixes to avoid visual wrinkles. Furthermore, you might also want to customize some visual attributes, such as colors and padding.

Table 9-3 lists some CSS classes you might want to experiment with to personalize the look and feel of the *typeahead.js* component.

Table 9-3 List of CSS classes to edit for customizing *typeahead.js*

CSS class	Description
twitter-typeahead	Styles the input field where the user types hints.
tt-hint	Styles the text that represents the delta between what you typed and the first hint. This class is used only when the hint property is set to true. (It is set to false by default.)
tt-dropdown-menu	Styles the drop-down popup where hints are listed.
tt-cursor	Styles highlighted suggestions in the drop-down box.
tt-highlight	Styles the portion of the text that matches the query string.

Figure 9-9 gives you an idea of what you can get out of custom CSS classes.

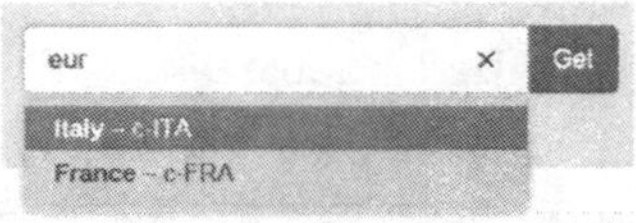

FIGURE 9-9 Bootstrap radio buttons

You can find the full list of common CSS fixes for effectively using *typeahead.js* with Bootstrap in this book's companion code. Note also that *typeahead.js* offers a powerful native mechanism to override critical CSS styles. It's based on the *classNames* setting, as shown here:

```
$('.typeahead').typeahead({
  classNames: {
    input: 'Your-input-class',         // input field
    hint: 'Your-hint-class',        // list item
    highlight: 'Your-highlight-class'    // highlighted list items
  }
});
```

Obviously, strings assigned to *classNames* entries must match available CSS classes of yours.

Adjusting the hint template

In Figure 9-9, the list items use some additional formatting. In particular, the name of the country/region is bold and the actual text displayed results from the combination of multiple data properties. With *typeahead.js*, you need a separate template engine to format list items. A popular template engine is *Handlebars*. You can get it from *http://handlebarsjs.com*. Here's how to use it with *typeahead.js*:

```
$('#queryString').typeahead(
    {
      minLength: 2,
      limit: 15
    },
```

```
    {
        displayKey: 'value',
        templates: {
            suggestion: Handlebars.compile('<p><strong>{{label}}</strong> - {{id}}</p>')
        }
        source: hints.ttAdapter()
    }
});
```

A *Handlebars* expression consists of a property name wrapped in double curly brackets. The template is some HTML text with one or more expressions embedded. In the preceding example, *label* and *id* are expected to be properties of the JSON object that represents the individual hint being displayed.

The code snippet just shown uses both the *displayKey* and *templates* properties. Actually, that's not entirely correct. The *templates* property replaces *displayKey* and sets a custom layout for the content of the hints rendered in the drop-down list.

Note that *typeahead.js* supports several types of templates, as summarized in Table 9-4.

Table 9-4 Templates supported by *typeahead* hints

Template	Description
notFound	The template to use when no hints can be found for the specified query
header	The template to introduce a collection of hints
footer	The template to summarize a collection of hints
suggestion	The template for individual hints

A template can be either a plain HTML string or a precompiled template. If it's a template, it will be passed the JSON object associated with the hint and, with the exception of the *suggestion* template, also the query string. Templates are applied to each dataset defined for the *typeahead.js* component.

> **Note** The use of *Handlebars* is not mandatory. You can use any other template engine you like (for example, *mustache.js*), or you can even write your own template engine in the form of a JavaScript function.

Dealing with multiple datasets

A dataset is a collection of related hints all associated with the query. In many cases, one dataset suffices, but the following code shows how to bind multiple datasets to a given input field:

```
$('#queryString').typeahead(
    {
        minLength: 2,
        limit: 15
    },
    {
        name: 'Dataset #1',
```

```
        displayKey: 'value',
        templates: {
            suggestion: Handlebars.compile('<p><strong>{{label}}</strong> - {{id}}</p>')
        }
        source: hints.ttAdapter()
    },
    {
        name: 'Dataset #2',
        displayKey: 'value',
        source: ...
    },
    {
        name: 'Dataset #3',
        displayKey: 'value',
        limit: 10,
        source: ...
    }
};
```

In a nutshell, when you initialize the *typeahead.js* component, you first pass the general settings and then the list of all datasets. Each dataset has a name, a display property, or a set of templates and even a maximum number of hints. Each dataset automatically attempts to refresh its collection of hints when the user types new text in the input field.

> **Tip** When the input field is empty, users typically see no suggestions. In some cases, though, it might be advisable to provide some default suggestions, even for empty queries. You can do that by setting the *minLength* option to 0 and having, at the same time, the remote endpoint return suggestions for empty queries.

Handling the *Selected* event

When the number of items to choose from is in the hundreds, any classic drop-down list is slow. Therefore, if you plan to use the autocomplete input field to select a specific value—say, the name of a product or a customer—a plain *typeahead.js* plugin is not enough. Some additional script code is required that binds to the *selected* event of the plugin and stores the user selection for later use.

The following code saves the selection to a hidden field (the *#queryCode* path) and tracks that a selection has been made using a local variable:

```
<script type="text/javascript">
  var typeaheadItemSelected = false;
  $('#queryString').on('typeahead:selected', function (e, datum) {
      $("#queryCode").val(datum.id);
      typeaheadItemSelected = true;
  });
</script>
```

The major benefit of an autocompletion input is that users can type some intelligible text and the system understands and associates that with a unique code, such as a product ID. The selected code must be stored safely to be used in future uploads. Most of the time, in fact, you need to use an autocomplete text box as a specialized form of a drop-down list with way too many items.

In the *selected* event handler, you retrieve the ID information from the *datum* object and store it safely in a hidden field. When the form that the autocompletion input fields belong to is posted, the selected ID is posted as well. The layout of the *datum* object—namely, the data item being selected from the drop-down list—depends on the schema of the data you receive from the server side.

Displaying text in the input field

What about the text being displayed in the input field? Most of the time, just setting the *displayKey* property in the configuration of the *typeahead.js* component does the trick. At any rate, though, you can set any value in the input field programmatically:

```
$("#queryString").val(datum.label);
```

In some cases, the autocompletion text box is the only element in an HTML form. This means that you might want to process any selected data as soon as the data is selected. By adding the following line to the *typeahead.js*'s *selected* event handler, you simulate a click on the submit button of the form:

```
$("#queryButton").click();
```

Sometimes users start typing in the input field and then stop without making any selection. When they return back and the input field regains the focus, what should you do? That mostly depends on the intended behavior of the input field. If you want to treat it just as a specialized form of a drop-down list and force users to type (with autocompletion) only specific strings there (for example, user names or products), you are better off clearing up the field when the input focus is moved back there:

```
$('#queryString').on('input', function () {
    if (typeaheadItemSelected) {
        typeaheadItemSelected = false;
        $('#queryString').val('');
        $("#queryCode").val('');
    }
});
```

The code snippet resets the Boolean guard that controls whether a selection is made in the specific input field and empties the input field and the companion hidden field that stores the value of the selection.

> **Important** In this example, I used a local JavaScript variable to store the state of the selection on a particular input field. That works as long as there's a single autocompletion input field per view. When you have two or more, you better use an attribute on the input element to track its selected state.

Date picking

In HTML5, there's a new INPUT element of type *date*. Based on that, you would probably expect that all browsers provide nearly the same experience and offer a date-picker facility. This is not the case for the time being, at least. Some browsers let you navigate up and down through arrow buttons; some browsers don't even provide any special support for dates. The experience is quite different across browsers.

A common workaround is doing feature detection with Modernizr and then plugging in some external component if the browser doesn't support date-picking facilities. I prefer to stick to Bootstrap and offer a consistent experience. Bootstrap doesn't offer a native date-picker component, but an external framework exists that works well with Bootstrap. Let's see how to use it. In particular, I'll be referring to the package you find at *http://www.nuget.org/packages/Bootstrap.Datepicker/1.5.0*.

The Bootstrap date-picker framework

The Bootstrap Date Picker package you get from NuGet contains a CSS file and a couple of JavaScript files, including the date-picking tool (*bootstrap-datepicker.min.js*), a helper library like *moment.min.js*, and ad hoc files for localization. Be sure to reference *moment.js*, date picker, and locales in this exact order. You need to deploy in production only the locales that you actually use:

```
<script type="text/javascript" src="~/content/scripts/moment.min.js")"></script>
<script type="text/javascript" src="~/content/scripts/bootstrap-datepicker.min.js")"></script>
@foreach(var l in localesOfInterest)
{
    <script type="text/javascript" src="~/content/scripts/locales/" + l + "></script>
}
```

In the code snippet, the variable *localesOfInterest* is assumed to be a collection of file names in the form of *bootstrap-datepicker.{0}.min.js*, where the parameter is a culture string such as *it*, *fr*, or *es*.

Binding the picker

Let's focus on an input field where you want users to enter an optional date. You can find this form in the profile page of some membership system, and the date to enter is the birthdate. The first thing to do is drop the *date* value from the *type* attribute of the INPUT element. That would stop browsers that support date pickers from using such facilities. Another attribute you want to add is *contenteditable*, and you want to set it to *false* to prevent manual editing in the field. In this way, any content that ends up in the field is either set from the picker or inserted via script.

The following markup produces what you see in Figure 9-10:

```
<div class="input-group">
    <input type="text" class="form-control" id="dateofbirth" name="dateofbirth"
        contenteditable="false"
        value="@Model.DateOfBirth.GetValueOrDefault().ToShortDateString()">
```

```
            <span class="input-group-btn">
                <button class="btn btn-dark" type="button" onclick="setNoBirthDate()">
                    Don't show
                </button>
            </span>
        </div>
</div>
```

The *value* attribute of the INPUT element is bound to a property of the view model that carries the date to show. The date type is assumed to be nullable and defaults to the empty string if no date is set. The button in the input group just clears the buffer when clicked:

```
$("#dateofbirth").val("");
```

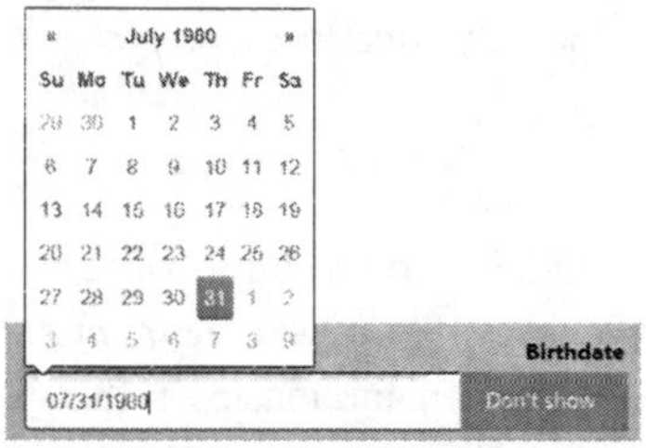

FIGURE 9-10 The Bootstrap Date Picker component in action

Configuration of the date picker

Just like many other rich script-based components, the date picker needs some initialization in order to function properly. The markup just shown is the first step; next is some script that ties together logic and DOM elements. Following the standard set by jQuery plugins, you can attach the picker to an input field with a parameter-less call and accept all default settings or specify your own preferences:

```
<script type="text/javascript">
    $(function () {
        $('#dateofbirth').datepicker();
    });
</script>
```

You specify you preferences through an object passed to the initializer:

```
@{
    var startBirthDate = new DateTime(1915, 1, 1).ToString("d", culture);
    var endBirthDate = DateTime.Today.AddYears(-5).ToString("d", culture);
}
...
```

```
<script type="text/javascript">
    $(function () {
        $('#dateofbirth').datepicker({
            language: 'it',
            startDate: '@startBirthDate',
            endDate: '@endBirthDate'
        });
    });
</script>
```

The most common parameters you want to customize are the language, start date, and end date that users can navigate through. Especially if you're using the input field to grab a birth date, you might want to delimit the interval to avoid meaningless dates such as dates for users not of a particular required age.

Custom components

Bootstrap doesn't offer any particular predefined styles to embellish and empower drop-down lists like those you obtain with SELECT/OPTION elements. Although a drop-down list can be styled easily using CSS settings, it will always look a bit inconsistent when used in the context of a Bootstrap user interface. At the same time, Bootstrap has so many facilities for creating drop-down content that arranging a drop-down list component is not a hard task. All it takes is an ad hoc markup template and a bit of JavaScript.

Creating the list

The following code snippet defines a drop-down menu in Bootstrap. It shows users a clickable button and an associated list that drops down. The button initially displays the text *Get one* followed by a caret symbol. When the user clicks the button, a menu populated with all list items shows up:

```
<div class="btn-group">
    <a class="btn btn-default dropdown-toggle"
        data-toggle="dropdown>
        Get one <span class="caret"></span></div>
    </a>
    <ul class="dropdown-menu">
        @foreach (var item in list)
        {
            <li><a href="#"><span>@item.Text</span></a></li>
        }
    </ul>
</div>
```

In Bootstrap, drop-down menus exist only to offer a list of hyperlinks to navigate to. If you package up a bit of JavaScript with the markup just shown, though, you can handle clicking on the hyperlinks and override navigation into user-interface changes. It's key to notice that for a Bootstrap drop-down menu to become a classic drop-down list, no hyperlinks should be defined on the list items. Ideally, you set the *href* attribute of anchors within LI elements to #. If you leave it empty, the item is still clickable but the mouse pointer changes as if it were plain text.

Figure 9-11 shows the overall behavior of the drop-down list.

FIGURE 9-11 Changing the caption of the button when a drop-down item is selected

Adding selection logic

In HTML, the regular SELECT element is considered an input element and browsers query it for the currently selected element before posting. This won't happen if you simply replace the SELECT element with Bootstrap's drop-down button group. At a minimum, you need to add a hidden input field marked with a unique ID. This ID will also identify the drop-down list as a whole. The hidden field must be populated via JavaScript.

The markup for the drop-down list changes slightly, as shown here:

```
<div class="btn-group">
    <a class="btn btn-default dropdown-toggle"
       data-toggle="dropdown">
            <input type="hidden" name="Id" id="Id" value="..." />
       Get one <span class="caret"></span></div>
    </a>
    <ul>
      <li>
        <a href="#" data-value="Value"> Text </a>
      </li>
    </ul>
</div>
```

Each anchor element in a UL/LI drop-down structure should be associated with the following code to react to users' clicking:

```
$(".dropdown-menu li a").click(function () {
    // Grab the selected text
    var selected = $(this).text();

    // Display the selected text
    $(this).parents('.btn-group')
        .find('.dropdown-toggle')
        .text(selected + '<span class="caret"></span>');

    // Get the value associated with the selected element
    var dataValue = $(this).attr("data-value");
```

```
    // Store the value in the hidden field
    $(this).parents('.btn-group')
        .find('input[type=hidden]')
        .val(dataValue);
});
```

Now that you have a bare-bones working solution, you're ready to face the next challenge: how to effectively use the drop-down component in real-world HTML pages.

Using a custom drop-down list in real pages

Razor offers opportunities to encapsulate reusable pieces of markup in HTML helpers. Most Razor helpers are defined in code as extension methods for the *HtmlHelper* class. Such components build up their HTML markup by using the ASP.NET MVC native *TagBuilder* class or plain string concatenation. However, in ASP.NET MVC you also can create markup-based reusable components. This option seems perfect for creating Bootstrap extensions.

Let's create a new file in the *App_Code* folder of the project and call it *BootstrapExtensions.cshtml*. (Note that while the file name is arbitrary, the *App_Code* folder is not.) The full source code is shown here:

```
@using System.Web.Mvc
@helper DropDown(string id,
        string title,
        SelectList list,
        string buttonStyle="btn-default",
        string width="auto",
        string caret="caret")
{
    var selectedText = title;
    var selectedValue = (string) list.SelectedValue ?? "";
    if (!String.IsNullOrWhiteSpace(selectedValue))
    {
        selectedText = (from item in list
                        where item.Value == selectedValue
                        select item.Text).FirstOrDefault();
    }

    <div class="btn-group" style="width:@width">
        <a class="btn @buttonStyle dropdown-toggle"
           data-toggle="dropdown"
           style="width:100%">
            <input type="hidden" name="@id" id="@id" value="@selectedValue" />
            <div class="bext-dropdown-selected">@selectedText</div>
            <div style="float:right"><span class="@caret"></span></div>
            <div class="clearfix"></div>
        </a>
```

```
        <ul class="dropdown-menu" style="width:100%">
            @foreach (var item in list)
            {
                <li>
                    <a href="#" data-value="@item.Value">@item.Text</a>
                </li>
            }
        </ul>
    </div>
}
```

You now have a new component called *DropDown* that can be used in Razor views. The constructor accepts a few parameters such as the ID of the drop-down component, the text to display when no item is selected, the list of items to show, and a few style properties. In your Razor files, you can use code as shown here:

```
@BootstrapExtensions.DropDown(
    "btn-select",
    "Get one",
    new SelectList(Model.Data, "Id", "Name"), "btn-primary btn-lg", "200px")
```

Using the custom drop-down list is not much different from using any of the predefined Razor HTML helpers, such as *Html.CheckBox* or *Html.Partial*.

To programmatically read the value of the element in the Bootstrap-derived drop-down list, you use the following script:

```
($("#btn-select").val()
```

The *#btn-select* expression identifies the hidden field buried in the folds of the markup structure. In particular, *btn-select* is the ID you passed as the first argument of the drop-down helper earlier in the code. From a drop-down list, you usually don't need to read the text of the selected item. However, if you just need that, this is how you accomplish that given the structure of the markup:

```
$("#btn-select").next().text()
```

The *next()* selector assumes that the hidden field comes in the hierarchy just before the DIV that contains the displayed text. If you alter the HTML template, the JavaScript code needs to be updated too.

Examining the weird case of check boxes

In plain ASP.NET MVC views, you can use check boxes in one of two ways. You can just add raw HTML markup, or you can use a Razor helper, as shown here:

```
<!-- Option #1 -->
<input type="checkbox" checked id="checkbox" name="checkbox" />

<!-- Option #2 -->
@Html.Checkbox("checkbox", true);
```

As weird as it might sound, the two options are not really equivalent when you put them in action in real pages. The reason is that the ASP.NET MVC model-binding layer has trouble parsing the raw HTML information posted by browsers when plain INPUT is used. For this reason, the *Html.CheckBox* helper includes a hidden field with the same ID that is used to post data in a format that makes Booleans understandable by the binding layer. The bottom line is that in ASP.NET MVC you should use *Html.CheckBox* instead of plain INPUT check-box elements.

Better yet, you can create custom Bootstrap check boxes that also offer a more consistent look and feel. It's simple. You can find ideas and help code at *http://getbootstrap.com*.

Summary

Ultimately, I believe that there are very few reasons for not using Bootstrap in a website. One good reason to use it is that you already have a template that unifies under a common look and feel most of the artifacts you use in pages. Things like menus, drop-down lists, buttons, check-boxes, tabs, and modal dialogs are a common presence in webpages and must be there in one (graphical) form or another.

Bootstrap offers some built-in facilities, but web designers can produce the same thing while making the overall appearance of the site pretty unique. This is a good reason for not using Bootstrap. At the same time, however, this is a good way to understand the power and role that Bootstrap plays in the modern web: either you use it or you use something that does what it does, just with a different look and feel.

With Bootstrap, you experience a relatively short learning curve, and many templates—variations of Bootstrap—exist for free, with even more available for a small fee. If you are a web designer or someone who intends to hire a web designer, you might and probably should request that the final template is Bootstrap-based.

This chapter offered an overall view of Bootstrap and covered its primary features and components. I tried to provide a realistic vision of Bootstrap and its uses in real sites. I'm not sure I covered all important aspects of it, though. I encourage you to check out more components, features, styles, and extensions directly from the Bootstrap documentation starting at *http://getbootstrap.com*.

As a final note, keep in mind that Bootstrap heralds an era of Responsive Web Design, a design methodology that makes a point of providing an ideal experience to users regardless of the screen size. Responsive Web Design is definitely a great idea—it's so great that it makes Bootstrap templates work with any sort of mobile devices. However, in much the same way Bootstrap doesn't remove the need for having some strong graphical ideas for the content, it also doesn't remove the need to sometimes treat some devices—especially smartphones and older cell phones—in a particular way through ad hoc mobile sites. I'll return to this point in Chapter 15.

CHAPTER 10

Organizing the ASP.NET MVC project

Intelligence is the ability to adapt to change.

—*Stephen Hawking*

As more and more developers take advantage of the various flavors of ASP.NET Core 1.0, using Microsoft Visual Studio to write, compile, and test an ASP.NET MVC application becomes just one possible option. When you create a new ASP.NET MVC project in Visual Studio, you end up running a sort of wizard that creates a new tree of folders based on a template. An ASP.NET MVC application requires a few specific folders and files and doesn't work, or works differently, if those folders are missing. A good example of a required folder is the *Views* folder, which contains HTML views and must be replicated as-is in production, contain a specific number of subfolders, and be aptly named.

Beyond the *Views* folder, however, the structure of the project is mostly up to the development team. Unless you use specific features such as startup initializers or custom HTML helpers, you don't have to stick to mandated names and folders.

Yet the organization of the project folders is an important part of the solution. So is the distribution of required functionalities across binaries and class libraries. In this chapter, I'll present a set of practices I use on an every-day basis. I don't expect you to agree with my opinion on each of them, but I hope that reading about my programming habits at least prompts you to reconsider your own habits and thereby directly or indirectly improves them.

Planning the project solution

An ASP.NET MVC project delivers a bunch of DLL files in the *Bin* folder. Such DLL files are of two types: your own application-specific DLL files, and files brought in by referenced NuGet packages, including ASP.NET platform binaries.

How many application-specific binaries do you need to build an ASP.NET MVC application? That depends on the project architecture you envision.

Mapping projects to the Layered Architecture pattern

In the cloud era we currently live in, when it comes to scalability, the primary consideration is how the code lends itself to be replicated. This focus implies a need to keep the amount of shared data limited to zero or the bare minimum and to avoid connections across processes. The more you can keep things in a single tier, the better. In other words, the more compact the project code is, the better.

Taking a look at the big picture

At a minimum, you need a project that produces the web-server application binary. In Chapter 5, "The layered architecture," I argued that layers are preferable to tiers because they're far easier to scale with today's technologies and practices. The Layered Architecture pattern identifies four key layers: presentation, application, domain, and infrastructure.

Figure 10-1 shows a possible way to set up a layered architecture in the context of an ASP.NET MVC solution.

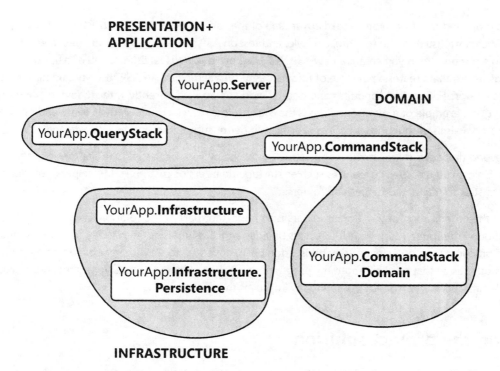

FIGURE 10-1 Mapping projects in an ASP.NET MVC solution to the Layered Architecture pattern

The figure presents a realistic ASP.NET MVC solution and its entire set of projects. Projects have been mapped to layers, which are represented by balloons. Each balloon represents a typical layer you want to have in the code. The *YourApp.Server* project is an ASP.NET MVC project and combines the presentation and application layers. The domain layer is made of three distinct class library projects: one for the query stack, command stack, and domain model.

> **Note** A Command Query Responsibility Segregation (CQRS) approach is used in the example. See Chapter 2, "Selecting the supporting architecture," for more information about CQRS.

Finally, the Infrastructure layer contains two class libraries——for persistence and other helper components you might need, such as caching, password hashing, dependency injection, logging, external services, and the like.

Presentation and application layers

In an ASP.NET MVC controller, classes are the first point of contact between the browser and server-side code. For this reason, they serve as the repository of any presentation logic you might have. You can orchestrate any workflow you need from within controllers, but complex workflows will make your controller classes rather bloated.

For this reason, you might want to keep controllers thinner and move code that orchestrates business tasks to an intermediate layer—the application layer. The application layer certainly can be a separate layer and a distinct class-library project. It's entirely your call. However, a common practice these days is to try to keep code as compact as possible. Also, it is more than acceptable to keep the presentation and application layers in the same project—you just use project folders to keep content separated.

Domain layer

As discussed in the first part of the book, keeping the command and query stacks separated is quickly becoming a standard architectural approach. As explained in Chapter 2, it helps keep things simple and avoids most complications.

If you opt for a CQRS design, you might want to have a class library for the query stack and stick any data transfer objects there that you might need. You also should have another class library for the command stack and place most of the code for domain services there. You likely will have a separate class library for the domain model.

Infrastructure layer

The infrastructure layer is mostly a wrapper layer around persistence, with data persisted via either relational or NoSQL databases. A general pattern for the layer consists of having an infrastructure class library and considering persistence as just one aspect of the infrastructure, possibly implemented in another specialized class library. In simple scenarios, though, you might just want to reduce the infrastructure layer to the persistence layer.

Application startup

Nearly every ASP.NET MVC application has a *global.asax* file that works as the container of handlers for system-level events. Most common events are application starting problems and application errors. You also can handle in *global.asax* events issues related to the start and end of sessions.

The *global.asax* file is a plain text file, and all it does is reference a custom class that contains handlers. Here's the markup for a typical *global.asax*:

```
<% @Application Codebehind="Global.asax.cs" Inherits="YourApp.MvcApplication" Language="C#" %>
```

The class *YourApp.MvcApplication* contains the actual handlers and inherits from the system-defined *HttpApplication* class. In the *YourApp.MvcApplication* class, you place all the code that fully configures and properly initializes your application.

Registering areas

A common pattern for initializing applications involves placing a bunch of calls in the *Application_Start* method in the *global.asax* class. At a minimum, you find the following code in the start handler. (Note that this code will be a bit different in ASP.NET Core 1.0 and the new runtime environment.)

```
protected void Application_Start()
{
    // Register ASP.NET MVC areas (if any)
    AreaRegistration.RegisterAllAreas();

    // Register routes for the application to listen
    RouteConfig.RegisterRoutes(RouteTable.Routes);
}
```

The first line deals with ASP.NET MVC areas, if any are supported by the specific application. If not, you just drop the first call in the code snippet. An ASP.NET MVC area is a functionally independent module of an ASP.NET MVC application and is recognized by a name. Essentially, an *area* is a subapplication within the main application that mimics the same folder structure and conventions of the parent MVC application. You might want to have areas in large applications, too, as a convenience to better manage the typically large number of controllers and views. Areas, therefore, are optional.

Each area has its own set of controllers, models, and views. To invoke a controller action under a given area, you just use a route where the area name precedes the controller name. The following code snippet shows the class that defines an area:

```
public class AdminAreaRegistration : AreaRegistration
{
    public override string AreaName
    {
        get { return "Admin"; }
    }
    public override void RegisterArea(AreaRegistrationContext context)
```

```
    {
        context.MapRoute(
            "Admin_default",
            "Admin/{controller}/{action}/{id}",
            new { action = "Index", id = UrlParameter.Optional }
        );
    }
}
```

In Visual Studio, you can use an ad hoc menu item from the solution box to create areas. The menu item pops up a dialog box in which you specify the name of the area, creates the appropriate folder structure, and autogenerates a class like the one just shown. You are welcome to edit the class to customize the routes for the area. The *RegisterAllAreas* method you see called in *global.asax* uses a bit of reflection to navigate into the project assemblies to find assemblies that contain classes that inherit from *AreaRegistration* class. For each of these types, it then calls the *RegisterArea* method.

Registering routes

In Chapter 8, "Core of ASP.NET MVC," I discussed application routes at length and how they're defined and managed. The *global.asax* file is where routes are loaded into the running application. The call in the *Application_Start* event handler ensures that all necessary routes are in place before the first request hits the application. Here's the default route configuration:

```
public class RouteConfig
{
    public static void RegisterRoutes(RouteCollection routes)
    {
        routes.IgnoreRoute("{resource}.axd/{*pathInfo}");
        routes.MapRoute(
            name: "Default",
            url: "{controller}/{action}/{id}",
            defaults: new { controller = "Home", action = "Index", id = UrlParameter.Optional }
        );
    }
}
```

Obviously, you can modify the default route as you want and add as many new routes as you like. In addition, be aware that all you need to do is add instances of the *Route* class to the *Routes* static collection of the *RouteTable* class. Doing that using the *MapRoute* extension method in the context of a *RouteConfig* class is a recommended pattern, and it's just as good as any other code that achieves the same result.

> **Important** Keep in mind that the code just shown works only in versions of ASP.NET MVC outside the new ASP.NET Core 1.0 runtime environment. As discussed in Chapter 7, "What's new in ASP.NET Core 1.0," the new runtime environment supports a slightly different syntax that doesn't need any *RouteConfig* class, even though the syntax for defining routes is similar.

Customizing the configuration

How to configure areas and routes is a general concern with any ASP.NET application. Each application, however, can have additional configuration needs. As mentioned, a popular convention in ASP.NET MVC is using *xxxConfig* classes equipped with static methods to perform any initialization that relates to a given functionality, such as resource bundling, Web API routes, action filters, localization, inversion of control (IoC) frameworks, and the initialization of specific components such as device-detection frameworks or service buses.

A typical task that needs to be configured in a web application is loading global data from some form of storage. Some general settings can be saved as key/value pairs directly in the *web.config* file. This approach is often taken for semiconstant values that change only occasionally or for features that need to be enabled or disabled in special situations.

Any other information that specifies the system should work in a particular way and is probably better stored in a separate data store, whether that's a plain Microsoft SQL Server database table or some form of cloud storage. All configuration data, ideally, is made available through global static properties exposed out of the application-specific *HttpApplication* object. Here's an example:

```
public class YourApplication : HttpApplication
{
    public static YourAppVersion Version { get; private set; }
    public static YourAppSettings Settings { get; private set; }
    public static IList<INewsProvider> NewsProviders { get; private set; }
    ...

    protected void Application_Start()
    {
        AreaRegistration.RegisterAllAreas();
        RouteConfig.RegisterRoutes(RouteTable.Routes);

        Version = ApplicationConfig.LoadVersionInformation();
        Settings = ApplicationConfig.LoadGeneralSettings();
        NewsProviders = ApplicationConfig.SetupNewsProviders();
        ...
    }

    ...
}
```

The full version number can be read from the *web.config* file, whereas settings and news providers can be read from storage. All information is globally available from within any part of the application.

> **Important** When you use globally accessible data, you should be careful to ensure that it is read-only information or at least that any changes made to the shared data don't break into undesirable side effects.

Multitenant applications

A multitenant application is a special flavor of a web application in which a single host website serves multiple clients or tenants, each making requests from a distinct URL. A blog engine is a great example of a multitenant application. Imagine you create, say, a WordPress blog and pay to have it run on your own domain. You are not getting your own copy of the blog engine deployed on your own server. More likely, you are instructing the blog multitenant infrastructure to map any requests that come from your known domain to a special configuration of the web application code based on the settings and data for that tenant.

In terms of configuration, an ASP.NET MVC multitenant application requires an extra step. For each action, the controller will parse the host information and load any data that configures the application instance to the needs and expectations of the requesting tenant. In addition to the shared configuration set at the application startup, you also have an extra step to be performed for each and every request. The host name is the discriminant used to load the right information. Here's some code for a sample controller action:

```
public class HomeController : Controller
{
    public ActionResult Index()
    {
        // Grab the name of the requesting host
        var host = Request.Url.DnsSafeHost;

        // Grab tenant-specific configuration
        var tenantSettings = TenantConfig.Load(host);

        // Incorporate the tenant-specific information in the response
        var model = DoSomeWorkAndGetViewModel(tenantSettings);
        return View(model);
    }
}
```

Note that the tenant work is required for every action. For this reason, in a real-world scenario you might want to move the common code into a base controller class to minimize the burden.

Understanding the ASP.NET Core 1.0 configuration

The brand new .NET Execution Environment (DNX) controls the execution of ASP.NET Core 1.0 applications. As a result, each ASP.NET Core 1.0 project is a DNX project and follows an ad hoc JSON-based syntax. The point of contact between an ASP.NET Core 1.0 application and the DNX pipeline is the ASP.NET Application Hosting package. The core of this package is the *Startup* class. The class is the convention used in ASP.NET Core 1.0 to initialize the pipeline and fully configure the application so that it's also based on information coming from the hosting environment:

```
public class Startup
{
    // Sets up middleware for the request pipeline (OWIN)
    public void Configure(IApplicationBuilder app)
    {
        ...
```

```
        }

        // Sets up services being used through the internal IoC infrastructure
        public void ConfigureServices(IServiceCollection services)
        {
            ...
        }
}
```

The *Configure* method configures the pipeline that each request goes through. It adds references to components being used to process the request. References are added through *UseXxx* extension methods defined on the *IApplicationBuilder* object. At a minimum, an ASP.NET MVC application contains the following:

```
public void Configure(IApplicationBuilder app)
{
    app.UseMvc();
}
```

If you intend to use convention-based routing, you specify here the routes you support:

```
public void Configure(IApplicationBuilder app)
{
    app.UseMvc(routes => {
        routes.MapRoute(
            name: "Default",
            template: "{controller=Home}/{action=Index}/{id?}");
    });
}
```

In the *ConfigureServices* method, you list the services being used by your application. Again, at a minimum, an ASP.NET MVC application contains the following:

```
public void ConfigureServices(IServiceCollection services)
{
    // Reference Entity Framework and SQL Server
    services.AddEntityFramework()
    services.AddSqlServer();

    // Reference ASP.NET MVC binaries
    services.AddMvc();
}
```

In the *ConfigureServices* method, you also have calls that work with the internal IoC framework and resolve interfaces to actual class names.

Examining application services

ASP.NET MVC is a framework designed to be testable and promotes important principles such as separation of concerns (SoC) and dependency injection (DI). ASP.NET MVC expects an application to be separated into parts known as the *controller*, the *view*, and the *model*.

Being forced to create a controller class doesn't mean you'll automatically achieve the right level of SoC, and it certainly doesn't mean you're writing testable code. ASP.NET MVC gets you off to a good start, but any further (required) layering is up to you.

Using fat-free controllers

Any request will likely trigger a workflow, and sometimes workflows are complex. If you orchestrate the workflow with all of its error handling and compensation logic from a single place—the controller method—you have a good chance to end up with a long method, perhaps 100 lines or more. Such a long method makes little sense.

To support your efforts in creating fat-free controllers, I recommend a strategy based on the following points:

- Relay any action to a controller-specific, worker-service class. This class is part of the application layer and is not expected to be reusable.

- Make methods of the worker-service class accept data as it comes from the model binder.

- Make methods of the worker-service class return data expressed as View-Model objects that are ready to be passed down to the view engine.

- Grab exceptions via attributes.

Let's see how I envision a worker-service class.

Using worker-service classes

A *worker service* is a helper class that goes hand in hand with the controller. You might reasonably expect to have a distinct worker-service class for each controller. On the other hand, the worker service is just an extension of a controller, and it results from moving the core behavior out of the controller class and into a distinct and testable class.

Figure 10-2 shows an architectural perspective of worker services in ASP.NET MVC.

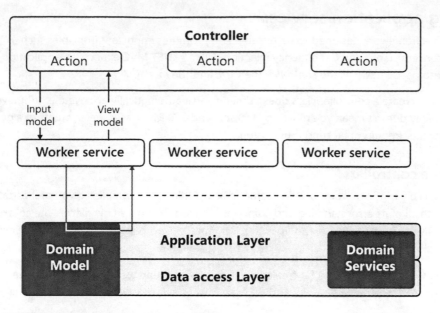

FIGURE 10-2 Worker services and controllers

With worker services implemented, a controller method becomes as simple as the one shown here:

```
public class HomeService : IHomeService
{
    public IndexViewModel GetIndexViewModel()
    {
        ...
    }
    ...
}


public class HomeController : Controller
{
    private IHomeService _homeService = new HomeService();

    public ActionResult Index(...)
    {
        var model = _homeService.GetIndexViewModel(...);
        return View(model);
    }
}
```

Whether or not to abstract the worker-service class to an interface is your call. Abstraction is a great thing if it brings concrete benefits. The preceding code also doesn't use any form of dependency injection as well. An example of handmade dependency injection is shown here:

```
public class HomeController : Controller
{
    private IHomeService _homeService
    public HomeController() : this(new HomeService()) {}
```

```
    public HomeController(IHomeService service)
    {
        _homeService = service;
    }

    public ActionResult Index(...)
    {
        var model = _homeService.GetIndexViewModel(...);
        return View(model);
    }
}
```

Determining the placement of worker-service classes

The worker-service classes are the point of connection between the presentation layer (for example, controllers) and the middle tier (for example, the domain and infrastructure). The collection of all worker-service classes form the application layer that I discussed in Chapter 5.

You can implement the application layer as a separate class library, but most of the time it can easily stay within the boundaries of the main ASP.NET MVC project. I just create a new project folder that I like to call *Application* and place all worker-service classes there. Because worker-service classes are just compiled classes that end up in a single binary DLL, any folder structure you come up with is more than acceptable if it works for you.

Adding in other assets

Models and resources are two types of assets an ASP.NET MVC application needs to define and have available. There are many ways to organize such assets in a project. The following sections summarize what I like to do in my own projects.

Using models

In general, any web application has to deal with four types of models. There's an *input model* that represents the collection of classes that describe data being passed to controller actions. There's a *view model* that groups all classes required to provide data for views to be rendered. Next, there's a *domain model* for business logic, and finally there's the *persistence model*, which you typically use with Entity Framework.

The domain and persistence models can sometimes coincide if you don't have much complicated logic or tend to isolate the execution of business logic in standalone components. If you have both models, the domain model should be defined in the domain layer and the persistence model should be defined in the infrastructure layer. Input and view models, instead, belong to the main ASP.NET MVC project.

Figure 10-3 shows a possible way to map models to layers.

ASP.NET MVC project	Presentation + Application	Input / View model
Class library	Domain layer	Domain model
Class library	Infrastructure	Persistence model

FIGURE 10-3 Mapping layers to models and project types in an ASP.NET MVC solution

Using resources

A web application uses four types of resources: CSS classes, script files, images, and fonts. The relative path to any resource must be replicated in production as long as the resource is requested as a physical file.

There are many ways to organize resources in an ASP.NET MVC project. At a minimum, you have a folder for each type of resource: images, fonts, styles, and scripts. I prefer to have these folders wrapped in a parent Content folder.

Creating presentation layouts

The markup generated by an ASP.NET MVC application is obtained through the services of a system component known as the *view engine*. The view engine gets an HTML template written in the Razor language and a specific data model object and then produces the final markup. A given template can be split into smaller, reusable pieces called *partial views*, and the location of templates can be customized by creating a custom view engine. Let's see how it works.

Splitting a template into partial views

In ASP.NET MVC, a *partial view* is just a plain HTML view template, except that it contains small chunks of markup. You use a partial view whenever you want to incorporate an existing smaller view into the view template you're writing. The concept is analogous to *IFRAME* elements in HTML.

Partial views typically go in the Shared folder under the Views folder. If a partial view is used only by a specific controller, you can store it in the same view folder as the controller. However, having a partial view that can be used by the views created via a single controller is somewhat limiting.

I recommend using partial views for two main reasons. First, it gets you reusable pieces of user interface. Second, it makes your view templates cleaner and a lot easier to read and understand. Here's the code you use to invoke a partial view:

```
@Html.Partial("pv_CustomerList")
```

Using a prefix to distinguish partial views from regular views is a common practice. Some developers just use the underscore to prefix the name. I tend to use the *pv_* prefix. More important than using the prefix, though, is naming the view. Using a plain string to name the view in the Razor templates, as well as in controller methods, is acceptable, but it makes your code brittle. I make a point of using constants to refer to names of views and partial views.

Custom view engines

In a large ASP.NET MVC application where you extensively make use of partial views, your Shared folder under Views soon gets swamped with partial views. When dozens of partial-view files are used, editing the right one might become an annoying task.

I would love to have the freedom to place all partial views in a distinct folder under the Views folder and perhaps keep them organized on a per-controller basis. This is simply not a supported feature. Well, not exactly. It isn't supported natively, but at the cost of writing your own personalized version of the view engine you can load partial views from wherever you like.

There are two ways to write a custom view engine. You can inherit from the base class *VirtualPathProviderViewEngine*, or you can derive your view engine from the Razor engine—the class *RazorViewEngine*. If you inherit from *VirtualPathProviderViewEngine*, you must provide your own implementation of the rendering process for views and partial views. You are responsible for locating the content of templates (whether it comes from physical files or database tables) and for rendering that to an HTML view. All in all, I consider this an advanced option that is only occasionally required in the real world, although it's a good feature to have.

If all you want to do is locate Razor partial views (or even layouts and views) from a different location than usual, you just need the following class. In the constructor, you assign new values to three properties: *PartialViewLocationFormats*, *ViewLocationFormats*, and *MasterLocationFormats*.

```
public class MyViewEngine : RazorViewEngine
{
    public MyViewEngine()
    {
        // Define the locations of partial views
        this.PartialViewLocationFormats = new string[]
        {
            "~/Views/{1}/{0}.cshtml",
            "~/Views/Shared/{0}.cshtml",
            "~/Views/Partial/{0}.cshtml",
            "~/Views/Partial/{1}/{0}.cshtml"
        };

        // Define the locations of views
        this.ViewLocationFormats = new string[]
        {
            "~/Views/{1}/{0}.cshtml",
            "~/Views/Shared/{0}.cshtml",
            "~/Views/Controller/{1}/{0}.cshtml"
        };
```

```
        // Define the locations of layouts
        this.MasterLocationFormats = new string[]
        {
            "~/Views/Shared/{0}.cshtml",
            "~/Views/Layout/{0}.cshtml"
        };
    }
}
```

The *{1}* placeholder indicates the controller name, and the *{0}* placeholder indicates the view name. You register the new view engine in *global.asax*, as shown next. You first clear all existing view engines to avoid conflicts and then add your new one:

```
protected void Application_Start()
{
    RouteConfig.RegisterRoutes(RouteTable.Routes);
    ...
    ViewEngines.Engines.Clear();
    ViewEngines.Engines.Add(new MyViewEngine());
}
```

Figure 10-4 presents a screenshot from an ASP.NET MVC project that uses the custom view engine. The structure of the Views folder, as you can see, is completely customized. You now have three main subfolders, one for each category of view you might have: *controller*, *partial*, and *layout*.

FIGURE 10-4 A completely redesigned structure for the Views folder

Finally, note that if you place layout files outside of the default Shared folder, you must edit the content of the *_ViewStart.cshtml* file as well and make it point to the new location. The *_ViewStart.cshtml* file contains the path of the default layout file to use when no layout file is passed to the view engine.

Serving resources more effectively

As webpages continue to offer ever-richer visual content, the cost of downloading related resources such as CSS, script files, and images grows significantly. Surely, for the most part these resources can be cached locally by the browser; yet, the initial footprint can really be hard to sustain. For script and CSS files, GZIP compression can be combined with *bundling* and *minification*, two smart techniques to significantly reduce the size and number of downloads.

A lot of currently available frameworks provide bundling and minification services with slightly different levels of extensibility and different feature sets. For the most part, they all offer the same capabilities—so picking one over the other is purely a matter of preference. If you're writing an ASP.NET MVC application, the natural choice for bundling and minification is the Microsoft ASP.NET Web Optimization framework, available through a NuGet package.

> **Note** You can apply bundling and minification together, but they remain independent processes. Depending on your needs, you can decide to only create bundles or minify individual files. Usually, however, you won't have any reason on production sites not to bundle and minify all CSS and JavaScript files. At debug time, though, it's an entirely different story: a minified or bundled resource is quite hard to read and step through, so you don't want bundling and minification enabled.

Working with Bundling

Bundling is the process of rolling up a number of distinct resources into a single downloadable resource. For example, a bundle might consist of multiple JavaScript or CSS files. In layout and view files when you reference the URL of the bundle, a single download occurs, but the DOM is ultimately affected by all content stored in the bundle.

Bundling related CSS files

Typically, you create bundles programmatically in *global.asax*. In accordance with the ASP.NET MVC initialization conventions, you can create a *BundleConfig* class in the *App_Start* folder and expose a static initialization method out of it, as shown here:

```
BundleConfig.RegisterBundles(BundleTable.Bundles);
```

A bundle is simply a collection of files—typically, style sheets or script files. Here's the code you need to group two CSS files into a single download:

```
public class BundleConfig
{
    public static void RegisterBundles(BundleCollection bundles)
    {
        bundles.Add(new Bundle("~/site-css")
                .Include("~/content/styles/site1.css",
                         "~/content/styles/site2.css"));
    }
}
```

You create a new *Bundle* class and pass the constructor the virtual path that will be used to reference the bundle from within a view or a layout file. To associate CSS files with the bundle, you use the *Include* method. The method takes an array of strings, each representing a virtual path:

```
bundles.Add(new Bundle("~/site-css")
        .Include("~/content/styles/*.css");
```

You can indicate CSS files explicitly, as in the first example, or you can indicate a pattern string, as demonstrated in the example just shown. Note that the *Bundle* class has an *IncludeDirectory* method you use to indicate the path to a given virtual directory, and possibly it has a pattern-matching string and a Boolean flag to also enable search on subdirectories.

Enabling bundles optimization

Bundling is a form of optimization. As such, it mostly makes sense to use it when the site is in production. The *EnableOptimizations* property on the *BundleTable* class is a convenient way to set up bundling as it should work in production. So be aware that until it is turned on explicitly, bundling is not active:

```
public static void RegisterBundles(BundleCollection bundles)
{
    bundles.Add(new Bundle("~/site-css").Include(
            "~/content/styles/site1.css",
            "~/content/styles/site2.css"));

    BundleTable.EnableOptimizations = true;
}
```

For the sake of demos, let's assume the following content for *site1.css*:

```
body {
    padding-top: 50px;
    padding-bottom: 20px;
}
/* Set padding to keep content from hitting the edges */
.body-content {
    padding-left: 15px;
    padding-right: 15px;
}
```

```
/* Set width on the form input elements since they're 100% wide by default */
input,
select,
textarea {
    max-width: 280px;
}
```

The file *site2.css*, instead, will have the following content:

```
.title {
    font-size: 3em;
}
```

If you're not interested in testing bundling while in development, you can also use directives as shown here:

```
#if DEBUG
    BundleTable.EnableOptimizations = false;
#else
    BundleTable.EnableOptimizations = true;
#endif
```

Let's see now what's required to reference a bundle in a Razor view.

Referencing CSS bundles in views

To reference a CSS bundle in any sort of a Razor view, you use the following code:

```
@Styles.Render("~/site-css")
```

The string you pass to the *Render* method is just the virtual path of a previously created CSS bundle. In a bundle, you can easily reference content delivery network (CDN) paths. Also note that choosing to use bundles doesn't force you to just use bundles. In the same view, in fact, you can have bundles as well as direct CSS requests, as shown here:

```
<head>
    <meta charset="utf-8" />
    <meta name="viewport" content="width=device-width, initial-scale=1.0">
    @Styles.Render("~/content/styles/bootstrap.min.css")
    @Styles.Render("~/site-css")
</head>
```

The Bootstrap CSS file is added as an individual, standalone download, and all other CSS files are bundled together.

Bundling script files

To bundle script files, you just pass JavaScript files to a newly created instance of the *Bundle* class, as shown here:

```
bundles.Add(new Bundle("~/site-core-scripts")
        .Include("~/content/scripts/jquery-1.10.2.min.js",
                "~/content/scripts/bootstrap.min.js"));
```

To reference a script bundle in a view, you use the *@Scripts* object:

```
@Scripts.Render("~/site-core-scripts")
```

Figure 10-5 shows the details of the browser's activity when bundles are used.

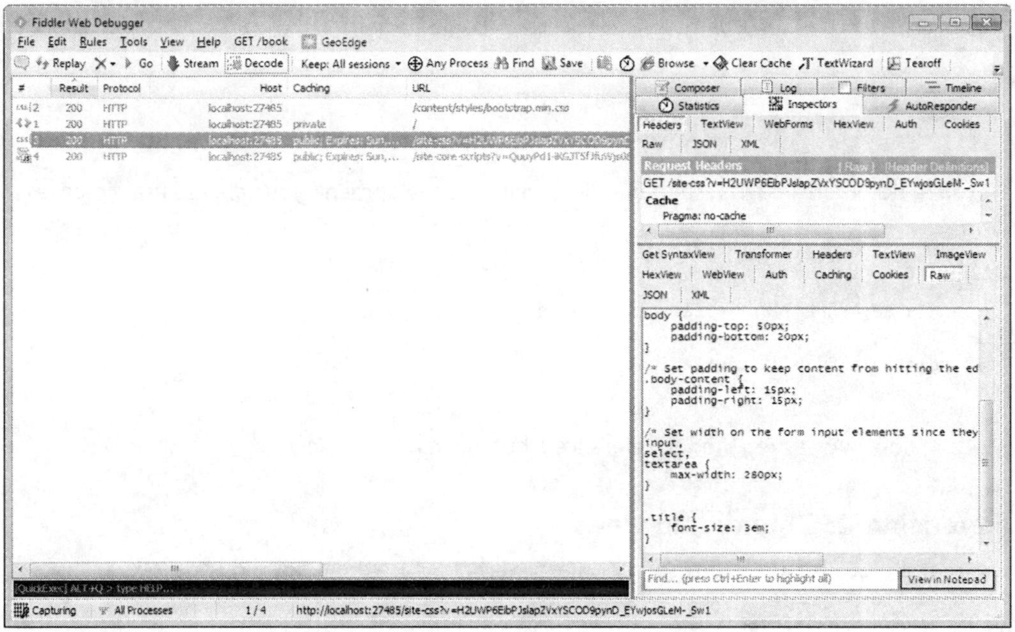

FIGURE 10-5 Browser activity when bundles are used

If you compare the details view of the */site-css* request in the figure with the previously declared content of the *site1.css* and *site2.css* files, you see that the downloaded content is just the combined content of the two files.

Bundle classes can work with CSS or JavaScript files with no differences. However, the *BundleCollection* class has a couple of features that are mostly useful when bundling script files: orderers and ignore lists.

Orderers and ignore lists

The *Bundle* class has a property named *Orderer* of type *IBundleOrderer*. As obvious as it might seem, an orderer is a component responsible for determining the actual order in which you want files to be bundled for download.

The default orderer is the *DefaultBundleOrderer* class. This class bundles files in the order that result from the settings of the *FileSetOrderList* property—another property of *BundleCollection*. The *FileSetOrderList* property is designed to be a collection of *BundleFileSetOrdering* classes. Each of these classes defines a pattern for files (for example, *jquery-**), and the order of *BundleFileSetOrdering* instances determines the actual order of files in the bundle. For example, given the default configuration, all jQuery files are always bundled before Modernizr files. Orderings for common groups of files (such as jQuery, jQuery UI, and Modernizr) are predefined. You can programmatically reset and update orderings at will.

> **Note** The impact of the *DefaultBundleOrderer* class on CSS files is more limited but not null. If you have a *reset.css* file, a *normalize.css* file, or both in your website, they are automatically bundled before any of your other CSS files, and *reset.css* always precedes *normalize.css*.
>
> The goal of having reset/normalize style sheets is to provide a standard set of style attributes for all HTML (reset) and HTML5 (normalize) elements so that your pages don't inherit browser-specific settings such as fonts, sizes, and margins. Although some recommended content exists for both CSS files, the actual content is up to you. If you have files with these names in your project, ASP.NET MVC makes an extra effort to ensure they are bundled before anything else.

If you want to override the default orderer and ignore predefined bundle-file-set orderings, you have two options. First, you can create your own orderer, which works on a per-bundle basis. Here's an example that just ignores predefined orderings:

```
public class SimpleOrderer : IBundleOrderer
{
    public IEnumerable<FileInfo> OrderFiles(
            BundleContext context, IEnumerable<FileInfo> files)
    {
        return files;
    }
}
```

You use it as illustrated here:

```
var bundle = new Bundle("~/all-css");
bundle.Orderer = new SimpleOrderer();
```

In addition, you can reset all orderings by using the following code:

```
bundles.ResetAll();
```

In this case, the effect of using the default orderer or the simple orderer shown earlier is the same. Be aware, though, that *ResetAll* also resets all current script orderings.

The second noteworthy feature is the ignore list. Defined through the *IgnoreList* property of the *BundleCollection* class, it defines the pattern-matching strings for files selected for inclusion in the bundle that should be ignored, instead. The major benefit of ignore lists is you can just specify **.js* in the bundle but use ignore lists to skip over, say, **.vsdoc.js* files. The default configuration for *IgnoreList* takes care of most common scenarios (including **.vsdoc.js* files) while giving you a chance to customize.

Using minification

Minification is a transformation applied to an individual resource. In particular, minification consists of removing all unnecessary characters from a text-based resource in a way that doesn't alter the expected functionality. This means removing comments, white-space characters, and new lines. In general, all such characters in a text file are usually added for readability but take up space without serving any functional purposes.

Readability is important for humans at debug time but is never an issue for browsers. The following string is a sample minified CSS class. It doesn't include any extra characters, and it is perfectly acceptable for a browser:

```
html,body{font-family:'segoe ui';font-size:1.5em;}html,body{background-color:#111;color:#48d1cc}
```

You reference minified CSS and JavaScript files exactly the same way as you reference bundles. Minification is just an additional transformation you make to an existing bundle. So the next question becomes: how do you add minification to CSS and JavaScript files?

Minifying CSS and scripts

The *Bundle* class you've used so far is concerned only with packing multiple resources together so that they are captured in a single download and cached. To add minification, you have two options. One is replacing the *Bundle* class with more specific classes, such as the *StyleBundle* and *ScriptBundle* classes. The other is populating the *Transforms* collection of the *Bundle* class with transformer components that just perform minification on CSS or script files.

Here's the definition of *ScriptBundle* and *StyleBundle* classes. Both inherit from *Bundle* and add a different constructor:

```
public ScriptBundle(string virtualPath)
        : base(virtualPath, new IBundleTransform[] { new JsMinify() })
{
}
public StyleBundle(string virtualPath)
        : base(virtualPath, new IBundleTransform[] { new CssMinify() })
{
}
```

A transformer component is an instance of a class that implements the *IBundleTransform* interface. Script minification is performed via the *JsMinify* class. CSS minification is performed via the *CssMinify* class. Note that the *CssMinify* and *JsMinify* classes are the default minifiers in ASP.NET MVC and are based on the WebGrease framework—one of the elements of the Microsoft ASP.NET Web Optimization framework. You can use a different couple of minifiers if you want. A minifier is simply a class that implements the *IBundleTransform* interface.

If you don't like using *ScriptBundle* and *StyleBundle* and prefer to use the same *Bundle* class, you can add transformers as shown here:

```
public class BundleConfig
{
    public static void RegisterBundles(BundleCollection bundles)
    {
        var cssBundle = new Bundle("~/site-css")
            .Include("~/content/styles/site1.css",
                "~/content/styles/site2.css");
        cssBundle.Transforms.Add(new CssMinify());
        bundles.Add(cssBundle);

        var scriptBundle = new Bundle("~/site-core-scripts")
            .Include("~/content/scripts/jquery-1.10.2.min.js",
                "~/content/scripts/bootstrap.min.js");
        scriptBundle.Transforms.Add(new JsMinify());
        bundles.Add(scriptBundle);

        BundleTable.EnableOptimizations = true;
    }
}
```

Multiple transformers defined for a bundle are applied in the order in which they appear.

Dealing with custom transformers

An interesting example of a custom transformer is the LESS transformer that compiles a LESS script down to CSS and then minifies it. Here's some sample code:

```
var lessBundle = new Bundle("~/site-less")
        .IncludeDirectory("~/content/less", "*.less");
lessBundle.Transforms.Add(new LessTransform());
lessBundle.Transforms.Add(new CssMinify());
bundles.Add(lessBundle);
```

The *LessTransform* class is responsible for turning a LESS file into plain CSS. You can do that programmatically through the services of the *dotless* NuGet package. Once you have the package installed, you can do the following:

```
public class LessTransform : IBundleTransform
{
    public void Process(BundleContext context, BundleResponse response)
    {
        response.Content = dotless.Core.Less.Parse(response.Content);
        response.ContentType = "text/css";
    }
}
```

If you use other intermediate languages for styles, such as CoffeeScript and SASS, you can create analogous classes yourself.

Examining other aspects

All applications need some form of error handling, and a significant share of applications need to restrict access to content to authorized users. In general, developers are quite sensitive to best practices for error handling and security. Every development team tends to consider their solution preferable to everything else they have run across. For this reason, I don't want to spend much time in this chapter providing a step-by-step guide to error handling and user authentication.

What I will do, instead, is summarize the key facts of error handling and user authentication, which will work as a checklist for any solution you might have seen already or that you can easily find by searching on Google and StackOverflow.

Exploring error handling

Error handling in ASP.NET MVC spans two main areas: the handling of program exceptions and route exceptions. The former is concerned with catching errors in controllers and views; the latter is more about redirection and HTTP errors.

Handling program exceptions

Any stack trace you can have in an ASP.NET MVC application originates from a method call in a controller class. Catching program exceptions, therefore, is catching errors from within controller classes. You can have a *try/catch* block surrounding the entire method body. It works, but it's ugly to see, too. A better option probably is overriding the *OnException* method from the base *Controller* class. Yet another option is using the *HandleError* attribute at the controller-class level. Better yet, the *HandleError* attribute—which is ultimately an action filter—can be set globally on every controller and action you can have.

If overridden in any controller class, the following method is invoked every time an unhandled exception occurs in the course of an action method:

```
protected override void OnException(ExceptionContext filterContext)
{
    // Switch to a view/layout that shows appropriate information about what happened.
    ...
}
```

Be aware that no exception that originates outside the controller will be caught by *OnException*. An excellent example of an exception not caught by *OnException* is a null reference exception that results in the model-binding layer. Another good example is a *route not found* exception.

If you don't like the explicit override of *OnException*, you can decorate the controller class (or just individual methods) with the *HandleError* attribute:

```
[HandleError]
public class HomeController
{
    ...
}
```

You can use properties on the attribute to select the exceptions to trap and views to redirect to:

```
[HandleError(ExceptionType=typeof(ArgumentException), View="generic")]
```

Each method can have multiple occurrences of the attribute, one for each exception you're interested in. By default, *HandleError* also redirects to the same view-named error I mentioned earlier. Note that such a view is purposely created by the ASP.NET MVC templates in Visual Studio.

When using *HandleError* at development time, you need to be aware that the attribute doesn't produce any effect unless you enable custom errors at the application level:

```
<customErrors mode="On">
</customErrors>
```

When you go live, remote users will correctly receive the selected error page regardless of whether or not you enable this. To test the feature, though, you need to change the configuration file.

HandleError can be applied automatically to any method of any controller class by registering it as a global filter in *global.asax*:

```
public class MvcApplication : System.Web.HttpApplication
{
    protected void Application_Start()
    {
        RegisterGlobalFilters(GlobalFilters.Filters);
        ...
    }
    public static void RegisterGlobalFilters(GlobalFilterCollection filters)
    {
        filters.Add(new HandleErrorAttribute());
    }
}
```

Global filters are automatically added to the list of filters before the action invoker calls out any action method.

Handling route exceptions

In addition to any program errors you detect, your application might throw exceptions because the URL of the incoming request doesn't match any of the mapped routes—either because of an invalid URL pattern (an invalid action or controller name) or a violated constraint. In this case, your users receive an HTTP 404 error. Letting users receive the default 404 ASP.NET page is something you might want to avoid for a number of reasons, primarily to be friendlier to end users.

The typical solution enforced by the ASP.NET framework consists of defining custom pages (or routes in ASP.NET MVC) for common HTTP codes such as 404 and 403. Whenever the user types or follows an invalid URL, she is redirected to another page where some useful information (hopefully) is provided. Here's how to register ad hoc routes in ASP.NET MVC:

```
<customErrors mode="On">
    <error statusCode="404" redirect="/error/show" />
    ...
</customErrors>
```

This trick works just fine, and there's no reason to question it from a purely functional perspective. So what's the problem, then?

The first problem is with security. By mapping HTTP errors to individualized views, hackers can distinguish between the different types of errors that can occur within an application and use this information for planning further attacks. Thus, you explicitly set the *defaultRedirect* attribute of the *<customErrors>* section to a given and fixed URL and ensure that no per-status codes are set.

A second issue with per-status code views has to do with search engine optimization (SEO). Imagine a search engine requesting a URL that doesn't exist in an application that implements custom error routing. The application first issues an HTTP 302 code and informs the caller that the resource has been temporarily moved to another location. At this point, the caller makes another attempt and finally lands on the error page. This approach is great for humans, who ultimately get a pretty message; it is less than optimal from an SEO perspective because it leads search engines to conclude that the content is not missing at all and that it's just harder than usual to retrieve. And an error page is cataloged as regular content and related to similar content.

On the other hand, route exceptions are a special type of error and deserve a special strategy that's distinct from program errors. Ultimately, route exceptions refer to some missing content.

Looking at all other possible errors

No matter which catch points you might have, an error can always find its way to the user. The *Application_Error* method in *global.asax* is invoked whenever an unhandled exception reaches the outermost shell of ASP.NET code. It's the final call for a developer's code before the yellow screen of death. You could do something useful in this event handler, such as sending an email or writing to the event log:

```
void Application_Error(Object sender, EventArgs e)
{
    var exception = Server.GetLastError();
    if (exception == null) return;

    var mail = new MailMessage { From = new MailAddress("noreply@yourserver.com") };
    mail.To.Add(new MailAddress("administrator@yourserver.com"));
    mail.Subject = "Site Error at " + DateTime.Now;
    mail.Body = "Error Description: " + exception.Message;
    var server = new SmtpClient { Host = "your.smtp.server" };
    server.Send(mail);
```

```
    // Clear the error
    Server.ClearError();

    // Redirect to a landing page
    Response.Redirect("home/landing");
}
```

Although you can always write the error handler yourself, ASP.NET developers often use Error Logging Modules and Handlers (ELMAH). Ultimately, ELMAH is an HTTP module that, once configured, intercepts the *Error* event at the application level and logs it according to the configuration of a number of back-end repositories. The bottom line is that with ELMAH you can handle errors in many more ways and change or add actions with limited work. ELMAH also offers some nice facilities, such as a webpage you can use to view all recorded exceptions and drill down into each of them.

ELMAH is an open-source project available at *http://code.google.com/p/elmah*. It also has numerous extensions, mostly in the area of repositories. To integrate it into your applications, the easiest path you can take is using the NuGet package.

Collecting all application exceptions

A common scenario is collecting all handled exceptions in a single repository and running some analysis on them to identify their frequency and their impact on users. More and more frequently, exception-handling code takes the following form:

```
try {
    // Some operation
}
catch(Exception exception) {
    // Step 1: Handle the exception
    // Step 2: Log the exception to some service
}
```

In the *catch* block, the first step is the canonical recovery step. The second step consists of uploading information about the exception to some server-side or cloud-based repository. Based on the capabilities of the repository API, you can just upload the exception details or more data taken from the current state of the application. The benefit is that such remote or cloud services might offer a visual dashboard to run analytics about the logged exceptions. A popular service of this kind is Microsoft Application Insights. Others are Exceptionless and Raygun. ELMAH also offers a similar logging capability.

Configuring user authentication

In ASP.NET MVC, you choose the authentication mechanism by using the *<authentication>* section in the root *web.config* file. Child subdirectories inherit the authentication mode chosen for the application. By default, ASP.NET MVC applications are configured to use Forms authentication. The following code snippet shows an excerpt from the autogenerated *web.config* file in ASP.NET MVC. (I just edited the logon URL.)

```
<authentication mode="Forms">
   <forms loginUrl="~/Auth/LogOn" timeout="2880" />
</authentication>
```

Configured in this way, the application redirects the user to the specified logon URL every time the user attempts to access a URL reserved for authenticated users. In ASP.NET MVC, you use the *Authorize* attribute every time you have a controller method that only "known" users can invoke. Here's how to use the *Authorize* attribute:

```
[Authorize]
public ActionResult Index()
{
   ...
}
```

You can apply the *Authorize* attribute to individual methods as well as the controller class as a whole. If you add the *Authorize* attribute to the controller class, any action methods on the controller will be available only to authenticated users. The attribute *AllowAnonymous* keeps the method publicly accessible no matter what the settings are at the controller level.

Comparing ways to authenticate users

To authenticate a user, you need some sort of a membership system that supplies methods to manage the account of any users, including checking provided credentials. Building a membership system means writing the software and the user interface to create a new user and update or delete existing users. It also means writing the software for editing any information associated with a user, such as the user's email address, password, and roles. That sounds like too much work, and any framework that can simplify the task is more than welcome. The latest, and probably most highly recommended, framework is Microsoft ASP.NET Identity. (See *http://www.asp.net/identity*.)

More often than not, though, all you need to do is just verify whether the provided user name and password match what's stored in some database. If the validation passes, you want to create the authentication cookie; if it doesn't, you need to send a gentle reply to that effect. Using an identity framework or writing a custom membership provider for such a simple task, frankly, is overkill. Here's a much simpler, yet equally effective way to go.

You create the table of users as you expect it to be and add an ad hoc repository class to centralize read and write access to the users table. Next, you add an account controller to the ASP.NET MVC application with at least a couple of methods, as shown here:

```
public ActionResult Login(LoginViewModel input, String returnUrl)
{
    // Gets posted credentials and proceeds with
    // actual validation
    ...
}
```

```
public ActionResult Logout(String defaultAction="Index", String defaultController="Home")
{
    // Logs out and redirects to the home page
    FormsAuthentication.SignOut();
    return RedirectToAction(defaultAction, defaultController);
}
```

The *Login* method will directly use the repository and make a simple query to see whether a record exists in the table with a matching user name and password. The method gets a Boolean answer and, in the case of a negative response, decides what the most appropriate message is to show to users. If the user exists, it then just uses the ASP.NET (or OWIN) API to create an authentication cookie:

```
FormsAuthentication.SetAuthCookie(userName, rememberMe);
```

For privacy reasons, developers need to consider hashing the password in the database and using the service to check the password. Here's an example:

```
// Check if user exists and credentials match
var found = _passwordHashingService.Validate(password, storedPassword);
if (!found)
{
    response.Message = Strings.AppLogin_InvalidCredentials;
    return response;
}
```

The following code shows a sample password hashing service:

```
public class DefaultPasswordHasher : IHashingService
{
    public bool Validate(string clearPassword, string hashedPassword)
    {
        return String.Equals(HashInternal(clearPassword),
                             hashedPassword,
                             StringComparison.InvariantCulture);
    }

    public string Hash(string clearPassword)
    {
        return HashInternal(clearPassword);
    }

    private string HashInternal(string password)
    {
        const string defaultSalt = "112358";
        var md5 = new MD5CryptoServiceProvider();
        var digest = md5.ComputeHash(
                    Encoding.UTF8.GetBytes(string.Concat(password, defaultSalt)));
        var base64Digest = Convert.ToBase64String(digest, 0, digest.Length);
        return base64Digest.Substring(0, base64Digest.Length - 2);
    }
}
```

This basic schema made of plain code, devoid of any external framework, is sufficient for simple cases. The more you need to support advanced features—such as roles, changing or resetting the password, password lock, and two-phase authentication—the more you might appreciate frameworks with built-in features. In this regard, ASP.NET Identity is the de facto standard, even though you can still use the old-faithful membership system of ASP.NET Web Forms.

Using social authentication

Most social networks use the OAuth protocol to carry authentication on behalf of client applications. Because of the common and standard protocol, a few companies started offering frameworks and services to do OAuth authentication against various social networks. This is beneficial for developers because you declaratively state which social networks you want to enable for authentication and code authentication only once using a unified API, instead of dealing with the heterogeneous API of Twitter, Facebook, Instagram, LinkedIn, and the like.

In some cases, though, you want to authenticate against only a single social network. In my opinion, in this case it is preferable to play by the rules of the specific OAuth API. Here's the code you need to perform Facebook authentication from within an ASP.NET MVC application:

```
public class LoginController : Controller
{
    public ActionResult Facebook()
    {
        var returnUri = new UriBuilder(Request.Url)
        {
            Path = Url.Action("FacebookAuthenticated", "Login")
        };

        var client = new FacebookClient();
        var fbLoginUri = client.GetLoginUrl(new
        {
            client_id = ConfigurationManager.AppSettings["fb_key"],
            redirect_uri = returnUri.Uri.AbsoluteUri,
            response_type = "code",
            display = "popup",
            scope = "email,publish_stream"
        });

        return Redirect(fbLoginUri.ToString());
    }

    public ActionResult FacebookAuthenticated(String returnUrl)
    {
        var redirectUri = new UriBuilder(Request.Url)
        {
            Path = Url.Action("FacebookAuthenticated", "Login")
        };
    var client = new FacebookClient();
    var oauthResult = client.ParseOAuthCallbackUrl(Request.Url);
```

```
    // Exchange the code for an access token
    dynamic result = client.Get("/oauth/access_token",
                        new
                        {
                            client_id = ConfigurationManager.AppSettings["fb_key"],
                            client_secret = ConfigurationManager.AppSettings["fb_secret"],
                            redirect_uri = redirectUri.Uri.AbsoluteUri,
                            code = oauthResult.Code
                        });

        var token = result.access_token;
        SaveAccessTokenToSomeCookie(Response, token);

        // Query Facebook for EXTRA claims about the user
        dynamic user = client.Get("/me", new
            { fields = "first_name,last_name,email", access_token = token });

        var userName = String.Format("{0} {1}", user.first_name, user.last_name);
        var cookie = FormsAuthentication.GetAuthCookie(userName, true);
        Response.AppendCookie(cookie);
        return Redirect(returnUrl ?? "/");
    }

    public ActionResult Signout(String defaultAction = "Index", String defaultController =
"Home")
    {
        FormsAuthentication.SignOut();
        DeleteCookieWithAccessToken(Request);
        return RedirectToAction(defaultAction, defaultController);
    }
}
```

Two prerequisites need to be met for the preceding code to work. One is that you properly register a Facebook application and hold the application ID and secret token. The second prerequisite is that you reference the Facebook C# SDK in the ASP.NET MVC application. You place a Login button in the view and make it point to the *Facebook* endpoint in the *LoginController* class.

The *Facebook* endpoint prepares the internal login URL for Facebook and makes a request. If the request is successful (for example, a matching application exists and is properly configured), the *FacebookAuthenticated* URL is called back. There, the code gets the access code from Facebook that is required to place authenticated calls to the Facebook back end on behalf of a given Facebook user. The code is cached to a private cookie (*SaveAccessTokenToSomeCookie*) and then used to get user information. Once the user information is available, the application creates the ASP.NET authentication cookie. During the logout process, the ASP.NET authentication cookie and the access token cookie are deleted.

Summary

In this chapter, I presented a few practices I use every day when building ASP.NET MVC applications. I started with the organization of folder projects and then discussed a few recommended techniques, such as bundling and error handling. I also touched on user authentication and project types.

I suggest you consider this chapter as a reference and look at it when you need guidance for some aspects of programming. The practices presented here are the results of my personal experience and my perspective on programming. And, as you might understand, experience and perspective are not necessarily the same for everyone!

CHAPTER 11

Presenting data

We need men who can dream of things that never were.

—*John F. Kennedy*

There are very few applications available in which the presentation layer is missing or not that important. In the vast majority of cases, the user interface and, even more, the user experience are all that matter to users. As far as web applications are concerned, the effectiveness of the user interface also depends on the time it takes to refresh the view when changes are applied or more information is requested. The full refresh of the page is an issue that Ajax-based techniques might provide significant help with.

In this chapter, I'll first review the structure of a Razor view—the template language used to arrange HTML views in ASP.NET MVC—and then move on to discuss how to display a list of data and page and scroll through it.

Structuring an HTML view

As you saw in Chapter 8, "Core of ASP.NET MVC," a view served by an ASP.NET MVC application can be described through a Razor template file. A Razor template can receive data to display in various ways, the most complete and general of which is through a view model object. A Razor template is often based on a master layout, and a master layout can be articulated in sections that can be over-ridden in derived views. Finally, a view can be made reusable if you serve it as a partial view. From a purely technical perspective, a partial view is in no way different from a view, except for the fact that a partial view is not based on a layout. Not only are partial views reusable in multiple views and layouts, but views and layouts are composable and easier to edit at any time because of partial views.

Let's examine other aspects of an HTML view in ASP.NET MVC.

Exploring the view model

The term *view model* refers to a class that carries all the data that a given Razor template will process and display. A view-model class is a plain data-transfer object (DTO), mostly made of properties and with nearly no behavior attached. Whether or not you have methods exposed out of a view-model class, however, is a design decision and also a matter of preference to some extent.

Properties of a view-model class, and related types, should be defined primarily to accommodate the needs of the view. This means it's likely that any properties can be a string and related content can be preformatted to a string. This is not mandatory, however. At the same time, it should be clear that a view-model class is a class that plays a specific role—carrying data for a view. A view-model class is a different thing than a domain-model class or a persistence-model class, though in some scenarios the same class can be used for just about everything. Distinguishing various models helps you to make sense of things and better handle complex real-world scenarios.

Defining a common base class

I suggest you define a common base class for all the classes that form the application's view model. Here's a good starting point:

```
public class ViewModelBase
{
    public ViewModelBase()
    {
        Title = "Modern Web Applications";
    }

    public string Title { get; set; }
}
```

At a minimum, such a base class will have a read-write property for the title of the view. In a more realistic scenario, the title of the page is composed to reflect the current path. Here's a slightly more sophisticated and realistic version:

```
public class ViewModelBase
{
    public ViewModelBase()
    {
        Title = YourApplication.DefaultAppTitle;
        Menu = new Menu();
    }

    public string Title { get; private set; }
    public Menu MainMenu { get; set; }

    public ViewModelBase SetTitle(string extra)
    {
        Title = extra.IsNullOrWhitespace()
            ? YourApplication.DefaultAppTitle
            : String.Format("{0} [{1}]", YourApplication.DefaultAppTitle, extra);
        return this;
    }
}
```

The title is set via a method that contains the logic to compose the application title with the suffix that's specific to the current path and status. Other properties can be added as well, such as *Menu*, which contains the menu items to render in the view. In general, the base class for the view model defines all properties that affect all views served by the application, including common elements such as menus, footer, header, and so forth.

Creating instances of the view model class

Whenever a controller method requests the rendering of a view, it indicates the Razor template to render and passes a view-model instance. Instances of a view-model class, therefore, are created under the supervision of the controller method. Because it is recommended to keep the controller class as lean as possible, filling out the view-model class is a task that can be delegated to a worker-service class, as in the following example:

```
public class HomeController : Controller
{
    private readonly HomeService _service = new HomeService();

    public ActionResult Index()
    {
        var model = _service.GetHomeViewModel();
        return View(model);
    }
}
```

I discussed the benefits brought by worker-service classes in Chapter 10, "Organizing the ASP.NET MVC project." Typically, you might want to have a view-model class for each Razor view, except those situations in which an existing class can be patently reused and shared among multiple views. Also, you likely will have worker-service classes go hand in hand with controller classes. Each worker-service class contains methods that orchestrate any requested task and return data ready for display. Sometimes further processing is required on the controller side before a view is invoked, but in general you want to keep the controller as thin as a basic wrapper around a worker service.

Here's a sample implementation of a worker-service method returning a view-model object:

```
public class CountryService
{
    public CountryListViewModel GetCountryListViewModel()
    {
        // Load the list of countries/regions from storage
        var repository = new CountryRepository();
        var model = new CountryListViewModel
        {
            Countries = repository.All().ToList()
        };

        // Perform here further queries and aggregation of data for display purposes.
        // The view model object contains ALL information for the view
        return model;
    }
}
```

Methods of the worker service typically accept data types resulting from model binding at the controller-method level. If requesting specific data is required for the implementation of the task (for example, data stored in the cache or session state), that data is explicitly passed by the controller as plain data. The worker-service class must be agnostic with regard to the HTTP context. In doing so, you ensure it will be fully testable.

```
public ActionResult List()
{
    // Retrieve data from the session state
    var currentPageIndex = (int) (Session["CurrentPageIndex"]);

    // Use session state information with the worker service
    var model = _service.GetListOfCountriesByPage(currentPageIndex);
    return View(model);
}
```

Ultimately, keeping the controller lean and mean involves creating an application layer that separates the presentation layer (where the controller lives) and the back end of the system, where the business logic lies.

Examining the page layout

Nearly every page of an ASP.NET application is based on a fixed layout. In ASP.NET Web Forms, you used to call the layout a *master page*. In ASP.NET MVC, instead, you just have *layout pages*.

Setting a layout page

The *View* method you invoke from a controller to render an HTML view has a few overloads. You can use one of these overloads to indicate the name of the layout page to use in the rendering of the view:

```
[ActionName("List")]
public ActionResult IndexViaGet()
{
    var model = _service.GetCountryListViewModel();
    return View("index", model, "layout");
}
```

The first parameter of the *View* method refers to the name of the Razor file you want to use as the template. It has to be a *.cshtml* file located under the Views project folder. If omitted, the view name defaults to the name of the controller action. In the sample code just shown, the action name is *List*. If the *ActionName* attribute is not specified, the action name defaults to the method name. If the *View* method takes the view name explicitly, that setting overrides any default values.

The layout page can be indicated by name following the same conventions as regular views. The layout page must also be a *.cshtml* file located under the Views project folder. Layouts are commonly shared by multiple views. For this reason, their typical location is the Shared folder under Views. You can also set the layout directly in the view using the following convention:

```
@{ Layout = "~/Views/Shared/YourLayout.cshtml"; }
```

Finally, you can indicate a default layout file that applies to all views where the layout is not explicitly set. You do that by adding a *_viewstart.cshtml* file to the Views folder with the following content:

```
@{ Layout = "~/Views/Shared/YourDefaultLayout.cshtml"; }
```

Note that in the code generated by Microsoft Visual Studio, the default layout file is named _Layout.cshtml. The leading underscore in the name is a convention to indicate layouts and partial views.

Defining the Head section of a page

The layout page is responsible for all common elements of a view. The layout references common stylesheet and script files and adds common meta tags. All of it goes in the HEAD section of an HTML page. Here's a realistic example:

```
<!DOCTYPE html>
<html>
<head>
    <meta charset="utf-8" />
    <meta name="viewport" content="width=device-width, initial-scale=1.0">
    <meta http-equiv="X-UA-Compatible" content="IE=edge">
    <meta name="description" content="What your web site is for ...">
    <meta name="author" content="Just you ...">
    <link rel="stylesheet" href="@Url.Content("~/content/styles/bootstrap.min.css")">
    <link rel="stylesheet" href="@Url.Content("~/content/styles/font-awesome.min.css")">
    <link rel="stylesheet" href="@Url.Content("~/content/styles/yoursite.css")">
    <link rel="stylesheet" href="http://fonts.googleapis.com/css?family=Montserrat:400,700">
    ...
</head>
...
</html>
```

In light of the proliferation of mobile browsers, nowadays it's mandatory to add the *viewport* meta tag to any page served out of a website. In addition, the HEAD section of a page will list all CSS files you want to reference from within all views bound to that layout. Today, that mostly means referencing the Bootstrap library and a glyph library that adds nice icons to style buttons, menus, and links. Bootstrap comes with its own set of glyph icons, but most sites prefer to add other sets of icons. A popular choice is FontAwesome from *http://fortawesome.github.io/Font-Awesome*. The HEAD section of a layout page is also the ideal place to download additional fonts.

> **Note** When used in a URL, the tilde (~) refers to the root path. For quite some time in Razor you had to use the *@Url.Content* function to expand the tilde into the root path of the site. This is no longer necessary if you use a version of ASP.NET MVC newer than version 4. Now you can just type the URL as "~/..." in the various HTML elements and the Razor engine will convert it for you. Note also that proper tilde conversion is relevant only if you deploy the site in a directory and, more importantly, it doesn't apply to JavaScript code.

Defining the website icon

A modern website devoid of an icon looks much less appealing than one with that little graphical touch. Having an icon doesn't make the site more functional, but because of the limited costs of adding an icon I see no reason for not having one. The standard way to define a favicon is the following:

```
<link rel="icon" href="~/yoursite.ico" type="image/x-icon">
```

With regard to the use of the tilde, note that automatic conversion takes place only if the markup is processed by the Razor engine. If you add the line just shown to a plain HTML page and view it from a browser, the tilde will be ignored or interpreted in a browser-specific way.

If no icon is specified in the page, for backward compatibility, nearly all browsers also look for a *favicon.ico* file in the root of the site. If any such file is found, it will be used. So probably the quickest way to add an icon to a site is just by dropping an *.ico* file in the root.

The following form of defining a site icon is deprecated:

```
<link rel="shortcut icon" href="~/yoursite.ico" type="image/x-icon">
```

That format was originally introduced with Internet Explorer. However, today the proprietary value in the *rel* attribute is ignored as long as the type attribute of the LINK element is set to *image/x-icon*.

When it comes to site icons, you might also want to add icons for mobile browsers. Here's how:

```
<link rel="icon" sizes="192x192" href="~/yoursite-192x192.png" type="image/png">
<link rel="apple-touch-icon" sizes="180x180" href="~/yoursite-apple-touch-icon-180x180.png">
```

That's the minimum configuration you want to add to cover Android and iOS browsers. To get a full pack of mobile-browser icons, you can go to *http://www.favicon-generator.org*, grab the files it generates for you, and include the markup it suggests. That guarantees coverage for most mobile scenarios.

Placing scripts in the right place

Putting more and more script in webpages means more and more script files to download. Browsers always download script files synchronously and with limited parallelism. Downloading all referenced script files can be a time-consuming operation; worse yet, any content following any SCRIPT tag is not processed until the script has been downloaded, parsed, and executed. Browsers implement synchronous downloads mostly to stay on the safe side. In fact, there's always the possibility that script files include instructions, such as JavaScript immediate functions or *document.write*, that could modify the status of the current DOM.

A common trick to speed page loading is placing all script references at the end of the page just before the closing *</body>* tag. However, note that all you improve by doing this is the user's perception that the page is loading faster. All it really means is that visible elements of the page display earlier and lengthy downloading that doesn't affect rendering is postponed to the end.

In my opinion, this general practice needs to be re-examined. What matters is laying out clearly which parts of the DOM are affected by which set of JavaScript files and arranging the structure of the view to match that. Even when you place several scripts at the bottom, the download is synchronous. So the page is quick to load and display, but it might be unresponsive for a few seconds until all scripts are effectively downloaded. For complex pages I'm going back to the old practice of having all scripts in the HEAD section and placing at the bottom only those that perform initialization of the DOM, such as jQuery plugin calls.

> **Note** To speed up the load of the page, you can also resort to *SCRIPT* attributes such as *async* and *defer*, which instruct the browser to download scripts asynchronously with the implicit assumption that no dependencies exist between DOM elements and script. When such dependencies exist, and also dependencies between script files exist, you can consider using a framework like RequireJS. (See *http://requirejs.org*.)

Creating the body of the layout

The layout sets the skeleton of a family of views. The skeleton typically contains common elements such as menus, a navigation bar, tabs, a header, a footer, a sidebar, and whatever else a view needs to present to the user in addition to its specific content.

In ASP.NET MVC, each view is rendered from scratch every time and all the data it needs must be retrieved in some way for each and every request. In Web Forms, instead, the viewstate carries most of the rendering data from the currently displayed page. The view-model class is the ideal place to store common elements of a layout to be shared by pages.

Earlier in the chapter, I introduced the *ViewModelBase* class as the parent of all view-model classes. A single root class works well when a single layout is used throughout the entire application. When multiple layouts are being used, you're better off adding a second layer of base view-model classes—one for each layout:

```
public class Layout1ModelBase : ViewModelBase { ... }
public class Layout2ModelBase : ViewModelBase { ... }
```

At a minimum, a layout page must incorporate one replaceable section for the view to render custom content. This section is identified by the *RenderBody* method call:

```
<body>
    <header> ... </header>
    <div>
        @RenderBody()
    </div>
    <footer> ... </footer>
</body>
```

If no *RenderBody* method call is found in the layout page, an exception is thrown.

Presenting the elements of a view

The *RenderBody* method defines a single point of injection within the layout. Although this is a common scenario, you might need to inject content into more than one location. This is where sections fit in. In addition, each section can be composed of partial views, and partial views can reference small factories of HTML code known as *HTML helpers* or, in the newest ASP.NET MVC 6, *tag helpers*.

Sections

In the layout template, you define a custom injection point by placing a call to *RenderSection* at the locations you want those sections to appear:

```
<body>
    <div class="page">
    @RenderBody()
    </div>
    <div id="footer">
       @RenderSection("footer")
    </div>
</body>
```

Each section is identified by name, and all sections are considered mandatory unless you mark them as optional:

```
<div id="footer">
   @RenderSection("footer", false)
</div>
```

The *RenderSection* method accepts an optional Boolean argument that denotes whether the section is required. The following code is functionally equivalent to the preceding code, but it's much better from a readability standpoint:

```
<div id="footer">
   @RenderSection("footer", required:false)
</div>
```

Each section can be given default content that will be used if the section is not overridden in the derived view:

```
@section footer {
    <p>Written by Dino Esposito</p>
}
```

You can define the content for a section anywhere in a Razor view template. In particular, a custom section can be defined within the HEAD element to let derived views add ad hoc CSS files and topmost script files. Another good place to have a section is right before the closing of the body element for late-loading script files:

```
<head>
    ...
   @RenderSection("adhoc_css", required:false)
```

```
    @RenderSection("adhoc_script_top", required:false)
</head>
<body>
    ...
    @RenderSection("adhoc_script_bottom", required:false)
</body>
```

Using sections to split CSS and script dependencies is not all that beneficial from a performance perspective because all CSS and script files are soon cached locally by the browser and won't really take time to download over and over. Using sections does help to keep the code clean, though, and to clarify the list of CSS and script files each view depends on.

Partial views

A partial view is a Razor view not bound to a layout. Because of its nature, a partial view is a reusable component made of code and markup. You can add one to your project via Visual Studio. (See Figure 11-1.) If you're familiar with Web Forms, it's the same as a user control.

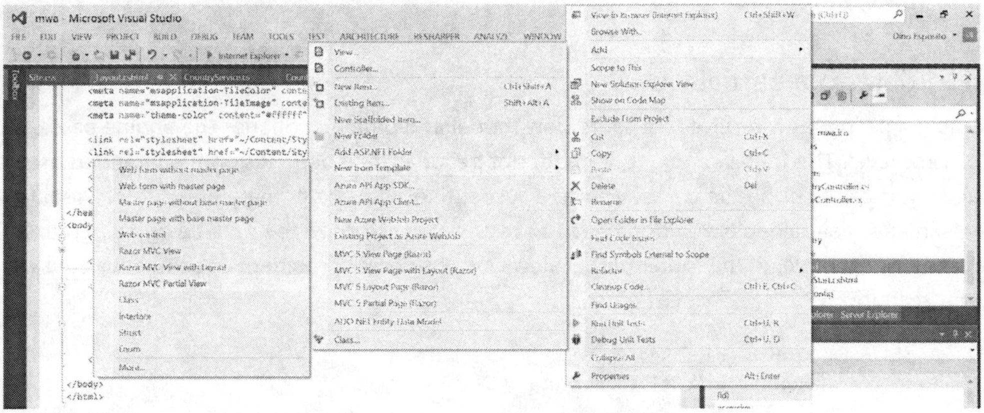

FIGURE 11-1 Adding a Razor partial view to an MVC project

The following code shows a simple but effective partial view:

```
<hr />
<footer>
    <p>&copy; @DateTime.Now.Year - Modern Web Applications with ASP.NET MVC</p>
</footer>
```

If you create a file that just contains the above markup and C# code and name it, say, _Footer.cshtml_, you can invoke it as shown here:

```
<div class="container body-content">
    @RenderBody()
    @Html.Partial("_Footer")
</div>
```

You use either the *Partial* or *RenderPartial* helper method to insert a partial view in a parent view. Both methods take the name of the partial view as an argument. The only difference between the two is that *Partial* returns an HTML-encoded string, whereas *RenderPartial* writes to the output stream and returns void. Because of this, the usage is slightly different:

```
@Html.Partial("_Footer")
@{ Html.RenderPartial("_Footer"); }
```

RenderPartial is perhaps slightly faster, but it doesn't allow further manipulation of the output as a string. You might prefer using *RenderPartial* when you compose distinct and standalone pieces of markup. Using *Partial* instead is the only option when you are iteratively concatenating markup to build the final piece. I'll return to this point with an example in a few moments.

The typical location for a partial view is the Shared folder under Views. This makes the partial view callable from within any controller action. However, you can also store a partial view under the controller-specific folder. In this case, only actions fired from within the specific controller can invoke the partial view.

Passing data to a partial view

By default, a partial view receives the same view model and data dictionaries the engine passes to the parent-view level. This behavior might or might not be ideal. It all depends on the intended use of the partial view. If you're using the partial view as a subroutine, with the primary purpose of keeping the code clean and maintainable, you don't need to restrict or customize the data being passed to it. This is the case, for example, of the footer partial view we considered a moment ago. But let's consider a different scenario:

```
<table class="table table-condensed">
    @foreach (var country in Model.Countries)
    {
        @Html.Partial("_CountryItem", country)
    }
</table>
```

Let's say you are building a table where each row displays some information about a country/region: capital, continent, name, and the like. The parent view receives the entire list of countries/regions from the controller, but the partial view deals only with a specific one. In such situations, you just need to pass ad hoc data to the partial view.

Here's the partial view:

```
@model Mwa.Persistence.Model.Country
<tr>
    <td>@Model.CountryName</td>
    <td>@Model.Capital</td>
    <td>Model.Continent</td>
</tr>
```

Note that in this case you must use *Partial* to render the view. *RenderPartial* won't work here because you need to iterate in order to build the actual markup you want to send to the output stream.

Using render actions

Complex views inevitably result from the composition of various child views. When a controller method triggers the rendering of a view, it must provide all data the view needs for the main structure and all the parts. Sometimes, this requires the controller to know a lot of details about parts of the application the class itself is not directly involved with. Want an example?

Suppose you have a menu to render in many of your views. Whatever action you take in relation to your application, the menu has to be rendered. Rendering the menu, therefore, is an action not directly related to the current ongoing request. How do you handle that? You can pass all data down to the view and use partial views to render menus and sidebars, or you can use render actions.

A *render action* is a controller method specifically designed to be called from within a view. A render action, therefore, is a regular method on the controller class that you invoke from the view by using one of the following HTML helpers: *Action* or *RenderAction*. Here's an example:

```
@Html.Action("action")
```

Action and *RenderAction* behave mostly in the same way—the only difference is that *Action* returns the markup as a string, whereas *RenderAction* writes directly to the output stream. The sample method shown next triggers a specific render action that provides data for the menu to render in the view:

```
public ActionResult Menu()
{
    var options = new MenuOptionsViewModel();
    options.Items.Add(new MenuOption {Url="...", Image="..."});
    options.Items.Add(new MenuOption {Url="...", Image="..."});
    return PartialView(options);
}
```

The content of the menu's partial view is not relevant here; all it does is get the model object and render an appropriate piece of markup.

Take a look at the view source code for one of the pages you might have in the application:

```
<div>
    ...
    @Html.RenderAction("Menu")
    ...
</div>
```

The *RenderAction* helper method calls the *Menu* method on the specified controller (or on the controller that ordered the current view to be rendered) and directs any response to the output stream. In this way, your code is more granular. The view receives just the data it needs for its specific purpose and calls back the controller for any surrounding piece of markup it needs to incorporate. The controller just exposes as separate methods pieces of logic to create menus and sidebars.

> **!** **Warning** Render actions can be a dangerous tool to use. Suppose that you have several widgets to render—such as a menu, header, footer, a couple of sidebars, and advertising boxes. If you use partial views, you typically arrange a single transaction to retrieve all the data you need and pass it in a single shot. If you use render actions for each widget, you also split the data retrieval into multiple steps. If not properly handled, this situation can lead to multiple transactions and overload.

Displaying a list of data items

Let's see now what it takes to accomplish a few common tasks in ASP.NET MVC that revolve around the presentation layer of a web application. The first example is rendering a classic grid of data.

Creating a grid view

As a framework, ASP.NET MVC makes a point of letting you gain full control of the HTML being rendered. This inevitably destroys the idea of having rich and smart controls, such as *GridView* or *ListView*, that offer advanced templating options as well as built-in paging and sorting capabilities. More work is required to get results but, at the same time, more freedom is possible as far as templates are concerned.

Rendering data as a plain grid

At its core, a data grid is a table of data. Therefore, in ASP.NET MVC you just create it as a plain HTML table, perhaps with some optional Bootstrap styles to make it look nicer. (See Figure 11-2.)

```
@model GridView.Models.View.CountryListViewModel
<h2>Countries of the World
    <span class="badge">@Model.Countries.Count found</span>
</h2>
<table class="table table-condensed">
    <thead>
        <th>Name</th>
        <th>Capital</th>
        <th>Continent</th>
    </thead>
    @foreach (var country in Model.Countries)
    {
        <tr>
            <td>@country.CountryName</td>
            <td>@country.Capital</td>
            <td>@country.Continent</td>
        </tr>
    }
</table>
```

The entire grid, or just each row, can be moved to a partial view to make the solution a bit more maintainable:

```
@model GridView.Models.View.CountryListViewModel
<h2>Countries of the World
    <span class="badge">@Model.Countries.Count found</span>
</h2>
@{ Html.RenderPartial("_CountryGrid", Model.Countries); }
```

The _CountryGrid partial view looks like this:

```
<table class="table table-condensed">
    <thead>
      <th>Name</th>
      <th>Capital</th>
      <th>Continent</th>
    </thead>
    @foreach (var country in Model)
    {
        @Html.Partial("_CountryItem", country)
    }
</table>
```

And finally, the _CountryItem partial view is the same as the one presented earlier while discussing ways to pass data to a partial view.

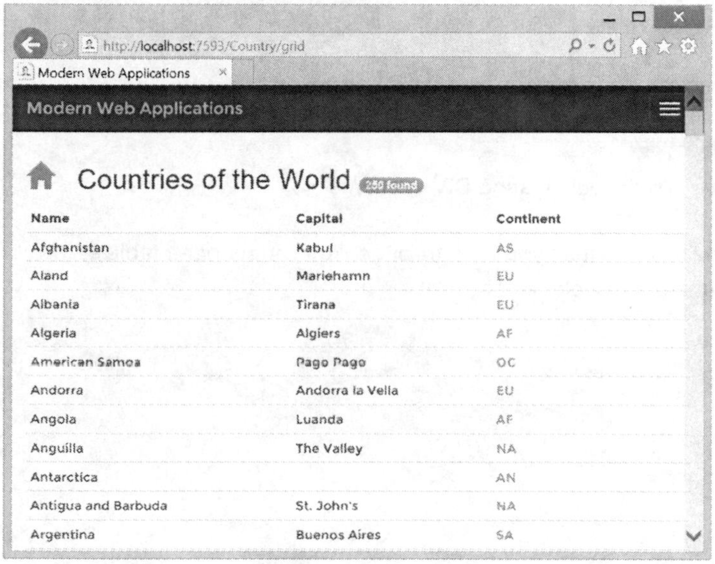

FIGURE 11-2 A plain and simple grid of data

Rendering data as tiles

In Web Forms, setting up a grid is quite trivial, but changing the layout to anything else can be quite cumbersome, especially if you want to achieve ad hoc views like those you find in some trendy websites. With ASP.NET MVC, you have full control over the HTML and can set up virtually any presentation layout with a limited (but not null) effort.

Here's how to present the same data list as a sequence of tiles rendered into a given container. (See Figure 11-3.)

FIGURE 11-3 Data rendered sequentially through floating DIV elements

The trick is what you do for each data item you loop through. You can render a table as in Figure 11-2 or you can create floating *DIV* elements:

```
<div id="tile-container">
@foreach (var country in Model.Countries)
{
    // Create a floating DIV
    <div style="float: left; ...">
      ...
    </div>
}
</div>
<div class="clearfix"></div>
```

Each DIV element renders its content—image and text as in the figure—and is styled with the *float* CSS attribute set to *left*. The net effect of the *float* attribute is that *DIV* elements are horizontally aligned one to the next instead of being rendered as blocks. The *clearfix* class applied at the bottom DIV is a Bootstrap class that restores the default block-style rendering of *DIV* elements. If you don't use Bootstrap, here's how you can achieve the same effect of the *clearfix* class:

```
<div style="clear: both" />
```

Server controls are powerful tools and accelerate development at the cost of accepting a few predefined layouts or looking for ad hoc custom controls. Next, I'll show you an even more representative example.

Rendering data in logical groups

Suppose the list of data you need to display is too long to be effectively consumed by users. Hence, you want to split it into logical groups. Say you want to organize a list of countries by continent or initials. In the end, it's similar to pagination except that some logic is required to create and display groups. A generic component that can be used is a tab list. In Bootstrap, you find all the low-level tools you need.

Let's see how to organize views to obtain the effect shown in Figure 11-4.

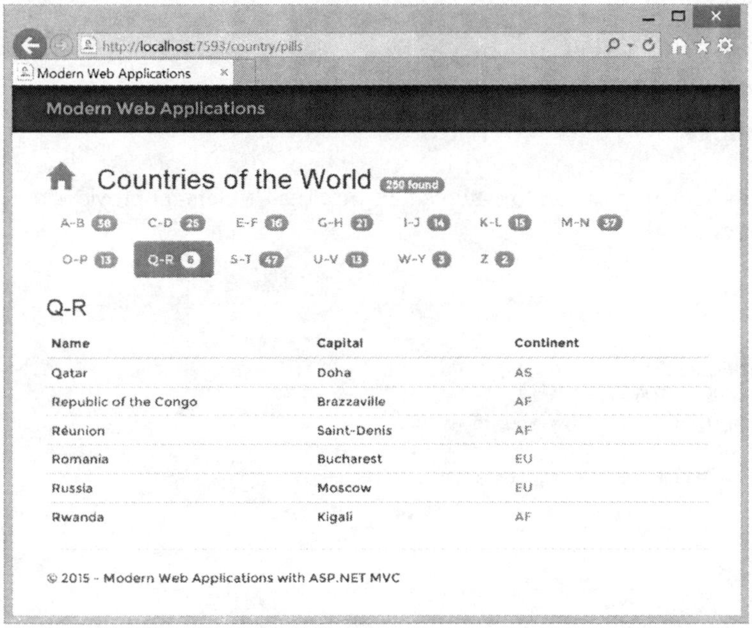

FIGURE 11-4 Logically grouped data

To obtain a view like the one shown in Figure 11-4, you need the controller to pass ad hoc data down to the view engine. The view must receive both the list of tab headers and the country/region list for each tab to render:

```
public ActionResult Pills()
{
    var model = _service.GetCountryGroupsViewModel();
    return View(model);
}
```

The worker service returns a view-model class defined as shown here:

```
public class CountryGroupsViewModel : ViewModelBase
{
    public CountryGroupsViewModel()
    {
        Groups = new List<CountryGroup>();
    }
    public IList<CountryGroup> Groups { get; set; }
}

public class CountryGroup
{
    public CountryGroup()
    {
        Header = "?";
        Countries = new List<Country>();
    }
    public string Header { get; set; }
    public IList<Country> Countries { get; set; }
}
```

The Razor view uses a few Bootstrap classes to set up a tab strip. The UL element provides the selectable tabs styled as pills:

```
<ul class="nav nav-pills">
    @foreach (var g in Model.Groups)
    {
        var isActive = (g.Header.StartsWith("A") ? "active" : "");
        <li role="presentation" class="@isActive">
            <a href="#group_@g.Header" data-toggle="tab">
                @g.Header
                <span class="badge">@g.Countries.Count()</span>
            </a>
        </li>
    }
</ul>
```

The following *DIV* element includes the list of child sections, each providing the detail view of a tab:

```
<div class="tab-content">
    @foreach (var g in Model.Groups)
    {
        var isActive = (g.Header.StartsWith("A") ? "active" : "");
```

```
            <div role="tabpanel" class="tab-pane @isActive" id="group_@g.Header">
                <h3>@g.Header</h3>
                @Html.Partial("_CountryGrid", g.Countries)
            </div>
    }
</div>
```

Working at a lower level of abstraction also involves spending more time thinking about the ideal organization of the data to show and the ideal navigation experience for users. When you have too-powerful components available, on the other hand, you inevitably tend to see data as a function of what those tools can do. It's a known pattern after all: when all you have is a hammer, everything you see looks like a nail.

Adding paging capabilities

Paging data is not overly complex, but it can be boring and that data is not always as reusable as one would expect. As you'll see in a moment, the pattern for paging through a list of data items is well established and mature, and a few high-quality NuGet packages also exist to streamline most of the tasks. Yet, there's always a bit of work that might be required every time to set up the user interface, provide ad hoc endpoints to collect data pages, or both.

Selecting a helper package

At its core, pagination is about selecting a slice of data out of a larger data set. In doing so, you also need to define the size of the page and track the current index. Finally, you need a paging toolbar to allow the user to jump to the previous or next page or just to a specific page. In Web Forms, paging was incorporated in rich data-bound controls such as *GridView* and *ListView*. In ASP.NET MVC, you have a few options when it comes to paging:

- Use a fully JavaScript solution.

- Use some third-party components for ASP.NET MVC.

- Build your own paging solution based on commonly available facilities.

One of the best 100 percent JavaScript solutions for paging a grid of data is Guriddo jqGrid. A demo of the product can be found at *http://www.guriddo.net/demo/guriddojs*. The library fully supports Bootstrap and is subject to a license fee. Incorporating the grid in a view requires only a bit of JavaScript. Overall, the effort is analogous to configuring a *GridView* in ASP.NET Web Forms. Here's the page layout:

```
<table id="grid"></table>
<div id="pager"></div>
<script>
    $(document).ready(function() {
        $("#grid").jqGrid({
            url: ...,
            colModel: [
                { label: 'Name', name: 'CountryName', key: true, width: 200 },
                ...
```

```
        ],
        rowNum: 30,
        pager: "#pager"
    });
  });
</script>
```

The component will query the specified URL for some JSON or JSONP data and populate the grid dynamically. The pager is also filled appropriately based on the size of the downloaded data set. Once the view is complete, paging and sorting are done out of the box.

Another option is looking into the offering of popular component vendors like Telerik. A demo of a powerful grid component that offers paging and sorting capabilities can be found here: *http://demos.telerik.com/aspnet-mvc/grid/index.*

The solution I'm presenting here is based on a NuGet package called PagedList. (See Figure 11-5.)

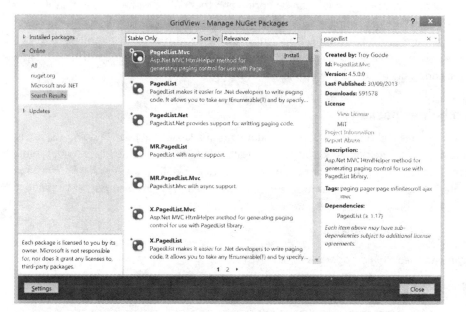

FIGURE 11-5 The PagedList NuGet package used in the sample project

URL-based paging

To arrange a paging solution based on the PagedList NuGet package, the most important thing you can do is expose a controller endpoint that can provide data for each requested page. Once the endpoint has been set, turning the grid of Figure 11-2 into a paging grid is as simple as this:

```
<div style="text-align:center">
    @Html.PagedListPager(
            Model.CountriesInPage,
            page => "/country/pagedgrid?p=" + page)
</div>
@{ Html.RenderPartial("_CountryGrid", Model.CountriesInPage.ToList()); }
```

The _CountryGrid partial view is the same one I used earlier in the chapter. The only difference is that it now receives only a page of data. The *Html.PagedListPager* is a function in the package that just renders the pager. (See Figure 11-6.)

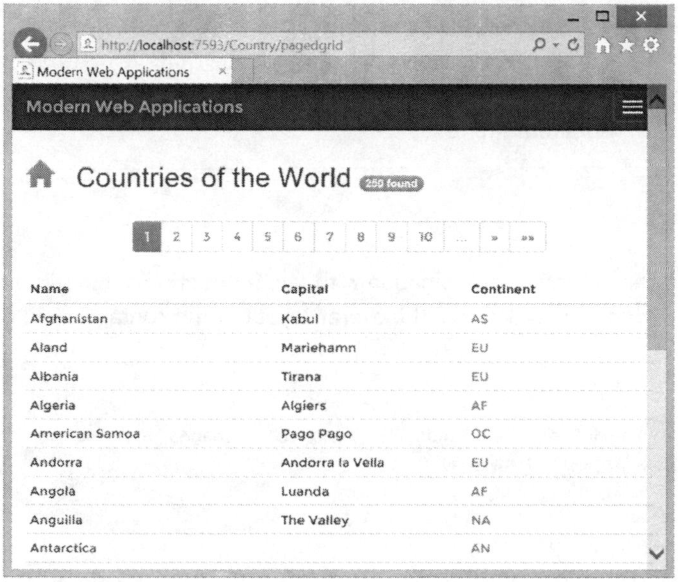

FIGURE 11-6 A paged grid

Each button in the pager is an anchor tag and points to a specific controller action. The controller action must accept a couple of parameters, such as the index of the page and the size of the pages:

```
public ActionResult PagedGrid(
    [Bind(Prefix = "p")] int pageIndex = 1,
    [Bind(Prefix = "s")] int pageSize = 20)
{
    var model = _service.GetPagedCountryListViewModel(pageIndex, pageSize);
    return View(model);
}
```

The hardest work is done by the service-layer method, which is responsible for filling out a view model, as shown here:

```
public class PagedCountryListViewModel : ViewModelBase
{
    public PagedList<Country> CountriesInPage { get; set; }
}
```

PagedList in the example is an ad hoc collection type defined in the NuGet package. It wraps up the data items to render as well as information about the page index and size. In the example, the view-model class receives only the data items to render in the view.

Ajax-based paging

The PagedList NuGet package also can be used in combination with JavaScript and Ajax to retrieve subsequent pages. When Ajax is used to page a data set, the overall layout of the container looks like this:

```
<div id="pager">
    <img id="loader" style="display:none" src="@Url.Content("~/content/images/loading.gif")" />
    <!-- dynamically populated upon page loading -->
</div>
<div id="grid">
    <!-- dynamically populated upon page loading -->
</div>

<script type="text/javascript">
    <!-- Load first page -->
</script>
```

The controller action is nearly the same as in the previous case. You still need an endpoint that knows how to retrieve a view model for a given page index. In this case, though, you have the additional problem of refreshing the DOM with retrieved data. In the solution you find implemented in the companion code of this book, both the page and its pager are rendered on the server and returned to the browser in a single response. Some ad hoc JavaScript code on the client page will take care of separating the markup of the pager from the markup of the page and update DOM segments independently. Here's an excerpt of the controller code:

```
public ActionResult Page(
    [Bind(Prefix = "p")] int pageIndex = 1,
    [Bind(Prefix = "s")] int pageSize = 10)
{
    var model = _service.GetPagedCountryListViewModel(pageIndex, pageSize);

    // Store the view model for EACH partial view (if models are of different types)
    ViewData["_CountryGrid"] = model.CountriesInPage.ToList();
    ViewData["_CountryGridPager"] = model;

    return new MultipleViewResult(
        PartialView("_CountryGridPager"),
        PartialView("_CountryGrid"));
}
```

The JavaScript code in the host page looks like this:

```
// Load first page
_p(1, 20);

function _p(pageIndex, pageSize) {
    new Paginator({
        urlBase: "/country/page",
        pageIndex: pageIndex,
        pageSize: pageSize,
        loaderSelector: $("#loader"),
        updater: function(chunks) {
            $("#pager").html(chunks[0]);
            $("#grid").html(chunks[1]);
        }
    }).select();
}
```

The *Paginator* JavaScript object is also defined in the project as a wrapper around an Ajax call to the controller's paging action:

```
var PaginatorSettings = function () {
    var that = {};
    that.urlBase = false;
    that.pageIndex = 1;
    that.pageSize = 10;
    that.loaderSelector = '';
    that.updater = '';
    return that;
}

var Paginator = function (options) {
    // Merge provided and default settings
    var settings = new PaginatorSettings();
    jQuery.extend(settings, options);

    this.select = function() {
        var url = settings.urlBase + "?p=" + settings.pageIndex + "&s=" + settings.pageSize;
        $(settings.loaderSelector).show();
        $.ajax({ url: url })
            .done(function(response) {
                $(settings.loaderSelector).hide();
                window.location.hash = settings.pageIndex;

                // Refresh page content and pager
                var splitter = new MultipleViewResult();
                var chunks = splitter.split(response);
                settings.updater(chunks);
            });
    };
}
```

As you might have noticed, the controller paging action merges the partial view of the page and the partial view of the pager. The _CountryGridPager_ partial view internally uses the *PagedList* helper method to render the pager:

```
@Html.PagedListPager(
    Model.CountriesInPage,
    page => "javascript:_p(" + page + "," + Model.CountriesInPage.PageSize + ")")
```

In summary, handcrafting paged grids with and without Ajax is possible, but in the economy of a real-world project your best option is spending some money on a professional component, especially if you're running short of time.

Adding scrolling capabilities to page elements

A modern webpage is rarely monolithic. More often than not, instead, it is made of a few DIV elements laid out together. Sometimes a DIV element is rendered as an independent block just the for the sake of programming or reusability. In some other cases, the *DIV* is there to delimit a fixed area of the page and show some given content only within the boundaries of the element. This introduces the need for scrolling. And scrolling can be horizontal or vertical.

Horizontal scrolling

Making an HTML DIV scroll horizontally has never been a big issue for developers. If it wasn't often used, that was only because most decision-makers considered it a bad practice of limited, or at least controversial, usability. The whole perspective of horizontal scrolling changed completely with the advent of mobile devices when the "swipe" gesture became natural. Although it's still controversial for a web view aimed at desktop devices, a DIV that extends for the entire width of the screen and lets users swipe to get more content is a powerful tool for tablet and smartphone interfaces.

Let's see how to revisit the grid example to make the list of countries/regions scroll horizontally with full support for the swipe gesture.

First and foremost, horizontal scrolling is a matter of having the right CSS in the right place. Here's the Razor structure of the scrollable element:

```
<div class="country-container">
@foreach (var country in Model.Countries)
{
    <!-- Render the data item here -->
}
</div>
```

The trick is all in the CSS class that decorates the *DIV* element:

```
.country-container {
    width: auto;
    height: 320px;
    border: 13px solid #555;
    overflow-x: scroll;
```

```
        overflow-y: hidden;
        white-space: nowrap;
        padding: 10px;
    }
```

The width of the element is set to auto, which means that it takes the size determined by the *content* and *container* elements. If too much content is available, a scrollbar will be added. No vertical scrollbar whatsoever will be added, regardless of the actual height of the content. (See Figure 11-7.)

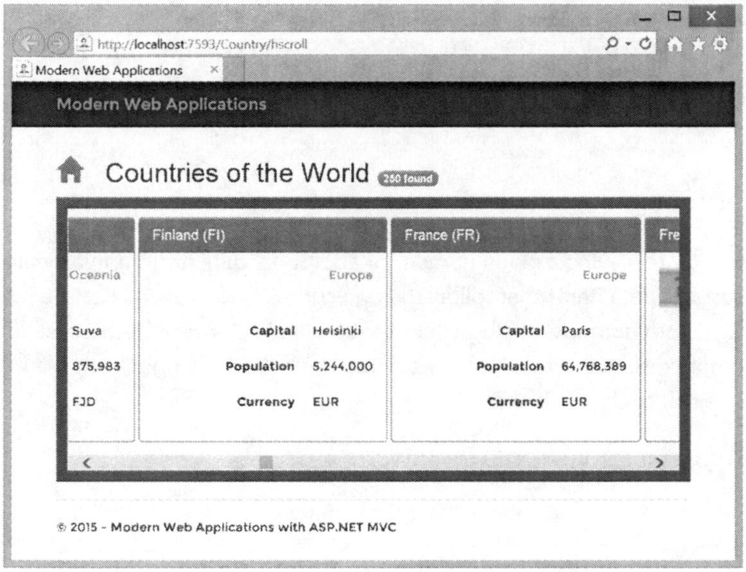

FIGURE 11-7 Horizontal scrolling of content

On-demand scrolling

For years, paging data meant giving users a list of buttons and expecting them to click to get more. Recently, some popular websites—most notably LinkedIn—introduced a different pattern: when the user scrolls beyond the bottom of the container, more content is downloaded and dynamically appended to the existing view. Let's see how to implement such a feature.

Let's start with the following Razor code that renders the initial page of a data grid:

```
@{
    const int maxInitialNumber = 40;
    const int chunkSize = 10;
}
<table id="list" class="table table-condensed" data-last="@maxInitialNumber">
    <thead>
        <th>Name</th>
        <th>Capital</th>
        <th>Continent</th>
    </thead>
    @Html.Partial("_CountryTableItems", Model.Countries.Take(maxInitialNumber).ToList())
</table>
```

The _CountryTableItems_ partial view just renders the table rows. The markup of the view has been isolated to a partial view file because you need to return an additional collection of rows when the user scrolls beyond the bottom. When this code runs, the user sees the first chunk of rows and can freely scroll through them using the browser's scrollbar.

Let's now add some script code to detect the bottom of the page:

```
<script type="text/javascript">
    $(window).on("scroll", function () {
        var scrollHeight = $(document).height();
        var scrollPosition = $(window).height() + $(window).scrollTop();
        if ((scrollHeight - scrollPosition) / scrollHeight === 0) {
            // Scrolling reached to the bottom of the page. Load more data...
            ...
        }
    });
</script>
```

On-demand scrolling works by retrieving a given number of additional data items. In particular, you might want to retrieve just the data items that follow the one currently displayed last. The index of the last item is stored as a custom *data-last* attribute into the scrollable element, in this case an HTML TABLE element. The script code that runs when the bottom is reached will figure out the index of the last element and place a call to the back end:

```
var from = parseInt($("#list").attr("data-last"));
var size = @chunkSize;
var url = "/country/more?from=" + from + "&howMany=" + size;
$.ajax({ url: url })
    .done(function (markup) {
        // Add downloaded data items to the current view
    });
```

The controller action is made to measure and likely accepts a starting index and the number of items to retrieve:

```
public ActionResult More(int from, int howMany = 10)
{
    var model = _service.GetCountryListViewModel();
    return PartialView("_CountryTableItems", model.Countries.Skip(from).Take(howMany).ToList());
}
```

The final touch is finding a way to dynamically append markup to an existing DOM. The way you achieve this depends on the nature of the scrollable element. If it's a TABLE element, the following code works fine:

```
$("#list").attr("data-last", from + size);
$("#list tr:last").after(markup);
```

You first update the *data-last* attribute and then append more rows to the table. (See Figure 11-8.)

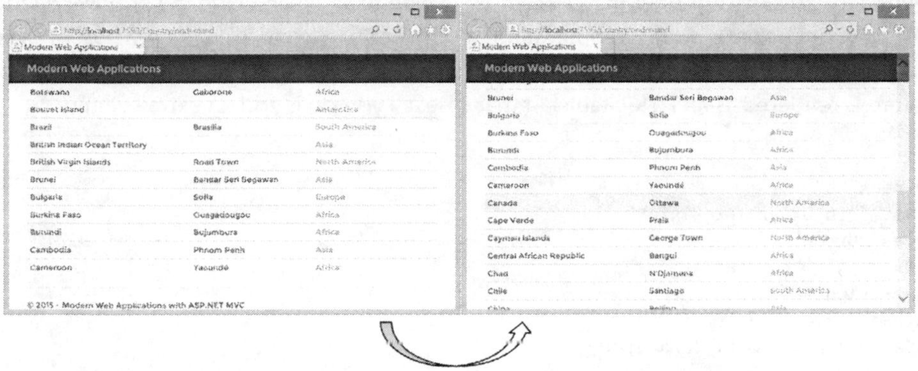

FIGURE 11-8 More data items added when scrolling reaches the bottom of the page

Adding a detail view

The canonical implementation of a master/detail view entails that from the master view the user selects a particular element and jumps to a separate page that provides additional information about that particular record. This pattern worked for years and still works beautifully today. The only problem with this pattern is that it can be cumbersome for users if the website is a heavy one and is particularly rich in graphical elements. In this case, jumping back and forth between master and detail pages can soon become an unpleasant experience. Let's explore a couple of alternatives.

Popover views

Bootstrap makes it particularly easy to add a *popover*, or an HTML-rich tooltip, to page elements. A popover contains additional information for a quick drill-down into the selected element. Note that a popover doesn't fully replace a full detail page, but it can be an effective middle way and might save the server a few roundtrips. At the same time, the overlay nature of the popover doesn't flood the user interface with too much second-level information.

There are two steps required to arrange a popover facility with Bootstrap. First, your list of data items must include toggle elements that trigger the popover. Second, you need to explicitly opt in to using the popover feature with a line of script. In Bootstrap, in fact, popovers are considered quite an intrusive feature, and for this reason opt-in is required.

Adding the toggle facility

The popover needs an explicit trigger that users interact with to show and hide the popover window. This is typically an anchor or a button. If you want the popover to appear just when the user hovers over any page element, you'd better use a rich Bootstrap tooltip. Suppose the list of data items to further explore is rendered as an HTML table. In that case, all you do is add an extra column:

```
<td>
    <a tabindex="0"
        class="btn btn-xs btn-info"
        role="button"
        data-toggle="popover"
        data-trigger="focus"
        data-placement="left"
        data-content="@Model.ToPanel()">
        More info
    </a>
</td>
```

The *data-trigger* attribute sets the expected interaction model. A value of *focus* indicates that the popover appears and disappears as the toggle element gets or loses the input focus. Other options are *hover* or *click*. The *data-placement* attribute indicates the position where the popover will show with respect to the toggle element. For more information, refer to the Bootstrap documentation: *http://getbootstrap.com/javascript/#popovers*.

Enabling popovers

As mentioned, popovers and tooltips in Bootstrap are opt-in features. This means that once the markup is fully configured nothing happens until the following script code is processed:

```
<script type="text/javascript">
    $('[data-toggle="popover"]').popover({
        html: true
    });
</script>
```

This script goes at the bottom of the page and needs to run once the page DOM has been fully initialized. It must follow jQuery and Bootstrap script references, though. The jQuery selector can generically capture all popover toggle elements in the page or just one in particular.

The final aspect to consider is the content you display through the popover. If you want it to include HTML formatted text, the *html* option property must be set to *true* as in the example.

Setting the popover content

The popover is designed to present relatively small pieces of secondary information that doesn't fit—for whatever reason—in the main user interface. In other words, you don't want to dynamically determine the content of the popover when it shows up. Bootstrap, however, fires proper events when the popover is about to show, is shown, or is dismissed.

As I see things, the appropriate way to use popovers is through some predefined HTML text that downloads with the host page (if you are in an ASP.NET MVC scenario) or is set up within the page DOM if you're in the context of a Single-Page Application (SPA). You can set the popover content via the *data-content* attribute of the toggle element. Alternatively, you can resort to a specific setting of the popover plugin:

```
<script type="text/javascript">
    $('[data-toggle="popover"]').popover({
        html: true,
        content: function() {
            return "Some text";
        }
    });
</script>
```

Most likely, the text you intend to display is found within the DOM but is specific to a given data item. How can you retrieve the specific data item the popover is being called on from within the plugin? Let's say you want to retrieve the popover content from a hidden DIV that exists for each data item. In the toggle element, you add a custom attribute that contains anything that uniquely identifies the data item—for example, a *data-id* attribute:

```
<td>
    <a tabindex="0"
        ...
        data-toggle="popover"
        data-trigger="focus"
        data-id="@Model.CountryCode">
        More info
    </a>
</td>
```

Next, in the plugin configuration you retrieve the attribute and build the selector for the DIV. The following example assumes your data item's additional DIVs are identified as *yourDiv_XXX*, where *XXX* is the ID of the data item:

```
<script type="text/javascript">
    $('[data-toggle="popover"]').popover({
        html: true,
        content: function() {
            var code = $(this).attr("data-id");
            return $("#yourDiv_" + code).html();
        }
    });
</script>
```

Figure 11-9 shows a popover in action.

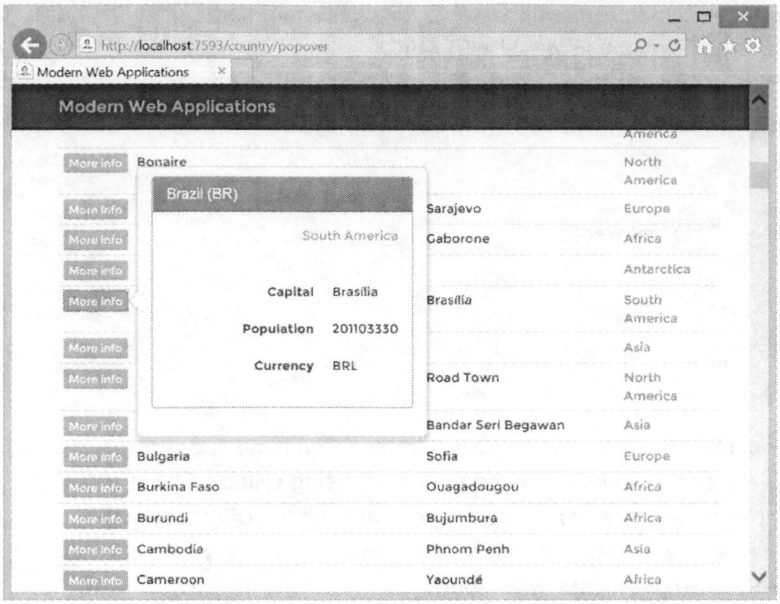

FIGURE 11-9 A Bootstrap-based popover in action

Drill-down views

Another common example of a detail view is when you click on a given item and a hidden section of the same page shows up to let users drill down into the item. Compared to popovers, a drill-down view typically presents a much more sophisticated layout that is not repeated for each bound data item. You have one DIV representing the viewer and dynamically retrieve information to show when an item is selected. In the end, the drill-down view presented here is analogous to the classic master/details pattern except that no browser-led navigation takes place.

Preparing the list

A drill-down view is articulated in a list that serves as the menu and a distinct viewer where details of the selected item will show up. The list must be made of clickable elements. Here's an example:

```
<table class="table table-condensed table-hover">
    @foreach (var country in Model.Countries)
    {
        <tr id="tr_@country.CountryCode" onclick="expand('@country.CountryCode')">
            <td>@country.CountryCode</td>
            <td>@country.CountryName</td>
        </tr>
    }
</table>
```

The TR elements are given a unique ID and *click* handler. By clicking anywhere on the table row, you run the script that will read the ID attribute and use that to place a remote call for further details. Here's a sample script:

```
function expand(code) {
    $("tr").removeClass("active");
    $("#tr_" + code).addClass("active");

    var url = "/country/details/" + code;
    $.getJSON(url).done(function (data) {
        $("#code").html(code);
        $("#name").html(data.CountryName);
        $("#flag").attr("src", "/content/images/flags/" + code + ".png");
        $("#continent").html(data.ContinentName);
        $("#population").html(data.Population);
        $("#area").html(data.AreaInSqKm);
        $("#languages").html(data.Languages);
        $("#currency").html(data.CurrencyCode);
        $("#drilldownViewer").collapse('show');
    });
}
```

The first two lines of the script just set the active state on the selected row. The rest of the code places a call to a remote endpoint for the JSON data of the country/region and then update elements of the viewer area.

Setting up the viewer

The viewer is a plain DIV element that can be optionally configured as a Bootstrap collapsible element:

```
<div id="drilldownViewer" class="collapse">
    <img id="flag"
        onerror="this.src='@Url.Content("~/content/images/flags/none.png")'" />
    <dl class="dl-horizontal">
      <dt>Name</dt>
      <dd><span id="name"></span></dd>
      <dt>Continent</dt>
      <dd><span id="continent"></span></dd>
      <dt>Population</dt>
      ...
    </dl>
</div>
```

Data retrieval occurs via jQuery and takes advantage of the built-in caching capabilities of the jQuery Ajax framework. Most of the time, the actual request for JSON data is resolved by looking into the local cache of the browser. This fact makes any performance concerns quite relative. (See Figure 11-10.)

Obviously, though, as a developer you have both the option of disabling the jQuery automatic Ajax caching or setting a proper caching policy on the server side that makes the downloaded content expire after a suitable amount of time.

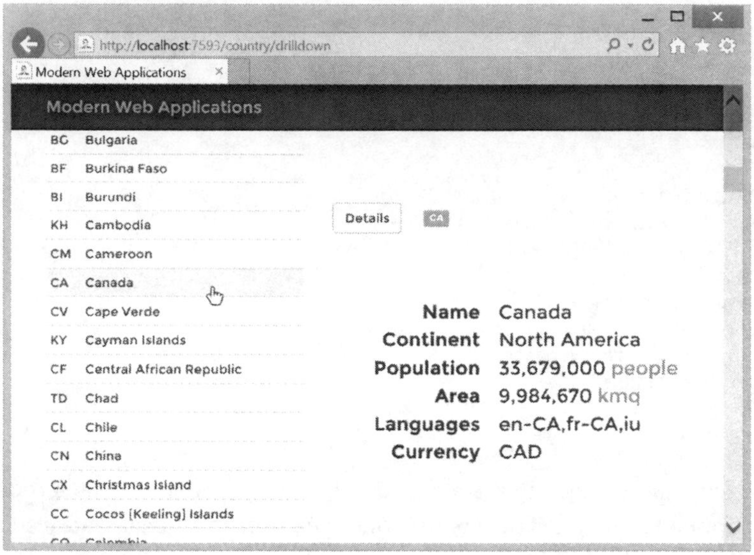

FIGURE 11-10 A drill-down view built with jQuery and Bootstrap

Tip More often than not, the list of data items is long and exceeds the visible area of the page. This means that when you scroll to reach a given data item, the drill-down viewer is pushed outside the screen. To avoid that, just set the *position* CSS attribute of the DIV element that contains the viewer to the value of *fixed*.

Note Another possible option for implementing detail views is modal dialog boxes. I am very careful about using modal dialogs for details views. It mostly depends on the expected frequency with which details are requested. A modal dialog needs be closed before another element can be selected. This makes the solution quite annoying and cumbersome for the user. In addition, modal dialogs are not that great in terms of usability on tablets and smartphones. It is not by chance, in fact, that popovers—a very lightweight form of modal dialogs—have been introduced with the iPad user interface.

Summary

Presenting data is what most webpages do most of the time. Presenting data is also a critical aspect of the overall user experience a site offers to users. You must be careful about navigation and paging through data, and also careful about sorting and filtering—all that's required for users to find the information they need quickly and effectively. ASP.NET MVC has been a game-changer in this regard, dismissing rich server controls and pushing the manual arrangement of HTML5 solutions.

In this chapter, I discussed a few common ASP.NET MVC techniques to build effective presentation layers. I mostly relied on Bootstrap, but I encourage you to use professional components for even more better-looking and easy-to-use user interfaces.

Editing data

It matters not what someone is born, but what they grow to be.

— *J. K. Rowling*

At its core, editing data from within an ASP.NET MVC application is easy. All you do is create an HTML form and post data from there to some HTTP endpoints. To be even more precise, it all boils down to arranging a POST (or even a GET) HTTP call to pass all necessary data. To place an HTTP call, you can use jQuery or plain Ajax facilities, but using an HTML form is still the most widely used approach.

In this chapter, I'll review a few common practices for posting data to a web server and for dealing with the system's feedback, whether that feedback is a plain confirmation or a list of errors.

A common form for the login page

In any realistic application, only authorized users are entitled to edit some server-held content. In the final part of Chapter 10, "Organizing the ASP.NET MVC project," I covered the basics of user authentication in ASP.NET MVC.

I didn't spend much time explaining the mechanics of the login page, though. Specifically, I didn't say much about the process of validating credentials and how login failure can be handled.

Presenting the form

Based on the information in the *web.config* file, the ASP.NET runtime redirects unauthenticated users to the login page. The return URL is appended to the query string. What users see next is the login page.

> **Note** What if a method that requires authentication, authorization, or both is also configured to support output caching? Output caching (specifically, the *OutputCache* attribute) instructs ASP.NET MVC to not really process the request every time and, instead, to return any cached response that was previously calculated and that is still valid (for example, not expired).
>
> If output caching is enabled, a user might request a protected URL already in the cache. ASP.NET MVC ensures that the *Authorize* attribute takes precedence over output caching. In particular, the output-caching layer returns any cached response for a method subject to *Authorize* only if the user is authenticated and authorized.

The login form

The login page is a plain HTML form with a few input fields such as a text box for the user name or email address, a text box for the password, and optionally a check box to determine the expiration date of the authentication cookie:

```
<form method="POST" action="@Url.Action("login", "account")">
    <input type="hidden" name="ReturnUrl" value="..." />

    <label for="username">Username</label>
    <input type="text" id="username" name="username" />

    <label for="username">Password</label>
    <input type="password" id="password" name="password" />

    <label>
        @Html.CheckBox("RememberMe")
        Remember me
    </label>
</form>
```

In a Razor view, you can output HTML elements as plain HTML or output them via a few predefined helpers that offer a higher-level syntax. Usually, there's no difference between helpers and plain HTML code, except when the HTML code required comprises multiple elements. This is precisely the case of *Html.CheckBox*. The core INPUT element of type check box won't upload a Boolean value and won't upload any value if the check box is not selected. Hence, to guarantee that the ASP.NET binding layer (discussed in Chapter 8, "Core of ASP.NET MVC") works effectively, you need an additional hidden *INPUT* field with the same ID as the check box. This is precisely what you achieve through a rather compact syntax when you use the *Html.CheckBox* helper.

Also, note the hidden field added in the form to store the return URL. When the ASP.NET runtime redirects the user to the login form, the return URL—namely, the originally requested URL—is appended to the query string. Hence, the controller method that processes the GET request on the *Login* method will successfully capture the return URL. By storing it in a hidden field, the code guarantees the return URL is also made available to the controller method that will handle the POST from the login page.

Posting from a login form

When the login form posts its content, the controller action method receives posted data. The binding mechanism presented in Chapter 8 makes it possible to write the following code:

```
[HttpPost]
[ActionName("login")]
public ActionResult LoginPost(LoginInputModel input, string returnUrl)
{
    // Validate credentials
    ...

    // If any error occurred ...
    ...

    // Jump to the next page
    ...
}
```

Note that for the preceding code to work it is required that *INPUT* fields have the *name* attribute set. The sole *id* attribute won't be enough.

The *LoginInputModel* class is an application-defined class that collects all data that flows out of the login form and becomes input for the controller action. If the validation process ends successfully, the user is redirected to the return URL or to some predefined URL. Otherwise, the login page must be displayed again with some additional information such as the number of login attempts and error messages. As a result, the data that flows in the login view when it gets displayed might be different from the input model.

Processing posted data

Processing credentials is the simple action of comparing the user name and password against stored credentials. This operation usually involves accessing a database table and understanding a given database schema. Comprehensive frameworks such as ASP.NET Identity provide a fixed database schema, but they also offer an abstract interface to override to provide the same functionality on top of different storage or a different database schema.

Generally, checking credentials is a process that can fail for two reasons. It can fail because the credentials entered are invalid (for example, empty, null, too short, too long, or badly formatted) or because the credentials given don't match the stored credentials. Based on which type of failure occurs, you implement a counter that blocks the account after a fixed number of failed attempts or just reports about those failed attempts.

Displaying login errors

When errors are detected during the validation of credentials, you might want to report this via messages and restore the form to the way it was before the user posted invalid data. ASP.NET MVC has some interesting facilities to achieve this, but it should be clear that this feature doesn't come for free as it does in ASP.NET Web Forms.

Consider the following body for the POST action of a login:

```
[HttpPost]
[ActionName("login")]
public ActionResult LoginPost(LoginInputModel input, string returnUrl)
{
    // Validate credentials to see if they're valid
    if (String.IsNullOrWhiteSpace(input.UserName) ||
        String.IsNullOrWhiteSpace(input.Password))
    {
        ModelState.AddModelError("", "Incomplete credentials");
    }
    ...    // More checks possible here

    // Validate credentials to see if they match a known user
    if (ModelState.IsValid)
    {
        if (_service.TryAuthenticate(input))
            return Redirect(returnUrl ?? "/");
        ModelState.AddModelError("", "Invalid credentials");
    }

    // Error occurred
    return RedirectToAction("login");
}
```

You can run a number of consistency checks and record an error message for each detected flaw. You can add error messages to the *ModelState* system dictionary. When you're done with this, you proceed with security checks only if the model state is empty. If security checks fail, you record another error in the model state and redirect to the original page carrying the gathered feedback.

Unfortunately, the code just shown is not able to carry any feedback. The reason is the *RedirectToAction* instruction at the end of the method. Later in the chapter, I'll get back to the reasons that suggest you exit a POST method with a redirect call rather than a plain rendering of a view. For now, it suffices to say that if you call *View*() instead of *RedirectToAction*, everything works as expected and the gathered feedback shows up nicely.

Redirecting to the view

A call to *RedirectToAction* introduces an additional HTTP 302 request. Because of that, the content of the *ModelState*, as well as the content of the input model, gets lost. To preserve this information across two successive requests, you must use the *TempData* dictionary:

```
// Error occurred
TempData["ModelState"] = ModelState;
return RedirectToAction("login");
```

The *TempData* dictionary is part of the ASP.NET MVC infrastructure. It is automatically persisted in the session state across two successive requests and then is automatically dropped. The dictionary was added to ASP.NET MVC to serve this specific programming pattern—ending POST statements with a redirect. If used in the POST, the dictionary must be retrieved in the GET:

```
[HttpGet]
[ActionName("login")]
public ActionResult LoginGet(string returnUrl = "/")
{
    var state = TempData["ModelState"] as ModelStateDictionary;
    ModelState.Merge(state);

    // Set default input model for display
    var input = LoginInputModel();
    var model = new LoginViewModel(input) {ReturnUrl = returnUrl};
    return View(model);
}
```

Names used to store data items in the dictionary are arbitrary. Figure 12-1 shows a login form posted with incomplete credentials.

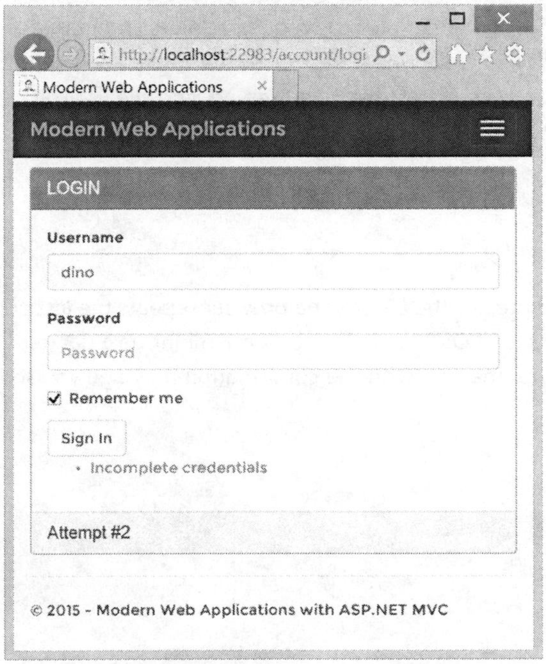

FIGURE 12-1 A login form that reports the system's feedback

> **Note** There's more to say about the dynamics of reporting a system's feedback to users during form posting. I'll just do that in the remainder of the chapter.

Input forms

In spite of appearances, the discussion over the login form and the authentication process already covered much of the story about the way users interact with the system through input forms. You've seen how to set up an HTML form and what happens when the form is posted to a controller action. The model-binding layer turns request parameters (such as *querystring*, *route*, and *form*) into comfortable C# classes that the controller can easily manage.

Any action the controller method performs on input data can be a success or a failure. If it's a failure, you need to inform the user of this using the system's feedback and preexisting data. It works the same way in a login form and in a data-entry form. The only point left to further investigate is why you might want to end a POST request with a redirect.

The Post-Redirect-Get pattern

Imagine the user fills out a form and submits it. The browser takes the instructions of the HTML FORM element literally and sets up a POST request. The server handles the request. Unless countermeasures are taken, the controller ends its processing effort by selecting a Razor view template and telling the view engine to render that to the output stream. The request has been served, and the user receives some HTML back. Everything is perfect and everybody is happy.

Until the user tries to refresh the page.

The F5 effect

When the user clicks *Refresh* from the menu or presses the F5 key, the browser repeats the last action. Refreshing the page right after having performed a POST operation, though, might be a danger-ous scenario. For this reason, all browsers prompt the user with the confirmation message you see in Figure 12-2.

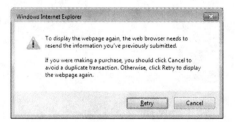

FIGURE 12-2 The confirmation message that browsers display when reposting a form

If the user goes ahead and retries, the last operation is repeated with really unpredictable effects. The user receives an exception (for example, a record is added with the same unique key), or the state of the system is inconsistently altered (for example, a copy of an existing record is added).

By applying the Post-Redirect-Get (PRG) pattern, you are guaranteed that the last action is always a GET, which eliminates the problem (or the annoyance) of getting the dialog box shown in Figure 12-2. The pattern, though, is also—and mainly—beneficial because it clearly separates command actions from query actions. The entire architecture of the application comes closer to modern patterns such as Command/Query Responsibility Segregation (CQRS).

Applying the PRG pattern

The first step on the way to applying PRG to ASP.NET MVC applications is neatly separating POST actions from GET actions. Here's how to rewrite the Edit action:

```
[HttpGet]
[ActionName("edit")]
public ActionResult EditViaGet(String id)
{
    // Retrieve the data item and display
    var model = _service.GetModelForEdit(id);
    return View("edit", model);
}

[HttpPost]
[ActionName("edit")]
public ActionResult EditViaPost(String id)
{
    // Execute the command
    ...

    // Instead of calling View(...), just redirect to the entry
    // point responsible for displaying data
    return RedirectToAction("edit", new {id = id});
}
```

Another pleasant side effect of the PRG pattern is that the displayed URL is a lot more significant. Users can even navigate to a different page, or different data item, by simply understanding the structure of URLs and typing.

Drawbacks of the PRG pattern

The PRG pattern is just a pattern. Just like any other pattern, it has its pros and cons. To use it, you have to slightly change some common programming habits. To at least consider that, you probably need to hear about the good parts of PRG first. My experience is that the PRG pattern helps a lot in keeping code clean and simple to architect. Well beyond the F5 effect, this is the primary benefit I've found and the main reason I keep on using it.

With PRG, the last action you perform in a form submission is always a GET. However, because the form submission started with a POST, you end up placing an additional intermediate request. For the mechanics of HTTP, that causes some loss of information. In particular, the state of the POST operation is no longer available when you're rendering the view in a GET operation.

The information you lose by redirecting to a view page instead of calling *View* at the bottom of a controller POST method is essentially the result of any validation you might have performed on posted data, including any information and messages you wanted to return as feedback. That information is handy if only you could invoke View instead of some redirect.

Unless you have static success/fail pages, this is an issue. The official solution that fixes the issue is using the *TempData* dictionary to persist the model state and, in general, any other information you can't retrieve in other ways in the subsequent GET method. The *TempData* dictionary has a short lifetime, and each key stays there only for the span of two successive requests. Where's the drawback, then?

Using *TempData* requires that data be serialized somewhere to survive the next request. The default implementation of *TempData* uses the session state. That's no big deal for single-server applications, but in the context of web farms and web roles, the less you use the session state, the easier you make your life.

PRG and web farms

To make a long story short, in a web-farm or cloud scenario, you need distributed session storage of the session state (external process or Microsoft SQL Server). Alternatively, you can resort to using cookies or distributed caching. ASP.NET MVC includes a simple provider mechanism to change the default implementation of *TempData*. The *TempData* implementation works on a per-controller basis. All you need to do is override the following method in any controller class in which you intend to have PRG:

```
protected override ITempDataProvider CreateTempDataProvider()
{
    return new YourTempDataProvider();
}
```

A custom *TempData* provider is a class that implements the *ITempDataProvider* interface:

```
interface ITempDataProvider
{
    IDictionary<string, object> LoadTempData(ControllerContext controllerContext);
    void SaveTempData(ControllerContext controllerContext, IDictionary<string, object> values);
}
```

A common way to customize the *TempData* dictionary is by using cookies. However, when you change the implementation of *TempData* and start adding cookies to the stream of requests, you should make sure that cookies are actually expired as soon as they're issued so that no further request will actually get them. An interesting discussion on the topic and links to sample code can be found on StackOverflow: *http://bit.ly/1jfyehd*.

Form validation

When you require users to fill in and submit a form, you make yourself responsible for accepting only valid data. At the end of the validation process, though, in ASP.NET you are left with the problem of notifying users of whatever was wrong with their input. In addition, the validation process is typically made of two phases: checking structural aspects (such as the type, range, length, and nullness) and checking the business consistency of the input data. The structural aspects, at least, can be checked through a framework that enables some flavors of declarative programming.

In ASP.NET MVC, this framework is known as *Data Annotations* and is now fully incorporated in the Microsoft .NET Framework.

Introducing data annotations

Data annotations are a set of attributes you can use to annotate public properties of any .NET class in a way that any interested client code can read and consume. Attributes fall into two main categories: display and validation. In this book, we're interested only in validation attributes.

In Chapter 8, you saw how controllers receive their input data through the model-binding subsystem. The model binder maps request data to model classes and, in doing so, it validates input values against validation attributes set on the model class. Validation occurs through a provider. The default validation provider is based on data annotations. The default validation provider is the *DataAnnotationsModelValidatorProvider* class. Let's see which attributes you can use that the default validation provider understands.

Table 12-1 lists the most commonly used data-annotation attributes that express a condition to verify on a model class.

Table 12-1 Data annotation attributes for validation

Attribute	Description
Compare	Checks whether two specified properties in the model have the same value.
CustomValidation	Checks the value against the specified custom function.
EnumDataType	Checks whether the value can be matched to any of the values in the specified enumerated type.
Range	Checks whether the value falls in the specified range. It defaults to numbers, but you can configure it to consider a range of dates, too.
RegularExpression	Checks whether the value matches the specified expression.
Remote	Makes an Ajax call to the server, and checks whether the value is acceptable.
Required	Checks whether a non-null value is assigned to the property. You can configure it to fail if an empty string is assigned.
StringLength	Checks whether the string is longer than the specified value.

All these attributes derive from the same base class: *ValidationAttribute*. You can also use this base class to create your own custom validation attributes. You use these attributes to decorate members of classes being used in input forms. For the whole mechanism to work, you need to have controller methods that bind data to such data types:

```
[HttpPost]
public ActionResult Edit(CountryInputModel input)
{
    ...
}
```

For any invalid posted value being mapped to an instance of the *CountryInputModel* class, the binder automatically creates an entry in the system's *ModelState* dictionary. Whether the posted value is valid or not depends on the outcome returned by the currently registered validation provider. The default validation provider bases its response on the annotations you set on the *CountryInputModel* model class.

Decorating an input model class

The following listing shows a sample class—the aforementioned *CountryInputModel* class—that makes extensive use of data annotations for validation purposes:

```
public class CountryInputModel : ViewModelBase
{
    public CountryInputModel()
    {
        Code = "??";
        Continent = Continent.Unknown;
        RegistrationNumber = String.Empty;
    }

    [Required(ErrorMessage = "Country name is required.")]
    [StringLength(50)]
    public String Name { get; set; }

    [Required(ErrorMessage = "Country code (ISO2) is required.")]
    [StringLength(2, MinimumLength = 2)]
    [RegularExpression(@"\b[A-Z]+", ErrorMessage = "ISO2 format")]
    public String Code { get; set; }

    [Required]
    public Continent Continent { get; set; }

    public Int32 Population { get; set; }
    public String RegistrationNumber { get; set; }
}
```

As you might have guessed, this class is only a distant relative of the *Country* class that you saw used in most examples in Chapter 11, "Presenting data." You can consider that *Country* class to be a domain class. The class you're decorating for input purposes is just a helper class whose only purpose in life is collecting data in a way that reflects the user's preferences as far as the interface is concerned.

Your next goal is to find an efficient way to edit the content of instances of this data type. ASP.NET MVC comes to the rescue with a long list of HTML helpers. Let's say that you have an *AdminController* class with a *New* method through which new countries/regions can be added to the system:

```
[HttpGet]
public ActionResult New()
{
    // Set default values to show in the form
    var model = new CountryInputModel();
    return View(model);
}
```

Let's have a look at the Razor view for editing.

Presenting the input form

The HTML form has the following layout. Most Bootstrap styles and filler elements (mostly DIV elements) have been removed from the listing for brevity and clarity:

```
<form method="POST" action="@Url.Action("new")">
    <fieldset>
        <legend>New Country</legend>

        @{ Html.RenderPartial("_Alert"); }

        <!-- Registration number -->
        <label for="name">Registration</label>
        <span type="text" id="registration"> @Model.RegistrationNumber </span>

        <!-- Name -->
        <label for="name">Name</label>
        @Html.TextBoxFor(m => m.Name, new { placeholder = "Name" })
        <span class="text-danger">@Html.ValidationMessageFor(m => m.Name)</span>

        <!-- Code -->
        <label for="name">Code</label>
        @Html.TextBoxFor(m => m.Code, new { placeholder = "Code" })
        <span class="text-danger">@Html.ValidationMessageFor(m => m.Code)</span>
        ...

        <!-- Continent -->
        <label for="name">Code</label>
        @Html.DropDownListFor(m => m.Continent,
                        new Continent().ToSelectList(@Model.Continent.As<int>()))
        <span class="text-danger">@Html.ValidationMessageFor(m => m.Continent)</span>

        <!-- Validation summary -->
        <span class="text-danger">@Html.ValidationSummary(true)</span>

        <!-- Submit button -->
        <button type="submit" class="btn btn-primary"> Save </button>
    </fieldset>
</form>
```

The most relevant thing to notice in the preceding code is the use of HTML helpers instead of plain HTML5 elements. What's the real difference between *Html.TextBoxFor* and the following mix of HTML and Razor code?

```
<input type="text"
       name="code" id="code"
       class="form-control" placeholder="ISO2"
       value="@Model.Code">
```

If you look at the plain markup generated, there's no difference at all. (See Figure 12-3.)

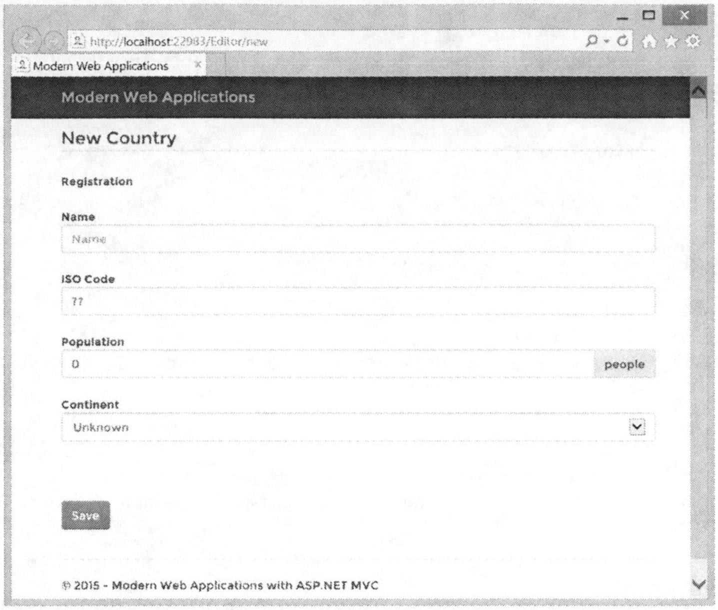

FIGURE 12-3 The form to add a new country to the system

If you look at what happens under the hood, the difference is significant. The HTML helper is a piece of code and not plain markup. As such, it does a lot of invisible work, all related to storing in the *value* attribute of the *INPUT* elements of the form the last value the user entered.

To show you why this is relevant, I need to take the example one step further and show you what happens when the user clicks the Save button and submits the input form.

Processing posted data

Imagine the following and rather classic scenario. The user types in some data and clicks the Submit button. The controller method receives the posted data and copies matching data into the properties of the input model type. The input model type, though, is decorated with data annotations, and posted values are then validated against those annotations. A note is taken for any invalid properties and saved to the *ModelState* dictionary.

Through the programming interface of the *ModelState* dictionary, the controller method checks whether the input model is in a valid state. If so, it proceeds with any necessary business operation, such as persistence. If the input model is not in a valid state, the controller method has two options to choose from:

■ Rendering a view with some error messages

■ Redirecting to a different controller action that will render the next view (the PRG pattern)

The former option will leave POST as the last action in the browser's cache, and it potentially exposes the user to the F5 effect. The latter option is clearer from a design perspective (commands and queries treated as distinct actions), but it loses information about the invalid state and also information about the posted data.

A controller that supports PRG will simply store the model state in the *TempData* dictionary and redirect. The redirected method will load the model state from the same *TempData* dictionary and render the view back. The *ModelState* dictionary contains all the information about errors and posted values, but a purely HTML5 view knows nothing about that. The ASP.NET MVC *xxxFor* helper methods, instead, perform the magic of reading the *ModelState* dictionary and set the value properties of input fields to reflect the last known state:

```
[HttpPost]
public ActionResult New(CountryInputModel data)
{
    if (ModelState.IsValid)
    {
        // Perform the command
        var model = _service.Save(data);
        if (model.LastActionResponse.Success)
          return RedirectToAction("...");
    }

    // Errors detected
    return RedirectToAction("new");
}
```

As a result, if you implement PRG and you want to keep any incorrect input in the form as the user fixes that, you must use *xxxFor* helper methods instead of plain HTML5 elements in your Razor views.

Showing validation messages

Among the *xxxFor* HTML helpers, you find *Html.ValidationMessageFor* and *Html.ValidationSummary*. The former displays the error message associated in the model state with the specified property:

```
<span class="text-danger">@Html.ValidationMessageFor(m => m.Continent)</span>
```

The latter, on the other hand, presents the summary of error messages stored in the model state. In terms of HTML, both helpers render out plain *SPAN* tags and can be placed wherever you like in the form. Typically, you place the validation message next to the specific input field and the summary at the top or the bottom of the form.

The nice thing is that after you decorate the input model with data annotations and instruct the controller method to deal with the model state, all you see in Figure 12-4 comes nearly for free.

The beauty of data annotations is that after you define attributes for a model type, you're pretty much done. Most of what follows happens automatically, thanks to the deep understanding of data annotations that the ASP.NET MVC infrastructure has. However, in this imperfect world, none of the things you really need are completely free. So it is for data annotations, which cover a lot of relatively simple situations very well, but leave some extra work for you to do on your own in many realistic applications. Let's explore a more advanced scenario.

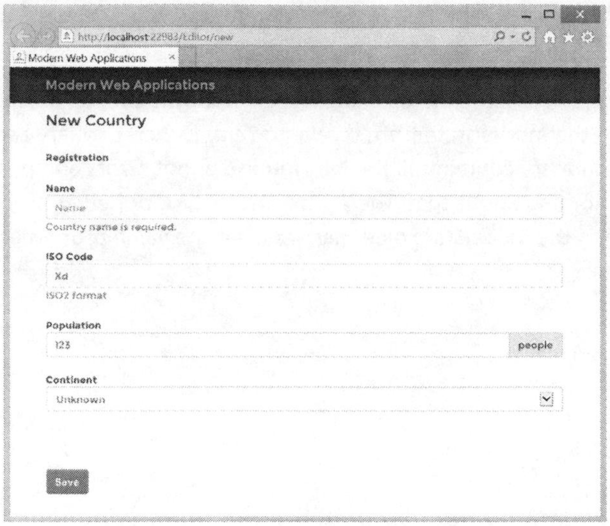

FIGURE 12-4 Dealing with the error messages in an input form

Performing cross-property validation

The data annotations I've covered so far are attributes you use to validate the content of a single field. This is definitely useful, but it doesn't help that much in a real-world scenario in which you likely need to validate the content of a property in light of the value stored in another property. Cross-property validation requires a bit of context-specific code.

To validate two or more properties at the same time, and one based on the value of the other, you need a global attribute at the level of the class—*CustomValidation*:

```
[CustomValidation(typeof(CountryInputModel), "Validate")]
public class CountryInputModel : ViewModelBase
{
    ...
}
```

Quite simply, the attribute specifies a method that is called during the process to do whatever else requires cross-property checks:

```
public static ValidationResult Validate(CountryInputModel data, ValidationContext context)
{
    if (data.Continent == Continent.Unknown && !data.Name.IsNullOrWhitespace())
        return new ValidationResult("Must indicate a continent.");
    return ValidationResult.Success;
}
```

Should you just define a global attribute and ignore individual properties? The point is that with individual properties it's far easier for you to display point-to-point error messages, as shown in Figure 12-4. To display error messages related to cross-property validation, you resort to the validation summary helper:

```
span class="text-danger">@Html.ValidationSummary(true)</span>
```

An interesting feature of *Html.ValidationSummary* is that if you call it with a Boolean value of *true* (as in the example), the list of displayed errors is limited to those that don't refer specifically to a property. This allows you to display cross-property validation messages and also helps you avoid duplicate messages. (See Figure 12-5.)

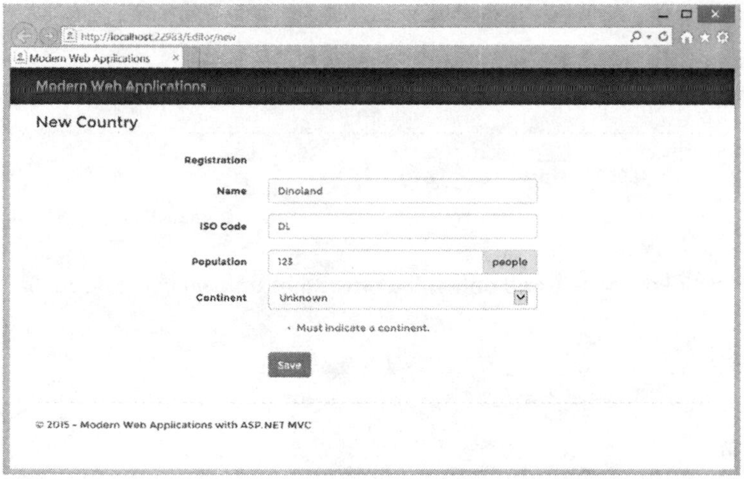

FIGURE 12-5 Cross-property validation

The next view

So far, I've discussed the validation phase of an input form. When the posted data satisfy all requirements, the *ModelState* dictionary is in a valid state and the controller proceeds to perform the actual operation requested by the user. This operation can complete successfully or it can fail. In both cases, feedback must be reported to the user.

A simple way to do this is by adding a couple of properties to the base view-model class so that they are always available in any view. Better yet, you can create a new *CommandResponse* class:

```
public class CommandResponse
{
    public bool Success { get; set; }
    public string UserMessage {get; set;
}
public class ViewModelBase
{
    ...
    public CommandResponse LastCommandResponse { get; set; }
}
```

The service method invoked by the controller, or the controller itself, writes the command response that ends up right in the view and is always displayed in the same manner. The net effect is that you can now easily create an HTML widget to display success or error messages:

```
<!-- _Alert -->
@if (Model.HasMessage())
{
    var style = Model.LastActionResponse.Success ? "alert-success" : "alert-danger";
    var rnd = new Random().Next(1000000, 1000000000);
    <div id="__alert__@rnd" class="alert alert-dismissable @style">
        <button type="button" class="close" data-dismiss="alert" aria-label="Close">
            <span aria-hidden="true">&times;</span>
        </button>
        @Model.LastActionResponse.UserMessage
    </div>

    <script type="text/javascript">
        $("#__alert__@rnd").delay(4000).slideUp();
    </script>
}
```

In any view, you just add the following line and obtain the effect that's shown in Figure 12-6:

```
@{ Html.RenderPartial("_Alert"); }
```

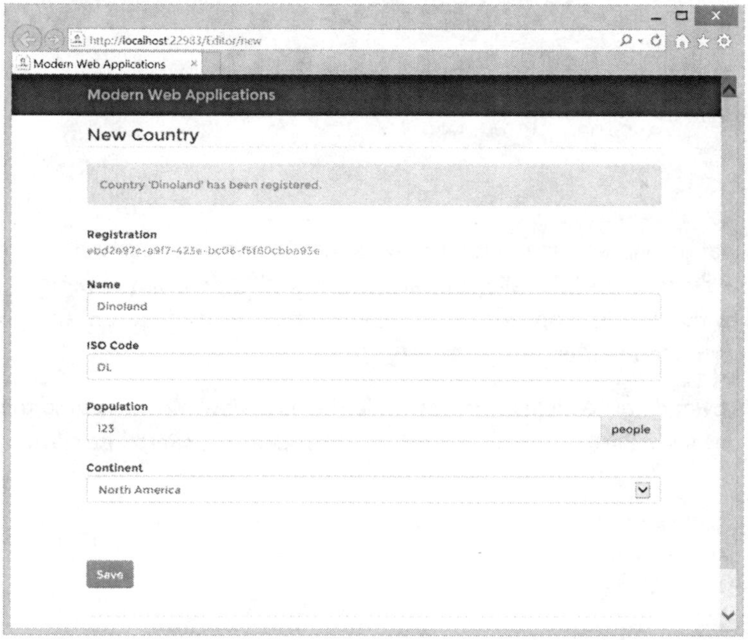

FIGURE 12-6 A reusable alert widget

The response is rendered at the top of the screen in a Bootstrap alert box that automatically disappears after a few seconds.

A custom attribute for PRG controllers

If you explore the source code distributed with the book, you'll see that some examples that revolve around input forms don't apparently deal with the *TempData* dictionary yet the produced effect of the code is exactly the same as it would be if the dictionary was used. Where's the trick?

To implement the PRG pattern and form validation, you need to perform just a couple of basic operations with the *TempData* dictionary. It's always the same operations, repeated over and over again, for each posting method of each controller.

ASP.NET MVC offers a facility to incorporate additional functionality into controller methods—action filters. Once compiled, an action filter takes the form of an attribute you use to decorate a controller method or a class. Internally, an action filter can override up to two methods: *OnActionExecuting* and *OnActionExecuted*. As the names suggest, the former override indicates code to execute right before the controller method is executed. The latter method defines code to execute upon completion of the controller method.

The action filter gains access to the entire controller pipeline and can read and modify the view model and model state. Note that *OnActionExecuted* runs after the controller method is finished but before the view is processed and generated. For this reason, any update to the model state or view model is fully reflected in the actual view.

The *Prg* attribute you find in the companion code of this book is a slight variation of an analogous component that was originally part of the MvcContrib project, which you can read more about at *http://mvccontrib.codeplex.com*. Using the attribute couldn't be easier:

```
[Authorize]
[Prg]
public class EditorController : Controller
{
    [HttpPost]
    public ActionResult New(CountryInputModel input)
    {
        if (ModelState.IsValid) {
            DoYourTask(input);
            return RedirectToAction("next-view");
        }
        return RedirectToAction("current-view-with-errors");
    }
}
```

The code here shows the resulting pattern for POST controller methods.

Modal input forms

In Chapter 11, I discussed a drill-down example in which details of a data entity were displayed in a sidebar as the user selected an item from a list. The same pattern is sometimes useful for editing data. It works well when the primary purpose of the view is to let users check and review information, and occasionally edit it if they are authorized to do so.

For a long time, editing data required jumping to a different page or URL where data entry takes place. In such views, input forms were built around the FORM tag and a browser-led content submission. This is the scenario we addressed so far. Is there a way to present to the user an input form without a full page refresh? Enter modal input forms.

Configuring a modal form

Ultimately, a modal form is simply a DIV displayed on top of everything else, making whatever lies underneath it unresponsive. In other words, here *modality* means that the user's attention is captured by the popup user interface. Arranging and displaying a modal form requires the content DIV and some JavaScript to show and hide it, paying attention to *z-index* and focus HTML attributes. Having a framework at hand, though, makes everything easier. Bootstrap provides excellent support for modals.

In Bootstrap, a *modal* is made of two elements: the trigger and the content. The content is a sparse DIV decorated with some ad hoc attributes. The DIV is laid out within the host view, typically at the bottom, and can be injected as inline markup or, better yet, as a distinct partial view:

```
<div>
    <!-- This is the template of the host view -->
</div>
@{ Html.RenderPartial("your_modal_view") }
```

Each modal has one or more triggers. A trigger is the user-interface element the user acts on to bring up the modal. In general, the trigger is a clickable element such as an anchor or a button. However, because the modal component in Bootstrap has its own programming interface and eventing model, you can programmatically bring up a modal as a reaction to whatever event or sequence of instructions you like. Here's the typical Bootstrap configuration of a modal form:

```
<!-- Trigger -->
<button class="btn btn-xs btn-danger"
        data-toggle="modal"
        data-target="#modalEditor"
        data-id="@country.CountryCode">
    <span class="glyphicon glyphicon-pencil"></span>
    EDIT
</button>
```

```
<!-- Modal content -->
<div class="modal" id="modalEditor">
    <div class="modal-dialog">
        <div class="modal-content">
            <div class="modal-header">
              ...
            </div>
            <div class="modal-body">
              ...
            </div>
            <div class="modal-footer">
              ...
            </div>
        </div>
    </div>
</div>
```

In the trigger element, the key attributes are *data-toggle* and *data-target*. The former tells Bootstrap about the behavior expected for any clicking. The *data-target* attribute contains the jQuery selector to the DIV to bring up.

The modal content is a special chunk of HTML markup. It's a container DIV marked with the *modal* class and contains a nested DIV styled as *modal-dialog* which, in turn, contains another DIV styled as *modal-content*. Within the modal content element, you can have any content you like to see displayed in front of the users. Typically, there are three child elements: a header, body, and footer. It's not mandatory, though. Having such containers primarily helps with padding and positioning, but it doesn't change any core functionality of the dialog.

Structuring common elements of a modal

It's good to give modal forms some common elements, such as a close button in the header and a list of active buttons in the header to perform operations. It's also recommended to set a title somewhere and reserve some space for feedback, if the user has any.

Here's the markup of a typical header. The ID of elements is totally arbitrary:

```
<button type="button" class="close" data-dismiss="modal">
    <span aria-hidden="true">&times;</span>
</button>
<h4 class="modal-title" id="titleOfTheForm"></h4>
```

The code here adds a close button to the header in much the same way you have one in Microsoft Windows. Also, it's common to add a similar button to the footer. The *data-dismiss* attribute tells Bootstrap to dismiss the dialog if the button is clicked:

```
<button type="button" class="btn btn-default" data-dismiss="modal">Close</button>
```

A modal can be used to just present information or to implement a modal input form. The content of the modal can be statically defined when the view is created, or it can be updated when the modal is about to show:

```
<div class="modal-content">
    <div class="modal-header">
        ...
    </div>
    <div class="modal-body">
        @Html.Partial("_ModalEditorForm")
    </div>
        <div class="modal-footer">
        ...
    </div>
</div>
```

The _ModalEditorForm referenced in the code snippet indicates the HTML form being used to edit the selected element. Input elements of the HTML form are set via JavaScript that intercepts the *show* event of the modal form.

Initializing the modal form

When the view that contains a modal form is loaded, some one-off initialization must occur. In particular, the initialization will attach the event handler for the *show* event, and for an input form, it will also set up the rules for client-side jQuery validation:

```
$(document).ready(function() {

    // ==> Register event handler for "show" event
    $("#modalEditor").on("show.bs.modal", function (e) {
        // Get code of clicked country
        var code = $(e.relatedTarget).attr("data-id");

        // Set title
        $("#titleOfTheForm").html(code);

        // Download details
        $.ajax({
            url: "/country/find/" + code,
            cache: false
        }).done(function (info) {
            $("#legend").html(info.CountryName);
            $("#code").val(info.CountryCode);
            $("#Population").val(info.Population);
            $("#AreaInKmSq").val(info.AreaInSqKm);
        });
    });

    // ==> Register jQuery validation rules (if any)
    ...
});
```

The idea is to download JSON data from the server with the details of the record to edit and use that information to populate the input fields of the popup HTML form. Every time the user triggers the modal, a download occurs and the same HTML markup is configured to show dynamic data.

> **Important** The use of jQuery caching is controversial here. If used extensively, it can generate nasty effects and give users the perception that the system is ignoring their commands. It is not unusual that users save data, the system says everything is OK, but then next time the same record is edited, the form offers the old data even though the system stored updated information. Well, I've been there, and it can really be annoying and frustrating. You solve the problem by disabling jQuery caching as in the example, but you do so at the cost of a new download every time.

Figure 12-7 presents the modified version of the drill-down example of Chapter 11, in which a button has been added to the menu to bring up a modal input form to edit some information.

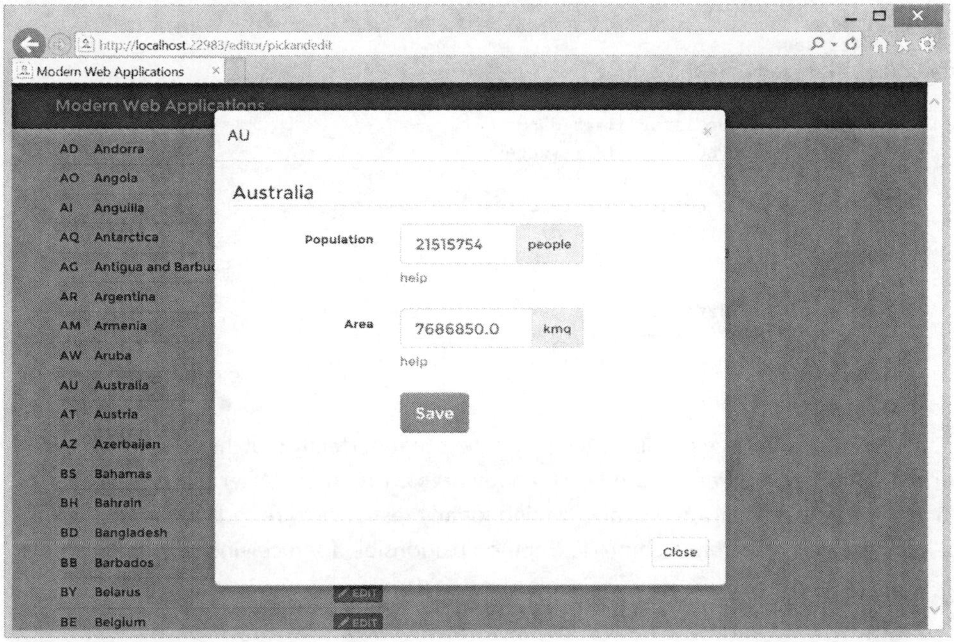

FIGURE 12-7 A modal input form in action

Posting from a modal form

Once the modal form is up and running, the user can freely edit any content. Let's assume for a moment that everything the user enters and types is acceptable input. How would you post data from a modal form? There are two basic approaches:

- Regular browser-led form posting and landing on a different page where any feedback (success or error messages) is displayed

- JavaScript-controlled form posting without leaving the form and with any feedback (success or error messages) reported back to the same form

In both cases, you can apply some nice validation effects on the form using jQuery validation.

The first posting option is trivial to code and is, in many regards, the default option. Ultimately, the popup is a DIV that contains a canonical HTML FORM element. As such, the FORM element refers to a server action and hosts a classic submit button. When the user clicks the submit button, the content of the form is collected and sent via a POST request. This is in no way different from classic form implementation. The effect for users is that they are taken to a different page after posting and need to navigate back to continue editing. This is not a drawback per se; it's just a common behavior that might or might not be appropriate in any given situation.

To post via JavaScript, you need to attach a click handler to a submit button and then serialize the content of the form to JSON. Here's some sample code:

```
function __saveChanges(form) {
// form here is assumed to be jQuery object, NOT a DOM reference to a FORM element!

var url = "/editor/save";
    var postData = form.serialize();
    $.post(url, postData, function (data) {
        $("#feedback").removeClass("alert-danger")
                      .removeClass("alert-success");
        if (data.toLowerCase() == "ok") {
            $("#feedback").addClass("alert-success")
                          .html("Data saved!");
            return;
        }
        $("#feedback").addClass("alert-danger")
                      .html("Something went wrong. Please retry!");
    });
}
```

The jQuery method *serialize* produces a string of text that perfectly matches the content of the HTML form and the browser format used in the body of POST requests. After that, it's all about setting up a POST request to a given URL and waiting for any response to refresh the modal form's user interface. Here's an excerpt from a controller method responsible for receiving such posted data:

```
public ActionResult Save(string code, string population, string area)
{
    // Perform action and get response/feedback
    var model = _service.PerformTask(...);

    if (Request.IsAjaxRequest())
    {
        var success = model.LastResponse.Success;
        return success ? Content("ok") : Content("fail");
    }

    //
    return RedirectToAction("pickandedit");
}
```

Note that the same controller method can be used to receive classic POST requests waiting for HTML and to receive Ajax POST requests waiting for plain data. The trick to distinguishing the type of request is the *IsAjaxRequest* method. Figure 12-8 shows the effect of a successful post from a modal form. Posting via JavaScript from a modal form is an excellent strategy when you intend to let users stay within the form for a long time and save data multiple times in the same working session.

IGURE 12-8 Posting from within a modal form

Note The sample application doesn't really save data and doesn't even attempt to perform any work when the user posts data. For the sake of the demonstration, it just decides randomly if the operation was successful or not. When you click Save in the form of Figure 12-8, you have more chances to fail than to succeed. Click repeatedly to experience the user interface in both cases: nothing bad will happen to the core project and back-end data.

Client-side validation

Whether you display an input form in a modal popup or embed it in a classic view, and regardless of the posting model of choice, you can enable client-side validation via jQuery. In general, form validation can occur both on the client side and the server side, and the side that really matters is the server. Having some quick checks performed on the client, however, is a form of optimization because it might save a few roundtrips to the server. In addition, it gives users the perception of greater responsiveness and better care of the system.

Client-side validation is effective because it gives users rather prompt feedback about what they're typing. It's a feature you can code yourself with a bit of JavaScript and a bunch of event handlers. However, as you saw already with data annotations for server-side validation, having a readymade framework can make things quicker to write and more reusable. The de-facto standard framework for client-side validation is jQuery Validation. You can install it as a NuGet package and just reference the *jquery.validate.min.js* file. Alternatively, you can get it from *http://jqueryvalidation.org/validate*.

To set up client-side validation, you need to attach validation rules to each form where you intend to use it. This is an operation you can conduct in the *ready* handler of the host page or view. Here's an example:

```
$("#CountryForm").validate({
    rules: {
        Population: { required: true, min: 0 },
        AreaInKmSq: { required: true, min: 0 }
    },
    messages: {
        Population: "Set population to 0 if not available.",
        AreaInKmSq: "Set area to 0 if not available."
    },
    errorContainer: "#validationSummary",
    errorLabelContainer: "#validationSummary ul",
    wrapper: "li",
    submitHandler: function (form) {
        var $form = $(form);      // Normalize to jQuery
        __saveChanges($form);
    }
});
```

In the code snippet, *CountryForm* is the ID of the HTML FORM element to validate, and property names in the *rules* and *messages* collections must match the ID of input elements in the form. You can refer to the framework's website for more details about the actual usage and supported forms of validation.

The validation framework also requires you to indicate where error messages should be displayed. The combination of *errorContainer*, *errorLabelContainer*, and *wrapper* properties indicates where and how individual messages will be displayed. In the example, error messages will appear boxed in a *LI* element and appended to the *UL* child element within the *validationSummary* element.

Finally, the *submitHandler* property can be used to automatically register a handler for the submit button of the validated form. In other words, if you use and configure jQuery Validation for a form, you also save yourself the burden of attaching a click handler to submit buttons. Figure 12-9 shows client-side validation in action.

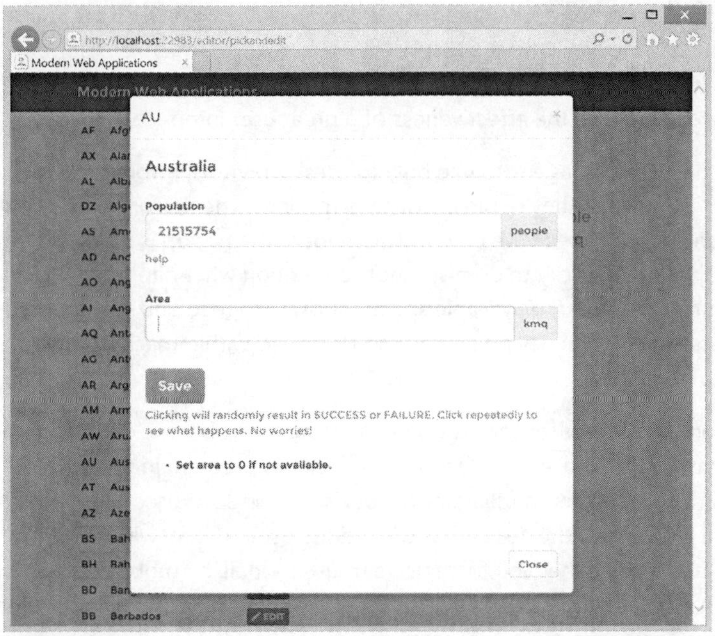

FIGURE 12-9 Client-side validation with jQuery

Examining the pros and cons of modal forms

No matter what gurus and pundits say about usability, it turns out that all that matters is the experience that users go through when they work with an HTML view. And experience is made of perception. Modal forms are definitely an option to consider when it comes to editing or drilling down into some information, and they are perceived to be better in some scenarios than in others. A modal is generally recommended for the following scenarios:

- Editing multiple input fields in a single shot. (This is precisely the scenario of the prior example.)

- Performing a single-step action like booking a resource, posting a comment, or registering information. (This is a slight variation of the previous point.)

- Creating quick previews of things like images, videos, or lists of data.

At the same time, a modal is much less effective, and even annoying, in situations like the following ones:

- Notification of the outcome of an operation (success or failure). As shown earlier, a dismissible alert text is much more favorable and even better if it disappears after a few seconds.

- Validation messages. (These are much better if displayed inline or in a single summary.)

- Quick and specific editing of small amounts of data, like a single field.

- Multistep, wizard-style operations.

My personal experience is that modal forms are helpful, but even when they're used properly they never turn a poorly usable user interface into a great one. In other words, they help but they're never a decisive factor that makes a user interface a great user interface. On the other hand, if modal popups are misused, they can really reduce the effectiveness of a great user interface.

Furthermore, I consider modal windows as a resource only for desktop views. I would not use modal screens on mobile devices, whether they're tablets or smartphones. The reason is fairly obvious: given the smaller screen and coarseness of the pointer (the finger), the popup is often cut off or takes too much of the screen and can be tricky to dismiss—not to mention what happens with on-screen keyboards, which can further reduce the available space for users to read and type. Moreover, most of the modal effectiveness comes from having everything displayed within reach. If you have to scroll a modal, it's better not to have it.

Not using modal windows on mobile devices touches on a far broader problem—detecting devices and serving intelligent markup to each form factor. (I'll cover this problem in Chapter 15, "Responsive design.") At this time, though, let me share a sort of a trick I've seen used as an effective shortcut by some UX experts. If the core of the design has been done using modal windows (say, mobile support is added at a later time), either you force users to use modals on mobile devices or replace modals with something else. Replacing modals falls in the range of topics related to multidevice design. The trick, therefore, is using modal windows as large as the entire screen on mobile devices. The application flow is unchanged, and you reduce the burden for the users to a bare minimum. (By the way, this is not much different from what happens in Cordova applications or jQuery Mobile websites.)

Quick tips for improving the user experience

Improving the user experience of websites is a huge topic that deserves its own books. I'm not willing to tackle it here because I consider myself no more than an enthusiast novice of software usability. I'm not going to discuss cognitive analysis or UX patterns, but I'd like to share a few concrete tips for everyday use that definitely will contribute to making the user experience of your sites more pleasant—at least, this has been the case for most of my users.

> **Note** If you're looking for a source of UX inspiration and a resource for learning and building a better user experience, I have a suggestion. Have a look at *http://www.givegoodux.com/think-first.*

Using date pickers is great, but...

Date pickers are nothing new in the world of software, and there's nothing that can be added to further explain them or justify their use. As far as the web is concerned, though, date pickers have an issue—lack of uniform support.

Browsers and Modernizr

I was so happy to find out that HTML5 introduced the specific *date* input type field. For quite some time, I hoped that all browsers would have aligned to using a nearly identical user interface for that. That was not the case. Internet Explorer doesn't even treat date input fields differently from plain text fields, and the situation is not different with Firefox and Safari. In addition, the user interface offered by browsers that support the feature (Chrome, Opera, Microsoft Edge, and a few mobile browsers) is slightly different. An excellent resource for learning about HTML5 support for browsers is *http://caniuse.com*.

Modernizr (see *http://modernizr.com*) works as a feature detector and tells you whether or not the current browser supports a given feature. Based on that, you then implement your own workaround. Here's a quick example of how to check whether the browser supports a type *date* input field. If it does not, you resort to some external date picker plugin:

```
$(function(){
    if(!Modernizr.inputtypes.date) {
        $("#givenInputDateField").someDatePickerPlugin();
    }
});
```

Frankly, in this particular case, I don't see the point of using Modernizr. The effect is that you use the same plugin on all browsers that don't have native support for *date* input fields and slightly different user interfaces on browsers that offer that. I'd like to offer the same experience to my users, and differences across browsers at the moment are still well beyond the plain graphical styles as for text-input boxes.

Another crucial point to consider is the level of customization that date input fields support. Depending on the specific input, you might want to restrict the range of dates and navigate by month or year. Entering a birth date is different from entering an invoice date or booking date. Although the HTML5 standard defines a few additional properties, I find that plugins do a better job and, more importantly, using plugins to bypass Modernizr makes the experience the same across all browsers.

Bootstrap Datepicker

Which plugin should you use? For years, jQuery UI has been the favorite choice of most developers. Today, Bootstrap is used in a growing number of websites as the tool of choice for creating better layouts and the most appropriate look and feel. Bootstrap doesn't have a native date-picker component, but a few projects exist to back it up. One is *http://github.com/eternicode/bootstrap-datepicker*, which is also available as a NuGet package, the Bootstrap Datepicker. The following code snippet shows the markup and script you need to have in place:

```
<input type="text" id="dateofbirth" name="dateofbirth" contenteditable="false" value="@
birthDate">
<script type="text/javascript">
    $(function () {
        $('#dateofbirth').datepicker({
            language: 'en',
            startDate: '@startBirthDate',
            endDate: '@endBirthDate',
            pickerPosition: "bottom-left",
            autoClose: true
        });
    });
</script>
```

In the INPUT markup, note that the *contenteditable* attribute is set to *false*, which makes the content of the field not editable outside the user interface. Just as significantly, the *type* attribute of the INPUT element is set to *text*.

The plugin nicely supports localization, and the date format reflects that. The NuGet package comes with a bunch of dependencies, but that's the price to pay for extreme customization these days. Here's some sample code that restricts the range of dates to those reasonable as birth dates in a business application:

```
var startBirthDate = new DateTime(1915, 1, 1).ToString("d", culture);
var endBirthDate = DateTime.Today.AddYears(-5).ToString("d", culture);
```

Figure 12-10 shows a (localized) example of the plugin.

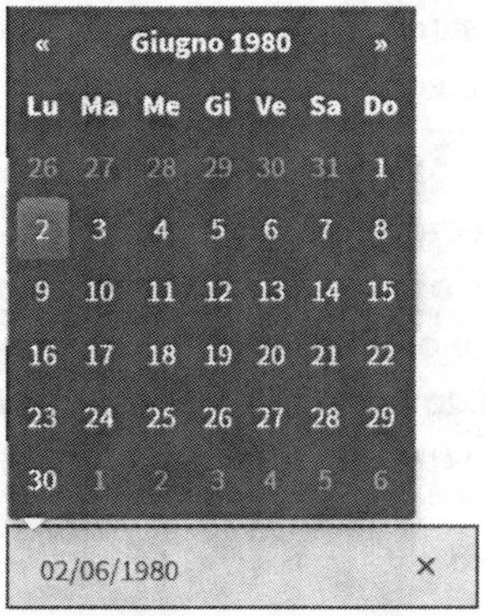

FIGURE 12-10 A bootstrap-based date-picker component

Presenting dates as plain text

This is a comment I first heard from a renowned mobile expert in a meeting about patterns and practices for web mobile development:

> The quickest way for users to enter a date in a mobile form is just typing numbers in sequence. Whether it is DDMMYY or something else is just a detail.

Well, ultimately, I find this so true.

Again, if you want or need to build a mobile optimized view, you can turn off any plugin and just declare the date field as a number input field. This approach also instructs the operating system to bring up the numeric keypad. As a further step, you might want to validate the entered text and try to guess a date to the extent that it is possible.

Date pickers are nice, and on mobile devices they are fully supported for dates. However, typing dates as text is still an option, and that's faster than picking a date, especially when the date is far from the default date displayed.

Using autocompletion instead of long drop-down lists

How many times did you write a form to select a country name? And how many times did you end up with an endless drop-down list? A million websites out there do exactly that, but is it really the most user-friendly way of doing that? Look carefully at what users (including yourself) really do to select a country from a long list: they move the focus to the drop-down list and then quickly type the first letters of the country name. If the desired country isn't already selected in the drop-down list after typing a few letters, it's only one or two keystrokes away.

Typing is boring, but once you decide to put your hands on the keyboard, it might be faster than any other option for certain tasks.

Why don't we use a plain text box for entering a country/region name? The primary reason is that we need to remove ambiguity in country/region names: for humans USA is the same as United States, and sometimes United Kingdom might be as acceptable as Great Britain. The language is also an issue: Italia is not the same as Italy and so forth. Finally, with a free text box, users can mistype names. With a drop-down list, instead, the page provides a fixed list of names and, more importantly, each entry is bound to a unique ID that identifies unambiguously the selected country/region.

What would be a better way to pick out a country/region name? Something like a smart autocomplete text box.

Introducing Bootstrap Typeahead

If you plan to use autocompletion features in a webpage, you'd better turn off the browser's native autocompletion before doing anything else:

```
<input type="text" autocomplete="off" />
```

Next, you pick out your favorite framework. My favorite is Typeahead, which you can get as a NuGet package. The JavaScript library comes with a minified JavaScript file and a CSS. I invite you to look at the slightly modified CSS file included with the sample code and make your own changes there.

Once you're up and running with Typeahead, here's what you need to have in your input form:

```
$('#country').typeahead(
    null,
    {
        displayKey: 'value',
        source: hints.ttAdapter()
    }
);
```

Typeahead accepts hints in various ways from both local and remote sources. The example I discuss here assumes you use a remote data source. The *null* you see in the configuration call refers to the settings of the call. By passing *null*, you accept all defaults. The second parameter defines the behavior of the component and specifies the display value field and the source of the data to drop down.

Here's a complete example of initialization:

```
<script type="text/javascript">
var hints = new Bloodhound({
        datumTokenizer: Bloodhound.tokenizers.obj.whitespace('value'),
        queryTokenizer: Bloodhound.tokenizers.whitespace,
        remote: yourRemoteUrl + "?query=%QUERY"
    });
    hints.initialize();

    $('#country').typeahead(
        null,
        {
            displayKey: 'value',
            source: hints.ttAdapter()
        }
    );
</script>
```

Bloodhound is a wrapper for the hints served to Typeahead. It comes as a part of the Typeahead bundle. All you do is get an instance of the Bloodhound engine and set it to the remote URL of your choice. That's typically your URL or an external URL that is Cross-Origin Resource Sharing enabled (CORS). In any case, the expression *%QUERY* must be used to refer to the text currently typed in the text box. As long as the remote URL returns a JSON collection with a property named like the strings provided to the tokenizer and the *displayKey* property (*value* in the example), you're all set.

Using the text box as a drop-down list

To achieve the goal of using the text box as a drop-down list that accepts only selected strings, a few more event handlers must be registered with Typeahead. The idea is to use a companion hidden field to save the unique ID of the picked element while showing the full name of the element in the text box. Next, any edits in the typed text forces clearing of the buffer until a new selection is made from the list.

In the same SCRIPT block as just shown, you add the following script:

```
$('#country).on('typeahead:selected', function (e, datum) {
    $("#country").attr("data-itemselected", 1);
    $("#countrycode").val(datum.id);
});

$('#country).on('blur', function() {
    var typeaheadItemSelected = $("#country").attr("data-itemselected");
    if (typeaheadItemSelected != 1) {
        $("#countrycode").val("");
        $('#country').val("");
    }
});

$('#country).on('input', function () {
    var typeaheadItemSelected = $("#country").attr("data-itemselected");
    if (typeaheadItemSelected == 1) {
        $("#country").attr("data-itemselected", 0);
        $("#countrycode").val('');
        $('#queryString').val('');
    }
});
```

In the example, the companion hidden field is named *countrycode*. When Typeahead fires the *selected* event—a hint picked from the list—the companion hidden field is set with the *id* property of the hint. The name *id* here is arbitrary; it's whatever unique property you have that identifies the hint. If it's a list of countries/regions, it will be the country code or any sort of primary key you might have. At the same time, you add a dynamic attribute (*data-itemselected*) to the text box to mark it as holding a value picked from the list of hints. Handlers of *blur* and *input* DOM events will reset content of the text box and hidden field if the user tabs away from the field without making a selection or just attempts to type free text in the field. (See Figure 12-11.)

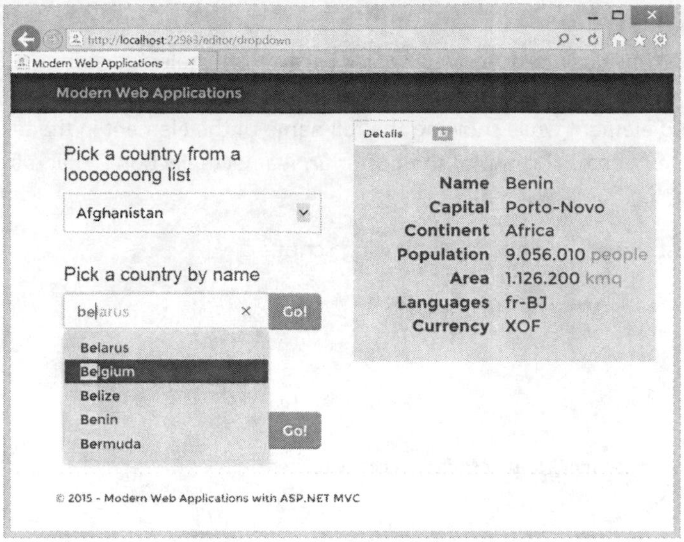

FIGURE 12-11 Using autocompletion to simulate a drop-down list

Miscellaneous tips for large input forms

How many times have you caught yourself in the middle of input forms that are too large and too cumbersome to deal with? As a developer, you sometimes need to collect a lot of data from users, and that's an issue. But, trust me, that's an issue for users too! I once heard a UX person say that the best way to make a feature highly usable is to make it unnecessary. I couldn't agree more.

Here are a few ideas to make large input forms a bit more usable:

- Use tabs to present only related blocks of input fields at one time. An all-encompassing HTML FORM element wraps up all tabs so that whenever you save, regardless of the tab you're in, everything is saved.

- Make it quick and easy for users to find the Save button. In the case of scrolling forms, a solution could be having buttons at the top and bottom. An even better solution is having the toolbar with the Save button scroll with the content of the form.

- Give special types of data such as images (for example, profile images) or passwords (for example, reset or changed passwords) their own Save button. Often, they are special operations performed independent of a general update of the entire record.

- Don't be afraid of using JavaScript buttons to store common values in edit field. An example is a No Date button next to a date-input field, or a Suggest Random Password button next to a password-editing field.

- If possible, implement an autosave feature.

- If possible, consider inline editing of small chunks of data.

It's a quick list, and I might have forgotten other tips I learned myself over the years. But I'm sure you can integrate this list with your own tips as well!

Summary

Editing data in a web application is mostly about dealing with HTML input forms. In this chapter, I approached data editing by focusing on core elements and patterns of today's applications. I assumed you had some basic knowledge of HTML and ASP.NET. I started the chapter talking about authentication and authorization—a rather unusual choice. On the other hand, though, you don't do any sort of editing in a web application without first authenticating a user and checking the user's permissions.

I discussed the PRG pattern and validation through data annotations. I also spent a bit of time presenting and illustrating the pros and cons of modal input forms and the use of smart JavaScript frameworks to improve the quality and usability of your forms. In this chapter, I only simulated data changes because I mostly focused on the interaction model between the front end and back end.

In the next chapter, I'll take some time to discuss Entity Framework and the whole theme of persistence in the context of web applications.

CHAPTER 13

Persistence and modeling

Get your facts first, and then you can distort them as much as you please.

—Mark Twain

Today, it's generally accepted to have a relational database management system (RDBMS) as the foundation of your software architecture. When an RDBMS serves as the foundation, the design and building of a software system is all about designing and building a data-access layer (DAL). In the Microsoft .NET Framework stack, a DAL is made of a bunch of classes using the ADO.NET API or Entity Framework to read from and write to a physical database.

What's the data model, and what is its role in the overall architecture?

The data model—and more often than not, the relational data model—is the first and most important step in carrying out the agenda of software architects. The data model—and more often than not, the relational data model—is an abstraction of the database schema.

This architectural pattern is still valid and still works, but it's becoming less effective every day. Or, to partially mitigate the dramatic impact of the previous sentence, it's becoming less effective every day for more and more types of applications. The point here is not that the (relational) data model is no longer the beating heart of the architecture, but that the (relational) data model is just one way of modeling data and applies to the bottom of a layered architecture—the infrastructure. (See Chapter 5, "The layered architecture.")

In this chapter, I'll first describe the various models you find across the layers of an ASP.NET architecture. Then I'll focus on common ways to implement persistence and common ways of dealing with data models for command and query operations.

Examining the different flavors of a model

I'm surprised to see that today the clear difference between *persistence model* and *domain model* still is disregarded or at least underestimated by a good number of software professionals. One reason for this lack of clarity is that way too many tutorials that claim to illustrate architectural and design practices still use examples that are too simple to make a meaningful distinction between those models. Using the Northwind database to build a good example of domain-driven design, for example, is pure nonsense. You cannot seriously take a physical database and be inspired to design a domain model with its own set of business rules. Likewise, you can't just use the classic Music or Movies application to effectively showcase the importance of a layered architecture.

In both cases, although for different reasons, you end up with a single data model that corresponds one to one with the physical database. There's nothing bad about using a single model for data used throughout the stack as long as you can effectively implement the requested features and are aware that various flavors of a data model exist.

The persistence model

I often make a point of not using at all the expression *data model*. I find it to be too generic because its real meaning too often strictly depends on the business context. If I need to refer to the data model used to read and save data on some type of persistent storage, I prefer to use the expression *persistence model*.

To fix in your mind an example of a persistence model, think of Entity Framework. The classes that Entity Framework infers for you from the database, or the classes you specify as the Code First model, are just part of a persistence model. Those are the classes used to go down to the database. Those classes need to correspond one to one with the database schema of choice. More often than not, though, they also need to correspond one to one with some existing and unmodifiable database schema.

How can you claim that you modeled the domain logic of a business context if you were forced to use an existing database?

So far, I've assumed that the database is a relational database, such as Microsoft SQL Server. A relational database imposes a few constraints on the model that another type of database—say, a NoSQL data store—wouldn't likely impose. A relational database is subject to the rules of the relational model and, subsequently, tends to normalize data, avoid redundancy, and favor indexing and type constraints. A NoSQL data store just saves objects for what they are. In this regard, if you use a NoSQL back end, the persistence model probably is already the sole model you want to work with. As long as you work in a relational environment, though, you should consider the classes used to read from and write to the database as the persistence model.

How much should a persistence model be visible outside the realm of the system's infrastructure?

The answer is simple: as much as you want, as long as it works. If the requirements you face allow for the same set of classes to be used at higher layers than the infrastructure, by all means, use them there. If the requirements don't allow for that, don't be afraid to create an additional model as you move up through the layers.

The domain model

A frequently quoted, but not often applied, slogan of Domain-Driven Design (DDD) is that classes in the domain model must be agnostic with regard to the database structure. Most of the time, this really means that the domain layer and infrastructure layer (where persistence takes place) must be using a different collection of classes.

However, the necessity of that really depends on the application being designed. If the same set of classes can be adapted to work both in the domain layer (business logic) and the infrastructure layer (persistence), why should you be artificially creating more complexity just to have two distinct models? The theory is that each layer might require its own specific data model with proper adapters for converting to and from it. The smaller number of lines of code you end up working with—without precluding or significantly compromising maintenance—the better!

Business rules

Overall, the core point of using a domain model is to have within it a set of classes that contain and expose business rules. A domain model uniquely serves the purpose of implementing business rules and pursues that through classes that express business concepts, business data, and behavior.

The focus on the behavior being a key part of a domain model is all in the fact that classes in a domain model express business concerns and tasks. Because this is the sole concern, it's obvious that a domain model is totally database agnostic in its design.

Having domain and persistence classes coincide with some adaptation is just a shortcut. Legal and legitimate, but a shortcut.

A simple domain modeling exercise

Imagine someone asks you to create a scoring system for some sport—just the trivial type of application that a referee or scorekeeper would use to track the progress of a game: points, faults, timeouts, periods, and all those kind of things. As an example, consider soccer. What do you think about the following class?

```
public class Match
{
    public string Team1 { get; set; }
    public string Team2 { get; set; }
    public int Goals1 { get; set; }
    public int Goals2 { get; set; }
    public int Period { get; set; }
    public MatchState State { get; set; }  /* Scheduled, InProgress, Finished */
}
```

It seems to contain all that you might need, and it's trivial to persist, too. The selected domain is way too simple for a design exercise, you might think.

When you design a domain model, you are actually designing an API for other developers to use, including yourself. You should take care to allow only operations that are legitimate and legal given the business rules and the characteristics of the domain.

Here's a short list of objections to the code just shown:

- The number of goals can be freely set, making –3 to 4 million a valid score.

- The period can be freely set, making it possible for anybody to assign any illegal value.

- The *MatchState* enumeration is nice to have, but it requires a sort of state machine. Only scheduled matches can take the value of *InProgress*, for example, and the value cannot be reverted.

- Goal properties can be set only if the match is in progress.

You might object that all those issues refer to business rules you would take care of in a separate component. That's absolutely fine and, in the end, this is just how we've designed systems for at least 15 years. In this case, though, you don't need a domain model. All you need are data-transfer objects (DTOs) to move data into and out of the business rules component.

Rewriting the solution to the exercise

The alternative is having a domain-model class like *Match* to incorporate the business rules. The first consequence of this design approach is that you don't want to have settable properties—you just want to have methods that match to business actions and internally validate the state and ensure it's always consistent with the business.

Here's another draft of the *Match* class:

```
public class Match
{
    // Read the state
    public string Team1 { get; private set; }
    public string Team2 { get; private set; }
    public int Goals1 { get; private set; }
    public int Goals2 { get; private set; }
    public int Period { get; private set; }
    public MatchState State { get; private set; }  /* Scheduled, InProgress, Finished */

    // Behavior (with business rules)
    public Match(string team1, string team2) { ... }
    public Match Start() { ... }
    public Match Finish() { ... }
    public Match StartPeriod() { ... }
    public Match EndPeriod() { ... }
    public Match Goal1() { ... }
    public Match Goal2() { ... }
    ...
}
```

The methods listed are not simply implicit setters of read-only public properties. They now fully respect the business rules. As an example, take a look at the method *Goal1*:

```
public Match Goal1()
{
    if (!IsInProgress())
        throw new ArgumentException("Can't score a goal if match is not in progress");
    Goals1 ++;
}
```

If the method still looks like a setter, consider that you might need to access multiple properties to validate rules and that the naming of the method is key in light of the Ubiquitous Language pattern I discussed in Chapter 1, "Conducting a thorough domain analysis."

The input model

The input model and view model seem to be the same thing, and most of the time they are implemented as if they were the same thing. Because a picture is worth a thousand words, I'll use Figure 13-1 to recall an illustration you encountered in Chapter 5.

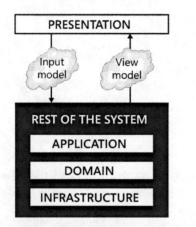

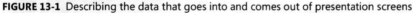

FIGURE 13-1 Describing the data that goes into and comes out of presentation screens

Together, the view model and the input model describe the flow of data that goes into and comes out of presentation screens. In ASP.NET MVC, the input model is relevant to the binding layer around controllers. The input model results from the union of all classes you use to receive data posted from HTML forms or Ajax calls. The view model, instead, is the union of all classes that contain data to be consumed in a Razor view.

The input model lives at the very top of the architecture and is never realistically related to domain-model or persistence-model classes. Note that the lack of relation doesn't mean it's wrong to use the same class that's being persisted to also collect data. It's not wrong: it's just unrealistic. If that happens to you in real life, well, good for you!

The view model

When it comes to actual coding, the input model and view model are often the same set of classes. Together, they represent and express the user's perception of the application and the tasks it has to perform.

In ASP.NET MVC, the view model and input model often coincide also because of the special nature of web applications with a strong server back end. When you generate an HTML response after executing a controller action, you pack into a view-model object all the data to be incorporated in the next view the user will see. But in the same moment in which the view is rendered within the browser and presented to the user, some HTML elements in the view turn into input elements. Subsequently, the same class happens to be part of the input and view models at the same time. This is especially true for view models used to render HTML forms. Here's an illustrative example:

```
[HttpPost]
[ActionName("login")]
public ActionResult LoginPost(LoginInputModel input, string returnUrl)
{
    // Validate credentials
    ...

    // Redirect (PRG pattern)
    return RedirectToAction("login");
}

[HttpGet]
[ActionName("login")]
public ActionResult LoginGet(string returnUrl)
{
    var model = new LoginViewModel() {ReturnUrl = returnUrl};
    return View(model);
}
```

The *LoginViewModel* class is used to prepare and initialize the login HTML form. When the login form is posted, the same content is presented back to the system in the form of an instance of the *LoginInputModel* class created by the ASP.NET MVC binding layer.

There's no valid reason for not trying to use the same physical class here. Yet, the input model and view model are conceptually different models.

Figure 13-2 summarizes the role of each flavor of data model in the context of a layered architecture as I depicted it in its entirety in Chapter 5. The recycling arrows added to the figure here indicate the presence of adapters to convert one model into another.

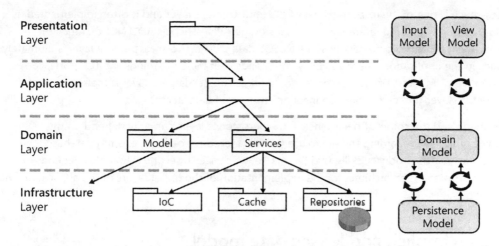

FIGURE 13-2 Flavors of data models in the context of a layered architecture

Designing a persistence layer

In Chapter 10, "Organization of the ASP.NET MVC project," I presented the same diagram as shown in Figure 13-3.

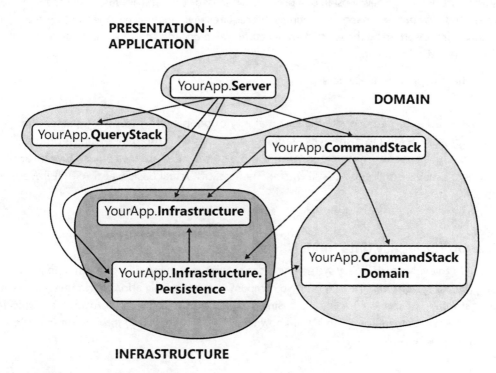

FIGURE 13-3 Identifying the persistence layer within a layered architecture

Persistence is one of the responsibilities of the infrastructure layer and is often implemented as a distinct assembly holding references to actual storage APIs—such as ADO.NET or, much more likely these days, Entity Framework or some NoSQL data stores. The infrastructure layer is ultimately the place in the application where you dirty your hands with concrete things like TCP ports, configuration files, URLs and, of course, connection strings. The persistence layer is the segment of the infrastructure layer that cares about connection strings and data-access APIs.

The shape and the colors of persistence in the persistence layer primarily depend on the constraints you have regarding the API to use (such as stored procedures, existing database schemas, specific RDBMS products, skills, budget, marketing policies). Secondarily, it also depends on the vision you promote as an architect for the implementation of the upper layers of the application and domain logic.

Using an implicit and legacy data model

The first scenario I will present is a relatively old-fashioned approach to designing a persistence layer. You don't have an explicit data model made of data-specific classes here; instead, you use generic data containers to move data in and out of the storage.

I referred this approach as *old-fashioned* for the sole reason that it dates back to a decade ago, a byproduct of the glorious days of ASP.NET 2.0. A significant share of today's production systems were created or heavily refactored at that time in the early 2000s. You don't typically touch a production system just because a new version of a product is released. You typically just apply changes that revolve around new business needs. Sometimes this requires making deep changes, but for the most part changes are absorbed by the existing architecture. Yet, a decade later, you might be feeling the need for some radical redesign.

This is what's happening these days.

Note As weird as it might sound, the vast majority of people who attend my classes and call me for help belong to a specific category: companies who run their business on top of very old, yet effective, systems. Some of these systems were put into place 15 years ago or more and have working parts still written in Microsoft Visual Basic 6 and ASP.NET Web Forms.

Motivation for legacy data models

When you try to evolve such legacy systems, you can't really do it in just a few months and just by replacing the old system with the new one. No company can reasonably afford to do that and accept the risk of stopping or severely limiting the business to install new production software. You typically start a long and winding journey with a well-known final destination and go through several milestones along the way.

In such a legacy context, the last token you are allowed to change is the database. You might extend it or perhaps introduce multiple storage technologies side by side (an approach known as *polyglot persistence*), but you still need to have an implicit data model in the persistence layer.

ADO.NET persistence

A decade ago, ADO.NET—the first data access API in the .NET Framework—introduced generic data container objects such as *DataSet* and *DataTable*. They're still there in the .NET Framework even though none of the most recent applications built from scratch have strict business reasons to use them.

Born from the ashes of successful ADO *Recordset* objects, *DataSet* objects don't push any explicit data models. They just elastically adapt to whatever database schema you have under the hood. The *DataSet*, as well as companion objects such as data readers, are some currency your persistence layer might exchange with the storage. The plain ADO.NET API, or the more comfortable Enterprise Library Data Access Application Block, is used to read and write data.

Using generic in-memory containers like *DataSet* objects, frankly, is no big deal for commands, when all you need is to write data persistently. You receive data to store from the upper layers and must first adapt it to storage formats. In this context, the *DataSet* model is as good as any other object model. The only good measure of the effectiveness of this choice is the performance.

LINQ-to-DataSet

Things are a bit more delicate for the read stack. Data fetched in the form of a DataSet object may or may not be ideal for presentation purposes. The *DataSet* model reflects the storage model; the presentation most likely doesn't. To address the issue, enter that special and little used flavor of LINQ called *LINQ-to-DataSet*.

You can use the powerful LINQ query syntax over the contents of *DataSet* and *DataTable* objects and comfortably extract data to more malleable C# classes. Here's an example:

```
// ds is a DataSet object you obtained in some way. For example, via ADO.NET
var customers = ds.Tables[0].AsEnumerable();
var orders = ds.Tables[1].AsEnumerable();

var data = from o in orders
           join c in customers
           on o.Field<string>("CustomerID")
              equals c.Field<string>("CustomerID")
           where o.Field<DateTime>("OrderDate").Year == 1998 &&
               o.Field<DateTime>("OrderDate").Month == 1 &&
               o.Field<DateTime>("OrderDate").Day < 10
           select new QuickOrderListItem {
              OrderID=o.Field<int>("OrderID"),
              Company=c.Field<string>("CompanyName")
           };
```

A new data-transfer object (class *QuickOrderListItem*) is built from a *DataSet* obtained in some way, most likely through a previous ADO.NET query or stored procedure call.

The benefit of this approach when you are refreshing a legacy system is evident. You maintain the existing data-access core (whether it's based on stored procedures or direct database access), and you still can evolve the rest of the architecture toward Command/Query Responsibility Segregation (CQRS) and more modern design patterns.

Using Entity Framework

As harsh as it might sound, I think that Entity Framework was neither born with, nor grew to build, a strong and well-defined personality. Is it a plain Object/Relational Mapper (O/RM) tool like the popular NHibernate was in the .NET space? Is it a more ambitious tool to create persistent object models when you're trying to represent a business domain? The word *Framework* in the name makes me lean toward the second option, and so do the memories I have of many conversations with Microsoft developers and product evangelists.

The fact is that, up to version 6, Entity Framework is an O/RM with the tacit ambition of being a domain-modeling tool. The tool is not bad per se, and it does its persistence work quite well, fitting nicely into most business scenarios.

The real problem I see is with the marketing of Entity Framework, which blurs the distinction between a domain model and a persistence model. As an architect, you might actually decide that a single model works for you in the system you're working on, but you might not see that the conceptual difference between the two is nefarious.

Modeling the business domain is an architect's task

As discussed in the section "The domain model" earlier in the chapter, modeling a business domain is an effort that completely abstracts from database concerns. It's an effort founded on the will of coding business rules in classes. Such classes end up representing entities and tasks in the business domain. Such classes would express the logic and the mechanics of the business. In this context, persistence is a completely cross-cutting concern.

The state determined by the interaction between such domain classes needs be persisted at some point. The state, therefore, must be read out of the domain model classes and saved to some data store. This is the work of the persistence layer. You can read the state out of domain classes and save it by using the following procedures:

■ Build a stored procedure or ADO.NET calls, and save to a relational database.

■ Save the state to NoSQL or to event data stores as plain objects.

■ Save the state to a relational database via the services of an O/RM tool such as Entity Framework.

For completeness, I should also mention a fourth option: save the state to some invisible remote back end exposed through web services.

What happens, exactly, when you use an O/RM tool?

Database-inferred data models

The saving options listed a moment ago can be graphically represented as shown in Figure 13-4.

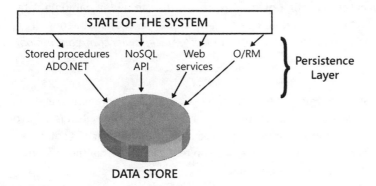

FIGURE 13-4 Flavors of a persistence layer

When the option is to use an O/RM, another helper object model comes into play that is strictly functional to the work the O/RM does. To read and save data, an O/RM needs an object model. All that an O/RM does, ultimately, is map properties of classes in the object model to columns of tables in the target database.

The O/RM helper object model might or might not be the same as the model you might have to represent the state of the system. The model you use to instruct the O/RM to persist data is the persistence model. The other is a model that expresses the domain logic and is agnostic with regard to database type and structure concerns.

The fundamental decision to make is whether you need to have distinct domain and persistence models or whether a single, all-encompassing model represents a good compromise in your specific scenario.

> **Important** If you decide that having a single model is preferable, you must be ready to accept compromises in terms of the structure and public interface of the domain model. In other words, when a single model is used, the database schema and underlying technology become constraints. As a result, the object model that expresses the domain logic might be spoiled and not as congruent and consistent as it should be.

Persistence and database segments

An O/RM framework works by opening a logical connection to the underlying data store and performing any sort of transaction within that context. In Entity Framework, such a logical connection is called a *DbContext*. It takes a different name in NHibernate—another popular .NET O/RM framework—where it's called a *Session*. Ultimately, a logical connection is actually a wrapper around a physical connection.

O/RMs were conceived to shield developers from the intricacies of SQL programming and to bypass the mismatch between classes and records. The public interface of a *DbContext* is made of data containers that represent in-memory proxies for physical data containers such as database tables. By acting on the members of such an interface, you can restrict at will what the consumer of the context can do. Consider the two classes shown here:

```
public class ApplicationDbContext : DbContext
{
    public ApplicationDbContext()
        : base("name=SomeConnectionStringEntry")
    {
    }
    public virtual DbSet<Order> Orders { get; set; }
    public virtual DbSet<Product> Products { get; set; }
}

public class Database : IDisposable
{
    private readonly ApplicationDbContext _context = new ApplicationDbContext();
    public IQueryable<Order> Orders
    {
        get { return _context.Orders; }
    }

    public void Dispose()
    {
        _context.Dispose();
    }
}
```

The first class shown is a canonical *DbContext* class that represents the operational context around the specified database connection string and classes bound to the schema. Any application that gains access to an instance of *ApplicationDbContext* gains full access to the referenced tables.

The second class is a read-only wrapper that fully encapsulates a canonical *DbContext* class—the same *ApplicationDbContext* class—and exposes only a subset of the tables and does so exclusively via a LINQ *IQueryable* interface:

```
using (var db = new Database())
```

```
{
    // There's no SaveChanges method available on the db instance.
    // Database is a read-only context for the same underlying database.
}
```

By creating wrappers around *DbContext* objects, you can expose segments of the database to different segments of your code.

> **Important** Segments of a given database exposed in this way through multiple *DbContext* objects are sometimes referred to as *DDD-bounded contexts*. As I see things, that's too much of a stretch. In DDD, a bounded context is a business concept that relates to the domain analysis. Because of that, it's completely agnostic with regard to database design and structure. I see in that, and appreciate, the same idea expressed here of segmenting access to a database. But I do believe that using the term *bounded context* only generates confusion. Even worse, generating confusion in such a delicate part of software architecture can really be costly.

Code First

Entity Framework Code First is a feature you use to take a code-centric approach to creating code that deals with databases. Essentially, it uses a set of (configurable) conventions to figure out the ideal database in which to save the classes you have in the model. Code First primarily works with new databases, but it supports migration packages to update a physical database when changes occur to the model.

The approach behind Code First will be a mainstream one in Entity Framework 7 and in the new wave of frameworks from Microsoft following the ASP.NET Core 1.0 revolution.

What's the real purpose of Code First?

There's some consensus in the industry that Code First is useful in DDD. The argument is that you focus on the classes that better express the business domain instead of creating the database first and matching classes to it. As I explained in the first part of the book and primarily in Chapter 1, DDD is primarily about discovering the behavior of the domain. So a DDD approach might lead you to describing the life of a sports match using a class like the second *Match* class I discussed earlier in the chapter.

That class has no writable properties and is not supposed to have any because of business constraints. It would be quite problematic for an O/RM to populate a fresh instance of that class automatically. Code First is probably the best way to create persistence models; domain models (and DDD) are quite different things.

> **Note** I want to point out that Code First is an excellent tool to programmatically create databases and to easily write applications that create their own database at startup. It can be an interesting feature to leverage to smooth out the setup of any software that goes

through a customization step when installed in some customer environment. One way to look at Code First is to view it as a modern version of a data-definition language (DDL).

The Repository pattern

Today, the persistence layer is traditionally implemented using the Repository pattern. A *repository* is a class where each method represents an action around the data source—whatever that source happens to be.

There's a huge amount of literature about the Repository pattern and its pros and cons. And just as much literature exists about the possible ways to implement it. In summary, my standing is that there's no patently wrong way to write a layer of repository classes. At worst, you end up with a few useless passthrough layers of code that just eat up CPU cycles in the name of some supposed increased clarity and elegance of code.

Generalities of the pattern

According to Martin Fowler, a repository is a component that mediates between the domain layer and lower layers in charge of persistence and uses a collection-like interface for accessing domain objects. (See *http://martinfowler.com/eaaCatalog/repository.html*.) This definition seems to closely match the public interface of the root context object that most O/RM frameworks expose—for example, the *DbContext* object of Entity Framework.

In a nutshell, a repository class provides the basic atomic tools for reading to and writing from a data store. It performs data access using one specific, data-access technology or multiple technologies, such as Entity Framework, NHibernate, ADO.NET, and similar products. (See Figure 13-5.)

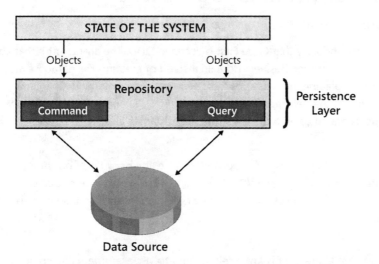

FIGURE 13-5 The repository as an implementation of the persistence layer

Consumers of repository classes

Repository classes can be consumed in many ways, depending on the rest of the architecture you have in place. It's acceptable that you invoke repositories from within the application layer. If you have domain logic implemented in a domain layer, repositories might be seen as the primary type of domain service. As shown in Figure 13-5, repositories are the interfacing layer between business logic (whether it's application or domain logic) and storage.

If you have a CQRS architecture, you typically need repositories only in the command stack and have one repository class for each group of related objects (or *aggregate*, to use DDD terminology). The command-stack repository will be limited to methods that write data and a couple of generic query methods: one to get an object by ID and possibly one to query all objects from a given database table. The read stack of a CQRS architecture is fairly thin, and it might even be acceptable that you invoke the *DbContext* object right from the application layer.

> **Important** Regardless of pattern names, the most important achievement here is that you isolate data-access logic in a closed black box that is easy to replace, for whatever reason: change of data store or just different persistence algorithms. You can refer to this layer any way you like. The name doesn't really matter as long as you have a single place in the project where you deal with connection strings.

My favorite way of implementing repositories

As I said earlier, I don't really think there's any patently wrong way of writing such data-access code in between business logic and storage. Anyway, I guess you might be curious to know how I do my own things.

Here are my key rules:

■ Encapsulate data-access API details (connection strings, *DbContext*, and configuration) within the repository classes so that upper layers know only about which read/write operations can be performed.

■ Have a repository class for each significant entity (or likely group of entities) in the business domain. In DDD jargon, a *significant entity* is referred to as an *aggregate*.

■ Preferably, give each repository class a task-oriented programming interface. This means having write and read methods that perform direct operations that are atomic from the perspective of the business. Often, instead, I see atomic behavior in the repository at the database level with operations such as Save, Delete, and Get.

- If you have long-running tasks and (distributed) transactions that exceed the boundaries of the data store, consider adapting the interface of repository classes so that, for example, multiple database operations can occur under the umbrella of the same *DbContext*.

To make more sense of the final point, have a look at the following code snippet:

```
public class OrderRepository : IOrderRepository
{
    protected ApplicationDbContext _database;
    public OrderRepository()
    {
        _database = new ApplicationDbContext();
    }

    public void Save(Order order)
    {
        _database.Orders.Add(order);
    }

    public void Commit()
    {
        _database.SaveChanges();
    }
    ...
}
```

When you code things this way, the repository is atomic with respect to business-oriented database operations. You can run multiple operations within the same transaction, but you can't combine order and, say, product operations in the same transaction. If that's crucial for you to do, just inject an externally created *DbContext* into the repository.

Polyglot persistence

It should not be seen as blasphemous to say that there might be scenarios today in which the venerable relational paradigm is less optimal than one expects. Such scenarios are probably less common than many think and affect far fewer applications than many claim to be affected. Yet such scenarios exist. When raising your gaze to look beyond the relational paradigm, though, it seems that the only other alternative is to use one of the NoSQL databases out there.

As I see things, the point here isn't simply to find reasons to call relational stores dead and replace them with your NoSQL product of choice. The point is to understand the mechanics of the system and the characteristics of the data being used. And, based on that, work out the best possible architecture and data-storage solution.

Polyglot persistence refers to using the most appropriate storage technology for each stack of the system and even for each operation.

Polyglot persistence by example

Polyglot persistence burst onto the stage with the advent of social networks. Can you imagine what it could mean to update indexes to guarantee consistency and durability on a multibillion-row database of Facebook users when someone likes a comment on a post that a friend of yours made? Given the numbers involved when dealing with social networks, that was just a nonissue; in fact, different approaches have been found, leading to what today we call *polyglot persistence*.

Dealing with variegated information

Let's review the canonical example used to illustrate polyglot persistence: an e-commerce system. In such a system, you reasonably might need to save the following information:

- Customers, orders, payments, shipments, products, and all information related to a business transaction.

- Preferences of users discovered as they navigate through the catalog of products or resulting from running business intelligence on top of their transactions.

- Documents representing invoices, maps of physical shops to help the user find the closest one, directions, pictures, receipts of delivery, and so on.

- Detailed logs of any user's activity; products the user viewed, bought, commented on, reviewed, or liked.

- Graph of users who bought the same and similar products, similar products, other products the user might be interested in buying, and users in the same geographical area.

Saving any such piece of information to a single relational database is certainly possible and probably still the first option that comes to mind. In addition, if a single database technology should be picked by policy, I dare say that relational databases are still the most recommendable option. But let's see what it could mean to be polyglot in persistence.

A canonical example of polyglot persistence

Polyglot persistence consists of mixing various stores and picking the right one for each type of information:

- You can store customers and orders to a SQL Server data store and access that information through Entity Framework or any other O/RM framework. Entity Framework, in particular, can be used also to transparently access an instance of a Microsoft Azure SQL Database in the cloud.

- User preferences can go to the Azure table storage and be accessed through an ad hoc layer that consumes Azure JSON endpoints.

- Documents could go to a document database such as RavenDB or MongoDB and would be consumed through the dedicated .NET API.

- The user's history can be saved to a column store such as Cassandra. Cassandra is unique in that it associates a key value with a varying number of name/value pairs. The nice thing is that any row stored to Cassandra can have a completely different structure than other records. The effect is similar to having a name/value dictionary where the value is a collection of name/value pairs.

- Hierarchical information can be stored to a graph database. An excellent choice today is Neo4j, and you can access and code it through the .NET client. The issue with hierarchical databases is not so much how you access it but how to organize, create, and maintain such a database.

The overall cost of polyglot persistence might be more than negligible at times. For the most part, you end up working with .NET clients that are relatively straightforward to use. Yet, when a lot of data is involved and performance issues show up, heterogeneous skills are required and shortage or lack of documentation is the norm rather than the exception.

Costs of polyglot persistence

The major benefit of polyglot persistence is the use of a heterogeneous storage architecture aimed at maximizing the performance of specific services. However, this can turn into a major weakness as you realize you need the skills to arrange possibly different operating systems and to learn to use new tools, new languages, and new ways to work.

Impact on customer support

For an organization with strong SQL Server skills, reconverting admin and DBA skills might be an issue and, at a minimum, it will be time consuming. Even if you hire new people, they must be really expert in the respective domains and they'll need time to get acquainted with the system and its possible intricacies. Furthermore, the more you're polyglot, the more people you might need to hire or, at least, the more skills you might need to acquire.

Finally, you never know how the system will react in production when real data (and not just test data) is used. It's likely that most of the existing knowledge base and case studies will be lost. You might reasonably expect diminished effectiveness of your customer support.

Points to consider

To evaluate costs and make an informative trade-off, here's a list of the points to consider. The perspective is that of a SQL Server shop considering NoSQL solutions:

- Tools you use to accomplish common tasks

- Maintenance of installed databases

- Customization of installed databases

Table 13-1, Table 13-2, and Table 13-3 use RavenDB as the representative of the NoSQL family. I suggest you take the following points as examples of issues but needing further investigation to understand how they fit in your particular scenario. Also, points and features discussed in these tables refer to a snapshot of products that might have evolved and improved by the time you read this.

TABLE 13-1 Tools comparison

Type of tool you use in SQL Server	NoSQL counterpart (RavenDB)
SQL Server Management Studio	RavenDB Studio allows you to create, encrypt, and replicate stores. It also offers logs and statistics.
SQL Server Profiler	RavenDB has an internal profiler exposed through an API. You can intercept the API in custom applications and also perf counters in Windows Management Instrumentation (WMI).
sqlcmd	Some command-line tools exist (for example, backup/recovery), but none like sqlcmd. RavenDB does expose an HTTP API you can invoke from the command line using curl.

TABLE 13-2 Maintenance operations comparison

Operation in SQL Server	NoSQL counterpart (RavenDB)
Backup	You do backup/recovery from within RavenDB Studio. Operations are also available through command-line utilities.
Shrink transaction log	Nothing like this exists.
Shrink database	RavenDB doesn't shrink files when you delete records. Shrink should be performed using system tools such as Esent utility. It's an offline operation, though.
Index defragmentation	Index manipulation happens through RavenDB Studio.

TABLE 13-3 Customization options comparison

Option in SQL Server	NoSQL counterpart (RavenDB)
Auto-growth	The data file will grow automatically.
Recovery model: simple, full	Full backup is common in RavenDB. You can manage backup via Windows to fine-tune it to your needs. You use Windows task scheduler to schedule activities. Backup can happen while the database is working and responding to requests, including writes. In the end, it works more or less like in SQL Server.

Polyglot persistence in the context of CQRS

The most basic form of CQRS uses a single database shared by command and query stacks. The beauty of CQRS, though, lies in the fact that you can optimize each stack separately. In this regard, you can optimize each stack to just use the database technology that best fits.

More sophisticated forms of CQRS, therefore, can implement polyglot persistence. The command stack focuses on mere storage of what happened and, in doing so, it can save data using NoSQL or, more likely, an event store to just save the state as a sequence of events.

At the same time, the query stack can be based on an RDBMS whose tables are synced up with the command stack and offer readymade data that's easy to query and present. If the command stack is saving data in the form of events, the synchronization is a matter of replaying events and building a custom projection of data to save in a relational schema.

The combination of the CQRS architecture with polyglot persistence is a powerful solution for systems that must guarantee high performance while being ready to scale up, even abruptly.

Summary

There's no application that doesn't have to read and/or write data. These tasks are performed by the persistence layer, which is ideally the only place in the application where connection strings and URLs are known and managed. The persistence layer is a relatively small and simple piece of the architecture, but the way it relates to the rest of the system is critical.

The key point I tried to make in this example is to clarify the difference between a persistence model—the set of classes you use to read from and write to a database via the services of an O/RM tool—and a domain model—namely, the set of classes you define to mirror the logic of the system and core tasks of the business.

Understanding such differences is critical for being an architect, regardless of the actual choices you make while designing a layered system.

User experience

CHAPTER 14

Creating more interactive views

There is nothing like returning to a place that remains unchanged to find the ways in which you yourself have altered.

—*Nelson Mandela*

Web content has always been interactive, ever since the beginning of HTML as a markup language. The sore spot today is not linking together related content hosted on different sources, but making the resulting experience as smooth and quick as possible for the user. My favorite definition of *user experience* expresses this concept: *the experience users go through when they interact with your views*.

Web views became rather bloated and cumbersome in the past decade, padded with a lot of graphics, images, videos, and advertising. In addition, the mobile-inherited attitude to just scroll for more content has led to creating longer and longer pages with content in a single view, a view that would have been split over multiple pages only a few years ago.

In the middle of the first decade of the 2000s, Ajax (which is short for a now rather weird term, *Asynchronous JavaScript and XML*) emerged as a must-have technology to refresh portions of the view without fully refreshing it and without reloading the huge amount of content in and around the view.

Originally devised to deal with XML, in the end Ajax works much more effectively with JSON (JavaScript Object Notation). JSON is a language-independent text format, but it uses programming conventions to wrap up any sort of data. With JSON, you transfer any text-based content over the wire regardless of clients and host platforms.

For web developers, and ASP.NET developers in particular, the challenge has become finding the most effective way to serve and consume JSON data from within client-side views. When it comes to this, there are a few points to be addressed:

- The infrastructure required to expose content

- Pulling content from remote data sources

- Data-binding techniques to inject any downloaded content in the current view

- Having remote data sources push data to clients

This chapter covers these points.

Exposing JSON content

I already presented in Chapter 8, "Core of ASP.NET MVC," a short code snippet aimed at exposing JSON content via a controller action. That is the simplest way of exposing JSON content from within an ASP.NET MVC application. In general, you can use HTTP handlers and even Web Forms ASPX pages to return JSON data. Any piece of code that can be reached by an HTTP request can be configured to return a response made of JSON.

JSON is plain text, but not free text. A typical JSON payload results from the serialization of some server-side object created in accordance with a few basic syntax rules. The nice thing about JSON is that the serialized text can be turned into a running JavaScript object by all types of browsers. To mark an HTTP response as JSON content, you use the *application/json* MIME type. For more information about JSON and its syntax, you can refer to *http://www.json.org*.

In the Microsoft .NET Framework, there are two popular libraries that can deal with JSON data. One is the *JavaScriptSerializer* class found in the *System.Web.Extensions.dll* assembly. The other is JSON.NET, which you can find at *http://www.newtonsoft.com/json* or install via NuGet.

Creating JSON endpoints

Any controller method can return JSON. All it needs to do is get JSON content and pass it to the system's action invoker for finalizing the request. Figure 14-1 shows the high-level pieces that work together to process an ASP.NET request. The figure also explains the different ways the system behaves when it's called to return HTML or JSON.

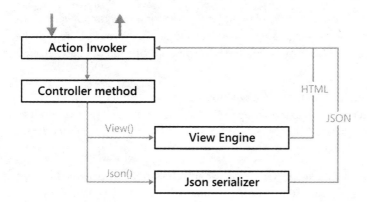

FIGURE 14-1 The varying behavior of a controller method that returns HTML or JSON

The *Json* Helper Method

All controller methods are required to return a type that inherits from *ActionResult*. In particular, a controller method can be written to return *JsonResult*, which is just a more specific class that inherits and extends *ActionResult*. An instance of *JsonResult* can be created via the *Json* helper method.

Here's a sample controller class that has one method that returns JSON data. An application service is used to retrieve data, and retrieved data is then serialized as JSON.

```
public class JsonController : Controller
{
    private readonly CountryService _countryService = new CountryService();

    public JsonResult Countries([Bind(Prefix="q")] string initial="")
    {
        var model = _countryService.GetCountryListViewModel(initial);
        return Json(model, JsonRequestBehavior.AllowGet);
    }
}
```

Given the code, you can now point the browser to, say, /json/countries?q=H and get the list of countries/regions in the world whose English name begins with H. The content type of the data you receive is JSON, as Figure 14-2 (captured with Fiddler) demonstrates.

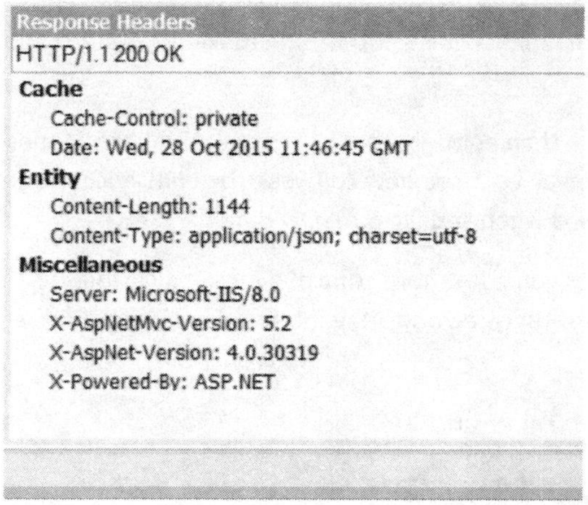

Response Headers
HTTP/1.1 200 OK
Cache
    Cache-Control: private
    Date: Wed, 28 Oct 2015 11:46:45 GMT
Entity
    Content-Length: 1144
    Content-Type: application/json; charset=utf-8
Miscellaneous
    Server: Microsoft-IIS/8.0
    X-AspNetMvc-Version: 5.2
    X-AspNet-Version: 4.0.30319
    X-Powered-By: ASP.NET

FIGURE 14-2 Headers of the response for the sample JSON URL

JSON hijacking possibility

The method *Json* accepts any .NET object and attempts to serialize it to a string. The second parameter—a value from the *JsonRequestBehavior* enumerated type—indicates whether ASP.NET MVC should return JSON data over an HTTP GET method. Note that, by default, no JSON data is returned by ASP.NET MVC over HTTP GET requests. This is a security measure aimed at reducing the likelihood of you falling victim to some JSON hijacking attack. (See *http://haacked.com/archive/2009/06/25/json-hijacking.aspx*.)

The fact is that the extra parameter of type *JsonRequestBehavior* doesn't really protect you in any way against a possible phishing attack like JSON hijacking. However, it serves the purpose of calling your attention to the fact you're exposing JSON data via a plain GET. If your data is sensitive and you want to make it harder to access, restrict the request to HTTP POST or non–HTTP GET verbs.

Also, note that JSON hijacking might affect you only if all or part of the original object serializes to JSON using arrays.

Inside the *JsonResult* class

The *Json* method is only a piece of syntactic sugar set around the constructor of the *JsonResult* class. The method creates a fresh new instance of the *JsonResult* class internally and hands it over to the action invoker for the actual production of the response.

The *JsonResult* class extends the base *ActionResult* with a couple of properties: *MaxJsonLength* and *RecursionLimit*. The former property indicates the maximum amount of JSON data the controller will ever return. The latter property refers to the maximum number of nesting levels allowed in the structure of the object being serialized. Both are nullable integer properties of the *JsonResult* class.

The internal implementation of the *JsonResult* class uses an instance of *JavaScriptSerializer* to perform the actual work of turning a .NET object into a JSON string. When the *Json* method is used to create an instance of the *JsonResult* class, no specific value is assigned to *MaxJsonLength* and *RecursionLimit*. As a result, both properties take default values: 2 MB for the maximum length and 100 nesting levels.

Although 100 nesting levels is realistically more than enough, the 2-MB limit might sometimes hit you and cause an exception at the controller level. Let's see how to tweak the controller's code to make sure that no length exceptions are ever raised when serializing JSON data.

Calling the *JsonResult* constructor directly gives you a lot more control over the available properties. In this way, you can comfortably pass settings down to the internal *JavaScriptSerializer* instance:

```
public JsonResult Countries([Bind(Prefix="q")] string initial="")
{
    var model = _countryService.GetCountryListViewModel(initial);
    return new JsonResult
    {
        MaxJsonLength = Int32.MaxValue,
        Data = model,
        ContentEncoding = Encoding.UTF8,
        JsonRequestBehavior = JsonRequestBehavior.AllowGet
    };
}
```

Yet another approach is performing the serialization yourself using your preferred serializer, either a *JavaScriptSerializer* class or JSON.NET:

```
var serializer = new JavaScriptSerializer {MaxJsonLength = Int32.MaxValue};
var result = new ContentResult
{
    Content = serializer.Serialize(model),
    ContentType = "application/json"
};
```

This approach is probably the most powerful because it lets you gain full control over the entire process. Not only can you control the maximum length of the data to process, you can also customize the JSON processor to register type converters and handlers for dates and null values.

Negotiating content

Even though in this chapter the focus is mostly on JSON, you likely still have some XML clients to accommodate. As you'll see later in the chapter, the ability to negotiate content with the caller is a strength of the ASP.NET Web API. However, even in a plain ASP.NET MVC controller class, serving JSON or XML is not really problematic. Here's some sample code:

```
public ActionResult Countries(
    [Bind(Prefix="q")] string initial = "",
    [Bind(Prefix="x")] bool formatXml = false)
{
    var model = _countryService.GetCountryListViewModel(initial);

    // Decide about content
    if (formatXml)
        return Content(new CountriesXmlFormatter().Serialize(model), "text/xml");
    return new JsonResult()
    {
        MaxJsonLength = Int32.MaxValue,
        Data = model,
        ContentEncoding = Encoding.UTF8,
        JsonRequestBehavior = JsonRequestBehavior.AllowGet
    };
}
```

The XML formatter is a custom class that can be written to serialize XML just the way you like for particular content. Here's an example:

```
public string Serialize(object data)
{
    var list = data as IList<Country>;
    if (list == null)
        return String.Empty;

    var builder = new StringBuilder();
    builder.AppendLine("<?xml version=\"1.0\" encoding=\"utf-8\"?>");
    builder.AppendLine("<countries>");
    foreach (var c in list)
    {
        builder.AppendFormat("<country>");
        builder.AppendFormat("<name>{0}</name>", c.CountryName);
        builder.AppendFormat("<capital>{0}</capital>", c.Capital);
        builder.AppendFormat("<continent>{0}</continent>", c.Continent);
        builder.AppendFormat("</country>");
    }
    builder.AppendLine("</countries>");
    return builder.ToString();
}
```

The XML serializer here is not generic, but in my experience that's just the point. Today, JSON works most of the time, and when you need XML it's because you just need some ad hoc XML schema that a generic XML serializer cannot produce.

Solving the cross-origin puzzle

As you might know, browsers apply the Same-Origin Policy to JavaScript calls they handle directly. This rule is relatively recent and was added to reduce to nearly zero the surface attack area for malicious users. The net effect of such restrictions is that you're prevented from making Ajax calls to a website hosted on a different domain than the requesting page.

JSON with Padding (JSONP) and Cross-Origin Resource Sharing (CORS) are two ways to address the problem. They have a different implementation and also different scopes.

> **Note** In addition to JSONP and CORS, you bypass the limitation of the Same-Origin Policy by using one of your controllers to serve as a proxy to the remote server you want to reach. The proxy approach works beautifully except that it requires a one-to-one mapping between external cross-origin endpoints and same-server endpoints. It's no big deal if you just have one or two endpoints. It involves significant development overhead if you have many more than that.

Using JSONP

Curiously, browsers take care of controlling Ajax calls and JSON data, but they still leave you complete freedom to deal with images and script elements. Whatever URL you use in an IMG or SCRIPT element, as long as it's reachable, will be blissfully downloaded. Tricky usage of the SCRIPT element lies behind the JSONP protocol, and it can be exploited to safely download JSON data via Ajax from sites that explicitly allow for it. Let's see what you should do in your website to enable callers from any site to call your public JSON endpoints.

The trick consists of returning the JSON content wrapped up in a script function call. In other words, when you use this trick, instead of the site simply returning plain JSON data, it would return the following string:

```
yourFunction("{plain JSON data}");
```

On the client side, you can call a JSONP endpoint if both of the following apply:

- You know the script function name that the server uses to wrap up JSON data, and you have such a function defined in your client page.

- You place the call from within a SCRIPT element.

After the site URL is invoked from within a SCRIPT tag, the browser receives what looks like a plain function call with a fixed input string. Because any downloaded script executes immediately, your local JavaScript function has the chance to process JSON data.

JSONP endpoints are documented, and documentation makes it clear what the function name is that's being used to wrap up any returned JSON data. Here's the previous endpoint rewritten to support JSONP:

```
public JsonpResult CountriesP([Bind(Prefix = "q")] string initial = "")
{
    var model = _countryService.GetCountryListViewModel(initial);
    return new JsonpResult()
    {
        MaxJsonLength = Int32.MaxValue,
        Data = model,
        ContentEncoding = Encoding.UTF8,
        JsonRequestBehavior = JsonRequestBehavior.AllowGet
    };
}
```

As you can see, the only difference is the use of *JsonpResult* instead of *JsonResult*. The *JsonpResult* class is a custom class that extends the native *JsonResult* and wraps up the JSON string being returned in a call to the specified JavaScript function:

```
public class JsonpResult : JsonResult
{
    private const String JsonpFunctionName = "callback";

    public override void ExecuteResult(ControllerContext context)
    {
        if (context == null)
            throw new ArgumentNullException("context");

        if ((JsonRequestBehavior == JsonRequestBehavior.DenyGet) &&
            String.Equals(context.HttpContext.Request.HttpMethod, "GET"))
            throw new InvalidOperationException();

        var response = context.HttpContext.Response;
        if (!String.IsNullOrEmpty(ContentType))
            response.ContentType = ContentType;
        else
            response.ContentType = "application/json";
        if (ContentEncoding != null)
            response.ContentEncoding = this.ContentEncoding;

        if (Data != null)
        {
            var serializer = new JavaScriptSerializer();
            var buffer = String.Format("{0}({1})", JsonpCallbackName, serializer.
Serialize(Data));
            response.Write(buffer);
        }
    }
}
```

To consume the JSONP data, you can just place an ad-hoc SCRIPT element somewhere in the page:

```
<script type="text/javascript" src="/json/countriesp?q=be"></script>
```

The effect of the script is that it invokes a client-side JavaScript function with the same name used by the server-side endpoint to wrap up the JSON data. In the example I've been using, that name is *callback*:

```
function callback(json) {
    var buffer = buildOutput(json);
    $("#jsonpResponse").html(buffer);
}
function buildOutput(json) {
    var buffer = "<ul>";
    for (var index in json.Countries) {
        var item = json.Countries[index];
        buffer += "<li>" + item.CountryName + "</li>";
    }
    buffer += "</ul>";
    return buffer;
}
```

Alternatively, you can use the services of the jQuery library by using the *$.getJSON* specific method or the more general *$.ajax* method. Here are the details of making a JSONP call:

```
$.getJSON("/json/countriesp?q=" + initial + "&xxx=?");
```

Note that in the *getJSON* call, you write things in the form of *"xxx=?"* only to force jQuery to place the call the JSONP way. The *xxx* string is arbitrary unless the remote endpoint allows you to pass the name of the JavaScript function you want to be called back. In this case, *xxx* becomes the name of the parameter as defined by the remote endpoint. The *"?"* placeholder is filled by jQuery with the name of a dynamically generated function that will then be called back:

```
$.ajax({
    url: "/json/countriesp?q=" + initial,
    cache: false,
    jsonpCallback: 'callback',
    contentType: "application/json",
    dataType: 'jsonp'
});
```

If you use *$.ajax*, you can pass the name of the client function to call back via the *jsonpCallback* parameter.

> **Note** I'll return to jQuery Ajax methods and provide more details in just a few moments. First, I'll bring to an end the discussion about accessing cross-origin resources.

Enabling CORS

JSONP is definitely a way to solve the problem of downloading data from a cross-origin endpoint, but it is a trick in the end and doesn't actually cover all possible scenarios. In particular, JSONP is not an option when you have some JavaScript framework that requires a URL to fetch and you want this URL to be outside your current website. In this case, using a proxy, although cumbersome, is the only safe approach. In summary, JSONP works beautifully to just grab and process remote data through a tricky API that uses the services of a temporary or fictitious SCRIPT element.

A more recent approach that is quickly becoming the standard is *CORS*. CORS is not supported on all possible browsers like JSONP is. On the other hand, it works on all browsers commonly used in at least the past five years. It's probably safe enough to use on any website.

CORS-aware browsers implement the following workflow when asked to connect to an external URL via JavaScript. They add a request header called *Origin*, set it to the current site, and perform the request. When data is received, browsers carefully check for one particular response header, called *Access-Control-Allow-Origin*. If the value of the header is *, the JavaScript call proceeds as usual and the downloaded response is made available within the page. Any value different from * is matched to the current origin URL. If a match is found, the request is successful; otherwise, it originates an error.

Note that all this logic is implemented within the browser's implementation of the *XMLHttpRequest* object. Browsers are not generally able to handle multiple origins, so any further logic to cover this scenario must be implemented on the server side. So much for the client—let's see what's required on the server to enable CORS.

CORS deals with adding a response header. In an ASP.NET MVC JSON endpoint, you can accomplish this task with an action filter or with a plain line of code as shown here:

```
Response.AddHeader("Access-Control-Allow-Origin", "*");
```

Better yet, you might want to replace * with the URL of the requesting origin. This code can be placed within each controller method and made a bit more sophisticated:

```
var origin = Request.Headers["Origin"];
if (String.IsNullOrWhiteSpace(origin)
    return;
if (Request.IsLocal || IsKnownOrigin(origin))
{
    Response.AddHeader("Access-Control-Allow-Origin", origin);
}
```

The placeholder *IsKnownOrigin* can simply check whether the specified URL belongs to some collection of known and allowed sites.

Starting with Internet Information Services 7 (IIS 7), you can even achieve the same goal (but you're limited to choosing all sites or just one specific site) using a section of the configuration file:

```
<system.webServer>
  <httpProtocol>
    <customHeaders>
      <add name="Access-Control-Allow-Origin" value="*" />
    </customHeaders>
  </httpProtocol>
</system.webServer>
```

Finally, note that you can also control the HTTP verbs through which the request is acceptable. The additional header is *Access-Control-Allow-Methods*. Multiple HTTP verbs can be specified by separating them with a comma. For more information on CORS, refer to *https://developer.mozilla.org/en-US/docs/Web/HTTP/Access_control_CORS*.

Designing a Web API

ASP.NET Web API is a framework expressly designed to support and simplify the building of HTTP services that can be consumed by a variety of clients—in particular, HTML pages and mobile applications. You can use Web API to build both RESTful and remote procedure call (RPC)-style HTTP services. It intersects various aspects of ASP.NET MVC, such as routing, security, controllers, and extensibility. At the same time, it has specific areas not directly supported by plain ASP.NET MVC.

> **Important** Up until ASP.NET Core 1.0, Web API and ASP.NET MVC used a different runtime environment in spite of similar class names and a similar overall architecture. In ASP.NET Core 1.0, the runtime environment will be the same and, in fact, any use of ASP.NET MVC and Web API becomes the same thing. In ASP.NET Core 1.0, there will be just one type of controller class, with a behavior that merges aspects of ASP.NET MVC controllers and Web API controllers.

Purpose of the ASP.NET Web API

When the world realized the power of web services, a standard protocol was worked out quickly and it became the currency that web services could exchange with callers. This protocol was SOAP, short for *Simple Object Access Protocol*. On top of that, a number of more in-depth specifications became a work-in-progress collectively known as *WS-* protocols*.

Windows Communication Foundation (WCF) was initially conceived to support SOAP and WS-* over a wide variety of transportation layers, including TCP, Microsoft Message Queuing (MSMQ), named pipes and, last but not least, HTTP.

It didn't take much to see that even though there was a clear motive and rationale for using WCF, developers were mostly using it as a shortcut to HTTP endpoints. This raised the need for the WCF infrastructure to more effectively support non-SOAP services and for it to be able to serve plain XML, text, and JSON over HTTP. Over the years, we first had the *webHttpBinding* binding mechanism from the WCF team and then bolted-on frameworks such as the REST starter kit.

In the end, it was essentially a matter of providing some syntactic sugar to make it easier to swallow the pill of using HTTP as a mere transportation layer. HTTP facilities on top of WCF didn't eliminate the true roadblocks that developers were facing, such as the notorious WCF overconfiguration and overuse of attributes and its structure not being specifically designed for testability.

The key change was separating multitransport services from plain HTTP services and removing all the heavy machinery of WCF to create a thin and HTTP-focused framework for HTTP services. This is Web API.

> **Important** As the focus for services shifts away from WCF, does it mean that WCF is a dead technology with no realistic application left? Of course, it doesn't. WCF is the only significant option when you really need to expose a service that can be invoked over protocols other than HTTP. WCF also remains a key solution when you really need advanced features such as security and transactionality.

Web API in the context of ASP.NET MVC

As you've seen so far, in ASP.NET MVC you can have HTTP services at the sole cost of adding a new controller class or a specific method to an existing controller class. This has always worked since the beginning of ASP.NET MVC. Why should you look at anything else?

The Web API framework relies on a different runtime environment that is totally separated from that of ASP.NET MVC. This has been done primarily to enable non–ASP.NET MVC applications (for example, Web Forms) to use Web API. The runtime environment, obviously, was largely inspired by ASP.NET MVC. Overall, though, it looks simpler and more to the point because it is expected to serve only JSON, not markup.

From the perspective of an ASP.NET developer, the following three points summarize the advantages that Web API sports over ASP.NET MVC:

- **Decoupling code from the serialization of results** This refers to the fact that a Web API controller requires you to simply return data from each method, without dealing with the serialization of the results within the method.

- **Content negotiation** A new family of components, called *formatters*, take care of the serialization of the data being returned to the requesting device. More interestingly, formatters are automatically selected based on the content of the Accept header of the incoming request. Built-in XML and JSON formatters are provided; replacing them is a simple matter of configuration. This feature simplifies the development of methods that can return the same raw data in various formats, most typically XML and JSON.

- **Hosting outside IIS** To some extent, content negotiation is a task that can be accomplished also in plain ASP.NET MVC. However, if you opt for implementing your HTTP services within an ASP.NET MVC application, you are bound to IIS as the web server. In other words, your API can't be hosted elsewhere. This is because ASP.NET MVC is inherently bound to IIS because it was primarily designed to serve as a framework for web applications. Web API, instead, does not require IIS, and you can self-host it in your own host process, such as a Windows service or a console application. (This aspect is why Web API services closely resemble WCF services.)

Having Web API inside an ASP.NET MVC application doesn't really add much programming power. So I believe Web API really becomes an option to consider in two cases:

- You need a layer of web services from within a non–ASP.NET MVC application—for example, Web Forms or desktop applications.

- You need a standalone service that sits in a service-oriented architecture and just serves content. This service can be hosted in IIS and provide no user interface, or it can be hosted in a Windows service or console application.

If you truly need an API—and you mostly need an API if you have multiple clients and operate in business-to-client (B2C) and business-to-business (B2B) scenarios—you likely face additional issues, such as versioning and authorization. If you truly need an API, ASP.NET Web API is an excellent option. If you just need to consume some JSON from your same user interface or a mobile application, you probably can blissfully avoid the extra costs of putting Web API in the middle.

In ASP.NET Core 1.0, there will be no difference between ASP.NET MVC and Web API.

Securing a standalone Web API

Securing a web application is simpler than securing a Web API module for just one reason: there are fewer scenarios to consider. An ASP.NET MVC application is aimed at end users; therefore, security mostly means authenticating users and ensuring that each authenticated user is presented only operations that user is authorized to perform.

When it comes to Web API, there are additional scenarios to look at. A Web API module is just an API that can be written for third-party developers to use. How would you control that the client is known and authorized? Let's review a few scenarios and approaches.

The host takes care of security

The simplest, but not necessarily most common, scenario for a Web API module is when the API and host are managed by the same team. In this case, the host is responsible for authenticating the user and avoiding that any user interface where a call to the API is possible is ever displayed.

Web API, therefore, assumes that any authentication takes place in the host—for example, within IIS through HTTP modules for authentication, whether they are built-in modules or custom modules. To address this scenario, you use the *Authorize* attribute on API controller classes or individual methods. This is nearly the same scenario you face in plain ASP.NET MVC applications.

Using Basic authentication

Outside of the scenario in which the host provides for authentication and authorization rules, it's all about incorporating the security layer in the Web API module. The simplest approach is leveraging the Basic authentication built into the web server. Basic authentication is based on the idea that user credentials are packaged in each and every request.

Basic authentication has pros and cons. It is supported on major browsers; it is an Internet standard; and it is simple to configure. Downsides are that credentials are sent with every request and, worse yet, they are sent as clear text.

Basic authentication expects that credentials are sent to be validated on the server. The request is then accepted only if credentials are valid. If credentials are not in the request, an interactive dialog box is displayed. Realistically, Basic authentication also requires a custom HTTP module to check credentials against accounts stored in some custom database.

> **Note** Basic authentication is simple and quite effective if combined with a layer that performs custom validation of credentials. To overcome the limitation of credentials sent as clear text, you should always implement a Basic authentication solution over HTTPS.

Using access tokens

The idea is that the Web API receives an access token—typically, a GUID or an alphanumeric string—validates it, and serves the request if the token is not expired and is valid for the application. There are various ways to issue to tokens and, subsequently, different security solutions.

The simplest scenario for tokens is that they are issued offline when a customer contacts you to use your API. You create the token and associate it with a particular customer. From now on, the customer is chargeable for the abuse or misuse of the API.

The Web API back end needs to have a layer that checks tokens. This layer can be added as plain code to any method or, better yet, configured to be a message handler. In Web API, a message handler is a component that examines the HTTP request and sets the *principal* on the request so that the *User* property on *ApiController* can be properly populated.

Using OAuth

A much more complex scenario is using OAuth authentication to restrict access to a Web API module. I covered OAuth in Chapter 6, "ASP.NET state of the art," when discussing how to use Facebook or Twitter to authenticate users of a site. The point here is to turn your Web API module into an OAuth server similar to what Twitter or Facebook does.

In the end, OAuth is a variation of the token scenario discussed a moment ago. The difference is that you need to have a distinct component that issues tokens online after checking the credentials of users. The authorization server mediates between the protected resources—the Web API—and the potential customers. Figure 14-3 shows the layout of a typical OAuth conversation.

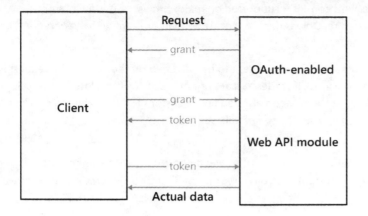

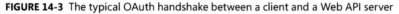

FIGURE 14-3 The typical OAuth handshake between a client and a Web API server

How would you code this in practice?

It is mostly up to you, but it probably requires having a web back end that acts as the authorization server. It will be responsible for issuing access tokens according to the credentials provided by authenticated users (a là Facebook). Next, you want to have a message handler in the Web API layer that processes the token and sets the principal to actually authorize the call. In the message handler, you can also introduce any mechanism to invalidate the token for any reason you consider worthwhile—expiration, misuse, or because the caller exceeded the allowed quota of calls.

Using a CORS Layer

Yet another solution to consider is CORS. As mentioned, CORS is a W3C standard that defines the behavior of webpages that intend to make Ajax requests to a different domain. CORS relaxes the same-origin policy that all browsers implement to restrict calls to the sole domain of the page that makes the call.

In Web API, you enable CORS through a new attribute named *EnableCors*. You can set the attribute on controllers as well as methods. For the attribute to be effective, you also need to call the *EnableCors* method on the *HttpConfiguration* object in *global.asax*:

```
using System.Web.Http.Cors;
public static class WebApiConfig
{
    public static void Register(HttpConfiguration config)
    {
        config.EnableCors();
    }
}
```

If you have CORS enabled at the controller level and want to disable it on a particular method, you just use the *DisableCors* attribute.

Pulling content

To make the web view more interactive, you need to be able to pull content programmatically from any accessible endpoint you know. This requires issuing out-of-band HTTP requests while bypassing the browser-window machinery. Browsers also offer a programmatic API for JavaScript developers to arrange autonomous calls to HTTP endpoints that don't alter in any way the content of the current document. This is the essence of Ajax.

The Ajax core

At its core, the Ajax functionality is built around the *XMLHttpRequest* object that all browsers implement. To be precise, the aforementioned object is offered by all recent browsers. Here's the code that guarantees full backward compatibility, including compatibility with very old versions of Internet Explorer:

```
var xhr;
if (window.XMLHttpRequest) {
    xhr = new XMLHttpRequest();
} else { // backward compatibility for browsers older than IE7
    xhttp = new ActiveXObject("Microsoft.XMLHTTP");
}
```

It's curious to notice that although Microsoft "invented" the underlying machinery of Ajax, it was still coded in Internet Explorer as an ActiveX object until Internet Explorer 7. And this was at a time when all other browsers offered the same functionality without having to enable ActiveX support.

Placing an HTTP request

The *XMLHttpRequest* object is the proxy through which your JavaScript code within a displayed web view establishes a connection and exchanges data with an HTTP listener. Preparing and placing the request are distinct operations. You prepare the request using the *open* method and place it using the *send* method:

```
xhr.open("GET", url);
xhr.send();
```

The first argument of *open* is the HTTP verb; the second argument is the target URL. You can also specify a third argument that indicates whether the request must be processed synchronously or asynchronously. If you want it to be asynchronous with respect to the remaining code of the page, set the argument to *true*:

```
xhr.open("GET", url, true);
```

To send form data, you typically use a POST and need to set additional headers, as shown here:

```
xhr.open("POST", url);
xhr.setRequestHeader("Content-type", "application/x-www-form-urlencoded");
xhr.send("firstname=Dino&lastname=Esposito");
```

In the case of a POST request, the *send* method also gets a string that represents the data being posted.

Processing the HTTP response

When the request goes synchronously, you can write the code to process the response right after calling the method *send*. The *responseText* property gives you the entire body of the response:

```
xhr.open("GET", url, false);
xhr.send();
console.log(xhr.responseText);
```

Note that by default *XMLHttpRequest* calls are asynchronous. In general, you should place synchronous calls only if in that way you get a true benefit that otherwise is hard to achieve.

In the case of asynchronous calls, though, your script code has to wait until the response is fully received:

```
xhr.onreadystatechange = function() {
    if (xhr.readyState == 4 && xhr.status == 200) {
    // Safely access xhr.responseText;
    }
}
xhttp.open("GET", url, true);  // Can omit true
xhttp.send();
```

You register a handler for the *onreadystatechange* event, and your code will be called when the response is ready. Your handler is also given a change to monitor intermediate states of the call. The call is completed successfully when the *readyState* property equals 4. The *status* property reflects the HTTP status code. It's set to 200 in the case of success.

Correct interpretation of a "success" status code

Note that receiving an HTTP 200 status code from the server doesn't mean that the operation you attempted was successful. If the server-side operation results, say, in an unhandled exception you'll get an HTTP 500 status. Similarly, you might get HTTP 404 if the URL is not found or HTTP 401 if the request is not authorized.

There are two scenarios to be taken into careful account. One is when the server detects some problem with the request and returns an error message in the context of a successful network operation. It is important, in fact, to separate the network level and the application level. The status code you get through *XMLHttpRequest* always refers to the success or failure of the network operation.

Another interesting scenario is CORS. When you place a JavaScript call to an external website, most of the time the network operation is successful, but the framework returns it as an error. (See Figure 14-4.)

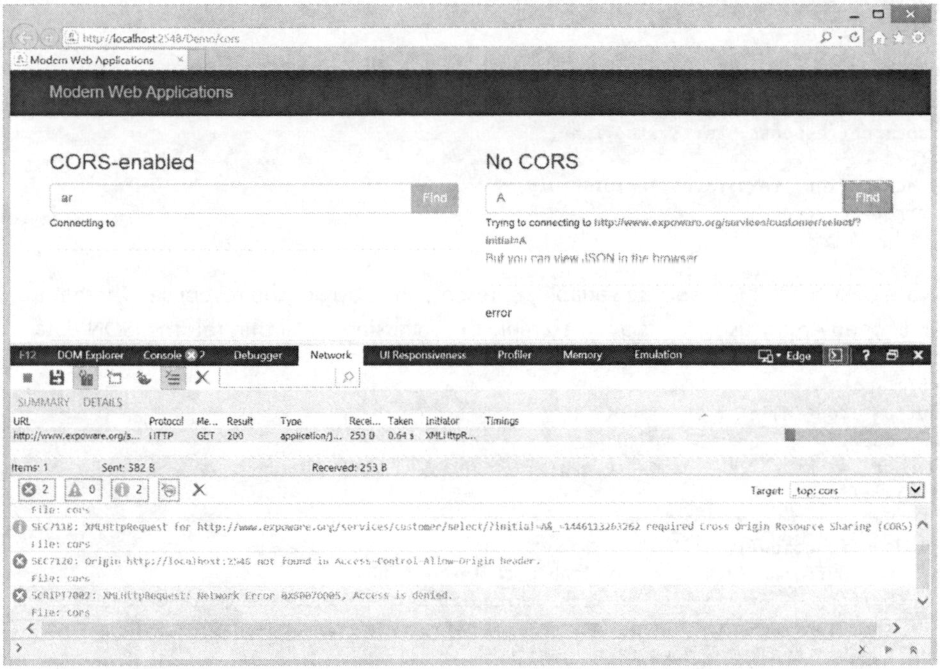

FIGURE 14-4 A CORS request that fails at the application level, even though it might still be successful at the network level

The jQuery tools

Most of the time, developers use jQuery facilities instead of the *XMLHttpRequest* object to place Ajax calls. The jQuery library wraps up the browser infrastructure and offers a nicer programming experience.

The *$.ajax* function

The central element of Ajax in jQuery is the *$.ajax* function, which performs an asynchronous call to the specified endpoint. The function takes two parameters—the URL and settings—and returns an object that wraps up the underlying *XMLHttpRequest* object used for the actual call. This object is *jqXHR*:

```
$.ajax( url [, settings ] )
```

The list of settings is long and includes primarily the properties *type*, *data*, and *dataType*. These properties let you set the HTTP verb, data to be sent to the server, and the data type the call expects to receive back from the server. For more information, refer to *http://api.jquery.com/jquery.ajax*.

To capture the response of an Ajax call, you can use functions *done*, *fail*, and *always* that are defined on the *jqXHR* object. The function *done* is invoked in the case of success; *fail* is called in the case of errors, and *always* is called when the operation completes (regardless of the result). Note that the analogous functions *success*, *error*, and *complete* are still in the documentation and still work, but they are deprecated:

```
$.ajax({
    url: ...
}).done(function(response, textStatus, xhr) {
    // Success
}).fail(function(xhr, textStatus, errorThrown) {
    // An error occurred
});
```

In the case of success, the response variable represents the body of the response, whether it's JSON, HTML, or anything else. Here's a full example of processing a call that returns JSON data:

```
$(function() {
    $("#button").on("click", function() {
        var query = $("#query").val();
        var url = "http://www.expoware.org/geo/country/all?q=" + query;
        $.ajax({
            url: url
        }).done(function(json) {
            var buffer = "<table class='table table-condensed'>";
            buffer += "<thead><th>Name</th><th>Capital</th><th>Continent</th></thead>";
            for (var index in json.Countries) {
                var country = json.Countries[index];
                buffer += "<tr>";
                buffer += "<td>" + country.CountryName + "</td>";
                buffer += "<td>" + country.Capital + "</td>";
                buffer += "<td>" + country.Continent + "</td>";
                buffer += "</tr>";
            }
            buffer += "</table>";
            $("#output").html(buffer);
        });
    });
});
```

The code defines a click handler for an HTML button element. When the button is clicked, the code reads the current value in a text box and prepares the URL to invoke. In the example, the URL is expected to be CORS enabled. The *done* handler receives the returned JSON and dynamically builds an HTML table to present the results. Finally, the results are injected into the body of the page. The JSON returned is the same that I discussed in an example earlier in the chapter. (See Figure 14-5.)

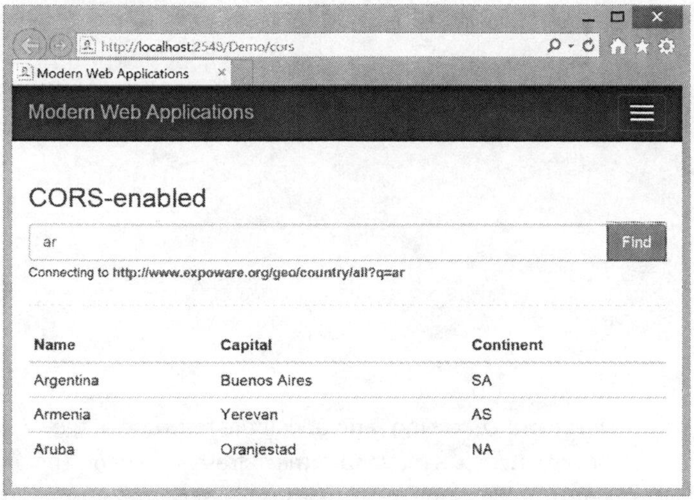

FIGURE 14-5 Placing an Ajax call and updating the page dynamically

Ajax shorthand functions

The jQuery library also offers more specific Ajax functions that use *$.ajax* just internally, but these functions offer a simpler and more specific programming ad hoc interface for the scenario. Table 14-1 presents the list of such Ajax shorthand functions. All such functions return a *jqXHR* object and rely on the *done*, *fail*, and *always* functions to process results.

TABLE 14-1 Ajax shorthand functions in jQuery

Function	Description	Documentation
$.get	Sends an HTTP GET request	http://api.jquery.com/jQuery.get
$.getJSON	Sends an HTTP GET request to collect JSON or JSONP data	http://api.jquery.com/jQuery.getjson
$.post	Sends an HTTP POST request	http://api.jquery.com/jQuery.post

Another interesting example of a shorthand function is *load*. (See *http://api.jquery.com/load*.) The function loads HTML data from the server and inserts it into the DOM elements that match the selector. Here's an example:

```
$("#content").load(url);
```

The request typically goes as a GET, but if you pass data as the second argument of the function it becomes a POST.

Ajax and caching

One of the reasons to always prefer the core *$.ajax* function instead of the various shorthand methods is that, by using the *$.ajax* function, you can always control caching. One of the settings you can indicate is *cache*, which accepts a Boolean value:

```
$.ajax({
    url: "http://...",
    type: "GET",
    cache: false
}).done(function(response) {
    // Update the current page
    ...
});
```

By default, the *cache* setting is *true*, meaning that caching is on and, if the response of the specified URL is still in the browser's cache, no attempt is made to retrieve fresher content. The default status of caching that affects all requests that don't indicate a specific setting is set through the *$.ajaxSetup* method. By default, caching is enabled for all Ajax calls.

Note that jQuery doesn't actually do any caching on its own. All jQuery does when you disable caching on an Ajax request is use header and additional query string values to prevent the browser or any proxies in the middle from returning any nonexpired response they might have.

Caching is no big deal, and it's a great feature, indeed, for plain GET requests of relatively static data. It might be the source of some headaches if you keep it on for resources that change and, say, in the context of some back-office application where all you do is edit records of data.

> **Note** I understood how critical the cache setting can be in the context of jQuery the day I used an application that offered to edit a record through a modal window. The modal window was retrieving data to initialize input fields via jQuery. The first time it all worked just great, and I edited the record and saved. I even got a successful message. Except that a second later while trying to make a second update to the same record, I brought up the modal again to find all input fields set as if the first update didn't work. The underlying database was OK; it was the side effect of too much caching on the client.

Binding data to the current DOM

Placing successful Ajax calls toward valid and well-designed endpoints is only the first step on the way to building more interactive web applications. A nontrivial point is how you refresh the existing content rendered in the browser to reflect the freshly downloaded data.

Direct binding

Browsers expose a Document Object Model (DOM) for the currently rendered content. This enables JavaScript code to edit the content on the fly, thus making the user's experience significantly better. Updating the DOM, however, might or might not be easy, depending on the structure of the downloaded data. One thing is updating a string or a number. It's quite a different thing to update a grid or the representation of some data that in the browser is also mixed up with a large quantity of markup.

If the data you receive can simply be attached to a specific location identified by ID, all you do in the *done* handler of the *$.ajax* call is this:

```
$("#position").html(freshData);
```

You can repeat similar calls as many times as you want and throughout the entire document. You can use all varieties of jQuery and DOM methods and set the new value as HTML or plain text.

More often than not, though, you place a remote call to get a collection of data and must show that as a grid or within a hierarchical layout. There's no magic that jQuery or any other framework can do for you. Ultimately, the data you download must be merged with the required layout, and the final result is inserted in the DOM:

```
// Preparing the markup
var buffer = "<table class='table table-condensed'>";
buffer += "<thead><th>Name</th><th>Capital</th><th>Continent</th></thead>";
for (var index in json.Countries) {
    var country = json.Countries[index];
    buffer += "<tr>";
    buffer += "<td>" + country.CountryName + "</td>";
    buffer += "<td>" + country.Capital + "</td>";
    buffer += "<td>" + country.Continent + "</td>";
    buffer += "</tr>";
}
buffer += "</table>";

// Displaying
$("#output").html(buffer);
```

Merging the downloaded data and the layout is a matter of creating an HTML string programmatically. You can do that by manually writing code as shown here. Or you can get support from some JavaScript template libraries.

JavaScript template libraries

Client-side data binding is a common but delicate aspect of single-page applications and, in general, of any JavaScript-intensive front end that operates over JSON data. When the ASP.NET MVC server prepares the view, data binding takes place on the server side within a comfortable Razor template. When plain data is downloaded to the client, the same artifacts must be operated on the client. Building HTML strings by concatenation is possible, but not exactly a reliable and maintainable approach.

As a result, various JavaScript template-based, data-binding libraries emerged over the past few years, with different levels of programming power and simplicity. Knockout is one of the most popular and powerful. For more information, see *http://knockoutjs.com*. Another viable option is mustache.js, although it's not as feature rich as Knockout. However, mustache.js has a smaller footprint and when minified and g-zipped, it accounts for approximately 10 KB of a download. (See *https://github.com/janl/mustache.js*.)

All client-side data-binding libraries take a template filled with data placeholders and inject data into it from a provided data model. A difference you notice between mustache.js and more popular but larger libraries, such as Knockout and the data-binding module of AngularJS, is that mustache.js requires the template to be provided as a separate element, embedded in a SCRIPT tag. Other libraries find the template in the body of the page where you'd like to have actual content injected.

A mustache.js template takes the following form:

```
<script id="country-template" type="text/template">
    <table class="table table-condensed">
        <thead>
            <th>Name</th>
            <th>Capital</th>
            <th>Continent</th>
        </thead>
        {{#Countries}}
        <tr>
            <td>{{CountryName}}</td>
            <td>{{Capital}}</td>
            <td>{{Continent}}</td>
        </tr>
        {{/Countries}}
    </table>
    {{^Countries}}
    No countries found
    {{/Countries}}
</script>
```

Data placeholders follow the *{{ ... }}* pattern. The name enclosed in double curly brackets references a property on the nearest object in scope. Each template is bound to a JavaScript object that represents the root data context. For example, *Countries* is expected to be a property on the programmatically bound object. A placeholder like *{{CountryName}}* refers to the property *CountryName* on the data element the iteration is on.

The # symbol prefixing a property tells the runtime to iterate over the content of that property, which is expected to be a collection of some type. Finally, the ^ symbol identifies the content to show if the property—expected to be a collection—is empty. To activate mustache.js on a template, you need the following code:

```
$(function() {
    $("#btnFinder").on("click", function () {
        var initial = $("#initial").val();
        $.ajax({
            url: "/json/countries?q=" + initial,
            cache: false
        }).done(function(json) {
            var dataTemplate = $("#country-template").html();
            $("#output").html(Mustache.to_html(dataTemplate, json));
        });
    });
})
```

The code first registers a click handler on a button. When the button is clicked, it collects initials from an input field, prepares a URL, and calls it via Ajax to grab JSON data. Finally, it gets the mustache.js template as a string and evaluates it on JSON data. (See Figure 14-6.)

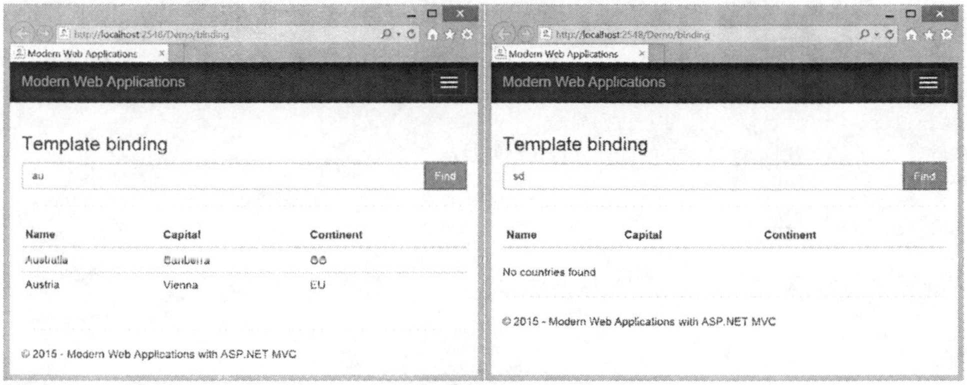

FIGURE 14-6 The effect of the sample mustache.js template

Pushing content to the client

So far, you've looked at interactive web content from the perspective of the user pulling information from some server environment. The other side of interactivity is when notifications are pushed from the server down to the client.

When I say "push notifications," you might immediately think of information being asynchronously displayed in your mobile devices when something somewhere happens that you declared your interest in. Push notifications only express an abstract concept and refer to some information that is detected on the server and, in some way, notifies clients. It says nothing about the actual implementation of the feature.

It turns out that push notifications often are simply the result of some client periodically checking for new data in some predefined location as agreed with the server. However, regardless of the network-level implementation details, an ASP.NET-related framework has been developed to simplify notifications from the server to the client. Its name is *ASP.NET SignalR*.

Concretely, ASP.NET SignalR addresses scenarios such as monitoring the progress of a server-side task or refreshing multiple segments of the user interface once a server-side operation has completed successfully.

ASP.NET SignalR at a glance

The first step toward using SignalR is installing the package from NuGet. ASP.NET SignalR has a client part and a server part. The client part is served as a jQuery plugin. The server part consists of a bunch of assemblies. One of the binaries is the OWIN library that is used to start and configure SignalR. Therefore, first you create a file called *startup.cs* in the project:

```
using Microsoft.Owin;
using Owin;
[assembly: OwinStartup(typeof(YourProject.Startup))]
namespace YourProject
{
    public class Startup
    {
        public void Configuration(IAppBuilder app)
        {
            app.MapSignalR();
        }
    }
}
```

The SignalR configuration is complete when you have linked the JavaScript core file in any of the web views where you intend to use its notifications:

```
<script type="text/javascript"
        src="~/content/scripts/jquery.signalR-2.2.0.min.js")"></script>
```

Next, you add the following script code, which actually sets up a connection between the client and server parts of the same instance of the library:

```
<script>
    $(function() {
        // Save  the reference to the SignalR hub
        var theHub = $.connection.yourAppHub;

        // Define here the functions which will be called back from
        // the server when notifications are available. These functions
        // are defined on the "theHub" object.
        ...

        // Start the SignalR client-side listener
        $.connection.hub.start().done(function () {
            // Here do any initialization work you may need
            ...
        });
    });
</script>
```

The *$.connection* object is the entry point in the SignalR jQuery plugin. It references an object—*yourAppHub* in the example—that is the client-side counterpart of the server-side ASP.NET SignalR console that server code will talk to. The *$.connection.hub* object is the wrapper for the communication infrastructure. By calling the method *start*, you start the listening process. When the method *start* returns, the connection is open and identified by a unique ID. Each connection links the server and one particular client browser. Any response generated on the server that might be interesting to the client will be broadcasted over this connection.

As an example, let's see how to use ASP.NET SignalR to monitor the status of a remote long-running task.

Monitoring remote tasks

Suppose you have a web view with a button that posts some data to the server for some operation to occur. The operation might take awhile to complete, so you don't want to refresh the entire page and you don't even want to present users directly with the final results. You want to show, instead, a progress bar that in real time indicates how much work has been done.

Sharing the communication channel

For this kind of notification, you need a one-to-one channel linking the client to the server thread that's taking care of the workflow. For this reason, you must have the SignalR connection ID before you start the remote task:

```
var connectionId;
$.connection.hub.start().done(function () {
    connectionId = $.connection.hub.id;
    $("#taskStarter").removeAttr("disabled");
});
```

Upon page loading, once the connection is established you save the ID to a global variable and enable the button that would start the potentially lengthy operation you want to monitor:

```
<button class="btn btn-primary" disabled="disabled" id="taskStarter" onclick="startTask()">
```

At this point, the user is able to click on the button and start working:

```
function startTask() {
    $.post("/task/lengthy/" + connectionId);
}
```

The net effect of this code is that the ASP.NET MVC endpoint that receives the call and is responsible for the task also knows the ID of the connection through which any transient feedback should be shared. Put another way, the ASP.NET MVC server-side environment now knows how to call back the JavaScript acting on a particular browser window.

Calling back the client

The following code simulates some work that takes awhile to complete and is articulated in steps to report back to the client. The simulation randomly generates a number of steps and waits two seconds for each step:

```
public void Lengthy([Bind(Prefix="id")] string connId)
{
    var steps = new Random().Next(3, 20);
    var increase = (int) 100/steps;

    var hub = new ProgressHub();
    hub.NotifyStart(connId);
    var total = 0;
    for (var i = 0; i < steps; i++)
    {
        Thread.Sleep(2000);
        total += increase;
        hub.NotifyProgress(connId, total);
    }
    hub.NotifyEnd(connId);
}
```

The most interesting part of the code is the class *ProgressHub*—the server-side part of the ASP.NET SignalR framework.

Every SignalR instance is built around a specific hub class that orchestrates the data exchange between the client and the server. In other words, the hub is the proxy sitting in between the server code and the ASP.NET SignalR infrastructure that knows how to reach out to connected clients.

Internals of a hub

A SignalR hub class doesn't contain any business logic. All it does is define a programming interface for the server code—the business code—to call back the original browser:

```
public class ProgressHub : Hub
{
    public void NotifyStart(string connId)
    {
        var hubContext = GlobalHost.ConnectionManager.GetHubContext<ProgressHub>();
        hubContext.Clients.Client(connId).initProgressBar();
    }

    public void NotifyProgress(string connId, int percentage)
    {
        var hubContext = GlobalHost.ConnectionManager.GetHubContext<ProgressHub>();
        hubContext.Clients.Client(connId).updateProgressBar(percentage, connId);
    }

    public void NotifyEnd(string connId)
    {
        var hubContext = GlobalHost.ConnectionManager.GetHubContext<ProgressHub>();
        hubContext.Clients.Client(connId).clearProgressBar();
    }
}
```

All methods in a hub have the same structure. They first grab a reference to the ASP.NET SignalR internal console and then place a call to all connected clients, or just to the one listening over the specified connection.

The ASP.NET SignalR API also allows you to define groups of clients and broadcast to all of them. In this example, the notification goes back just to the client that opened the connection with that ID.

Updating the user interface in real time

The methods invoked—*updateProgressBar*, for example—are just placeholders for JavaScript functions defined on the client. There's no server-side implementation for *updateProgressBar* and similar methods. You are welcome to give these methods any arbitrary name as long as they match JavaScript functions defined on the client SignalR hub:

```
theHub.client.initProgressBar = function () {
    $("#notification").show();
    theHub.client.updateProgressBar(0);
};


theHub.client.updateProgressBar = function (percentage, connId) {
    $("#workDone").text(percentage);
    $("#taskId").text(connId);
    $('.progress-bar').css('width', percentage + '%').attr('aria-valuenow', percentage);
};

theHub.client.clearProgressBar = function () {
    theHub.client.updateProgressBar(100);
    window.setTimeout(function() {
        $("#notification").hide();
    }, 2000);
};
```

Once the control is passed back to the JavaScript code, updating the user interface is as easy as updating the DOM. Figure 14-7 shows the sample application updating a progress bar created with Bootstrap. The connection ID is shown underneath the progress bar:

```
<div class-"progress">
    <div class="progress-bar" role="progressbar"
            aria-valuenow="0"
            aria-valuemin="0"
            aria-valuemax="100">
        <span class="sr-only" id="workDone"></span>
    </div>
</div>
```

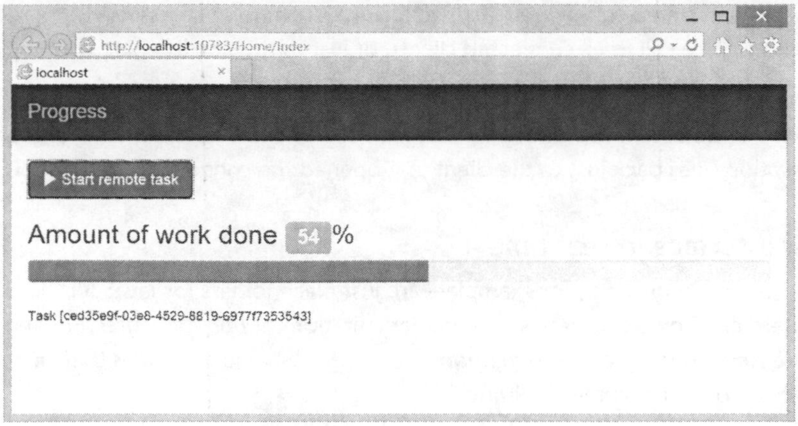

FIGURE 14-7 Monitoring a remote task using SignalR

Other scenarios for ASP.NET SignalR

ASP.NET SignalR can be used to serve client applications nearly any sort of dynamic change they might need. Here are some details about a few other common scenarios.

Refreshing the view after a modal update

In much the same way, you can use SignalR to instantaneously refresh the user interface of a webpage once some updates have been made to the server. I commonly use this technique to refresh the underlying page when I edit a record using a modal window.

Obviously, all changes you make to the DOM are limited to the current DOM. However, because the operation has been successful, the next time the user physically refreshes the page in the browser it still shows the same data!

Broadcasting changes to all users

Sometimes your server operates in a one-to-many scenario, and all it needs to do is broadcast its detected changes to all clients currently displaying a given page. I use this pattern in pages that track scoring in live sports events.

In this case, you don't need to deal with the connection ID that links a particular client and the server. In the server-side hub, you just call the JavaScript placeholder right from the *Clients* property:

```
// Broadcast to all listening clients
hubContext.Clients.All.update();
```

Similarly, you can broadcast to groups. Note that groups must be defined programmatically at the startup of the hub.

Counting online users

Interestingly, the *Clients.All* property can be used to broadcast to all connected clients, but it cannot be used to enumerate and count clients. There are other ways to do that within ASP.NET SignalR. The hub class you use to push events back to connected clients inherits from a system-provided class—the *Hub* class.

The *Hub* class has a few overridable methods related to tracking connected users. Here's a sample hub class you can use to also track online users:

```
public class SampleHub : Hub
{
    // Use this variable to track user count
    private static int _userCount = 0;

    // Public hub methods
    ...

    // Overridable hub methods
    public override Task OnConnected()
    {
        userCount ++;
    }

    public override Task OnReconnected()
    {
        userCount ++;
    }

    public override Task OnDisconnected(bool stopCalled)
    {
        userCount --;
    }
}
```

There are three methods you can override: *OnConnected*, *OnReconnected*, and *OnDisconnected*. As the names clearly suggest, these methods are called when browser sessions connect, reconnect, or disconnect from the SignalR hub. By adding some code to these overrides, you can call back the client to update some user interface as soon as the user count changes.

Summary

Interactivity is a must in modern web development and can be achieved in two main ways. One consists of choosing a full-fledged framework that teaches you a new programming paradigm and delivers a flavor of a single-page application. AngularJS is the most popular of such comprehensive frameworks.

However, a great deal of interactivity can also be obtained using a more traditional programming paradigm within the ASP.NET platform. Interactivity is based on having and exposing JSON endpoints and using some Ajax framework to connect and download information. At that point, it is all about updating the current DOM with fresh content. In this chapter, we reviewed common techniques to expose and download JSON data and also looked at ASP.NET SignalR, a relatively new way to refresh the DOM and push notifications to live webpages.

CHAPTER 15

Pros and cons of responsive design

I am not bound to please thee with my answers.

—William Shakespeare

Abstractly speaking, a responsive website is a website that adjusts the content it displays to the size of the actual viewport being used. Such a feature is so easy for salespeople to sell. They go to a customer and illustrate the wonders of a brand new website that auto-magically adapts to whatever device end users might happen to use, today and tomorrow.

It's a strong selling point, with nearly no chance for anyone to successfully rebut it.

For this reason, websites that can adapt displayed content to the requesting device are a must-have these days. It's not simply a matter of wanting to look nice and smart—it's a pure matter of business. As often happens, though, the devil is not so much in the strategy but in the details of the tactics.

How should you build a website that adapts any content to the size of the viewing device? Enter Responsive Web Design (RWD).

Foundation of Responsive Web Design

In general, *adaptive* and *responsive* can be used interchangeably as if they were synonyms. Effectively, some dictionaries—specifically the Merriam-Webster—define as "responsive" anything that shows the capacity for adaptation. In web development, though, the term *responsive* sometimes refers to something specific beyond the conceptual level and that is more of an implementation detail.

By describing something as *responsive*, salespeople and customers mean that the site displays nicely on whatever devices are used to navigate it. For developers and designers, on the other hand, a *responsive* site is an adaptive site built using a particular set of technologies and practices that go under the comprehensive name of *Responsive Web Design*.

In this chapter, I'll explore the pros and cons of RWD, calling attention to possible issues you'll encounter if you blindly employ RWD to serve mobile views.

A brief history of RWD

Up until a decade ago, the world of web development was split in two: desktop browsers in one camp and everything else in the other camp. The "everything else" camp included cell phones and a few small palm devices, like Windows CE devices. Early versions of ASP.NET even shipped with a distinct set of controls with a minimal browser-detection engine and mobile-optimized rendering. Mobile controls never became popular because mobile devices were hardly ever used to browse the web.

It all changed when Apple shipped the iPhone. And it changed even more when the iPad was shipped, thus splitting even the mobile camp into two segments: smartphones and tablets. Add in the growing number of brands and models of smart cell phones and you get the big picture. The built-in detection engine centered on the expression-based analysis of user agent strings became quite unmanageable. With the number of user agent strings (and variations thereof) in the order of the thousands, determining the ideal content to serve to a device could have easily become a hellish browser nightmare.

A radically different approach was therefore required.

Ethan Marcotte proposed an approach he called Responsive Web Design. Since then, the acronym RWD has become increasingly popular and the practices behind the RWD method have been perceived as the only way to get a responsive website that adapts to the host device. Ultimately, RWD is an approach that works, and it is largely supported by popular design frameworks like Bootstrap. (See Chapter 9, "Core of Bootstrap.") At the same time, though, RWD is just one possible approach—and perhaps not even the most effective one when it comes to mobile devices.

RWD is relatively easy to achieve, whether you do it through manual coding or adaptive HTML templates you get out of the box from designers. Whether it's also the most effective way to serve mobile content is an aspect that must be carefully investigated on a per-project basis.

CSS media queries

There are three pillars of the RWD approach: fluid grids, flexible images, and CSS media queries. The idea behind a *fluid grid* is that as the outermost container changes its size, the entire content in it reflows and adjusts to the new size. RWD is all about laying out content that can be easily re-rendered in a new, smaller or larger, container. Images can be easily resized via HTML attributes, but in this way they are just stretched regardless of artistic considerations and the size of the download.

CSS media queries are the glue required to assemble the visibility of HTML elements and floating styles, and even the size of containers.

Media types

CSS media queries is a well-known Worldwide Web Consortium (W3C) standard, and it has been around for a few years now. The term *media* refers to HTML-defined media types, the most popular and widely used of which are *screen* and *print*. The HTML standard defines many more media types, including *handheld*. The *handheld* type, at first, seems to be perfect for restricting the application of a CSS style sheet to just handheld devices. Unfortunately, no vendors of smartphones support that media type.

> **Note** When Apple released the iPhone, the company made a thoughtful choice in not supporting the *handheld* media type because—it said—the resolution of handheld devices suggested by W3C is way smaller than the iPhone's. Other vendors just followed Apple's lead, thus restricting the set of media types to not much more than *screen* and *print* and forcing the introduction of a query language around the *screen* media type to differentiate output across devices.
>
> It will probably never happen, but it would be nice to have smartphone browsers reconsider themselves to be handheld devices. That would entirely change the meaning and the numbers behind the definition.

Used in a LINK element, the *media* attribute indicates the context where the CSS file being downloaded will be used. The default value of *screen* indicates, as the name suggests, that the referenced CSS file is used while displaying the page on the screen. The value of *print*, instead, indicates that the referenced CSS file is used while printing the page. Typically, the print CSS differs from the screen CSS because of background images, fonts, and graphical styles.

A simple query language for screen devices

Being restricted to using just one core media type—screen—to face the explosion of devices a basic query language was created to let the use of different style sheets per scenario. This is just what the CSS media queries standard really represents.

A browser that supports CSS 3 accepts a Boolean expression in the *media* attribute and selects the referenced CSS file only if the expression evaluates to true. To have a sensible Boolean expression, you need to have parameters to combine together with AND and OR operators. Table 15-1 presents the most popular and used keywords that any CSS media queries enabled browser support.

FIGURE 15-1 Core properties defined in the CSS 3 media queries standard

Properties	Description
width, *height*	Refer to the width and height in pixels of the rendering viewport area—typically, the browser's window.
orientation	Returns the string portrait when height is greater than or equal to width. Otherwise, it returns landscape.
device-width *device-height*	Properties refer to the width and height of the physical device screen. On most mobile devices where applications run full-screen, these values match the width and height properties.
aspect-ratio	Indicates the ratio between width and height. Typically, it's a value such as "16/9."
device-aspect-ratio	Indicates the ratio between device-width and device-height. Typically, it's a value such as "16/9."

The full list of properties you can use in CSS media queries expressions is available at *http://www.w3.org/TR/css3-mediaqueries*.

The upcoming CSS media queries level 4 standard

A newer version of the CSS media queries standard is in the works, and newer properties are being added to make it easier to tailor style sheets according to specific device form factors. Properties featured in Table 15-2 are being added to the new standard.

TABLE 15-2 New properties being defined in the CSS media queries level 4 standard

Properties	Description
scripting	Refers to whether scripting languages, such as JavaScript, are supported in the current document.
pointer	Refers to the accuracy of a pointing device such as a mouse. Feasible values are none | coarse | fine. The value coarse refers to touch-based devices, such as tablets. The value fine, instead, refers typically to mouse support.
hover	Refers to the user's ability to hover a pointer over elements on the page. Feasible values are none | on-demand | hover. The value hover refers to tooltips and desktop devices. On-demand, instead, refers to situations like long-clicking to bring up more details.
resolution	Refers to the resolution of the output device—typically, the density of the pixels. It can be measured using various units, including dppx, cm, and dpi.

One of the benefits of the newer version is that detecting non-desktop devices comes easier if you test *hover* and *pointer*. For example, the property *hover* that equals "hover" clearly denotes support for tooltips and then desktop browsers. The property set to a value of "on-demand" will likely suggest the device is an Android device because Android is the platform where long-clicking is a default feature. At the same time, the property *pointer* set to the value of "coarse" suggests that the underlying device is a touch device, likely a tablet.

Conditional style sheets via media queries

Let's see how to use media queries properties to switch CSS files on the fly. Here's an example of a media queries expression:

```
<link type="text/css" rel="stylesheet" href="view480.css"
    media="only screen and (max-width: 480px)">
```

The browser will link the file *view480.css* only if the media expression evaluates to *true*. In the example, this happens if the actual screen size (the browser's viewport) is at most 480 pixels wide. Ideally, a web page will host multiple LINK elements, each pointing to a different style sheet for specific conditions. The evaluation process doesn't stop at the first match but proceeds through the entire list of CSS references. It's up to the page author to ensure that the media query of only one LINK element evaluates to *true*. Browsers re-evaluate the list of linked CSS files whenever the window is resized, whether it's resized because of a mouse action or a rotation of the screen.

Once the browser detects that the screen size or orientation has changed, it picks up the CSS file that best fits. The content of the page is re-rendered in accordance with the instructions in the current style sheet. Media queries properties—such as *width*, *height*, and *orientation*—change dynamically. Other properties—especially those coming in CSS Media Queries Level 4 standard—are static because they depend on the nature of the device.

> **Important** CSS media queries work in two ways. One way to make the desktop experience more pleasant for users is to have the content displayed remain usable regardless of the size of the browser window. The other way is to provide a pleasant experience to users visiting the website with a particular, non-desktop device. This happens without developers needing to deal with the intricacies of user agent strings.
>
> In a nutshell, RWD makes no distinction between a desktop browser resized to 480 pixels and a full-screen browser displayed on a smartphone. All that matters is the screen size, but smartphones and notebooks might work over different forms of connectivity (Wi-Fi, 3G) and be significantly different in terms of CPU power. This is the point that best represents the essence of RWD. And it is RWD's major strength as well as its most significant weakness.

Handcrafting a grid system with media queries

Most responsive websites these days are based on some responsive framework—most likely, Bootstrap. As you saw in Chapter 9, Bootstrap comes with its own media queries expressions and splits the screen into four main segments.

You can certainly overwrite the Bootstrap settings or not use Bootstrap at all. In this case, you just end up with a bunch of CSS styles that implement a homemade grid system. As mentioned, a grid system is the core of a responsive design. Here's a quick example:

```
.mycontainer {
    clear: both;
    padding: 0;
    margin: 0;
}

/* General settings of a column in the container  */
.col {
    display: block;
    float: left;
}

/* Column settings depending on the position: 4 elements  */
.span4_index4 {
    width: 25%;
}
```

```
.span4_index3 {
    width: 25%;
    background: #ddd;
}
.span4_index2 {
    width: 25%;
}
.span4_index1 {
    width: 25%;
    background: #ddd;
}

/* 2x2 under 800px */
@media only screen and (max-width: 800px) {
    .span4_index4 {
        width: 50%;
    }
    .span4_index3 {
        width: 50%;
    }
    .span4_index2 {
        width: 50%;
    }
    .span4_index1 {
        width: 50%;
    }
}

/* Vertical align below 400px */
@media only screen and (max-width: 400px) {
    .span4_index4 {
        width: 100%;
    }
    .span4_index3 {
        width: 100%;
    }
    .span4_index2 {
        width: 100%;
    }
    .span4_index1 {
        width: 100%;
    }
}
```

The *col* CSS class defines the foundation of a logical screen column, and *span4_* classes refer to a vision of the screen as a grid of up to four columns, knowns as *spans*. Span classes are numbered from 1 to 4 and equally split the available space. Media queries come into play to decide how many columns you want at a given screen size.

In the preceding example, you have two explicit conditions, plus the defaults:

```
@media only screen and (max-width: 800px) { ... }
@media only screen and (max-width: 400px) { ... }
```

By default, there will be four columns. However, if the maximum width of the screen is below 800 pixels, there will be two columns per row. If the screen width is less than 400 pixels, there will be just one column per row. Here's the HTML of the page. (See Figure 15-1.)

```
<div class="mycontainer">
    <div class="col span4_index1">
        Column #1
    </div>
    <div class="col span4_index2">
        Column #2
    </div>
    <div class="col span4_index3">
        Column #3
    </div>
    <div class="col span4_index4">
        Column #4
    </div>
</div>
```

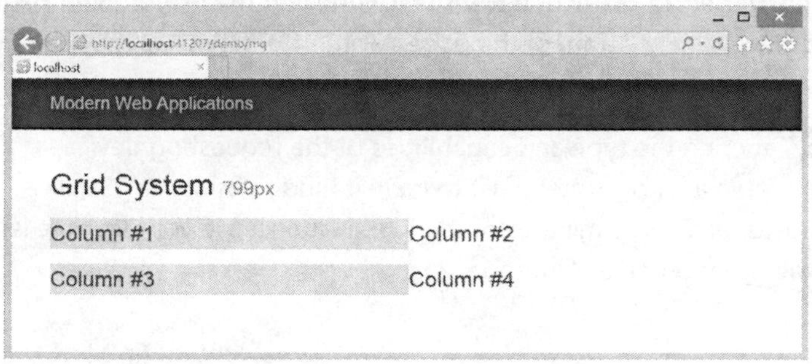

FIGURE 15-1 A simple grid system entirely handcrafted

RWD and device independence

Many developers and technical managers remember very well what a nightmare it was a decade ago to build websites for various browsers. There was a time when, say, Internet Explorer had a different set of features than Firefox, Safari, or perhaps just an earlier version of itself. That made authoring markup for pages a real mess. If the browser fragmentation of a decade ago scared you, be well aware that fragmentation in the mobile space is far worse.

Detecting devices is hard? Don't do that, then. Be smart and use Responsive Web Design instead. That is the slogan of RWD fanatics. RWD surely serves the purpose of letting you deliver usable content to mobile devices without it even knowing the target device is not a desktop computer. The question is whether RWD is always efficient.

You can't say that it absolutely is always efficient; it varies with projects, contexts, and business scenarios.

The RWD paradox: Serve any, ignore all

When you connect to a website, the server sends a bunch of markup content your way. According to RWD, you don't need to perform an analysis of the user agent string and can blissfully ignore the characteristics of the requesting browser. According to RWD, the server serves the same content regardless of the requesting URL, user agent, hosting server platform, and capabilities of the device. Next, once the content has been safely downloaded on the client, some magic happens.

All that can happen within the context of a client web browser is all that you can do with the CSS syntax and attributes:

- Reposition a few HTML elements within their containers.

- Flow elements toward the left or right edge of the container.

- Resize container elements, using a fixed number or percentages.

But more than everything else, you can use CSS to show and hide elements. And the show/ hide capability is the most frequently used. In real-world websites, when you resize a browser page, sometimes containers are moved toward the bottom of the page. More often, though, they just get hidden.

The paradox of RWD is that by ignoring the type and capabilities of the requesting device, you force the server to potentially serve a lot of content just to have it hidden by some CSS class. Users consume bandwidth and waste seconds or minutes of their life just because your website is downloading content that they will never see! (See Figure 15-2.)

Same content (in MB)

100% downloaded content is used

~**80%** downloaded content is used

~ **40%** downloaded content is used

FIGURE 15-2 The same content being downloaded to any user agent, regardless of the device

The fairytale of mobile-first design

At the foundation of RWD, there's the axiom that you should design your templates in a mobile-first manner. A mobile-first approach essentially dictates that you first arrange the view template that fits on smaller screens and then you proceed to adding more and more content as you target larger screens.

This approach might work if you're a designer, but as a web developer you always end up having a single chunk of content to serve. And that content is always for the largest screen the application supports.

Overall, a mobile-first approach versus a mobile-last approach, which is the same as *progressive enhancement* versus *graceful degradation*, is mostly an argument for designers and is largely a matter of personal preference. It depends on how you like to learn about a new system.

From a purely development perspective, instead, a mobile-first strategy brings no benefits because it still requires the server to serve all the content—unless some good device detection is done.

Adapting RWD to non-desktop devices

RWD is a great resource and a fantastic solution as long as you remain in the realm of high-end devices as far as computing power, graphics, and screen real estate are concerned. On a desktop computer, you want to download the entire content of the page. You pay the cost once, and it's likely not even a huge cost because you're probably connected to some fast Wi-Fi network.

In this context, if you are still able to get relevant information from a resized browser's window, that's a great feature of the website. The same mechanics that allow you to nicely resize browser windows also enables you to serve mobile browsers apparently without further effort.

Except that a resized desktop browser window and a full-screen smartphone browser are quite different things.

> **Important** Numbers are not an opinion, and neither are quantities in physics. A 15-inch screen, like the one you find on a notebook or desktop computer, is still as large as a few 5-inch smartphone screens placed in a row. That's not an opinion, and it's not even a matter of resolution. Large or small screens make a whole lot of difference for design and even use-cases. Sometimes your perception of the application changes if you view it through the lens of mobile users. You get no device-specific design and analysis if you blindly go with RWD.

When using RWD to serve content to non-desktop devices, there are a few areas of your development work that must optimized. First in line is how you deal with images.

Dealing with images

As long as it's affordable for you to move only a few HTML containers around to accommodate smaller screens, CSS is a formidable tool to use. Within an HTML container—typically, block-level elements such as *DIV* elements—you can have plain text, markup text, and images.

For different reasons, both text and images should be reviewed carefully and tested on any size of screen you're going to consider. In particular, dealing with images within a responsive website might be quite problematic.

Let's find out why and identify workarounds.

Moving beyond the *IMG* element

As of HTML5, you have just one way to add an image to a webpage—using the *IMG* element. The *IMG* element can point to a given image in one of two ways:

- A single URL (the most common way)

- An embedded Base64 text stream

When the URL refers directly to an image file, the file is downloaded, cached, and then resized to whatever combination of *width* and *height* attributes the CSS style indicates. At first sight, this is perfect. By acting on width and height and expressing them as percentages, you can fit the image nicely into the container, keeping the aspect ratio and proportions within the page.

Although it's functional, this approach is often simplistic for a couple of reasons:

- You download images that are likely far larger than needed on some devices.

- A large image might represent close-up or far-off content, which makes it difficult for a reader to make sense of a small resize of the same image.

Why should you download a 2-MB image on a small device when a small fraction of it would be more than acceptable? You can save bandwidth and have the device render the page a lot more quickly. Even when the size of the download is not your primary concern, consider that typically a 2-MB image can contain a lot of details (for example, a close-up shot of something) or very few details (for example, a far-off shot of a landscape).

When resized to a thumbnail, the image might be a confusing mess of pixels or a flat desert of nearly a single solid color. When resizing an image for a website, you want to be sure that the image carries exactly the meaning it is supposed to have. In this case, the device and its screen width do matter a lot.

Toward responsive images

Ideally, you use different images for different devices and screen widths. Ideally, the browser bears the burden of selecting and downloading the most appropriate image from a range of choices, based on media types and media attributes. Something like responsive images.

In fact, in the near future, browsers are expected to support a new HTML element for images that is not limited to a single source file. According to the W3C vision of responsive images, this is a draft of what you can expect to see in the next generation of web browsers:

```
<picture alt="">
  <source media="(min-width: 800px)" srcset="large-1.jpg 1x, large-2.jpg 2x">
  <source media="(min-width: 600px)" srcset="med-1.jpg 1x, med-2.jpg 2x">
  <source srcset="small-1.jpg 1x, small-2.jpg 2x">
  <img src="small-1.jpg">
</picture>
```

The PICTURE element works at two levels, letting you optimize both bandwidth via the *srcset* attribute and art direction via the *source* element. Art direction is the business consideration that ensures the content of the image is the best for a given context. In other words, art direction is the human factor that establishes the ideal content given the context and real estate.

The content of *srcset* is managed by the browser, which uses its own algorithm to pick the most appropriate image size-wise. The *source* element, instead, works similarly to media queries: the page author dictates the image to pick on a per-scenario basis.

When art direction does matter

To form a concrete picture of the role that art direction plays in the selection of the most appropriate image, have a look at Figure 15-3. The page is publicly available at *http://www.expoware.org/wit.html*. I took the image from the top row of bleachers of a tennis stadium.

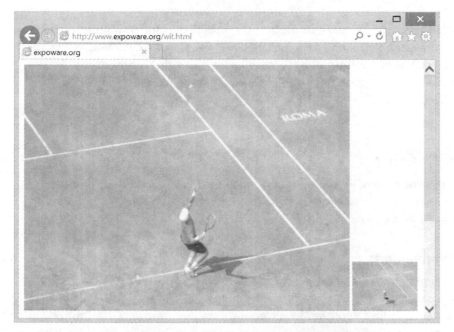

FIGURE 15-3 An automatically generated thumbnail without manual artwork

Because the image presents a far-off scene on a relatively flat and static background, a plain resize might produce a solid square box with nearly no distinguishable content. The original image can still be consistently resized to 100 by 100, but that requires human attention.

Hidden costs of the PICTURE element

At the moment, the PICTURE element is an experimental HTML element and is natively supported only in a narrow range of browsers, including versions of Chrome, Firefox, and Opera released since late 2014. No support exists in Internet Explorer and Safari, but Microsoft Edge has support for it.

On the mobile side of browsers, the situation is analogous. You have the PICTURE element on Android devices and wherever the Opera browser is available. A Modernizr polyfill exists, though, to let you use the element on a broader range of browsers. (See *http://scottjehl.github.io/picturefill*.)

In the end, unless you have a long list of old browsers to support, using the PICTURE element is definitely an option worth considering. Using the PICTURE element, however, is not free of issues and might have some hidden costs.

The strength of the PICTURE element lies in the fact that it lets browsers intelligently select the most appropriate image from a range of options. Maintaining multiple versions of the same logical picture requires extra work from designers and results in storing multiple images on the server. That's probably no big deal for relatively static images, such as background images or images that are only occasionally updated. Using the PICTURE element to back up the implementation of dynamic galleries can be quite expensive.

> **Note** An interesting workaround that sits in between PICTURE and IMG is represented by the ImageEngine Lite service. ImageEngine Lite is a server-side tool that acts as a proxy and automatically resizes and serves a source image in a way that is appropriate for the device. I'll cover ImageEngine Lite in more detail in the next chapter. For more information, check out *http://web.wurfl.io*.

Dealing with fonts

RWD is about reflowing content in containers of varying size. What about the size of the text contained therein? Let's start reviewing how things go within Bootstrap—a commonly used framework for responsive views.

Fixed and relative units

In Bootstrap, settings for font size and line height are placed at the BODY level and change slightly for other text elements such as P. CSS classes are also provided to increase or decrease the font size, such as *small* and *lead*. Up until Bootstrap 3.x, all font sizes are expressed in pixels. This is expected to change with Bootstrap 4.

The decision to use pixels in Bootstrap is debatable, but it was definitely a reasonable decision at the time it was made. Developers think primarily in terms of pixels, and pixels provide absolute control over text and ensure consistent rendering across all browsers. An alternate approach would have been to express the font size through relative measurements such as EM or REM units.

The difference between EM and REM is pretty subtle. Both units express font size as a fraction of something: EM sets it as a fraction of the font size of the nearest parent, whereas REM always looks at the font size set at the HTML level. By using REM font sizes, you care about actual numbers only in one place—at the root—and then everything else will automatically scale:

```
html { font-size: 14px; }
h1 { font-size: 3rem; }
h2 { font-size: 2.5rem; }
h3 { font-size: 2rem; }
```

Note that the primary argument in favor of REM fonts is their accessibility. A pixel-based font size doesn't scale automatically as operating system–level and browser-level fonts are increased by, say, people with vision problems. Fonts measured through EM, instead, increase as a percentage of the browser's font size. This means that EM units don't prevent accessibility, but building accessible solutions over EM units requires more work because pixels should never come around at any HTML level.

In a general-purpose framework like Bootstrap, using EM fonts all the way through would have probably raised a lot of issues across a variety of browsers. In the end, EM fonts remain a great option for websites with a strong emphasis on accessibility. REM fonts, on the other hand, make sense if you don't want to handle visual breakpoints yourself. In this case, you set a pixel-based font at the HTML level and forget about numbers.

Viewport units

Another option to express font size is to do it through viewport units. A viewport unit measures font size as a percentage of the viewport size:

```
h1 { font-size: 5.9vw; }
```

In the example, the size of H1 elements is set to 5.9 percent of the browser's window width. It goes without saying that as the browser window is resized the dimension of the font changes. All this happens automatically without any other CSS tricks on your end.

There are a few variations of viewport units (VWs).

You can use VW to set the font size as a percentage of viewport width. Or you can use VH to specify viewport height, instead. Finally, you can use VMIN or VMAX to specify either the minimum or maximum difference between the width and the height of the viewport.

Changes in Bootstrap 4

The primary reason why the authors of Bootstrap didn't go with the REM option right from the beginning was related to browser compatibility. For example, Internet Explorer 8 has no support for REM measurements. Going with the REM option would have then made Internet Explorer 8 incompatible with Bootstrap.

Bootstrap 3 is therefore built on pixels, but that doesn't prevent you from using REM or EM fonts on your end. Bootstrap 4 will drop support for Internet Explorer 8. Subsequently, you can embrace the best font-size logic with no constraints. If you intend to guarantee Internet Explorer 8 support, you'd better stick to Bootstrap 3.x.

Dealing with orientation

One of the primary reasons to have a responsive site is so that device users can consume the content with extreme ease. When viewed on, say, a tablet, a site must be able to survive orientation changes, from portrait to landscape and vice versa.

How do you detect a change of orientation, and how do you deal with that? First and foremost, this is not an aspect of programming you can detect on the server side. This is only a state you can become aware of on the client side.

Using media queries

From the perspective of the site, a change in orientation is a plain resize of the window that sets a different height and width. Depending on the content you have, a different CSS might be enough to address the change. If CSS is enough to address the required changes, the best you can do is add a couple of media queries expressions, as shown here:

```
@media screen and (orientation: portrait) {
    /* portrait-specific styles */
}
@media screen and (orientation: landscape) {
    /* landscape-specific styles */
}
```

If you're using Bootstrap, most of the time you don't need to take any measures to support portrait and landscape explicitly because it will be detected and treated as a plain resize. In more complex situations, though, just switching CSS files might not be enough and some client-side JavaScript work will be required.

Detecting a browser's event

You can programmatically detect a change in orientation using the *orientationchange* event or just the *resize* event for browsers that don't offer the other, more specific, event. When you detect a change of size, you don't know directly from it if the layout is *portrait* or *landscape*. However, you can easily figure it out with some simple math.

Yet another option is using the *matchMedia* object on the browser's *window* object:

```
var orientation = window.matchMedia("(orientation: portrait)");
orientation.addListener(function(portrait) {
    if(portrait.matches) {
        // Adapt content to Portrait
    }
    else {
        // Adapt content to Landscape
    }
});
```

The *matchMedia* object is supported on most recent browsers.

Summary

There's no question that responsive web views are an absolute must-have these days. Responsive Web Design is a programming practice you can follow to create fully responsive web views. Because this approach is backed by popular frameworks such as Bootstrap, creating responsive views is an affordable effort for nearly everybody. Note, though, that Bootstrap performs no magic—it just offers ad hoc tools that developers and designers can use to arrange responsive views.

This is to say that responsive views are no picnic and don't work the same in all possible scenarios. Fluid grids lie at the foundation of Responsive Web Design. Fluid grids are essentially resizable containers that can reflow any content written to be reflowed. The relatively simple idea of a fluid grid requires a lot of sophisticated code and essentially the ability to switch CSS style sheets on the fly.

This is where CSS media queries fit in. Media queries select a CSS style sheet based on a Boolean expression written around a few browser properties. The most important of these properties is the screen width. Differentiating content based only on screen width doesn't take into account the actual capabilities of the underlying devices. RWD, in fact, makes a point of ignoring the device—all it does is serve different layouts based on screen width.

In this chapter, I reviewed the core mechanics of media queries. (Chapter 9 contains more details on how to create fluid grids in real-world applications.) In the second half of this chapter, I discussed aspects to improve in a RWD solution.

In the next chapter, I'll explore solutions that include device detection and a mobile-centric strategy.

CHAPTER 16

Making websites mobile-friendly

The future belongs to those who prepare for it today.

—*Malcolm X*

I n software, the term *mobile* is usually associated with native applications for a particular platform, such as Apple iOS, Microsoft Windows Phone, or Android. A common vision is that you should aim for having apps for some platforms and ensure that the website can be comfortably viewed on smartphones and (mini) tablets. Most recent devices can comfortably display nearly any website. This leads many executives to address mobile with just a few native apps, thus completely ignoring the subtler issues of mobile web.

My vision is different. I don't argue with having (or not having) mobile apps, because that aspect is too business-specific to be addressed in general terms. But I do argue in favor of providing a mobile-friendly website, which is indeed quite important. More precisely, I argue that no company should content itself with a website that just shows up and can be read on a smartphone. The user experience (UX) you can provide with a mobile-optimized design of the site is significantly better than just providing pinch-and-zoom functionality for the user to fill in forms and read news.

In Chapter 15, "Pros and cons of responsive design," I already discussed the role that fluid grids and CSS media queries play in generating a website's screens in different sizes. In this chapter, I'll touch on HTML5 and feature detection before moving to the review technologies and approaches for optimizing websites for specific classes of devices such as smartphones.

Adapting views to the actual device

Mobile users tend to have high expectations when they navigate to websites from their mobile devices. They expect websites to provide an experience similar to that of native iPhone or Android apps. For example, they expect to have touch-enabled controls and popular widgets such as pick lists, sideway menus, and toggle switches. These widgets don't exist (yet?) as native elements of HTML. They must be simulated by using rich component controls that output a mix of JavaScript and markup every time.

The bottom line is that it's one thing to create a plain site by making the best possible use of HTML, CSS, and JavaScript; it is quite another to make a compelling mobile site that looks like a native application or, at a minimum, behaves like one. Achieving that goal is an even greater challenge when you consider that a mobile website is expected to have a small subset of features compared to a full site and sometimes also requires different use-cases. The good news is that some of the development issues can be minimized by making good use of HTML5.

The best of HTML5 for mobile scenarios

On average, mobile browsers offer great support for HTML5 elements. This means that at least on devices that fall under the umbrella of *smartphones* or *tablets*, you can default to HTML5 elements without worrying about workarounds and shims. Two aspects of HTML5 are particularly relevant for mobile development: input types and geolocation.

New input types

Currently, HTML (and subsequently browsers) supports only plain text as input. There's quite a bit of difference between dates, numbers, and even email addresses, not to mention predefined values. Today, developers are responsible for preventing users from typing unwanted characters by implementing client-side validation of the entered text. The jQuery library has several plugins that simplify the task, but this just reinforces the point—input is a delicate matter.

HTML5 comes with a plethora of new values for the attribute type of the INPUT element. In addition the INPUT has several new attributes that are mostly related to these new input types. Here are a few examples:

```
<input type="date" />
<input type="time" />
<input type="range" />
<input type="number" />
<input type="search" />
<input type="color" />
<input type="email" />
<input type="url" />
<input type="tel" />
```

What's the real effect of these new input types? The intended effect—though not completely standardized yet—is that browsers provide an ad hoc UI so that users can comfortably enter a date, time, or number.

Desktop browsers do not always honor these new input types, and the experience they provide is not always uniform. Things are much better in the mobile space. First and foremost, on mobile devices users typically browse the web with the default browser. Subsequently, the experience is always uniform and specific to the device.

In particular, input fields like *email*, *url*, and *tel* push mobile browsers on smartphones to automatically adjust the input scope of the keyboard. Figure 16-1 shows the effect of typing on a *tel* input field on an Android device: the keyboard defaults to numbers and phone-related symbols.

FIGURE 16-1 The *tel* input field on an Android smartphone

These days, not all browsers provide the same experience. Although they mostly agree on the user interface associated with the various input types, some key differences exist that might require developers to add script-based custom polyfills. As an example, consider the *date* type. No version of Internet Explorer or Safari offer any special support whatsoever for dates. Also in this case, things go much better with mobile devices, as the screenshot in Figure 16-2 demonstrates.

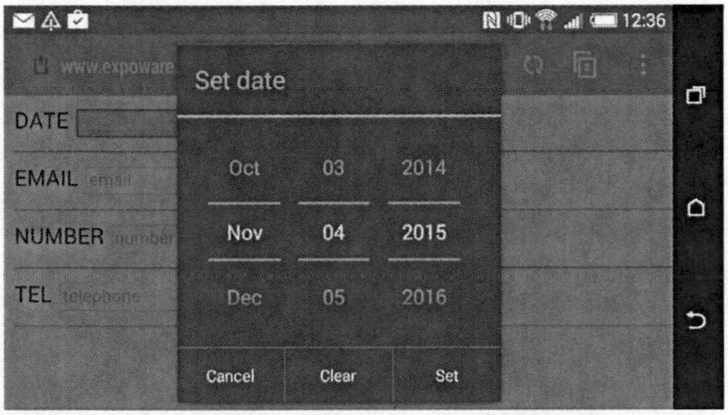

FIGURE 16-2 The date input field on an Android smartphone

In general, mobile browsers on recent smartphones are quite respectful of HTML5 elements; therefore, developers should be ready to use proper input types.

Geolocation

Geolocation is an HTML standard that is widely supported by both desktop and mobile browsers. As mentioned, sometimes the mobile version of a website needs to have ad hoc use-cases users won't find on the full version of the site. When this happens, it's quite likely that geolocation of users is involved in the mobile-only use-case. Here's some sample code:

```
<script type="text/javascript"
        src="http://maps.googleapis.com/maps/api/js?sensor=true"></script>
<script type="text/javascript">
    function initialize() {
    navigator.geolocation.getCurrentPosition(
            showMap,
            function(e) {alert(e.message);},
            {enableHighAccuracy:true, timeout:10000, maximumAge:0 });
    }

    function showMap(position) {
        var point = new google.maps.LatLng(position.coords.latitude, position.coords.longitude);
        var myOptions = {
            zoom: 16,
            center: point,
            mapTypeId: google.maps.MapTypeId.ROADMAP
        };
        var map = new google.maps.Map(document.getElementById("map_canvas"), myOptions);
        var marker = new google.maps.Marker({
                position: point,
              map: map,
            title: "You are here" });
    }
</script>
<body onload="initialize()">
   <div id="map_canvas" style="width:100%; height:100%"></div>
</body>
```

The page asks for user permission about geolocalization and then shows the exact geographical position of the device on a map.

Feature detection

Responsive Web Design (RWD) sprung to life from the following example of lateral thinking. Detecting devices is hard? Well, then don't do that. You grab a few snippets of basic information available on the client side (for example, the size of the browser window), set up ad hoc style sheets, and let the browser reflow content in the page accordingly. This originated the idea of feature detection and created a popular library—Modernizr—and a website just as popular, *http://caniuse.com*.

What Modernizr can do for you

The idea behind feature detection is simple and, to some extent, even smart. You don't even attempt to detect the actual capabilities of the requesting device, which is known to be cumbersome and difficult. It even poses serious issues with regard to the maintainability of the solution.

Equipped with a feature-detection library, you decide what to display based only on what you can detect programmatically on the device. Instead of detecting the user agent, and blindly assuming that such devices don't support a given feature, you just let an ad hoc library like Modernizr find out for you whether the feature is actually available on the current browser, regardless of the host device. (See *http://modernizr.com*.)

For example, instead of maintaining a list of which browsers (and related user agent strings) support date input fields, you just check with Modernizr whether date input fields are available on the current browser. Here's some illustrative script code:

```
<script type="text/javascript">
Modernizr.load({
    test: Modernizr.inputtypes.date,
    nope: ['jquery-ui.min.js', 'jquery-ui.css'],
    complete: function () {
        $('input[type=date]').datepicker({
            dateFormat: 'yy-mm-dd'
        });
    }
});
</script>
```

You tell Modernizr to test the date-input type. If the test fails, you download jQuery UI files and run the *complete* callback function to set up the jQuery UI date-picker plugin for all INPUT elements in the page of date types. This approach allows you to blissfully use HTML5 markup in your page regardless of the effect on end users:

```
<input type="date" />
```

Feature detection offers the significant plus that you, as a developer, have just one site to design and maintain. The burden of adapting content responsively is pushed to graphical designers or to ad hoc libraries such as Modernizr.

Modernizr consists of a JavaScript library with some code that runs upon the loading of the page and checks whether the current browser is able to offer certain HTML5 and CSS3 functionalities. Modernizr exposes its findings programmatically so that the code in the page can query the library and intelligently adapt the output.

Modernizr does a great job, but it doesn't cover the entire range of issues you face when optimizing a website for mobile users. Modernizr is limited to what you can programmatically detect as JavaScript functions, which might or might not be exposed out of *navigator* or *window* browser objects.

In other words, Modernizr is not able to tell you about the form factor of the device—whether the device is a smartphone or a tablet or a smart TV. Someday browsers will expose this information and then Modernizr will be able to add this service too; but that day is not today. By applying some logic to the results you get from Modernizr, you can reliably guess whether the browser is for a mobile device or desktop device. You can't get beyond that point, though.

Therefore, if you really need to do something specific for smartphones, tablets, or both, Modernizr is not of much help.

The major strength of feature detection, which we can summarize as "one *site* fits all," is also likely to be the major weakness, though. Is just one site what you really want? Do you really want to serve the "same" site to smartphones, tablets, laptops, and smart TVs? The answer to this question invariably is specific to each business. In general terms, it can only be a resounding, "It depends."

Enter client-side, lightweight device detection via user agent strings.

Client-side device detection

Optimizing a website for mobile devices doesn't usually mean letting users have the same experience as a native app for their favorite platform. A mobile website is rarely specific to iOS, Android, or Windows Phone operating systems. A mobile website, instead, is devised and designed in such a way any mobile browser can give users a good experience.

At present, to reliably figure out whether the device is a desktop computer or less powerful type of device, there's no other way than sniffing the user agent string.

Handmade user-agent sniffing

There a few online resources that provide reliable heuristics to detect—they claim—mobile browsers. They use a combination of two core techniques: analysis of the user agent string and a cross-check of some properties of the browser's *navigator* object. In particular, you might want to take a look at the following URLs for more information:

- *http://www.quirksmode.org/js/detect.html*

- *http://detectmobilebrowsers.com*

In particular, the script you find on the second website uses a tricky regular expression to check for a long list of keywords known to be related to mobile devices. The script does work and is available for a variety of web platforms, including plain JavaScript and ASP.NET. It has two nontrivial drawbacks, though.

One is the date of the last update you find on the webpage. The last time I checked, it was over a year old. It might be better by the time you read this, yet it leaves unaltered the perception that keeping the regular expression up to date is expensive and must be done frequently.

The other drawback is that the script attempts to tell you only whether the user agent is known to identify a mobile device as opposed to a desktop device. It lacks logic, and it lacks the programming power to identify more specifically the class of the requesting device and its known capabilities.

If you're looking for a free client-side solution to sniff user agent strings, I suggest you look at WURFL.JS. (See *http://web.wurfl.io*.) Among other benefits, WURFL.JS is not based on any regular expressions that you have responsibility for keeping up to date.

Using WURFL.JS

In spite of the name, WURFL.JS is not a static JavaScript file you can host on the premises or upload to your cloud site. WURFL.JS is an HTTP endpoint you link to your web views through a regular SCRIPT element.

To get the WURFL.JS services, therefore, you only need to add the following line to any HTML views you have that need to know about the actual device:

```
<script type="text/javascript" src="//wurfl.io/wurfl.js"></script>
```

The browser knows nothing about the nature of the WURFL.JS endpoint. The browser just attempts to download and execute any script code it can get from the specified URL. The WURFL server that receives a request uses the user agent of the calling device to figure out its actual capabilities. The WURFL server relies on the services of the WURFL framework—a powerful device data repository and a cross-platform API used by Facebook, Google, and PayPal.

The net effect of calling the aforementioned HTTP endpoint is injecting a tailor-made JavaScript object into the browser DOM. Here's an example of what you get:

```
var WURFL = {
    "complete_device_name":"iPhone 5",
    "is_mobile":false,
    "form_factor":"Smartphone"
};
```

The server-side endpoint receives the user agent string sent with the request and analyzes it thoroughly. It then selects the three pieces of information shown in Table 16-1 and arranges a JavaScript string to return.

TABLE 16-1 WURFL.JS Properties

Property	Description
complete_device_name	Descriptive name for the detected device. The name includes vendor information and the device name (for example, iPhone 6).
form_factor	Indicates the class of the detected device. It's any of the following strings: Desktop, App, Tablet, Smartphone, Feature Phone, Smart-TV, Robot, Other non-Mobile, and Other Mobile.
is_mobile	If the value is true, it indicates that the device is not a desktop device.

Figure 16-3 shows WURFL.JS in action on a public test page at *http://www.expoware.org/wjs.htm*.

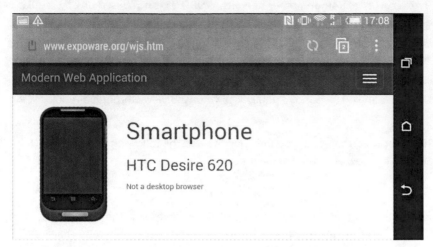

FIGURE 16-3 Device detection according to WURFL.JS

In terms of performance, WURFL.JS is fairly efficient; it does a lot of caching and doesn't really check any user agent it receives. While in development, though, you can switch off the cache by adding *debug=true* to the URL.

> **Important** The WURFL.JS framework is free to use as long as the website is publicly available. If used in production, though, it might possibly become a bottleneck in case of high volumes of traffic. In this case, you might want to consider a commercial option that reserves more bandwidth and also gives you access to a longer list of device properties. For more information, check out *http://www.scientiamobile.com*.

Mixing client-side detection and responsive pages

WURFL.JS can be used in many scenarios, including browser personalization, enhancing analytics, and optimizing advertising. Further, if you are a front-end developer and implementing device detection on the server side is not an option for you, WURFL.JS is your savior. For more examples, check out the WURFL.JS documentation at *http://web.wurfl.io*.

Let's briefly consider a few scenarios where you want to use client device detection. One is when downloading images that are appropriate, in size and content, for the device. You can go with code like this:

```
<script>
    if (WURFL.form_factor == "smartphone") {
        $("#myImage").attr("src", "...");
    }
</script>
```

Similarly, you can use the WURFL object to redirect to a specific mobile site if the requesting device looks like a smartphone:

```
<script>
    if (WURFL.form_factor == "smartphone") {
        window.location.href = "...";
    }
</script>
```

WURFL.JS gives you clues about the actual device, but for the time being there's no way to mix CSS media queries and external information such as device-specific details. A responsive design driven by actual user agents rather than media queries parameters is still possible, but you must do it entirely on your own. The most common way to use WURFL.JS is within the context of a Bootstrap, or any other RWD solutions. You get the device details and, via JavaScript, enable or disable specific features or download ad hoc content.

> **Note** In the companion code that comes with the book, you find an example that uses WURFL.JS to figure out which area of the website to point users to. The example is a simple proof-of-concept, but it can be enlarged to work in a scenario in which most of the site is a classic RWD site except for a few areas that are duplicated based on the form factor of the device.

A look into the future

Client Hints is the colloquial name of a draft that is emerging for a unified standard way for browsers and servers to negotiate content. The model that's the inspiration is the model behind the widely used *Accept-** HTTP headers. With each request, the browser sends in a few extra headers; the server reads those headers and can use them to adapt the content being returned.

At the current stage of the draft, you can have a header suggesting the desired width of the content and the client's maximum speed in download. These two pieces of information could be enough to make the server aware of most critical situations we face today, such as small screen devices over 3G connections. In most cases, in fact, it's not even crucial to know if it's a smart-phone or another type of device. Today, and even more in the future, content created according to RWD principles would likely be good anywhere except for use with very slow connections and very low-resolution devices, including old iPhone devices.

Client Hints goes in this direction. Some early documentation about Client Hints and prospective headers being defined for exchange is available at *http://igrigorik.github.io/http-client-hints*.

Device-friendly images

In the last chapter, I touched on the problem of serving appropriate images to devices. "Appropriate" means essentially two things: appropriate size and appropriately resized content that still makes the image relevant in the context in which it is used. The PICTURE element is gaining traction, and with it comes the need for developers and site administrators to maintain multiple copies of the same logical image to be used depending on the current screen size.

Another option that, unlike the PICTURE element, doesn't pose any compatibility issue is using the ImageEngine platform.

The ImageEngine platform

ImageEngine is an image-resizing tool exposed as a service. It is particularly well suited for mobile scenarios where it can significantly reduce the image payload of views, thus reducing the load time. The platform operates as a sort of content delivery network (CDN) because it sits in between your server application and the client browser and serves images to clients on behalf of the server. (See Figure 16-4.)

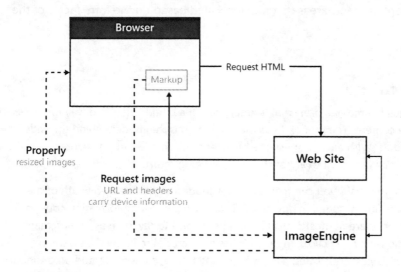

FIGURE 16-4 The overall architecture of the ImageEngine platform

The primary purpose of the ImageEngine platform is to reduce the traffic generated by images. In this regard, it presents itself as an ideal tool for mobile websites. However, ImageEngine is not limited to that. First and foremost, you can serve images resized as you wish to any device or desktop. Second, you can use ImageEngine as an online resizer tool with a URL-based programmatic interface. Finally, you can use ImageEngine as your smart image-only CDN and save yourself the burden of maintaining multiple versions of the same image to speed up load time on various screen sizes.

Resizing images automatically

To use ImageEngine, you need a free account. The account identifies you with a name and helps the server keep your traffic distinct from other users. Before you create an account, though, you can play with the test account. In a Razor view, you display images on webpages as shown here:

```
<img src="~/content/images/autumn.jpg">
```

When you use ImageEngine, you replace it with the following markup:

```
<img src="//try.imgeng.in/http://www.yoursite.com/content/images/autumn.jpg">
```

Once you have your account, you simply replace *try* with your account name. If the account name is, say, *contoso* the URL of the image becomes this:

```
<img src="//contoso.imgeng.in/http://www.yoursite.com/content/images/autumn.jpg">
```

ImageEngine supports a number of parameters, including cropping and sizing to given dimensions. Not only can it resize to the size it considers ideal for the device, it can also accept specific suggestions, as detailed in Table 16-2. Parameters are inserted in the resulting URL.

TABLE 16-2 URL parameters of the ImageEngine tool

URL Parameter	Description
w_NNN	Sets the desired width of the image in pixels. Sample URL: //contoso.imgeng.in/w_200/IMAGE_URL
h_NNN	Sets the desired height of the image in pixels. Sample URL: //contoso.imgeng.in/h_200/IMAGE_URL
pc_NN	Sets the desired percentage of reduction for the image. Sample URL: //contoso.imgeng.in/pc_30/IMAGE_URL
m_XXX	Sets the resize mode of the image. Acceptable values are box (default), cropbox, letterbox, and stretch. Sample URL: //contoso.imgeng.in/m_cropbox/w_300/h_300/IMAGE_URL
f_XXX	Sets the desired output format of the image. Acceptable values are png, jpg, webp, gif, and bmp. By default, the image is returned in the original format. Sample URL: //contoso.imgeng.in/f_webp/IMAGE_URL

Note that width, height, and percentage are mutually exclusive. If *none* is indicated, the image is resized to the dimensions suggested by the detected user agent. Multiple parameters can be combined as segments of the URL. For example, the following URL resizes the image in a 300 by 300 cropping appropriately from the center of the image in case the original dimensions don't return a square. The order of parameters is unimportant.

```
//contoso.imgeng.in/w_300/h_300/m_cropbox/IMAGE_URL
```

Compared to the upcoming PICTURE element, ImageEngine doesn't let you serve really different images, so if art direction is involved you really need to host and serve physically different images that can be further preprocessed via ImageEngine. If you don't have art direction concerns, though, ImageEngine saves you the burden of resizing manually and saves bandwidth.

ImageEngine is a free platform, but for more information you can check out *http://web.wurfl.io*.

 Note In the companion code for the book, you also find the source code of a jQuery plugin that simplifies the creation of the necessary URL for the ImageEngine tool.

Serving device-friendly views

If RWD doesn't completely fulfill your expectations, even with client-side adjustments done with WURFL.JS and ImageEngine, there's nothing else left for you to do other than trying server-side device detection. A rather primitive form of device detection (it was actually browser detection) was already implemented in the very first version of ASP.NET through a collection of XML *.browser* files.

Today, given the huge number of devices, user agents, and edge cases, a simple collection of individual files is no longer enough to do realistic and reliable device detection. If it's an asset for your application, you need to be ready to pay for a professional service.

What's the best way to offer mobile content?

Before I explore one of the server-side options available for ASP.NET MVC, let me first summarize the approaches you can take today to serve mobile content effectively.

Option #1: Responsive HTML templates

If you start today with a brand new website, I'd definitely recommend you use Bootstrap to have a responsive template in all your views. Using a responsive HTML template ensures not only that your views display nicely when the user resizes the desktop browser window, but you also have basic coverage for mobile users. At a minimum, in fact, mobile users will receive the same views that desktop users receive when they resize the browser.

It might not be ideal from a performance perspective, but if devices are new and fast enough, and connectivity is not really bad, the effect is acceptable. I wouldn't recommend this route for websites in which mobile interactivity is a core part of the business, but in most cases it just works.

Option #2: Add client-side enhancements

If you have the time and budget, you might want to improve the quality of responsive views and optimize the way images are handled, as well as add some mobile-specific features if you detect appropriate devices. This step goes in the general direction of offering the best possible user experience and encompasses both feature and device detection.

Most of the tools and frameworks you might want to employ at this stage don't strictly require a subscription or a paid license. However, if you're using them to achieve a performance goal, you might want to ensure you don't share your bandwidth with the rest of the planet. If you plan to run products like ImageEngine or WURFL.JS in production, I suggest you monitor the actual performance and consider a commercial service-level agreement.

Option #3: Creating an ad-hoc mobile site

At the current stage of mobile technology, the number of devices that can happily display pages equipped with jQuery, Bootstrap, and AngularJS is already significant and growing. This means that probably the full website, if responsive, can be effectively used by users browsing with a tablet.

Note that this is not something that happens automatically—it largely depends on some design choices you might have made. For example, modal forms and popups don't usually work that great on tablets and don't satisfy mobile users as well as they satisfy desktop users. Also, the thickness of the finger used on a touch-based device like a tablet is not the same as the mouse pointer. At a minimum, you want to change the CSS style sheets when on tablets. And this just one of those little things that media queries cannot do. To make this simple change, you need to know more about the device and use things like WURFL.JS.

What about smartphones?

Even the most modern and cutting-edge smartphone will have a screen width of five or six inches: much smaller than a tablet or a PC. You can't realistically expect to serve the same full site to smartphone users. The browser might even be able to show it and make it usable, but the experience will be less than ideal.

If you really care about devices and mobile users, you might want to have an ad-hoc website at least for smartphones, where you completely rethink the use-cases and the implementation. If this seems like it's just extra work to you, either your project doesn't strictly need ad hoc mobile coverage or you're missing something important about it.

An ad-hoc mobile website is also an excellent option to choose when you want to offer a mobile experience on top of an existing, legacy website that is not very responsive.

Redirecting to mobile websites

Suppose now you have two websites—the full site, whether responsive or not, and the mobile site, sometimes referred to in literature as an *m-site*. How would you reach them? The real world is full of examples that approach this problem in different ways, while still achieving good business results.

I believe we might all agree that having a single public URL for the website would be great. Users have only to remember the www thing and the software does the magic of silently switching to the most appropriate content available. Companies that don't do so—we might agree—might be facing some business pain.

Amazon does exactly this, but it's a relatively recent move.

When you visit amazon.com from a desktop device, no matter how you resize the window, you still get the full site. The template is not responsive, and if you resize it, most of the content is just cut off from view. If you visit the site and send a mobile user agent, you see the difference. You can reproduce the experience by changing the user agent string of, say, Internet Explorer to that of Windows Phone. The content in the browser immediately switches to what you would get if you point your mobile browser to the site. In the back end of the Amazon website, there's clearly some form of device detection that is used to simply point to a different set of views.

In simpler scenarios, you can consider having some device detection that redirects to a physically separated website under a different URL. Also, this solution is acceptable because it still gets users where they need to be, but at the cost of always typing the same general www URL.

From a development perspective, you can consider the ad hoc mobile website as a different project. Having it as a different project is a great achievement: you can develop it with ad hoc technologies and frameworks, outsource it to external companies, have different people work on it, and have it done at any later time.

In all these cases, though, you need to have a library you can use to do device detection on the server side, whether it's ASP.NET, Java, PHP, or something else.

Server-side detection

The easiest way to add server-side detection to an ASP.NET MVC application is via the WURFL library, and the easiest way to get the library in the project is through NuGet.

Installing the WURFL framework

Figure 16-5 shows the list of NuGet packages for the library. As you can see, there are two options: the cloud API and the on-premises API.

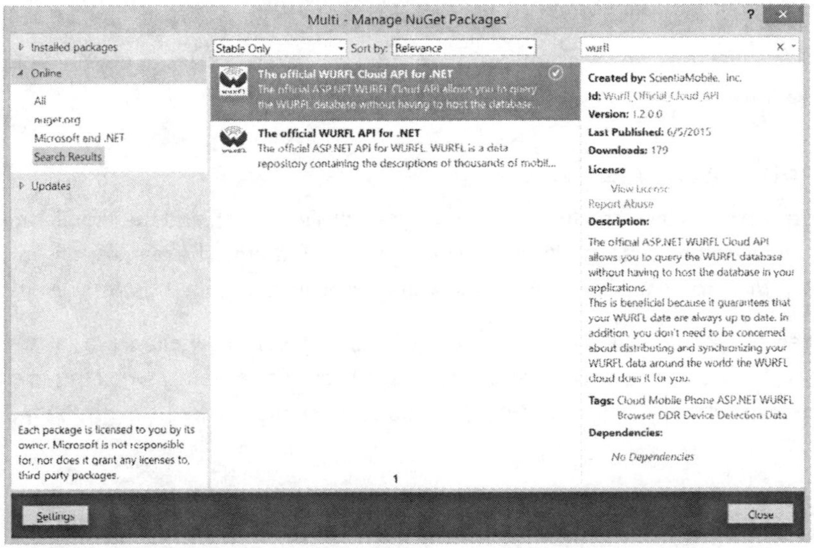

FIGURE 16-5 List of WURFL NuGet packages

If you opt for the on-premises API, you need a license before you move to production. Because you host the API side by side with the application, the on-premises API ensures optimal performance and, once caching is in place, nearly instant access time. The package downloads with the device database, which might not be the most up to date. It is your responsibility to keep it up to date as new drops are released. You can get the latest public chunk of the device database at any time from *http://wurfl.sourceforge.net*. However, once you set up a license you get weekly drops available from your account on *http://www.scientiamobile.com*.

The cloud API requires you to set up a free account, and you can use up to five capabilities of your choice. When you create the account, you're given an API key to use in any programmatic calls you make to the API.

Testing the WURFL cloud API

When you configure your WURFL cloud account, you can choose up to five capabilities (according to the free plan) from the list of over 500 device capabilities that WURFL offers. If you simply want to route views to the most relevant form factors (for example, smartphones, tablets, and large screens), the capabilities described in Table 16-3 should be enough.

TABLE 16-3 Basic WURFL capabilities for routing views

Capability	Description
is_wireless_device	Returns true if the requesting device is NOT a desktop browser. Note that true is returned as a string.
is_tablet	Returns true if the requesting device is known to be a tablet. The is_wireless_device capability still returns true. Note that true is returned as a string.
is_smartphone	Returns true if the requesting device is known to be a smartphone. The is_wireless_device capability still returns true. Note that true is returned as a string.
complete_device_name	Returns the commercial name of the requesting device.
advertised_device_os	Returns the commercial name of the operating system. The version number is not included. If you need it, you should add another specific capability: advertised_device_os_version.

You must add these capabilities to your account before you can get their values for the requesting device. The number of capabilities you're allowed to add depends on the level of your subscription. You can change capabilities at any time and however many times you like. Note that once you change capabilities, requests might take a few moments to refresh results because of internal caching. (See Figure 16-6.)

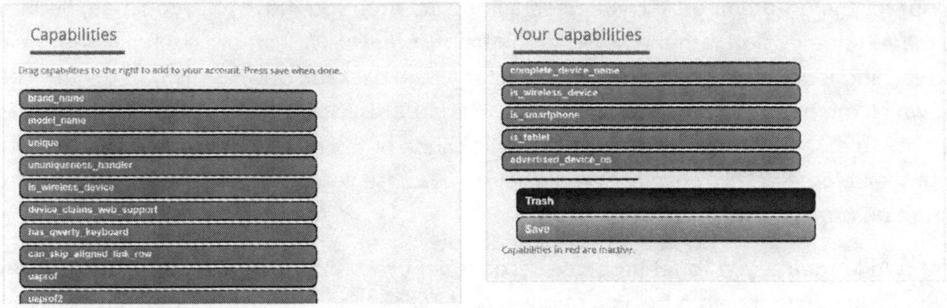

FIGURE 16-6 The WURFL cloud user dashboard for selecting capabilities

Here's some sample code that reports in a web view the values of selected capabilities. When the home page of the sample site is invoked, the controller invokes the API and packages results in a view model object:

```
private WurflService _service = new WurflService();
public ActionResult Index()
{
    var model = _service.GetDataByRequest(HttpContext);
    return View(model);
}
```

The *WurflService* class is a helper class in the application layer of the application. (See Chapter 5.) The class just takes logic away from the controller class:

```
public class WurflService
{
    public DeviceInfoViewModel GetDataByRequest(HttpContextBase context)
    {
        var config = new DefaultCloudClientConfig
        {
            ApiKey = "your API key here"
        };
        var manager = new CloudClientManager(config);
        var info = manager.GetDeviceInfo(context, new[]
        {
            "is_smartphone",
            "is_wireless_device",
            "is_tablet",
            "complete_device_name",
            "advertised_device_os"
        });
        var model = new DeviceInfoViewModel
                        {
                            DeviceId = info.Id,
                            DateOfRequest = info.WurflLastUpdate.ToString(),
                            Capabilities = info.Capabilities,
                            Errors = info.Errors,
                            Source = info.ResponseOrigin
                        };
        return model;
    }
}
```

Figure 16-7 shows the results you get when you test the sample view by simulating an Apple iPad device.

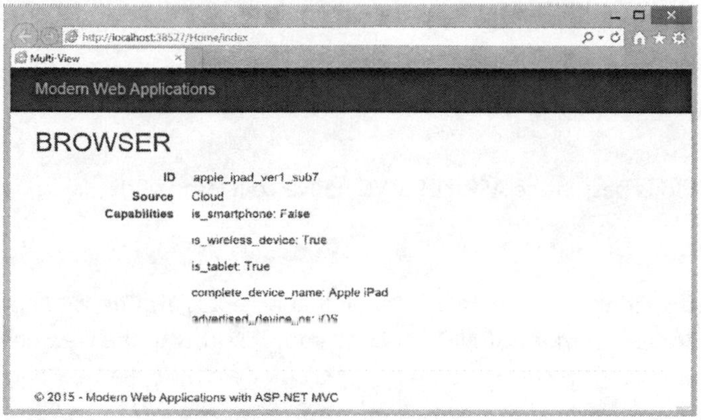

FIGURE 16-7 Device information as detected by the WURFL Cloud API

Routing views based on detected devices

ASP.NET MVC has effective mechanisms to let you switch views based on runtime conditions—*display modes*. In general, display modes are not a device-specific feature in the sense that you also can use them to switch to a grayscale or demo version of the site. With display modes, the logic to route to a given view is always up to the coder and, because of this, display modes are a formidable tool to use to route views based on the capabilities of detected devices.

If you intend to build a single website for multiple devices, you just arrange multiple sets of views—one for each form factor you support. Each form factor, then, has its own display mode, and WURFL helps to ensure that the requesting device is mapped to the proper display mode. This means that a tablet will get the tablet view of a given page (if any) and a smartphone will get its own view, as well.

The following code will go in *global.asax* to create display modes at the application startup. As mentioned, probably the most effective way to build a website these days is to make it responsive for all form factors except smartphones. Here's the code that sets up two display modes: desktop and smartphone. Desktop mode is set as the default, meaning that it will be used unless the device proves to be a smartphone:

```
public static void RegisterDisplayModes(IList<IDisplayMode> displayModes)
{
    var modeDesktop = new DefaultDisplayMode("")
    {
        ContextCondition = (c => c.Request.IsDesktop())
    };
```

```
        var modeSmartphone = new DefaultDisplayMode("smartphone")
        {
            ContextCondition = (c => c.Request.IsSmartphone())
        };

        displayModes.Clear();
        displayModes.Add(modeSmartphone);
        displayModes.Add(modeDesktop);
}
```

The *RegisterDisplayModes* method is passed the ASP.NET MVC native collection of display modes:

```
RegisterDisplayModes(DisplayModeProvider.Instance.Modes);
```

A display mode is given by a suffix string and a lambda function that accepts *HttpContext* and returns a Boolean. If the returned Boolean is *true*, ASP.NET MVC will add the suffix to the view name. As a result, if the lambda associated with the *modeSmartphone* display mode is *true*, the view engine will look for, say, *index.smartphone.cshtml* instead of *index.cshtml*.

ASP.NET MVC display modes

The *Request* object has also been extended with a few mode-specific methods such as *IsSmartphone* and *IsDesktop*. They are plain extension methods. The implementation of *IsDesktop* is trivial. The implementation of *IsSmartphone* uses the WURFL Cloud API internally:

```
public static Boolean IsDesktop(this HttpRequestBase request)
{
    return true;
}
public static Boolean IsSmartphone(this HttpRequestBase request)
{
    var info = MvcApplication.WurflContext.GetDeviceInfo(
                request.UserAgent, new[] { "is_smartphone" });
    return info.Capabilities["is_smartphone"].ToBool();;
}
```

Compared to the use of the WURFL cloud API shown earlier, I just managed to save to a global object the manager object—the static instance of the *CloudClientManager* class. I also added an *index.smartphone.cshtml* page to the project. When you navigate with a smartphone, you get something like what's shown in Figure 16-8.

FIGURE 16-8 The page served to smartphones

Note that the URL doesn't change depending on the device, and there's no redirection whatsoever. The processing of the request is the same: the controller gets the request, computes view data, identifies the root view name, and passes it down to the view engine. The name of the view, though, if display modes are active, is preprocessed and a suffix is appended based on the conditions set. If the device is detected to be a smartphone but no Razor view is found that is specific to smartphones, the default page is served.

Important Display modes are an extremely powerful feature in ASP.NET MVC because they let you develop the default site and then add a smartphone view where you need and, more importantly, when you need. If the mobile site is completely different, you might want to have only a smartphone-specific home page and have every link from there point to smartphone-unique pages. Therefore, the duplication of content is very limited.

Summary

A server-side solution is inherently more flexible than a purely client-side, RWD-based solution. The reason for this is that it allows you to check the device before anything is sent down the wire. In this way, the website can intelligently decide the most appropriate content. In practice, though, serving device-specific views is never an easy thing, and the core issue is not the mechanism used to detect the underlying device. The problem is the cost.

Device detection doesn't mean serving a different version of pages for each browser or device. It more realistically means maintaining, at most, three or four collections of views for the most common form factors: desktops, smartphones, tablets, legacy phones, and perhaps very large screens. Multiple pages are handled at a cost, no doubt.

The approach that sounds the most reasonable today consists of having a default responsive solution and a separate smartphone-specific website with just the use-cases that are relevant to mobile users. You can achieve this by deploying two distinct websites and using some client-side detection to redirect. Or you can use a server-side approach, which gives you more control over the behavior and also scales a lot more easily and flexibly in case you decide to accommodate more form factors.

Either way, as a developer you can't neglect the user experience on mobile devices and you can't blissfully conclude that a responsive template is all you need. Responsive design is just one answer; and it's probably not even entirely correct.

Index

Symbols

M

W

About the author

DINO ESPOSITO is CTO and co-founder of Crionet, a startup providing software and IT services to professional tennis and sports companies. Dino still does a lot of training and consulting and is the author of several other books on web and mobile development. His most recent book is *Architecting Applications for the Enterprise, Second Edition*, written along with Andrea Saltarello. A Pluralsight author, Dino speaks regularly at industry conferences and community events. You can follow Dino on Twitter at @despos and through his blog at *http://software2cents.wordpress.com*.

Now that you've read the book...

Tell us what you think!

Was it useful?
Did it teach you what you wanted to learn?
Was there room for improvement?

Let us know at http://aka.ms/tellpress

Your feedback goes directly to the staff at Microsoft Press,
and we read every one of your responses. Thanks in advance!

CPSIA information can be obtained
at www.ICGtesting.com
Printed in the USA
LVOW09s1319250618
581775LV00009B/27/P